QUESTIONS BLACK PARENTS ASK . . .

- Why would my five-year-old say her daddy's "too black"?
- Should black children be taught to be angry in order to fight racism?
- My daughter was called "nigger" and came home crying. What should I do?
- My son stopped playing tennis because his friends told him that it was a white man's game. I think he should play whatever he likes. What do you think?
- Fighting is a big problem among teenage boys in our neighborhood over such insignificant issues as "He stepped on my shoes." I fear for my child's life. What can I do?
- Our two daughters call us "Uncle Toms." We're hurt and angry. How should we respond?

Dr. James P. Comer of Yale Child Study Center and Dr. Alvin F. Poussaint of Harvard Medical School, who are themselves African-Americans, answer these and nearly 1,000 other questions connected to the day-to-day concerns and challenges black children face. Using a helpful question-and-answer format, Drs. Comer and Poussaint, two of America's leading child-care experts, draw on their many years of working with concerned black parents and educators to create the first authoritative, comprehensive child-care manual specifically for black children—a milestone work that belongs in every home and school library.

JAMES P. COMER, M.D., one of the most respected figures in American education, is Professor of Psychiatry at the Yale Child Study Center. A regular columnist for *Parents* magazine, he is also the author of *Maggie's American Dream* (Plume). He lives in New Haven, Connecticut.

ALVIN F. POUSSAINT, M.D., currently Professor of Psychiatry at Harvard Medical School, was a consultant to NBC's "The Cosby Show," and has written for *Ebony*, *The New York Times*, and *Psychology Today*, among other publications. He lives in Boston.

OTHER BOOKS BY JAMES P. COMER, M.D.

Black Child Care
(co-authored with Alvin F. Poussaint, M.D.)
Maggie's American Dream:
The Life and Times of a Black Family
School Power: Implications of an Intervention Project

OTHER BOOKS BY ALVIN F. POUSSAINT, M.D.

Why Blacks Kill Blacks
Black Child Care (co-authored with James P. Comer, M.D.)

RAISING BLACK CHILDREN

Two Leading Psychiatrists Confront the Educational, Social, and Emotional Problems Facing Black Children

James P. Comer, M.D. and Alvin F. Poussaint, M.D.

A PLUME BOOK

PLUME
Published by the Penguin Group
Penguin Books USA Inc., 375 Hudson Street,
New York, New York 10014, U.S.A.
Penguin Books Ltd, 27 Wrights Lane, London W8 5TZ, England
Penguin Books Australia Ltd, Ringwood, Victoria, Australia
Penguin Books Canada Ltd, 10 Alcorn Avenue,
Toronto, Ontario, Canada M4V 3B2
Penguin Books (N.Z.) Ltd, 182–190 Wairau Road, Auckland 10, New Zealand

Penguin Books Ltd, Registered Offices:
Harmondsworth, Middlesex, England

First published by Plume, an imprint of New American
Library, a division of Penguin Books USA Inc. Previous edition published
as *Black Child Care*.

First Plume Printing, November, 1992

10 9 8 7 6 5 4 3

Ⓟ REGISTERED TRADEMARK—MARCA REGISTRADA

LIBRARY OF CONGRESS CATALOGING IN PUBLICATION DATA:
Comer, James P.
    Raising Black children : questions and answers for parents and
teachers / James P. Comer, Alvin F. Poussaint.
        p. cm.
    ISBN 0-452-26839-7 (pbk.)
    1. Child rearing—United States—Miscellanea. 2. Afro-American
children—Miscellanea. 3. Adolescence—Miscellanea. 4. Education—
United States—Miscellanea. I. Poussaint, Alvin F. II. Title.
HQ769.C6323 1992
649'.1'08996073—dc20   92–53563
                                                           CIP

Printed in the United States of America
Set in Palatino
Designed by Eve L. Kirch

To our parents, extended families,
and all the parents, teachers, and children
who have helped us learn about children.

We would like to thank those who have assisted us in preparing this revision of *Black Child Care*. We especially appreciate the assistance provided by our administrative assistants, Ms. Etta G. Burke and Ms. Barbara B. Sweeny. Without the help of these and others, this revision would have remained a bright but unfinished idea.

However, we, the authors remain solely responsible for the contents of both the original and revision—its strengths and its weaknesses. We hope that you will experience the same joy and hope for the black child in reading this revised edition as we did in writing it.

Contents

CHAPTER 1

About This Book

This book is for all people who are involved in the important job of helping African-American children develop in a healthy way.

As black psychiatrists, we are constantly being asked questions about rearing black children—in the office, at schools, at social gatherings. Prior to the 1970s, these questions were almost never raised. Blacks and whites alike, for different reasons, pretended that all children—in fact, all people—were the same. Rearing a black child was just like rearing a white child. Some people still make that claim.

We believe there is a difference. Growing up black in America, where most policy-making and attitudes are influenced and controlled by whites who are often antagonistic or indifferent to the needs of blacks, poses many special problems for black parents and their children. The black awareness movement of the 1970s brought these problems out into the open. Increasing numbers of people are now conscious of the need to prepare black children to deal with the questions and issues of race in a way that will be the most beneficial to their overall emotional, social, and psychological growth and development.

What is the basic problem facing black parents? The responsibility of all parents is to help their children develop in a way that will equip them to function well as individuals, family members, and citizens. Parents are most able and willing to do this when they have a sense of belonging in the larger society. This sense of belonging can only be felt when the rights of parents are protected and obstacles to earning a living and respect are not placed in their way. Belonging to the whole provides individuals with a sense of security. A sense of belonging makes it easy and proper for parents to accept the values and ways of the society and pass them on to their children.

In America, however, racist attitudes and actions deny blacks a oneness with society and the security that comes from this feeling. Racism forces blacks to fight for the respect that whites take for granted and often bars blacks from earning an adequate income. Hence many black parents question and have mixed feelings about passing on the values and ways of a society that says in so many ways, "We do not value black men and women, boys and girls, as much as we do whites."

As black parents, we generally don't spend much time thinking about this larger problem of rejection because we are so busy trying to answer and solve the day-to-day questions and problems that the situation creates. For example, should black children repeat the Pledge of Allegiance to the American flag? The question itself indicates our mixed feelings about our place in the nation. This same doubtfulness shows up when we challenge mainstream or middle-class, that is, "white" ways. The need to preserve our culture and community springs from a desire to maintain a real and psychological place, where we are accepted, respected, and protected. For this reason we are concerned about whether "white psychology and child-rearing approaches" will change us, hurt us, destroy our culture.

The push by some to establish separate schools for black males is an effort to address these concerns. The same issues underlie the interest in the Afro-centric curriculum for African-American children. The belief is that black children—males viewed as more threatening and therefore experiencing more rejection and repression—need an environment that constructively and positively affirms them . . . the racial self as a part of the individual self, and vice versa. The belief is that an improved academic performance is possible with such self-esteem.

How to deal with our feelings of aggression and to what extent we should adapt standards established by whites are additional issues of great concern to black parents. Many blacks feel that we have been too passive in the past; that we are going to have to fight more aggressively for the rights, respect, and opportunity we want for ourselves and our children. We ask ourselves to what extent adaptation is compatible with black needs. These questions of aggression and adaptation and how to deal with them effectively in raising our children will be dealt with in several chapters in this book.

Besides the previously mentioned concerns, black parents must also deal with all of the child-rearing issues that face every parent. At the same time, they must also take into account and be prepared to cope with the many new issues posed by rapidly changing attitudes and values within our society regarding such vital matters as family life, sex, and authority. All of these concerns have been intensified by the rise of illegal drug use, crime, and AIDS (Acquired Immunodeficiency Syndrome). As a result, the issues and questions facing black parents are many and varied. We also receive numerous questions from whites who in one way or another are involved with the development of black children—as teachers, social workers, parents, and friends.

Typical of the race-related questions we have been asked are the following:

"My fifteen-year-old daughter attends a high school that is about fifteen percent black. She was recently elected to the student council, but some of the black students called her 'Aunt Tomassina' for running for office. She is all mixed up about it. How can I help her?"

"My husband refers to all whites on television as 'ice people.' Can't that cause a problem for our children when they have contact with whites?"

"I read in a sex book that blacks are more susceptible to venereal disease and that the susceptibility is inherited. Is that true? If it is true, should I warn my teenagers of that fact?"

"How can I, a white teacher, help a black child establish a positive black identity?"

In the area of general child care and child rearing, queries include:

"My child is two years of age and he still isn't toilet trained. What should I do?"

"How do you help disadvantaged children develop self-confidence in school?"

"Can a mother who works outside of the home give a child adequate emotional support?"

"My daughter was a very happy child and a good student in elementary school. This year she went to junior high school and we have had nothing but trouble. There is no obvious problem. What do you think is going on?"

And in trying to deal with specific problems raised by our troubled society, parents and others involved with children ask us such things as:

"What should I tell my teenagers about sex in this sex-crazy age?"

"How can I help my child stay away from drugs when they are so common in the neighborhood?"

"How does a teacher help a child become a good citizen when the teacher has no authority in the child's eyes?"

Where do we turn for answers to these and other questions? Despite the large number of child-care books on the market, most of them are geared toward the middle-income white family. Few discuss race-related issues of child rearing. Few discuss low-income children and families. Because race- and income-related issues do cause special problems, it is essential that a child-rearing approach that takes these important factors into consideration be available. That is why we decided to write this book.

It would be presumptuous of anyone to think that they could or should give absolute and final "answers." We are not going to try. We have a point of view, based on years of experience in the field, which we will present. We have confidence in the "good sense" of parents, and we don't want you to become dependent on this or any other book to the point that you don't think for yourself. An African proverb says, "If you catch fish for a man, he will be grateful to you and dependent on you forever. If you show him how to catch fish, he will catch his own and be proud of himself." "Answers" alone would be catching your fish for you.

On the other hand, it is possible to have good sense yet lack certain insights into how children grow or why we as adults react to them in certain ways—thus causing us even more trouble with our children. For this reason we are going to talk about how children mature and how that growth affects their emotional, psychological, and social development. Our intent is to share with you some of the latest findings and thinking in the child-development field. We hope that you will select and use what appears appropriate for you and your child. We believe that the more you are in tune with yourself and your child, the better your chances of keeping things under control, of being the kind of parent you would like to be—the kind of parent your child needs and deserves.

Excerpts from a previous edition of this book were published in *Ebony* magazine. One parent wrote a letter to the editor criticizing us for being "too wishy-washy," or conditional, and not giving hard-and-fast answers. The growing-up process is dynamic and changing. Thus, although parents need to be firm at times, they also need to be flexible and capable of responding to certain changing conditions. We have structured this book to help you think about what is going on with your child and how to respond in a positive way. Hard-and-fast answers would often put you out of touch with your child's need at a given time.

We have designed this book to serve as a practical reference guide for parents. The bulk of it is devoted to a stage-by-stage study of the black child's development from infancy through adolescence, with special emphasis on the role of parents and teachers of school-age children. By way of background, we will begin with a brief summary of the historical experience of black youth in America.

The tendency to compare blacks with whites as if white behavior represented the norm still exists in the minds and writings of many, including many blacks. This is because the white-controlled media have highlighted black problems but have seldom discussed the reasons for their existence. (In fact, the media have only recently begun to portray healthy and successful black families.) Yet knowing the causes of black family problems and how to overcome them, as well as having an awareness of black family and community strengths, can affect how black parents think about themselves and, in turn, influence the kind of care they give their young. It can also affect how white teachers and others view black youth.

We will use the question-and-response format throughout the book. In our daily work we are constantly receiving questions and giving responses, and we have found that most parents find this approach the most useful. We, in turn, feel that this is the most simple and direct method by which to present you, the reader, with the facts. In addition, after you read the book, you may want to refer back to various sections as specific problems arise. The question-and-response style should provide a convenient way to locate your query and our response.

CHAPTER 2

America and the Black Child

THE BLACK CHILD AND SLAVERY

How were black children treated during slavery?

Black children were abused and denied a happy childhood and the opportunity to develop to their fullest potential. During slavery, they were put to work at very early ages picking cotton in the fields. As house slaves, they cared for members of the mistress' family, including children and adults with mental or physical disabilities.

These black children who served as helpmates and personal servants to white children were often assigned to them for twenty-four hours a day. Slave children slept on the floor beside the beds of white children and reported to the master if their charges were in distress. During play, white children often used the slave child to test objects of curiosity or go first into strange places. Slave children attended to every minor need of the white children. When other white children came to visit, the black children were at their command as well. Black children were also used as playmates but were often shunned, depending on the occasion.

How did black parents handle this situation?

Black slaves did not have sufficient opportunity to rear their own children, because they were made to work either in the fields or in the house of the slave master. Often they were responsible for the rearing of the white children. This meant devoting special attention to the physical and emotional needs of the white child, whereas their own black child was either back at the cabin being attended by other children or, if older, helping the mother care for the white slave master's child, or tending a white child on his own.

How did black children manage to survive as well as they did up through the Civil War?

Black children survived because of the love, support, and determination of the black family. However, many black children did not survive. Because of the poor health care provided for the slave parent and child, many suffered grave illnesses and injuries, which resulted in lifelong physical impairments.

THE BLACK CHILD TODAY

How have black children fared since Emancipation?

Even after slavery was legally abolished, black children were one of the most mistreated and neglected groups in American society. They have consistently borne the devastating effects of white racism. Many have shouldered the double burden of growing up both poor and black. Some have been damaged so severely early in life that their chances for a happy, productive adulthood have been small. But as a result of the intensification of the Civil Rights Movement in the 1960s and 1970s, some black children are now receiving high-quality developmental, educational, and social opportunities. On the other hand, because of the political climate of the 1980s, conditions for many have worsened.

How early do social conditions begin to affect the development of the black child?

A child's life expectancy is to some extent determined before birth. The health of the mother while she is pregnant affects the well-being of the child. Black women have often carried their babies without the benefit of a balanced diet and adequate medical care. Children born of malnourished mothers are often weak and sickly, running a high risk of mental retardation and delayed physical development. Black women have suffered more from anemia and other complications of pregnancy than have white women. The care received by the mother and infant at the time of birth also affects a child's development. Black women have consistently lacked adequate access to doctors and medical facilities at the time of delivery. In many parts of the country, their children have been delivered by untrained midwives. Prenatal complications and physical birth injuries have resulted in brain-damaged and otherwise disabled children. As a result the infant mortality rate for black children has always been many times the white rate. Today, the black infant mortality rate is about twice that estimated for whites. This is due partly to poverty and the high number of teenage pregnancies. Infants of teenagers are at risk for having a low birth weight, which increases the risk of other health problems. Some babies are also damaged by a pregnant woman's abuse of illicit drugs and alcohol.

How else has the black child's welfare been influenced by social and economic factors?

The economic hardships that traditionally plagued the black family have directly affected the black child in a number of ways. In some parts of America, blacks still live in shacks without running water or toilets. Some homes lack heat and have dirt floors. It is difficult, if not impossible, to maintain the necessary sanitary standards in caring for a baby. In many city ghettos, families are crowded together in dilapidated tenements infested with rats and cockroaches. Food, clothes, shoes, and other basic items are often scarce. Such aids to a child's motor and intellectual development as toys, books, and play areas are frequently unattainable. Because they cannot afford to buy toys and games for their children, some black parents have had to invent activities to teach and amuse them, which may be a blessing in disguise. But the drug and crime culture that became so prevalent during the 1980s has severely impaired the health and well-being of many black children.

How true is the charge that black parents have traditionally neglected their offspring?

Frequently both parents have had to work because black fam-

ilies have been overburdened with social hardships and because
wages were low. This has meant that black children left at home
usually have had to assume many responsibilities at a very early
age. The black child at age five and six is often expected to watch
over the younger children, run errands, and help with house-
work. At age eight and nine, many have odd jobs—as field
hands, newsboys, shoeshine boys—to supplement the family
income. Often they earn their own money for candy and other
treats. In many Southern towns, the children of black share-
croppers were exploited as a source of cheap or free labor. In
the past, schedules of black schools were so arranged that black
children could be released to pick cotton and other crops during
harvest seasons. Their education was secondary to meeting the
labor needs of the plantation bosses.

Do black children feel that their parents are unable to protect them?

In some cases, yes. This was particularly true in the past
when children quickly learned that authority lay in the hands of
whites and that blacks had no protection against white violence
and lawlessness. Even in his own home the black child saw
evidence of the white man's control over the economic and social
well-being of his family. The black child was likely to grow up
regarding his parents as weak figures under the domination of
the white man. Also, persistently unemployed and teenage parents are often unable to be protective. In fact, some black children
have turned to the drug culture to earn money for themselves
and their families. Today, black children who live in poverty are
more likely to view their parents as powerless.

How have black children been trained to cope with white oppression?

In the past, black children were taught the rituals of servitude
and docility from the time they could talk. These rituals included
addressing all whites, adults and children alike, with a "yes sir"
or "no sir." In turn they were called names like "tar baby" or
"Little Black Sambo" and otherwise cruelly mocked and tor-
mented by whites. Today the black child is still made to feel
inferior to whites. From his earliest days he senses that his life

is viewed cheaply by white society and that he enjoys little protection at its hands. For example, black youths are frequently the victims of racially motivated police abuse at an early age.

How has the black child managed to adapt through the years in a society that so profoundly threatens his self-esteem?

The black child has been forced to learn to live in two cultures—his own minority culture and the majority one. He has had to teach himself to contain his aggression around whites, while freely expressing it among blacks. Although some people call this a survival technique, it contributes to black-on-black violence.

Does the black child resort to other such tactics for self-preservation?

Yes. Over the years black children have become skilled in the use of a variety of techniques in their struggle for survival and well-being in a hostile and unjust society. They have had to learn to be practical as well as cunning. They have had to learn how to win some sort of acceptance from belligerent whites. Black children have often assumed the responsibilities and burdens of adulthood at a very early age. Many have had little of what we call a childhood. In the black world, adolescence starts early in life, and unlike most white youngsters, many black children do not enjoy the luxury of a period of playtime and learning which extends into their late teens.

EDUCATION AND THE BLACK CHILD

In view of the general situation, how have so many black children managed to get an education?

Thanks to sheer determination, black parents have sent their youngsters through school, college, and on to great achievement despite the fact that schools have deliberately educated black children to assume menial roles in society. Much of the credit is due, as well, to black children themselves, who through their inner strength have refused to accept forever being "boys" and "girls."

In the past, what happened to those black youngsters who were denied an education?

Many black boys denied a chance for an education were able to earn a living and support themselves through heavy manual labor—agricultural and industrial. Black women had to accept low-paying, often backbreaking domestic work. As long as the economy could absorb undereducated people, such youngsters were able to grow up and meet their adult responsibilities as heads of households despite the low pay and hard work. But this has been more difficult since the 1960s, when the better-paying jobs began to require a higher level of education.

Isn't it fair to say then that things are much better now for black children than they were thirty years ago?

Yes, but although opportunities are better for many, too many are in trouble because of the reversal in the 1980s of gains made during the 1970s. Opportunities have opened up in professional areas other than medicine, law, religion, teaching, nursing, and social work. Today there are many more opportunities in science, engineering, and business. There are efforts to recruit blacks in almost every professional and technical area and business. Blacks are excelling in the arts and in athletics in ways that were only dreamed of thirty years ago. Black children must be encouraged to enter and achieve in all fields. But we must help black boys in particular understand that professional athletics is generally not an obtainable goal. Only 1 percent of fourth-year college athletes become professional rookies, and the careers of most of these men don't last more than two years. Too many youngsters spend too much time in athletics and too little time applying themselves in academic areas. They can be shown that it is possible and necessary to achieve academically *and* in athletics.

How can we best prepare our youngsters for this new age?

In order to take advantage of new opportunities we must raise strong, well-educated, and computer-literate black children. There is no longer a need for docility. It should be replaced with

an attitude of black pride, self-confidence, and appropriate assertiveness. Good child-rearing practices have become a crucial
element in assuring the future of black Americans. Children
raised in an atmosphere of love and security, even in the poorest
homes, will be prepared to face the challenges of tomorrow.

Without family and community support, however, children
cannot thrive. The family—mother, father, grandparents, cou-
sins, uncles, and aunts—passes on to a growing child both the
strengths of the old culture and the rules and techniques essential
for successful adaptation in the modern world. Because of the
serious problems within many communities, family guidance and
support is more important than ever.

CHAPTER 3

The Infant

ESTABLISHING YOUR INFANT'S IDENTITY

What is the age range of infancy?
About two years.

Is this period of life as important as later periods?
It is one of the most important. During this period the infant must establish a relationship with a caretaker, which becomes a blueprint for future relationships with other people. It is now that the biological, social, and emotional patterns are established which, with modification, will remain with the infant for the rest of his or her life.

Should black children be brought up in the same way as white children?
Our basic child-rearing practices should be the same as those of other groups. There will always be some differences between groups however, because we all bring our different cultures to bear in the job of child rearing.

Good child-rearing principles are fundamentally the same for all, because the basic needs of children are universal. Youngsters need food, clothing, shelter, and protection from physical and psychological damage. They need to be able to trust and feel affection for one or more adults from whom they can learn. They need to be taught to control their aggressive and impulsive energy in order to be able to learn, work, and play in gradually more mature ways. In providing for the psychological well-being of our children, we, as black parents, will occasionally need to act in special ways. (We will discuss such situations as they arise throughout the book.) But this is no different from what other groups have done through such means as religious schools and indoctrination of one kind or another.

Modern life forces groups of every kind to maintain the flexibility necessary to accept changes. As long as such changes protect and provide for the best interest of our children, there is little reason for concern. Black parents must realize that culture changes are normal and do not mean culture loss.

Does white psychology apply to black people?

There is no distinct black psychology or white psychology. However, psychological practices in the United States have been white-dominated and are often culturally biased and racist. Many psychological tests, standardized on white people, are inappropriately applied to blacks, causing them to appear less intelligent or deficient. These types of abuses must be corrected. Nonetheless, blacks and whites alike experience aggression, affection, independence, dependency. Everything that the black mind is capable of, the white mind is capable of. What appear as differences are the results of experience and training. When used correctly, many psychological principles are applicable to all.

We blacks have a concern about the threat of training or "brainwashing" black children to be passive or nonaggressive. We fear this has or can lead to acceptance of and adjustment to an unjust society. This concern has led to some confusion about the value of certain psychological principles, particularly those of aggression control and adaptation referred to in Chapter 1. These principles do not mean "accept and adjust" to everything. Control of aggression means handling it so that it works for you rather than against you, in any way necessary for as long as necessary. Adaptation simply means coping with the world around you, and changing it if necessary, even by militant struggle if there is no other way.

If the basic rearing of infants is similar everywhere, why then is it important to include a discussion of infants when discussing black child development?

Infant care determines a child's primary, core, and most important identity. A child's first self-image depends upon the responses of others; the child will feel he or she is a positive or good person when relationships with important people—parents, caretakers, other family—around the child are good. These early positive feelings about the self help the child to learn and do one thing after another. Each success adds to the positive feeling about the self. This positive feeling makes it easier to keep on learning and doing despite an occasional failure. In time an unshakable core of positive feeling about the self develops. The child has an inner feeling that says, "I am a person. I am an able person. I am a good person." At this point a primary, positive identity has been established.

How can black parents help their child develop a positive primary identity?

As the child grows older, learning black history and experiencing black culture can strengthen his pride and broaden his sense of identity. Teaching a child strategies to deal with racism and the negative feelings about being black that racism incurs is very helpful. But nothing can substitute for the love, care, and training that the child needs from birth onward.

With such preparation black children are able to maintain positive feelings about themselves when growing up in racist environments, whereas those without proper preparation often have low levels of self-esteem. That is why some cling to "blackness" as an end in itself (which may be better than nothing), but "blackness" alone cannot sustain them. That's why some people who claim great pride in being black also do destructive things to themselves, other blacks, and the black community at large. Although they reason, "Black is beautiful, I am black, therefore I am beautiful," they can't make it work for them. A positive black identity (secondary identity) must be built on an inner core of pride and positive feelings (primary identity), or it may fade away under the harsh light of life's realities.

Have black parents been successful in handling identity problems in the past?

Black parents, for the most part, have traditionally helped their children develop this positive inner core. That is why so many blacks in every walk of life function so well. As we mentioned in Chapter 1, however, we want to share some insights from our training and experiences to help black parents become more effective in dealing with the familiar burden of racism. We, as a people, will be able to lighten their burden only when enough black youngsters can resist becoming the victims of racism and force society to abandon racist social policies and attitudes.

We are not saying give up the fight (whatever your methods) to change society now. We are saying that simultaneous with that fight, we must try and guide more black children through the obstacle course of racism that exists today. That is why a close look at what we can do as parents, caretakers, and friends, from before birth onward, is very important.

How can I promote racial pride in my infant?

Although infants become aware of color and feature differences, these things have no meaning to them. Unless they are taught in a very direct and specific way, they have little or no interest in the issue of skin color or racial variations until around three years of age. Race is a complicated concept that they learn over time. It is not helpful to try to explain the concept of race to an infant.

But you can discuss color and race-related issues in a natural way. For example, you can talk about body parts and functions to your child in a way that includes skin color. Thus, when you are helping your child learn colors—and after he has learned the meaning of "arm"—you can indicate "brown" or "black," pointing to his arm or to your arm. He will eventually learn that it is an arm of brown color.

Race is a subject you should discuss with your child in an easy and natural way. Providing your infant with both black and white dolls helps to make black, brown, and white normal—like the real world. When the question of color arises later, it can be discussed in a positive, relaxed manner because you have not previously ignored or overdramatized it.

If you attend an African-American church, belong to organizations that utilize Africa-based ritual such as the Kwanzaa celebration, or other race-conscious activities, your children will absorb the feeling and the meaning of these experiences. They will not be conscious of the racial aspect of them until you or others make them aware later on. Such activities, together with good basic child care, can be helpful in countering the negative information about race your child is likely to receive later on, as long as he or she continues to develop a positive sense of personal adequacy, and as long as important others help the child deal with the negative racial attitudes that arise later on. In short, the ethnocentric cultural experience is not a vaccination. When children reach eight or nine years of age and begin to compare themselves with others, and to place themselves in the large scheme of things, help in establishing a positive racial identity is crucial, and can be most successful regardless of what has gone before. This is true because the child's development and social situation makes eight or nine the critical moment for teaching, experiencing, and learning.

YOU AND YOUR UNBORN CHILD

What can be done before birth?
There is much to be done even before pregnancy. The beauty of having a baby has been overrated. A child is a major responsibility that will be with you over the next twenty to twenty-five years of your life. Parents can receive great pleasure from helping their children grow. There are certain experiences and memories that only a parent can have. On the other hand, there will be places parents can't go and things they can't do because they have children. Unless a couple is ready to take on a major responsibility and make sacrifices, they should not become parents.

Since having a baby changes a person's life in far-reaching ways, the decision to do so should not be made in haste or result from an "accident." It should not be based on such reasons as trying to save a shaky marriage, religious beliefs alone, or attempting to add future soldiers to the black cause. The only valid reason to have a baby is that you are ready, willing, and able to share yourself and your relationship with your partner with a child—and you are prepared to help that child grow in a healthy way, whatever may be involved.

What can parents do to help their child before birth?

As an expectant mother, your good health is your child's good health. Your diet, blood pressure, weight, and exercise patterns do affect your baby. The better you feel about having a baby, the more likely you are to take good care of yourself— which is a good reason to be sure that babies are wanted and pregnancies are planned.

Evidence now suggests that when things are going well, the expectant mother need not see the doctor or nurse as often as was once thought necessary. But you should be under medical supervision throughout your pregnancy. Even today, too many black mothers see their doctor for the first time at delivery. This increases the chances of birth injury, defect, and death.

It is important for fathers and other relatives to be supportive of expectant mothers—without making mother the baby! Give some time to your wife, father-to-be. It's your baby, too. If you are not willing to do your bit now as well as after the baby arrives, you shouldn't be having a child.

Also, it is the obligation of the mother and father to establish and practice good health habits before, during, and after the pregnancy. It is best not to take any drugs—legal or illegal— during pregnancy, if possible. If there are medical problems that require medications, it is important to be under a doctor's care and to follow instructions carefully. Also, remember that cigarettes, alcohol, and cocaine ("crack") can produce severe birth defects. Women should not drink alcohol, smoke, or take illicit drugs during pregnancy. Mothers who ingest large quantities of alcohol can produce children with stunted growth and mental retardation; this condition is termed *fetal alcohol syndrome*. Pregnant women who smoke are more likely to have premature and low birth-weight infants. "Crack" babies may have severe neurological and emotional impairment. These children may be extremely irritable and have difficulty in forming normal emotional contacts. Such infants may require special patience and management. The avoidance of sexually transmitted diseases, particularly AIDS, is critical. Your child's life can be at risk and future health impaired unless you protect yourself.

THE PROBLEM OF POSTNATAL DEPRESSION

We wanted and planned the baby. I had good support. I still got depressed. Why?

Depression after childbirth under the best of circumstances is not unusual, and doctors are not absolutely sure of the cause. The emotional buildup—anticipation, excitement, fear—and then the normal letdown when it finally happens is thought to be the major cause. Chemical changes also play a role. When all else is well, the depression soon passes.

With first babies, there is often an additional factor. The mother asks herself: "Can I be a good mother?" With the support of others and contact with your baby, your doubts will soon pass.

HELPING BABY GROW

What does a baby inherit or receive from parents?

A baby inherits all physical characteristics plus mental and motor or movement capacities. The vast majority of human beings inherit mental and movement potentials that fall within a very narrow range. Many of the eventual differences in ability and performance between people depend on "what you do with what you got" or, more accurately, what a child's environment —parents, school, society—help and permit the child to do with what he or she inherited.

Only a very small amount of the known genetic material, maybe 1 to 2 percent, is responsible for the physical characteristics that distinguish one group or one person from another. In other words, only 1 to 2 percent of genetic material is involved in creating the physical differences between races—blacks, whites, browns, and yellows.

What must I help my baby accomplish in the first two years of life?

You must help your baby achieve increasing motor (muscle) control, language, and social development. In addition, the baby must become dependent, secure, and trusting enough to receive protection and learn from others. At the same time, he must become independent enough to explore himself and his environment. You must help your infant develop the desire to gain one new skill after another—to observe, listen, think, learn, remember, and generally develop both mind and body. Where circumstances permit, it is important that fathers be involved as much as possible.

What is there about the relationship between me and my baby that makes it possible for me to influence this development?

Because a baby is completely dependent at birth, you must meet her every need. As you feed, bathe, and diaper your infant, an attachment of great force normally develops between you and your baby. In fact, it need not be the mother who performs these particular functions. The baby soon attaches pleasure and security with whoever the caretaking person may be.

The child becomes extremely close to the mother, father, or caretaker by three months of age. It is not until about nine months that the baby begins to move toward separateness again, but even then maintains a close tie. She wants to please you, and therefore you are in a position to help your child gradually learn to control or delay the immediate need to satisfy every urge or impulse. This permits the child to give time and attention to accomplishing increasingly difficult tasks, and also permits you to interact with her! When the caretaker-child bond is not well established, physical, social, and emotional growth and general development are hampered.

What is the time schedule of this development in the first two years?

(A) *Motor development (muscle control).* The ability to suck is the only well-developed motor activity a child is born with. Obviously this makes feeding and growth possible. You must help develop all other motor functions. We will discuss ways to do this on pages 27–29.

Motor development (muscle control) proceeds form the head or neck down. By four weeks the baby is able to control eye movement and looks directly at nearby objects or people. By three months the baby is able to look around in all directions. At about the fourth month, or sixteen weeks, the baby is able to control movement of his head. His hands are now open rather than closed. About the seventh or eighth month, the baby can now sit up. He can grasp and manipulate objects with his hands and makes raking motions toward objects out of reach. At about nine months, the baby can crawl and, soon after, creep. By ten months he is able to pull himself to his feet by using the side of his playpen or other fixed objects. He can now release objects from his hands with some difficulty. By the end of a year, most babies begin to walk, and have better control of their hands and upper body.

By eighteen months, the baby walks without falling, can sit down readily, and has improved eye-to-hand coordination, which makes stacking three or four blocks or similar activities possible. The two-year-old walks with greater control and is not "all over the place," walking for the sake of walking. When the two-year-old walks, it's because he has someplace to go!

(B) *Speech development.* Speech development starts at birth, perhaps even before, although we have no way to be sure. Infants make and respond to sounds from the beginning. A baby listens to the voice of the caretaker in the first few weeks. By the fifth or sixth week he begins to make repetitive sounds called babbling. By the sixteenth week a baby is cooing and making sounds in response to the words and presence of those interacting with him. The infant is now clearly imitating what he hears. By twenty-four weeks babies have learned the basic sounds of their native language, whether it is English, French, Chinese, or any other. By the twenty-eighth week a baby is using his voice with gusto. There is a clear desire to have others respond and to make others understand. By the tenth month your baby is able to say one or two words and will respond to his name. On request he will often wave "bye-bye" and shows caution or stops what he is doing when told "no-no."

By twelve months a baby jabbers away and appears to enjoy hearing himself. This jabbering becomes increasingly expressive and takes on a conversational tone. By eighteen months a baby begins to use key words to express a need and obtain a desired response. For example: "Eat" will mean, "I am hungry. I would like to be fed." "Potty" will mean, "I am ready to have a bowel movement. Help me with my potty." The value of language becomes apparent to the child through these requests and the responses he receives. Language also helps the child become more and more integrated with the people and the world around him. Thus he is motivated to learn more and more words, to name objects, to inquire about the names of unfamiliar things.

The two-year-old can say "I," and has mastered two or three sentences but generally uses phrases. Language, through adult-child interaction, gradually becomes a way to understand or have a concept. This ability leads to thinking and reasoning.

Just as with motor control, there are ways in which you can help your infant improve his language skills. We will discuss these on pages 31–33. In this and other areas of training, however, it must be stressed that the parent should not become discouraged if he meets with success one day and failure the next. That's normal. Calmly start your training all over. Over-reacting to the normal course of events may cause the baby to feel failure where none exists, except for a parent's frustration. It is particularly harmful to spank a baby, or to refer to your baby as stupid, even in jest, and before he understands the meaning of the word. The tone and the manner send a harmful message. And spanking your child may lead to rebellious non-compliance with your demands for toilet training.

(C) *Social and personal development*. Social and personal development begin with the child's discovery of an outside world as well as the discovery that he is a separate and distinct individual. Improved control of the eyes and hands permits increased exploration of the self, other people, clothing, and crib toys. Language development increases the interaction with the caretaker and speeds social and personal development.

A baby recognizes and responds to a human face at about one or two months of age, and at about the same age the baby smiles in response to your smile. Your baby will attempt to reach your face, will appear surprised and frightened when it disappears, and will attempt to follow it. A "ham" from the beginning, he will smile at his reflection in a mirror. The baby imitates the movements of adults and loves to be tickled and gently bounced, but he can become frightened when physical play gets too rough.

After the first six months, the infant will show interest in games in which you hide small objects and he looks for them. He will try to repeat what an adult has just done while playing a game. He becomes more and more an "actor." During the ninth to eighteenth months, the baby comes into his own. He is now very much aware of himself as separate and distinct from other people. Even before he walks, he explores everything he can get his hands on. Once he is walking, exploration is the rule. He goes in all directions and gets into everything. He wants to make decisions for himself and quickly learns to say no. At the same time he will often cooperate to please you.

To gain attention and to establish his separateness, he begins to show his clothing and personal articles to everybody, as if to say, "This is me, right?" He continues to figure out who he is, where he fits in, and how he relates to the rest of the world—generally his family at this point.

Again, all of this behavior may be delayed when the caretaker-child bond is not good.

THE ABSENT PARENT

I must work. Will I harm my baby by leaving him with a caretaker?

Not if you have a good caretaker. In the past, it was thought that mothers should not work, but should stay home with their children. It was believed that an exclusive relationship between mother and baby was necessary for good child development. Evidence now suggests that as long as there are not too many adults involved, or caretakers do not change too rapidly, babies will do very well. It is important, however, that you care for your child regularly during available time after work. Temporary separations and reunions between mother and child help the child learn to deal with strangers more easily.

What about vacations or extended periods away from the baby during the first year?

Keep in mind that it is extremely important for your child to make an attachment to parents during the first year of life. Children who do not have this period of total attachment and dependency often show a longing for dependency and a desire to be cared for, as well as a higher level of anxiety, later in life. Although it is true that some children, particularly if they are cared for by a single familiar caretaker during your absence, will not show any ill effects, we nevertheless advise you to avoid extended absences during the first year.

Illness requiring hospitalization forces some mothers to be away from their babies. A single caretaker should be sought during this period to keep the baby's environment as predictable and secure as possible.

I often feel depressed. Can this harm my baby?

Depressed or stressed mothers are "away" even when they are present. It is hard for you to make your child feel secure and able to relate to things and people if you are stressed out or depressed. This is a destructive situation.

It is best to try to avoid conditions that lead to depression. This is one reason why we mentioned earlier that having babies should be planned. They should come at a time when you're likely to have the support of friends and relatives, and when you are not under a great deal of stress. It is important to have the support of relatives and friends so that an occasional evening or day away from the baby is possible. Father can spare mother and vice versa, depending on who is most involved and in need of a break. This is especially necessary if you have a very active baby.

People without family or friends who are willing to help, or lacking money to pay for help are most vulnerable. This is more often the case with very young mothers isolated from their families, and it's a good reason to postpone having children until a better income and support situation can be created. Sometimes mothers in such a situation can work out an arrangement in which they relieve each other from time to time, or create a support network through a local church, clinic, or community center.

VARIATIONS IN INFANT DEVELOPMENT

The baby down the street, the same age as mine, is walking and my baby is not. Am I doing something wrong?

Probably not. Each child appears to have a time clock of his or her own, which is determined from within. In addition, personal differences in activity levels and temperament show up from the very beginning. Only extreme cases of malnutrition or serious mishandling slow a child's growth. Babies grow and develop in spurts, with rapid growth and change, then level off, only to take off again. Most of what you observe as slow growth is actually a period between spurts. If the baby down the street is ahead of yours in some way, don't be alarmed; your baby's time will come. Some children, because of low birth weight or damage from drugs and inherited disabilities, may not develop normally. However, routine visits to the well-baby clinic will enable the doctor to assess whether there are any developmental abnormalities.

Are babies who develop faster smarter than others?

Rate of development is no indication of the level of intelligence. With good care, slow developers will eventually move to the level of ability of which they are capable.

Isn't there some evidence that black babies gain control of their bodies faster than white babies?

There are conflicting reports about this. Evidence does exist to show that motor development takes place faster during the first year among many African babies than among many European babies. Some observers feel that this is because African babies are carried on the mother's back; others believe that it is due to genetic differences. But because Africa and Europe are such vast areas and only a few studies have been done, we shouldn't make too much of these findings. Closer to home, some observers have reported that black American babies have better control of the neck at birth. It is almost impossible, however, to determine whether there are inherited differences in body movement control between black and white American babies.

Does faster motor development mean a lower degree of intelligence?

Experts agree that advanced motor or physical development is not a sign of lower mental ability. This outdated theory has been thoroughly disproved. There are simply too many bright children from all groups who have very rapid motor development. The old physical-mental argument is probably a remnant of Western culture's tendency to value mental activity over physical activity. In other cultures, those who were physically gifted were thought to be gifted mentally. We feel that this latter theory is more accurate. If your child is active and develops body control faster than he or she should according to the book, be grateful.

WAYS TO ENCOURAGE MOTOR DEVELOPMENT

How can I help stimulate my infant's motor or movement control?

Much of this can be done in the normal course of playing with your baby. Rocking the baby to your own singing or to recorded music will encourage motor development. Enticing toys just out of reach will encourage movement. After the child's hand opens up in the second or third month, place objects of different size, shape, consistency, and noisemaking ability in it. This will promote muscle use in the child's hand. Playing with the bath cloth, your clothing, his clothing, the crib rail, and other objects helps the child learn to use his hands. Moving his legs and arms, pulling him up, and holding your child in a standing position will help him discover and try to use these muscles.

A cradle gym is an excellent toy for helping a baby develop eye-muscle control and arm and hand coordination. Bright or noisemaking objects will attract the baby's interest, and he will try to grab or follow them with his eyes. Changing the position of these objects and substituting new objects from time to time will maintain the baby's interest. If you make your own cradle gym out of household items, be certain that it is safe. Beware of sharp objects or materials small enough for the baby to swallow! Once the child is out of the crib, a baby walker permits him to move about in safety. Because a walker does limit the baby's movement, however, it should only be used for short periods of time when you can watch what the child is doing.

What about feeding himself?

When your baby makes reasonably good attempts to feed himself, encourage it. Not only does this promote a feeling of independence, it also permits him to develop greater skill in using his hands. Some mothers feel that babies are so messy that it's easier to feed them, but this prevents the baby from developing independence and delays the development of movement control. In teaching all skills, it's best to show the child how to do it first and then let him practice. Put the spoon to his mouth yourself and then let baby try it, helping only when necessary.

Is "destructive" behavior sometimes permissible?

Children love to tear up newspapers, magazines, and anything else they can get their hands on. Some parents feel that this is messy and destructive behavior, but it is really a safe release of aggression, an exercise for the hand muscles, and a learning experience. Let them sit on the floor and tear up things you don't want. With your "no-no" as they approach the bookcase, they will learn what is fair game for the "tear mill" and what is not. Speaking of the floor and bookcases, be certain to place dangerous objects out of reach when your baby is out of the crib. Furniture that can be tipped over should be removed.

What about activities for the walking child?

The walking child will want more interesting things to do. The toy he can pull along, as if he's taking it someplace very important, is one he will like most. You can make your own toys out of empty ice-cream cartons, hair rollers, small boxes, or even pots and pans, if you don't mind the noise. Perhaps of equal pleasure to pulling a toy is pounding a block. Pounding in a peg with a wooden hammer is also a favorite activity; it promotes arm and shoulder muscle development and eye-hand coordination. Rolling a ball back and forth is another beneficial and pleasurable pastime.

Outdoors, sand and water play is the runaway favorite of the eighteen-month-old set. Slopping around in the resulting mess is close to godliness, and good for the release of tensions. It also encourages the use of the hands and offers the possibility of creative building and learning.

Around eighteen months, the infant also gets a great deal of pleasure from drawing with large crayons. Do not look for great artistic achievements, however. The development of your child's muscle and nervous system, at this point, will not permit it. A child is able to copy a circle only after about two years of age, a cross at about three years of age, a square at about five years of age, and a diamond at about seven years of age. But scribbling is wonderful fun and good for developing the hand. The child enjoys the act of creation, and it is important to applaud or clap—for the effort rather than the outcome. Clapping and showing signs of delight—smiling, hugging, and such—will encourage your child to try in a number of activities.

Around eighteen months your child will want to walk up and down stairs and jump off. It helps to hold at least one hand at first. It is also important to discourage heroic efforts such as jumping more stairs than he can handle. About the same time a baby will try to climb onto chairs, tables, or anything else he can reach. When you must rescue your little explorer from a precarious position, swift action in a calm manner, and afterward a clear, short explanation of the danger is helpful. Screams startle the child and can cause the fall you were afraid of. Prolonged scoldings, usually reflecting your anxiety over "what could have happened," are not helpful and they do not prevent future possible disasters.

PROTECTING YOUR INFANT: HOW MUCH AND WHEN

How can I keep my baby from harm?
Infants don't plan to get into trouble. They simply don't know what is dangerous or what can become dangerous. If you can

anticipate danger by placing harmful objects out of reach, for example, this will help. Once an infant has been exposed to danger he will need a simple explanation that relieves his fear and increases his knowledge so that he can gradually learn to avoid dangerous activities. But because babies can't yet "remember," they can't always transfer their learning from one situation to another; you must remind them over and over again. Be gentle: Angry scoldings can shake their confidence and reduce the desire to explore. Exploration aids learning and motor development.

Can't too much concern about safety hurt a child's development?

Safety should always be in the back of a parent's mind— something that we think about when the baby is in the crib, and especially when he or she is not. We should anticipate such dangerous situations as those already mentioned—sharp objects and tipping furniture. When you "think safety," it is possible to help your child learn from the beginning that paint peelings, caustic cleaners, and other dangerous materials are a "no-no." But once you have done all you can to ensure safety, a relaxed, calm attitude is necessary. Fear and overconcern can cause you to keep your child from taking the ordinary risks and suffering the ordinary frustration and pain a child needs in order to learn.

Some people have argued that black children will face greater hardships in life than whites, and therefore that soothing and comforting them after falls, fights, or frustrations is not good for them. It has also been argued that many white children, particularly those from middle-class families, are not tough or independent enough because they receive too much soothing, comforting, care, and attention, and are not allowed to take enough chances. Some parents—black, white, upper- and lower-income groups—do overprotect their children. Conversely, some parents are neglectful and cruel in the name of making their offspring tough.

There is a balance that must be struck. It is helpful for a child to experience danger, frustration, failure, and pain occasionally, but not to the point of being afraid to act. Don't get upset about every minor accident or fall. Smile so that the child understands that falling is natural when learning to walk; she will pick herself up and keep going. Enduring extreme frustration and repeated negative experiences do not give your child a psychological inoculation against future hardship. The will to "keep on keeping on" starts with support, protection, and encouragement from important loved ones. The will to go on disappears when nobody cares.

What about protection from teasing by older children?

The infant can be hurt by teasing. At this stage he has little self-confidence. We know of a case in which a teenage sister laughed at an eighteen-month-old child sitting on the potty. It was several months before anyone could get the child to use the potty again. In the meantime, he had his BMs in a corner of the room. You should encourage other children in the family to understand how important it is to respect the child's early efforts to crawl, walk, learn, and use the potty. A child doesn't start developing a self-image when he is five, ten, or fifteen. It begins to develop from the moment of birth and can be easily damaged early on in life.

ENCOURAGING LANGUAGE SKILLS

How can I aid language development?

Like motor development, language development starts at birth. Your baby speaks to you with gurgles, coos, and ga-gas. Gurgling, cooing, and ga-ga-ing back in a pleased and enthusiastic way promotes more sounds. When your baby starts to make sounds close to words, imitating the sound and later pronouncing the words slowly and distinctly will help him eventually pronounce the word. For example, "da da da" becomes "dada" and, finally, "Daddy."

Should I use baby talk?

Imitating and modifying the child's words is useful, but it is also important to talk to your child just as you would talk to anyone else. In this way the child is exposed to the rhythm and flow of speech. She begins to enjoy the sound of a pleasant conversational tone, and will enjoy listening to conversations between you and others. In fact, babies learn the fundamental sounds of their particular language by six months. The baby enjoys your speaking to her and will babble back and smile as if she understands. In the process she learns new words and develops a conversation pattern.

Talking to your baby about what you're doing while you're doing it is very helpful. Understanding language comes, in part, through the activity with which it is associated. If you say "Lift up your arm" when nothing is going on, your child won't understand you. But if you say "Lift up your arm" in order to put her arm in a sleeve while you are dressing her, she will soon understand the words and idea or concept. The more she understands, the more she will want to use language to make you understand her. Such phrases as "Let me stand you up, Janie" when you're doing so, or "Let's take those clothes off" not only establish language as a way to communicate but involve the child in the activity, so as to make her feel that she is involved in things that are done to her and for her. In this regard, it is also helpful to name objects—"bottle," "ball"—when a child is involved with them. This enables the child to name and call for those objects, giving her a greater sense of control and power. It also serves as a preparation for describing and classifying the world later on.

In what other ways can I encourage speech?

Singing or reading to the baby also helps promote language development. The most important thing here is the association of words with a pleasant experience. Your infant will want to snuggle up close to you and/or sit on your lap and let you read while he tries to turn the pages. He will enjoy this closeness to you and the pleasant sound of your voice, and this will result in a sense of security. Large, bright pictures are attractive to children as young as five or six months. Infants will listen as you pronounce the names of the objects in the picture, and will try to repeat the sound. Reading and language associated with such pleasant circumstances receive a positive emotional charge.

We believe that much of the motivation to read and use language starts in, or close to, the cradle.

Whether reading or singing, the child should be the center of the activity. Looking at him, pointing out things to him, being pleased when he joins in the singing or successfully names certain objects—all give the child a sense of well-being and encourage the use of more language. Name and finger games like This Little Piggy Went to Market not only help your child learn language but explore the body. They also provide essential close physical contact.

At what age will an infant "follow" orders?

Even before your baby learns to respond to directions, you can begin to encourage her to try things such as wave bye-bye or come to you in response to calling her name. Most children begin to respond to simple commands by nine months of age. Don't feel discouraged if yours does not, or responds one day but not the next. It takes a great deal of repetition for children to learn. Very often they will wave bye-bye consistently when you practice with them alone. Just when you want to show your neighbor how smart your child is, he will look at you as if you're crazy when you ask him to wave bye-bye. Don't try to force him or make him feel that he is a failure. Simply start training him all over again.

And remember, although it helps to understand that your play and activities with your child promote his development, it is equally important not to become too "teachy" about it. Relax, have fun, and interact with your child as the spirit moves you —or the crying calls you—but don't get hung up on rigid time schedules for promoting motor and language development.

STIMULATING THE INFANT MIND

What can I do to help my baby begin to think and learn?

Interest created by body movement or motor activity automatically puts your child's mind into gear. It starts almost accidentally. The baby's body goes through natural motions such as thumb sucking, which are pleasurable, and the act is repeated. Exploration continues. Your baby will examine everything she gets her hands on. She is doing more than being curious. She is learning about how things feel, how they work, how they're put together. Give her objects to explore of different size, taste, color, texture, and sound. Changing the kinds of objects she is exposed to is helpful. Your baby will tire of familiar things. Putting toys or objects eight to twelve inches in front of the very young baby's face and moving them encourages her to look around.

How can I best use words to help baby learn?

Naming objects gives your child words. Words used in connection with activities lead to understanding concepts and learning to think. For example, the word "water" is stated as a child touches water. Wet, the characteristic of water, may also be mentioned. A spill can lead to the concept of water as something wet, which flows, which can get on your skin and make you uncomfortable, and which sometimes makes Mommy angry. Eventually all of these meanings are sorted out and the differences and best usage are understood. A child who hears a lot of language and who is exposed to a lot of feeling, touching, and seeing experiences to which she can relate the words (and you can help her) will develop more concepts and start to become a good thinker earlier than a child who is hearing, doing, and receiving less.

Using words that describe the characteristics of objects—tall, short, hard, soft, cold, wet, and so on—is useful. These concepts can be taught during play, feeding, or other everyday activities. You can point out that your coffee is hot. After the baby has learned that a toy car is a toy car, you can move the car quickly and label the activity "fast." If the baby goes under a chair, you can say "under." As the baby climbs over the chair you can say "over," thus helping the baby learn new words and new concepts.

Having your baby identify parts of his own body, the same parts of your body, and similar parts in pictures helps the baby learn similarity and how to transfer learning from one situation to another. Using words like "after" you do this, or "before" you do that, or we will have a cookie "now" helps the baby learn the concept of time—the fact that there is a past, present, and future.

What about learning through play?

Through play your baby gradually learns that rattles, coins, and other objects are permanent. Peek-a-boo is an all-time favorite game with young children, and it helps them learn the concept of permanence. Hiding objects under sheets or guessing what hand the coin is in becomes great fun around a year to eighteen months of age. Having the child find the hidden object helps the child form a mental picture of it and to understand that things exist even when they are out of sight.

Numerous other concepts can be used to help your child develop through play and in the course of everyday activities. When you have three objects of different size in your hand, you can ask the child which one is big, which middle-sized, and which little. Two piles of paper on the table containing different numbers of sheets provides an opportunity to discuss the concept of more or less. The baby can learn colors by naming the color of objects in a room. Small objects of the same color can be matched, thus teaching the concept of matching characteristics —color, size, and shape. Putting pictures or puzzles together and taking them apart teaches the concept of whole and part. Tapping on objects made of different materials creates different noises and stimulates interest while the child learns about the objects in question.

What else can I teach my infant?

One of the most important things you must help your baby with is learning to wait or tolerate delay. Babies are impatient: they want what they want when they want it, often yesterday, and not a moment later. At the same time they love you deeply—you represent all the security they have in the world. They don't want to lose this safe feeling, and if you ask them to "wait just a minute" or say, "Let me get this for Johnny and then I will get the milk," they will not only learn words but the concept of waiting. They will begin to learn to cooperate and gain the all-important ability to delay immediate gratification. This is necessary for continued and more complex kinds of learning. Once your child learns to wait . . . a little . . . you are free of some of his tyranny. This is the first step in negotiations about your rights, his rights, your needs, his needs. You are laying the groundwork for similar future negotiations with others. Although it is important for you to encourage the child to explore his environment, to learn to understand language and concepts and to think, it is also important for the child to use his own imagination. Encouraging your child to play alone permits him to use his own imagination and think creatively.

In Chapter 6, in which we discuss intelligence testing, we indicate that verbal, analytic, and conceptual (use of ideas) thinking can be learned. We believe that underdevelopment of language and conceptual, analytic thinking—largely because there has been little need for it by blacks or whites in unskilled positions—is partly responsible for differences in test scores (which are not true indicators of intelligence) between groups. More attention to the development of language and thinking in infancy can improve later scores and school achievement without harming creativity and intuitive abilities. We will discuss this in greater detail later.

Can baby be overstimulated or overencouraged?

Yes, but let's define what we mean by stimulation. We mean the kinds of activities parents can engage in to "turn on" their babies and bring about good motor, language, and learning development. If you are too insistent or persist when a baby is tired, he will become irritable, cry in distress, or signal in one way or another that he's had enough! Overstimulation by a caretaking person who "reads" the baby well is unlikely. But a noisy environment, very loud music, loud arguments, and a great deal of activity in the home can overstimulate a child. Babies don't fare well amid chaos, conflict, and confusion. Inner organization of sights, sounds, and thought is difficult under these circumstances. On the other hand, infants don't learn without adequate stimulation.

Don't some child-development experts think that black babies are understimulated?

It is true that some people have discussed understimulation as a special problem among blacks. Understimulation has nothing to do with race, however. Many parents, black or white, who are overly stressed, are unable to feel warmth toward their children and therefore do not play with or adequately stimulate them. Because of the current social and economic conditions in America, the black population may have more than its share of parents who live stressful lives.

Working mothers, while doing well from a psychological standpoint, may be too tired or busy to interact properly with the baby. A great number of black mothers must work, and in such cases it is very important for the father and other relatives to help out. It is better for mothers or fathers to work less—if possible—when fatigue interferes with child care.

Some people, regardless of race or background, simply don't think that it's important to do anything other than feed and clothe their infant in a loving way. They feel that they should talk with babies only when they can understand. Obviously this is not true and, in fact, prevents the infant from developing language ability.

Can parents benefit from child-development programs?

Some groups regard programs designed to help parents acquire skills to aid in their children's development as an insult or an indictment of the parents' capabilities. It's possible that some program directors have not had the appropriate attitudes. But (pardon the pun) we hope that the baby will not be thrown out with the bathwater. To do away with such programs is to deny some black parents what most middle-income white parents obtain in books or from doctors. Get a trustworthy program director, but let's encourage black children to use large crayons to develop small hand muscles at eighteen months rather than coming to kindergarten unable to do so. We see this situation much too often!

THE INFANT AND HIS ENVIRONMENT

How can I help with my baby's social development?

Many of the things you do to promote motor and language development at the same time promote self-awareness and social development. Calling the child by his name from the very beginning, even playing name games once he is old enough to respond, is very helpful—for example, "Where's Lakisha?" or "Where is Jessie?" Beaming with satisfaction, your child will identify himself as the person you are searching for. The first birthday offers a good opportunity to help the child establish a positive identity, to understand himself as somebody of worth and value. This is his day! He won't understand the full meaning of it all, but he'll know it's for him; he's an individual. He is very worthwhile.

At about twelve months of age children begin to make costumes out of anything available and act in front of a mirror. This activity aids self-identification. Creating a place in the room that is available for them and their possessions is also beneficial in this regard. Many parents today are concerned about an undue stress on individualism and may worry about this practice. Children need some privacy, however, some time and some place they can call their own, a place where they are separate and safe from others. In addition, children aren't really ready to share much until a bit later. They are still very much wrapped up in themselves. For the one-year-old, it is more important to help establish an initial positive identity and a sense of security than it is to promote sharing. Unless "mine" and "yours" is forced on him too soon, he will be ready and willing to share and cooperate later on.

How can I get my child to do things by himself?

Some children will have trouble getting interested in anything on certain days. Taking a few moments to help him get started can save you a lot of trouble later on. Frustrated and bored, he is likely to act up. When you want the child to work alone, after you have gotten him started, saying something like "Now I think you'll enjoy doing that by yourself" usually works. You may want to assure the child that you will be back.

What about good manners?

Helping your child learn what to say or do in certain social situations is important. This training begins with the words "bye-bye," "hello," "please," "thank you," and then gradually becomes more complex. These responses, when properly used, will win your child's approval and respect. Most parents help their children learn these responses as a matter of course. But we also see youngsters who have not learned these and other appropriate social responses even after they are in school. These children are often thought to be rude and crude. They are uncomfortable, aware that they aren't doing something "right," and have negative feelings about themselves. Because of their rude behavior, adults sometimes respond to them in a negative manner, and they, in turn, respond negatively. This negativity can lead to learning and discipline problems.

It is sometimes argued that "good manners" are part of middle-class behavior, and that poor people shouldn't be expected to respond in the same way. This makes for an interesting argument. But if children are not taught polite ways of relating, problems arise. More than ever before it is important to be able to function in a socially acceptable way in a variety of social settings. Job, personal, and family security often depend on it. Given the fact that modern life requires greater togetherness, physically if not spiritually, social skills have become extremely important. Parents and schools have a responsibility to help children develop these skills. If a child is taught how to behave properly at a day-care center or in school, as long as the child's home life is not "put down," the child will not find it difficult to get along at home.

COMMON PROBLEMS AND THEIR SOLUTIONS

How will I know when my infant's overall development is not going well?

The newborn will have excessive feeding and digestive problems. Fretful sleeping is also an indication that there is something wrong. Excessive crying and irritability as well as a kind of overall body tension is another indication of problems. Such babies are difficult to comfort. Most of all, you will feel overly anxious. A part of you will be angry because you are not getting the satisfaction from your infant that you had hoped for.

Often—particularly with a firstborn—the mother simply

needs to relax. Sometimes the baby is not getting enough food. Sometimes the mother is too tired, and a little help from relatives will improve the situation. Sometimes professional counseling is necessary. Your pediatrician, family, or clinic doctor can help you sort out the problem and advise you about what steps to take.

My seven-month-old is afraid of strangers. Is that an indication that he has a problem?

No. In fact, be careful not to force your baby to respond to outsiders. He has become familiar with brother, sister, father, and other relatives whom he sees frequently. But the stranger represents danger. Most children develop some hesitancy about going to a stranger after six months of life. This is particularly true around eight months of age, when the child has a good mental image of the mother or caretaker and associates this face with security. He is still unfamiliar with the rest of the world, and therefore is frightened by it. Your reassurance that it is okay when meeting strangers will help.

Many babies will want to carry their security blanket or teddy bear with them as they explore their environment, meet strangers, or experience new situations. It's important not to ridicule them about this. These objects have been associated with secure times and security-giving people, and are reassuring in new situations.

Children who go to a day-care program early, or are exposed to many different people, may not have a problem relating to strangers. But this is not necessarily a good sign; there can be too many people in a child's life. But when a child is being well cared for generally, at home or in day-care, stranger-anxiety is nothing to worry about.

Things were fine before my baby began to walk, but now everything seems to be going wrong. Why?

Parents frequently feel this way when they don't adjust to the role change required when their child begins to walk. It is important that this adjustment be made, because it becomes a blueprint for later relationships.

Prior to the time that the child could get about on her own, you had to care for her. It was largely a giving relationship. You didn't have to do much to stop or limit the baby. As a matter of fact, it was just the opposite. You were constantly encouraging her to sit, to stand, to crawl. Once she begins to walk, things change. The walker is everywhere—into, under, and on top of everything. Now, in addition to giving, you must set limits and take away. "No, no" becomes the pattern.

The child doesn't know what is dangerous to her and precious to others. You must now protect both her and your valued possessions. Time and time again you say, "no, no." "No, no" when she touches the glass vase with her clumsy little hands. "No, no" when she sits on your clean couch with food—and can't always find her mouth. She bangs her hand against the glass in the window and you say, "No, no." Just as you get tired of saying these words, she gets tired of hearing them! Yet you must help your child learn how to get along in her world.

How can I deal with this conflict?

It is important to "seize the time" to show your baby how to function capably within certain limits without frustrating her every activity and without destroying her budding sense of independence. Her assertive, exploring behavior is her way of feeling, "I can do things for myself. I am a capable individual." This is exactly what we want her to feel, but we have to be able to live with her while she is "coming into her own."

Teaching your baby to learn how to get along in the world without trampling on your rights helps your child begin to develop self-control and to accept responsibility for her behavior. If the child doesn't get locked in a continual power struggle with you over limits, then motivation and direction from within can follow more quickly. Mutual good feelings between mother and child can continue. On the other hand, if you are in constant battle with your child, you will soon become frustrated and unhappy. One part of your child enjoys the fight, but the other part is frightened and unhappy about it. Most important, she is developing a relationship pattern that may cause her trouble later on.

What is the best way to avoid power struggles?

Remember that your baby can't anticipate much. He doesn't understand the full effect of his behavior on others. He needs help in finding ways to behave that are not so troublesome to him or to others. Giving explanations for "why" with your "no-no's," raising suggestive questions, and preparing your child for what you are going to demand of him are the best approaches. "No-no . . . glass break . . . cut baby," delivered with appropriate gestures gives the baby information and motivation that are more useful and powerful than "no-no" alone. You may have to say the same thing on many different occasions, but eventually the baby will stop banging the glass because he understands the reason behind your demand, and he learns to transfer this understanding to other situations. In this way he learns to think, learns to protect himself, and increases his ability to function without you. At the same time, you can prevent many future problems from arising.

With the older infant, if you try to put the round block in the round hole rather than the square hole for him, he may get angry or at least be disappointed that he couldn't do it for himself. He may keep trying to put it in the square hole "just because you got in his business." But if you say, "Johnny, what about this one?" your help will be more readily accepted. He learns to study and analyze a problem, and eventually learns to think before acting. With similar questions you can help him think about other ways to accomplish other goals. Most important, he is doing it for himself. It is one more proof of his ability and one more brick in his foundation of self-confidence, one more impetus to spend his time and energy acting on his own rather than resisting what you try to do for him or what you try to make him do. If this pattern can be established now, there will be fewer problems later on.

Preparation for the next activity cuts down on resistance and conflict. For example, you might say: "Pretty soon we'll stop and wash our hands," or "It's about time for crackers." Explanations cut down on anxiety and acting up. "I'm going across the way to get some sugar and I'll be right back." Suggestions rather than commands are useful: "The blocks go in the box" is less likely to provoke resistance than "Put the blocks away." You can always command when suggestion doesn't work.

What other methods can I use?
Getting your baby in the habit of cleaning up, washing hands,

or whatever you consider necessary is important. She realizes that this is a way to please you and to be a self-reliant person. Doing a task alongside your child in the beginning not only shows her how it is done, but it helps to get her used to the habit.

Children learn from imitation. You might say, "Okay, let's pick up now," and then pick up scattered play material with her. Praise—"Beautiful" or "Great job!"—makes it an achievement worth repeating the next day. Later, "I expect that pretty soon you can clean up by yourself." To reward her success, a big hug is in order.

Your undivided attention at the moment you want your child to respond is important. If you say, "Stop that, Janie," from across the room while talking and drinking coffee with Mrs. Jones, chances are good that Janie won't stop. If instead you put down your cup, address Janie directly, and point out calmly why you want her to stop—or suggest another, more acceptable activity—she is more likely to respond to your request. If she continues what she is doing or stops momentarily and then begins again, it will be necessary to go over and start her on another activity. Be careful that you don't spend too much time with Mrs. Jones. The "trouble" Janie is causing may be a question: "Who is more important, me or Mrs. Jones?" On the other hand, all parents need to spend some time with friends.

It is important to act before you become frustrated and angry. Not only is your loss of control a victory for Janie over "Goliath" but it is a situation in which you are likely to overreact and punish her severely when the matter could have been handled without any punishment. In saving a step, you may lose a mile. The way in which you speak makes a great deal of difference. Your calm confidence that Janie is going to accept your suggestions and ideas is extremely important. A hesitant voice on the one hand or a harsh, commanding one on the other is an invitation to battle. But remember, these are not mechanical operations. Your interactions with your child will be most successful if you approach them with enthusiasm and spontaneity.

Are there particular times that are likely to lead to conflict?

Yes. Mealtime and bedtime are among the most likely to create problems. Toilet training is the time when troublesome relationships between parent and child are most apparent. It is also an event that can worsen already difficult situations. When you or the baby are overtired, anxious, or frustrated, "war" is more likely.

(A) *Feeding*. Feeding, whether by breast or bottle, can and should be a warm, relaxed time. Doctors recommend breast feeding as a beneficial and preferred method of feeding for mothers who are physically able to do so. At birth your baby can take in enough milk to keep him satisfied for about four hours. This permits setting up a schedule of about six feedings a day. You need not be absolutely rigid about it, but a schedule permits you to plan and be ready for the call. You should set aside enough time for feeding so that it can be a time of quiet pleasure. Cuddling, singing, cooing, and burping afterward all make for a pleasant experience. When the baby is on a bottle, fathers can share in feeding the baby.

Your comfort increases the baby's comfort; therefore, as the baby can take in more, you will want to eliminate the feeding hours that disrupt your sleep. Babies typically are fed every four hours around the clock. Breast-fed infants may require more frequent feedings, because breast milk is digested more quickly. You should be flexible about your baby's feeding schedule, adjusting the schedule to the baby's needs. Usually at around four or five months, your baby can take more food and can sleep through the night. When the time appears right, you may want to delay your response to his stirring or crying in the middle of the night. If he falls back to sleep, you've got it made. If the demand is strong, feed your baby and try again another night. The next step, when possible, is to adjust the early morning feeding to a later hour.

You need not worry about overeating at the infant stage. From the beginning your baby will turn away when she has had enough. Don't turn her head back, pry her mouth open, and jam in food. She doesn't need it. You need not worry about what seems to be a loss of appetite between twelve and twenty-four months. The average birth weight is about seven pounds, and this is usually doubled during the first five months; small babies usually gain more and larger ones usually gain less. Infants tend to gain about a pound a month after five months of age and then about one-half pound a month in the second year. Therefore, less food is needed after a year.

At the age of about twelve months, your baby is likely to become highly selective about food. It appears to be the child's way of saying, "I'll make up my own mind!" You may begin to worry about whether your child is getting enough of "the right things." Keep up the vitamins, but don't panic. Babies have a way of getting what they need. If you don't get upset about it, you won't get into a struggle in which your infant becomes fearful or refuses to eat. By the second or third year he will again be eating a wide variety of foods.

(B) *Sleep.* At first, your baby seems to sleep whenever he is not eating. By nine or ten months of age the baby is down to morning and afternoon naps. By eighteen months your baby will require only one nap during daytime hours. Shortly thereafter your baby may develop some sleep problems.

Your baby has a lot going on at about eighteen months of age. You are probably involved in toilet training, setting limits on his increasing activities, and expecting more of him. He has fears and doubts in spite of his apparent self-confidence. His mind is working overtime, but he is unable to understand all that is going on. At this stage he believes that his angry thoughts and actions can hurt you. This all contributes to a fear of falling asleep at night.

Engaging in sexual intercourse in the presence of a young infant adds to this problem. The six-month-old infant does not understand what's going on. But it looks dangerous and violent, and the source of his security appears to be getting hurt. If possible, try to get your child's crib out of your bedroom by five months.

The infant who has trouble falling asleep should be comforted. Putting children to bed with a quiet song or story will prevent some sleep problems. Assurance that he is fine and you are fine and his daddy's fine and brother is fine and sister is fine is useful. Rubbing his back slowly and affectionately will relieve tension. Be certain that something as simple (but dangerous) as an open diaper pin is not causing the trouble. The cry of distress is different—more urgent—when the infant is in pain.

If baby cries, try to avoid removing him from his crib or bed or picking him up for as long as possible. You are asking for trouble if you place him in your bed. Be confident in your ability as a "sandman." Your fear that baby will not go to sleep may cause you to hug and squeeze too much. If you secretly feel that your efforts won't work, they probably won't. The baby will wake up and demand to be held again. Eventually you'll get tired and angry, and you and yours will soon be in a "sho' nuff" struggle.

When you must—because the demand is extreme—hold a wakeful baby, don't hold him too long. If you must bring him into your bed, place him back in his own as soon as he falls soundly asleep. Prepare and reassure the infant: "Pretty soon you will be able to sleep in your own bed all night long. Isn't that nice . . . a big boy!" When sleep problems occur for the first time simultaneously with toilet training, it is advisable to ease up on training—go slower, but don't stop.

Any change or possible threat—such as the mother's absence or a new baby in the home—may cause sleep problems. Calm, gentle support and assurance is always the best approach. You may notice a lot of lost-and-found play, "losing" items and finding them, during this period. You may see the child facing a lot of imaginary dangers, or falling down and recovering in his play. Don't stop such play. This is one of his ways of dealing with the fears of losing his mother and father.

(C) *Toilet training*. Toilet training can easily lead to conflict between you and your baby. One major problem is a frequent tendency to start training before the baby is ready. A second problem is the fact that many adults consider urinating and bowel movements a kind of "nasty business," without even being aware that they feel this way. We often want our babies to hurry up and get the whole business over with. As a result we press too hard, show fear of failure, or ignore the matter. Some parents push their child because day-care centers generally require a child to be toilet trained. Untrained children need home babysitters who can be located through friends, churches, and community social agencies.

Most children do not have good control of the bladder and bowel muscles until eighteen months to two years of age. Pressuring a child to perform well before he or she is able can lead to anger, disappointment, and loss of self-confidence—a fear that you will be angry with him, punish him, or leave him. He may also fear that his anger will hurt you. In addition, the eighteen-month-old still is not absolutely sure about what belongs to his body. Some may think that the feces is a part of them being flushed away. After all, "Mommy was upset and disappointed with me, and maybe she knows that I was angry with her, and now she is going to throw a part of me away."

If this is not the case, withholding those precious pellets (they must be precious, look how much Mommy wants them) is certainly a good way to "fix" that demanding parent. Confused, frightened, and angry, your child may either hold back or display wildly active and antagonistic behavior during this period.

It is best to wait until around eighteen months of age before you begin to start toilet training your child. Some children won't be ready until much later, two to two-and-a-half years. Most children will help to train themselves with the calm support and help of their parents. Remember, early achievement of this task does not indicate mental or physical excellence. A pleasant response when your child indicates that it is potty time tells him that it is an activity as normal and nice as any other. A calm, confident manner indicates that you have no doubt in his ability. Once he understands what he is supposed to do, continuing with some activity of your own a reasonable distance away shows your confidence. Praise for success—not too much, not too little—is helpful. When he doesn't quite make it to the potty, reassure him that he will get there next time.

Sometimes you can figure out the schedule of your child's BMs and put him on the potty before he soils. But the child himself has not gained control over his bowel functions. Help him learn how to tell you the time is near, what to do, and how to let you know he's finished. Children often misbehave because they have not been told what to do in certain situations. It is best to treat the feces as neither "good stuff" nor "bad stuff." Approval should be given for the way he handles himself, not for what he produces. Any mess or play with his BM should be responded to with an explanation and not with horror, a threat, or a put-down like, "Look what you did!" Calmly but firmly stated, "We don't play in the BM" is more positive and to the point.

Some psychiatrists have said that black children can have negative feelings about their skin color because their feces is brown. We think this is a misinterpretation of what occurs. Any apparent relationship is more related to whether toilet time was a pleasant experience than to the color of the feces. African psychiatrists see no evidence of this attitude in areas where all the people are black. We believe that this is one situation in which traditional theory is misapplied.

When training your boy to use the toilet, it is probably not advisable to hold his penis (or organ of pleasure) and direct the stream. There is a tendency to do this to prevent his wetting himself and the floor, especially at night when he is half-asleep. You might, when necessary, want to hold a receptacle (urinal or bottle) up to the penis to avoid spillage. But first urge him to "hold his own."

"Organ of pleasure"; how does he know about that? He doesn't know about sexual intercourse. But he does know that from the very beginning he got a pleasant sensation around the penis when it was being washed. The same sensation occurred when he played with it, or when stimulation caused an erection. It is a part of the body he will want to preserve. This does not mean that you must refrain from holding it at all costs, nor does it mean that you must be hesitant or timid about washing the area. Neither should you get upset if he plays with his penis occasionally.

But encouraging him from the beginning to hold his own penis is advisable. Wash the penis with no more or less concentration than the rest of the body. Later, because playing (masturbation) in public is not socially acceptable, you must calmly but firmly indicate the situations in which you don't want your son or your daughter playing with their genitals. This is usually not a real concern until a child is three or four. We will discuss masturbation in more detail within this age group.

THE QUESTION OF PERMISSIVENESS

Is it wrong to show anger? You stress handling everything with calm confidence.

When the infant is very young, only extended crying is likely to cause you anger. The walking child has more opportunity to get on your nerves. Every parent gets angry from time to time. The right amount of anger will let your child know that you have reached your limit. However, too much anger too frequently expressed can frighten and confuse your baby, particularly when you express it in an inconsistent way. (By that we mean the same act that angered you an hour ago does not appear to anger you now.) Exposure to too much anger can reduce a baby's confidence and her willingness to explore, learn, and express herself.

Most of a child's frustrating behavior occurs because she has little memory, little ability to figure things out, and little ability to restrain herself from certain acts even when she knows she should. Getting angry at her is much less effective than reminding her of what you expect, giving her information, and helping her restrain her tendency to act. Most troublesome situations can be handled without angry responses. A calm approach decreases the possibility of struggles between parent and child, which in turn can lead to even greater frustration and anger on your part. "Be cool." Yet a jam sandwich or a dirty hand on your clean laundry, or some similar problem, is going to get the better of you from time to time, and that's okay.

Is it harmful to spank a child?

Some well-behaved, well-balanced people were never, or rarely, spanked as children. Some well-behaved, well-adjusted people were spanked fairly often. Children who were spanked by thoughtful, loving parents rarely have problems as a result of spanking. But if your child can achieve good control and behave well without spanking, why do it? If you will take the time, come close, and look directly at your child while making your displeasure and expectations known, you can motivate your child to take responsibility for his behavior in a way that spanking alone will never do. The idea is not to frighten the child with angry faces or dirty looks, but to get across the notion that you mean what you say.

Many children are relieved and feel less guilty after a spanking. With a spanking, they "pay their debt" and often continue misbehaving. They have not been required to take any responsibility for controlling their troublesome impulses or acts. A better control of undesirable behavior, with a more beneficial long-range effect, can be achieved through talking to your child. Letting him know that you are unhappy with a particular act, that it is the act you consider bad, not him as a person, is the best approach. Let your child know that you think he can do better; that he can control himself; that he can avoid misbehaving. Through these expectations, you are giving him a chance to be responsible for his conduct. You are saying, "I believe in you. You are capable." Reasonable behavior becomes something that your child will want to achieve for himself. It becomes a way to demonstrate his capabilities to himself. This is the beginning of the development of inner control.

Talking to himself about acceptable and unacceptable behavior is one way your two- or three-year-old avoids unacceptable behavior next time. The cutest sight in the world is the two-year-old in front of your flower vase, no adults around, arm and hand out, saying, "No touch." Your words are helping him control himself—and use words.

What are some of the problems involved with spanking?

The most troublesome situation occurs when a parent spanks a child without just cause or "uses" a child. It often happens like this: Father had a bad day at work, Mother is tired, and an argument develops. One party is losing the argument or there is just no way out of it without someone losing face. At this point, Johnny climbs up on the "forbidden" table and he gets a spanking. Often the general tension is thus relieved and the argument stops. Johnny may have acted as he did because children get frightened and often become active and destructive when parents argue. They sometimes feel that they caused the argument. Children soon learn that they can stop the fighting by "being bad," thus becoming the focus of attention. At the same time, they understand that they didn't deserve the whipping, yet they can't do anything about it. They simply develop hurtful rage and anger toward their parents and themselves. This is even more likely to happen when there is little trust or love between parent and child.

Another problem: by being hit by you when you are angry, children learn to hit others when they are angry. Later, when you try to help your child learn to talk out a problem rather than fight, you will be trying to undo a response that you helped establish in the first place.

Occasionally you will lose control and spank your child even when you do not intend to. Some parents are able to apologize for their loss of control, but at the same time point out to the child how his behavior made them strike out in anger; the child need not have acted as he did; that if he does not want to be spanked or yelled at, he should not run up and down the steps or do whatever it was that caused your display of temper. Again, however, when there is love and trust between parents and children, spanking may not have a negative effect. But, in general, we do not recommend spanking.

Are you saying that parents should not be strict?

If strictness is your style or temperament and you feel most comfortable as a strict, stern person, that may be the best approach for you. The important thing is that in some way your child must be able to feel and understand your love and concern for her. You can be strict and yet be relatively calm. You can even be strict and stern without spanking.

There is a difference between being strict and being excessively harsh, arbitrary, and unfair. It is these latter tendencies that are likely to create problems. They promote rage, anger, unruly, and otherwise undesirable behavior in children. As mentioned previously, inconsistent responses—strictness one time and permissiveness the next, for the same kind of offense—add confusion, doubt, and suspicion to the child's feelings of anger and rage.

New child-rearing approaches are designed to help children develop more inner control, discipline, direction, and motivation, rather than depending on others to direct their behavior. On the other hand, children who are permitted to do whatever they want to are unlikely to develop effective life skills as are those who receive too much adult control.

I was reared by strict parents. I feel I am too strict with my baby. How can I change?

The way you respond to your child has a lot to do with what you think your role as a parent should be. Parents tend to consider themselves as either the owners, the servants, or the developers of their children. "Owners" tend to command, demand, and control their children. They often feel that it is difficult for their children to learn to be cooperative; that children are naturally stubborn and resistant, and parents must make them do things. Responding to them in this way often angers or enrages the child and brings about the behavior you are trying to avoid.

The "servant" parents tend to be permissive. They take everything the child can "dish out." They permit their children to hold tyrannical reign over the entire family, often believing such behavior to be "cute." Such children often become selfish and abusive. They frequently remain impulsive, are unable to concentrate, settle down, learn, or accomplish much. They are often very anxious and afraid that their behavior will get them into trouble.

The "developer" viewpoint is most beneficial. As a developer, you do not think of your child as your possession but as an individual with rights and needs of his or her own. As a developer, you view your child as a "ball of potential," ready to unfold and blossom with your assistance. You help your child gradually develop skills. You give children increased freedom, independence, and opportunity to function on their own as they demonstrate the understanding and ability to do so. You may occasionally have to back up and set limits when they demonstrate they can't handle a situation.

As a "developer," you don't want to make your child do anything. You don't want to let your child do everything. You want him to grow in a way that makes it pleasurable for you and the rest of the family to live with him. You want your child to develop in a positive way and satisfying way. You feel from the outset that you can prepare your child for a worthwhile life if you provide the necessary information and encouragement. Your role remains the same throughout his childhood, changing only in a way that's appropriate for a particular age. If you keep the "developer" viewpoint in mind, you can examine your behavior as your child matures to see whether the way you handle various situations is helping him learn.

Isn't it true that some child-care experts feel that black parents tend to be too strict?

Yes. Under harsh social conditions of the past many black parents felt that they had to force their children to obey so that they would not violate any of the racial rules and bring harm to themselves or their families. This led some parents to establish too many hard-and-fast rules with severe punishment for even minor disobedience. An attitude, and even a language of control developed: "Shut up," "Mind your manners," and so on. Often there is too little exploration or explanation given. These control instructions can discourage the curiosity, exploration, and possible risks needed for the kind of learning that leads to success in school.

Don't many black parents feel that middle-income white parents are too permissive?

Yes. We have heard this feeling expressed among black parents of all income groups. Black teachers are frequently critical of what they feel is permissive management of children by some white teachers, although this feeling is not typical of the vast majority of parents or teachers, black or white. But we ourselves believe that too many middle-income people—more often than not white—have carried permissiveness too far.

Why is inner control important?

It requires much more inner control to function well in today's world than it did in the past. In earlier times, many people lived on farms and in small towns. Jobs did not require a great deal of independent thought or decision making. There was no television to take you to faraway places and bombard you with ideas that were different from those in your own community. There was relatively little travel and little communication between people of different lifestyles. Children did not have to be taught to handle new and rapidly changing situations. Parents, teachers, clergy, and police had unquestioned authority.

Conditions are much different today. In a mobile, rapidly changing, and divided society, there is less "outside the family" pressure to accept responsibility and to live by the law. Also, children now face many more dangerous pressures than ever before—drug use, early and unsafe sex, gang involvement, and so on. We must develop and maintain our attitudes, values, traditions, and life direction much more on our own. Thus, it is important that children be brought up in ways that will teach them to accept responsibility and handle new and changing situations by themselves—with few outside guidelines or pressures. It can be done.

For example, in some schoolrooms, when a teacher is absent, classroom activities and behavior break down almost completely. In other cases the class goes on almost as if the teacher were present. Some parents complain that if they leave their children alone at home for fifteen minutes, their house will be in shambles. Other parents can be gone longer and return to find the house in relatively good order. In both situations the children involved are better able to care for themselves if they have developed inner control, self-motivation, and self-direction. Children who have not developed these inner qualities face great difficulty when the parent, teacher, or other source of external control is absent. Children who develop inner controls are better able to function as adults.

The development of inner control, direction, and motivation does not start at five or at fifteen years. It begins with the way you teach your child to wait for his bottle or to stop taking the toy of the boy next door. We have already given examples of how you can teach your child to accept responsibility for his or her behavior. We will continue to do so throughout this book.

CHAPTER 4

The Preschool Child: Ages Two to Four

SPECIAL PROBLEMS OF THE TWO-YEAR-OLD

Why does my two-year-old show so much frustration, fear, and anger?

Your two-year-old is "the great pretender." He has just gotten his legs together. He knows a few words. He has begun to figure out that he is an individual. Now he wants to be and act just like you—big, strong, capable, and knowledgeable. But the truth is that he is a David without a slingshot or a rock, in a land of Goliaths. He is only now learning to feed and clothe himself, to control his bowels and bladder. Every fall or mishap reminds him of how incapable he is—and too much help from you reminds him as well.

You are helping him explore his environment and protecting him from danger for his own good. But he doesn't understand that you must—that it's your job as a parent. You are his personal giant, frustrating and "helping." He resents this and occasionally gets angry with you. He attacks you and sometimes tries to drive you away. At the same time he is afraid that he may go too far. It's a case of not being able to get along with you or without you. His mind permits him to think that he can control the world—or that you can control the world.

Most of a child's thinking is magical and unrealistic. A stoplight turned red just as a father stepped off a curb and all the cars stopped. His two-year-old daughter said, "Do that 'gin, Dad, do that 'gin!" With such thinking it's easy to see why your child may think that his angry feelings can hurt people—including you. But you are his helpmate, the source of all his security. The "great pretender" knows deep down that he can't make it all by himself. He needs you, yet he thinks he can hurt and lose you. Thus fears and anxieties mark this age.

Is there any way to decrease these "around two" feelings of fearfulness and frustration? ﹨

If you talk calmly to your child about what you expect rather than lashing out at him, he will soon learn that you are not retaliating for his bad wishes. Through your firm but tolerant management of his anger and temper tantrums, he will gradually learn that his thoughts can't hurt. But be careful not to overprotect your child. If you respond anxiously to every fall and every cry, your behavior suggests that there is something to be afraid of. If he falls, gets up, survives a number of minor disasters, he gradually learns that the world is not too dangerous.

No matter what I say to my two-year-old, his answer is no. How can I manage his feelings of aggression?

From the moment you begin to help your child learn to wait, to walk (in certain situations) rather than run, to borrow a toy instead of taking it, to ask another child to return a toy instead of punching him in the nose, you are bound to meet resistance. Your child will fight your attempt to modify and refine his raw, aggressive energy and make it available for positive use. This resistance will reach its peak with the two-year-old in the form of stubborn, negative, "no" behavior. He is breaking away from the dependency of the first year, taking his independent, let-me-do-it-for-myself stand, which often means doing whatever he wants to do, whenever he wants to do it, to whomever he wants to do it. And there you are trying to help him become an acceptable human being. Who needs you?

In dealing with your two-year-old, always try to be firm but fair. Make sure your demands are reasonable. Don't take his attacks (hitting, refusing, and such) personally. Let him do what he can do without harming himself, you, others, or valuable property. Help him succeed at what he is trying to accomplish whenever he attempts to do too much. Stop him—in a firm manner but whenever possible without undue anger—when enough is enough. A firm, no-nonsense voice and eye-to-eye contact is better than a heavy hand and a lot of ranting and raving.

How do you handle "no! no! no! no!"? Banter or kidding is often effective—not ridicule. You might say something like, "Johnny's name is Mr. No. No." Use your common sense and sense of humor to make your child aware that you know that he knows he's playing a game—and it's not getting you upset. If he's involved in a task like washing up, helping him see that it's for himself and not for you will let you both off the hook. "Leroy sounds like he's cleaning up for Daddy, but let's see now, Daddy's not dirty, Leroy's dirty." He'll soon catch on. He should do his own thing for his own good, not for others.

Unfortunately, aggression and its control is not a problem limited to the two-year-old. It comes up again and again with your preschooler as he matures. Since it is something you will be dealing with for many years, let's stop for a moment and examine this important area of behavior more closely.

AGGRESSION AND THE PRESCHOOLER

You said earlier that aggression can be healthy. How?

Aggression in everyday language is interpreted to mean an unjust attack of some kind, ranging from a personal argument to large-scale war. But at the same time aggression is really a kind of life energy. It is very much like gasoline. A spark put to gasoline on the ground can be destructive to everything nearby. But the gasoline in your fuel tank provides the energy necessary to run your car. Human beings need this energy to make their way in the world. But it must be modified and channeled, much like crude oil is refined and put in the gas tank.

Whenever a young child is faced with an obstacle or problem, he attacks it with raw physical energy (aggression). If this response is not modified, conflict and chaos result. Parents, caretakers, teachers, and others must help the young child gradually turn raw aggressive energy into the fuel for curiosity, determination, learning, work, and play. They must help the child modify, refine, and control his energy so that it can be used at the proper time and in ways in keeping with the rules of the society.

How far should physical aggression be allowed to go?

Some parents feel that it is okay for children to destroy furniture or to attack other children as a healthy expression of their aggression. A parent who feels this way must be prepared when others find Walter's or Doris's expression of aggression unacceptable. In fact, they won't welcome such an unruly child in their home. You shouldn't be offended if a parent tells her Yusef and Alvina to hit Walter or Doris back. Who wants their children to be treated like punching bags, servants, or slaves?

Children will learn where, how, and when to show their anger as soon as you make your expectations clear. They will learn that it's okay to display their temper in the basement, outdoors, or in their room, but not in the living room. The point is they need an outlet for aggressive behavior, and you should provide this opportunity under conditions that are acceptable for you and good for your child. But at the same time, children need guidelines, rules, and limits, provided without undue anger and preaching.

My child bangs up all our furniture. Should I permit this?

We don't believe that children should be allowed to destroy furniture. We discussed in Chapter 3 the fact that certain kinds of "destructive" behavior are permissible, and that your child should have certain areas and things that she can destroy. But why should she destroy your valuables, even if you can afford to replace them? A child must learn that some things can be destroyed and some things should be preserved. "There is a time and place for everything" is an important lesson for adult life. We also believe that aggressive acts should be stopped when they are dangerous to your child or to others. The two-year-old in particular will use the scissors, blocks, or anything else she can get her hands on as a weapon when frustrated or angry. She will be embarrassed, ashamed, and feel bad about herself if you do not prevent her from hurting herself or others.

A word of caution about handling aggression: Where there is no danger, even though aggressive behavior is excessive, rude, or mean, don't be too quick to interfere if several children are involved. Very often children can work out conflicts by themselves, particularly the three- and four-year-olds. They really don't want to hurt each other. Working it out themselves is good practice in learning to negotiate with others in order to obtain their own rights without compromising the needs and rights of others. Intervene only after it is clear that they cannot handle the matter.

Can I make my child passive, a "Milquetoast," by controlling his aggression?

Not unless you are excessively harsh in controlling your child's aggression. (Although severe treatment sometimes increases rather than decreases aggressive, acting-up behavior, or causes a child to resist in other ways—not hear, not cooperate, or not obey the strong-arm parent's wishes.) Passivity is brought about in a different way.

Those parents who do everything for their children, so that there is no need for children to do things for themselves, are more likely to cause passive behavior in their children. Parents who are passive or withdrawn themselves often have passive children.

Children who have not been taught to deal with such feelings as jealousy and death fears often hold back their feelings and actions. This can reduce curiosity, exploration, and aggression to the point of passivity. Such children may become quiet, obedient, and undemanding, even when their rights and needs are being disregarded. If your child doesn't protest under these circumstances, you should be concerned. Such "holding in" and "holding back" can lead to failure in learning and school problems later on.

Looking back on black history, isn't this the age at which black children, particularly males, were forced into line?

Yes. In the past, because aggressive black males were likely to be in danger, some parents, knowingly and unknowingly, tried to suppress normal aggressive behavior in their preschool children. In order to survive in a hostile world, youngsters were taught to obey authority figures, right or wrong, fair or unfair.

This approach created many black children and adults who

were afraid to stand up for their rights and needs and who eventually learned to see no injustice, and automatically complied with anybody in a position of authority, right or wrong. The passive approach often backfired and created or reinforced the negative, excessively aggressive behavior it was supposed to correct. As mentioned earlier, this sometimes happens when children are spanked and scolded without good reason.

These two reactions to strict, crushing discipline can be found in caricatures such as "Dumb Sambo," "Geraldine," "Bad Nigger," and "Uncle Tom"—all types and stereotypes that were products of slavery and oppression.

To equip black children for the modern world, shouldn't we be training them to be more aggressive?

Permitting early negative behavior, anger, and aggression to be expressed without any check or effort to turn it into socially acceptable, useful energy is just as harmful as trying to suppress it. A child disciplined in this manner will not develop the inner control discussed in Chapter 3. Eventually family, friends, strangers—of all races—can become victims of the child's anger and aggression. In fact, a child through harmful acts to himself, or due to harmful reactions his behavior causes, can become the victim of his own anger and aggression. The records of many violent people show that their families and people of their own racial groups are the most common victims of their rage.

Patient, firm, and fair management of a young child's angry, aggressive behavior is necessary. When properly managed, the child is still free and better able to choose his own value system, so that as an adult he will have the ability to work within the political and economic system he believes in, through the method of his choice. He will still be able to be aggressive when necessary, but will be able to control his aggression. If development continues well, he can be even more effective in dealing with racism and bigotry.

But shouldn't black children be taught to be angry in order to fight racism?

We must help children become aware of their rights and opportunities, and we must help them acquire the skills needed to take advantage of these rights and opportunities. We must help them learn to identify and fight racism. But we don't have to help them become angry. Anger is a healthy human emotion. When youngsters are denied their rights and opportunities, anger will come naturally—unless they are forced to repress their feelings. Fortunately, most black children today are more expressive.

Making children supersensitive to all injustice in a world full of injustices will cause them to be indiscriminately reactive and angry—or reactive and angry whether it will help or not—reactive and angry when, in fact, the offense was unintended or minor. Anger consumes energy that is needed for establishing and carrying out life plans. We see teenagers aware and concerned about injustice and racism but with little or no knowledge of how to fight it. They are paralyzed, often to the point where they can't function. Constant reaction to racist acts leads to frustration, more anger, and then more than anger—hostility. Hostility is not like healthy anger. It is a fixed mind-set rather than a healthy emotional reaction. It is not helpful in the fight against racism.

Teenagers can fight racism by participating in community action groups and civil rights organizations. In school they can join African-American groups and also promote multiculturalism. When needed, they should join protests against racism.

Are street gangs the result of anger?

In part, but gang formation is more complicated. Many gang members feel neglected and rejected by families, schools, and society, and therefore are angry. But belonging to a gang also helps young people to feel good about themselves, to survive and thrive without mature and responsible adult guidance and support. Colors, territory, rituals, mutual support and loyalty, and such are all efforts to belong, to find a sense of adequacy, identity, and purpose independent of parents, families, social networks, and the society the young people feel hurt and rejected by.

Although the behavior should not be justified and cannot be tolerated, they hurt others because they feel hurt. Because some gang members have had difficult childhoods, they often lack any feelings for others, and they can do harm to people without feeling guilt. Because their development has not been good, they become undisciplined and despite good intentions, they can do harm to each other. Although street gangs more often develop among disadvantaged children from families under stress, gangs that are formed among white middle-class children now exist, because in some way they feel neglected and rejected. These gangs sometimes emulate the behavior of gangs from poor neighborhoods.

Gangs from all groups have often gotten involved in illegal activities to earn money. In recent years teen gangs have often become involved with drug trafficking, in some cases even taking on an organizational structure that emulates business corporations. Many behaviors of gang members suggest that with adequate supervision, education, and mainstream opportunities they could have been highly successful citizens. But once gang activity is established it becomes a force of its own and attracts young people who would prefer another way of life if they had a chance. Unfortunately, too little effort is being made to prevent gang activity.

RACE AND THE PRESCHOOLER

Why is the three- and four-year-old more aware of race than the infant?

During their first two years of life, children are not totally aware that they are individuals, separate and distinct from other people. By three years of age, the child is better able to understand himself and his world. He becomes conscious of himself and conscious of others as separate from himself. Now is the time that he or she will want to know: "Who am I?" "What kind of person am I?" He will become very interested in how he is like or different from others. He will question and be concerned about such things as similarities and differences in skin color and hair.

Should I bring up the issue of race with my three-year-old?

You need not sit your child down to talk about race. Children see blacks and whites on television. They may, depending on where you live, or where you take your child, see or play with people of different colors and races. They will hear your everyday conversations about race, your mention of "blacks" or "whites." Their sense of observation and interest in understanding what you are talking about will cause them to raise questions: "What is black?" "Am I black?" "Am I white?" This provides you with an opportunity to answer in a natural, calm, and—most important—confident manner.

A simple answer to a three- or four-year-old, "You are black . . . like Mommy (or Daddy)," is best. You may prefer "African-American" or some other term. The "like Daddy" or "like Mommy" relates the issue of race to yourself. You are your child's source of pleasure and security and therefore somebody very positive. If you show enthusiasm about the fact that you are black, your child will sense that being black must be both positive and good.

Is there anything else I should say or do?

A simple reply is all that is necessary in the beginning. A child of three or four still can't comprehend complicated explanations. In addition, if you give long answers, appear upset, ignore the question, or bring up the issue over and over again, your child may sense that you are anxious about the subject of race. As a result, he may either avoid the issue completely or use it as one more way to tease and control you. For example, he might play the game of saying he doesn't like being black just to annoy you.

The concept of race and an individual's feeling about it develops gradually. If your response, direct or indirect, does not indicate that all talk about race is forbidden, the child will feel free to ask for more information on the subject in the future. Increasing knowledge and awareness in this area does not ensure that your child will develop a positive racial identity. In fact, either extreme preoccupation with or neglect of the race issue can actually create undue anxiety about the danger of being black.

Being black in a country full of antiblack feeling and action presents real problems, but these problems need not be discussed until your child is able to understand and deal with such information. But whenever you discuss prejudice, it is important to strike a balance between too much and too little attention to the issue of race; otherwise, you can defeat your own purpose.

We know many black children who have a positive racial identity, whose parents responded only to casual opportunities to discuss race. These youngsters are comfortable with all groups. They can discuss race issues easily. They show a very mature concern about racism and injustice by the age of ten. Conversely, we know children who have been bombarded with discussions about race, almost from birth, and who are insecure about being black—even in all-black settings.

My five-year-old has never mentioned race to me. Why?

If you don't hear inquiries about race by four or five years, it is probably wise to think about what you are doing to discourage your child's interest in the question. You can introduce a discussion about race by talking about it when opportunities present themselves—blacks on television, news about black affairs, a new black teacher in the school or on the job. If this doesn't work—although it rarely fails—you might mention to a child of four or five that you have not heard him bring up the issue of race and ask whether it is a problem for him. Even here, a low-key discussion, not bombardment, is best. Once your child knows that it is okay to talk about race, he will.

Are there ways a child can develop a negative racial identity, even with reasonable discussion and apparent parental enthusiasm?

Yes. You can send your child mixed messages. If you talk about the beauty of blackness on one hand and say derogatory things about blacks on the other, your child will see through your "front." It is normal when we laugh at ourselves as individuals and as a group from time to time. There is a big difference, however, between this behavior and constant and hostile animosity toward our own race. The latter feelings create problems.

Children can sense the difference between kidding and group

deprecation. They can tell when their parents' real message is: "Black is not really good, but I am black, and therefore, I must pretend it is good." They must protect themselves and their parents; therefore, they in turn may talk "black is good." But they will have mixed feelings, anxiety, and anger—some directed at you—about being black.

The most troublesome situations arise when a black child has been told that black is beautiful and then has his own rights and needs ignored or abused by his own black parents. In this situation the child will feel rage, rage, and triple rage!

The first time my four-year-old raised a question about race, he said, "I'm white." Does this mean that he doesn't like being black?

Maybe yes and maybe no. But don't panic. This is not an unusual first response among children who are in a small minority in their neighborhood or in school. Children often want to be just like those they want to be friendly with. This reaction can also occur in a predominantly black community, because we are a minority in America. The television brings the nation to your child. We have seen white children who want to be brown or black like their therapist. We have seen young school-age white children who want to be brown or black like their favorite football heroes.

A response to "I'm white" could be, "No, you are black . . . like Daddy and Mommy." If your child is light-skinned, he is likely to offer you his hand or arm as evidence of his whiteness. You can point out that although the skin is light brown (or whatever), he is a member of the black or African-American group. You can explain that black is the name of the group, and that color within the group ranges from white to black. Again your enthusiasm and your reassurance—without being phony —will make it okay. Your child may not fully understand this concept until older.

Even with three- or four-year-olds, it's occasionally important for adults to intervene to make certain that the rights and needs of all children are being respected when they are in a group situation. Otherwise, difference—sometimes racial and sometimes otherwise—does become a basis for abuse and exclusion.

Four-year-olds become comfortable with two or three people, and can be cruel (without adult influence) in their exclusion of others. In fact, you may have to encourage your child to accept a more timid youngster into a play group. He might well be the one who is making life miserable for the newcomer, black or white. We will discuss this more fully later in this chapter.

What if my child says she wants to be white because someone is calling her "nigger"?

You should point out that nigger is a name that some people call black people when they want to make them feel bad. Urge her not to feel bad. Explain that she is not a nigger or anything else bad. The same explanation that was used previously should follow, this time—because *she* is under attack—emphasize that you feel good about being black. You should speak to the offending child's parents, if possible, and to the child, if the parents are unavailable or are unresponsive. You might explain to your child that the white child is being bad in calling names.

If your child settles the dispute on the playground in her own way, so be it.

What do I say if she says she wants straight blond hair?

In a relaxed and unemotional manner, point out that she is black and that most black people have nice curly black hair, and that most white people have straight hair—brown, blond, black. At this age what you convey in your voice and manner will either make it okay or create a problem. You will hear the same issue raised again at an older age, at which time an explanation suitable for that age should be given—still in a calm manner. You should be prepared for other questions about race or belonging when a statement like this is made.

You should never tease or belittle your child because she says that she wants to be white or have long blond hair. Teasing hurts deeply and produces destructive guilt.

SEX AND THE PRESCHOOLER

When are children first interested in sex? What do you tell them?

Children usually become interested in the differences between boys and girls at about three and a half to four years of age. Recall that this is about the same time they become interested in racial differences—and for the same reason. This is the age when a child becomes conscious of himself and others. This is a time of great curiosity about many things. A girl may ask (and maybe a boy) "What is that?" pointing to a penis. They may want to know why boys have them and girls do not. Answer such questions truthfully: "Because when they are grownups boys can give the seed to make a baby. Girls can receive the seed and keep it inside where the baby can grow." Under no circumstances should girls be told that they are lacking, missing, or deficient of genitals. They should understand that their genitals are different from, but just as important as a boy's.

How should I deal with questions about sexual intercourse?

Children often become curious about sexual intercourse by observing animals—either dogs or cage-contained animals. It is best to respond to animal sex as normal and not as something shocking. Don't call children to observe, and don't drive them away or cover the cage. It is best to answer a specific question in a way a child of that age can understand, and wait to explain more fully when he asks again. Answering the "tough" question "What are they doing?" is really very easy. "They are having sex," said without embarrassment, is a good reply. If the next question is, "What for?" you can explain that that is the way they have babies. In this way, you will not discourage the child from discussing the subject through "overtalk" or "undertalk." He will come back to it when he is interested and able to understand different and more complex aspects of the subject.

DISCIPLINING THE PRESCHOOL CHILD

What kind of discipline is best?

We indicated in Chapter 3 that we're not in favor of spanking children. Talk and time-out are more useful.

Some black children are severely punished by parents and relatives for little reason. The purpose of discipline or punishment is to help your child behave in a way that enables him to become a better person; to get along with others without "dumping" on them and without being "dumped" on. Punishment, whether by denial of privilege, or other means, should take place only when it is necessary to achieve these purposes. The more your child can be helped to behave well without punishment, the better it will be for him, and for you.

When you must do more than scold, a denial of privilege is best. A common error here is what we call "overkill." A week's denial of privilege means almost nothing to preschool children. They will forget they are being punished. Punishment is most effective when it closely follows the undesirable act and thus gets the child's full attention, but doesn't go on so long that the child forgets what it is for. If you forbid children to do something they need or something that you want to do, such as take a walk, you are denying yourself pleasure and denying them an important outlet of energy. You will be amazed at the effectiveness of a punishment as simple as having your child sit in another room—"until you can control yourself." If you suggest that they can come back when they feel they are ready, they will often sit for a reasonable length of time and reenter, saying, "I okay now, Mommy." This approach also enables them to control their inaction. They are settling themselves. It helps them take responsibility for their own behavior.

Should I try to shame my child when he misbehaves?

No. Please don't say, "Shame on you, you're a bad boy." Making your child feel bad about himself will not improve his self-image. Again, it's helpful to convey the message that you don't like or won't accept undesirable behavior, but that you like and accept the child. "I like you, but I don't like what you did."

Nagging, scolding, and complaining are not useful either. Some black parents try to shame and provoke guilt in their children by constantly pointing out sacrifices they are making even in the face of discrimination in the work world. It is important for children to understand some of these realities, but not in the context of scolding. The most frequent comment we hear from children is that their parents nag too much. Nagging, scolding, and complaining still don't stop the undesired behavior—in fact, they can increase it.

I always seem to be punishing my child. Is something wrong?

Harsh and frequent punishment often produces hostility and frequent misbehavior. If you must punish the child frequently, something is not working right somewhere. It's possible that the punishment has become the child's way to get attention from you rather than getting attention by performing in a desirable way. Perhaps you are not praising desirable behavior enough. Are you praising his scribbling, his setting the table, his or her many efforts to be able to do things—to be grown-up? Attention, applause, commenting that you are glad that he was able to do this or that are important rewards. Make certain the message is clear. A reward, such as a special treat on a day a child has been particularly difficult, is not helpful, because there is no reason for the child to give up bad behavior if "crime pays."

Children will begin to behave and perform in acceptable ways when they sense that you believe they will do so. For example, "Let's clean up your room," said with confidence, is more likely to get results than a hesitant request, as if you don't expect that it will happen, or standing with your arms folded with an angry expression on your face, or ruler in hand, to make it happen. In fact, helping your child clean up his room, or whatever the job, establishes the habit. Once started, the child will often do it by himself. When your relationship is relaxed and positive, you will not need to use punishment to get cooperation. For example, after you clean the playroom together a few times, your child will often follow your lead and begin cleaning up by himself. Just the comment, "What do we do when we finish playing?" can produce a clean room once the habit is established.

When I deny or punish my three-year-old, she appeals to her father and usually gets her way. Isn't this harmful?

Yes. Parents should present a united front to their children —but not against their children. Always make an effort to be fair. But children of three and four are very manipulative. They want what they want and they'll do what they have to do to get it. One three-year-old appealed to her father after a "no" response from her mother. When Father agreed with Mother, our little lady shot for the weak spot with this comment: "But, Dad, you're the boss!" Manipulation is normal at three but troublesome at seven. If it is not checked at three, it may be a way of life at seven and twenty-seven. In addition, your child loses the opportunity to learn to live with the normal and just denials we all face. After all, none of us can have everything, and a child must learn to accept this fact.

In addition, children who "get by" through manipulation often do not develop an ability to take an honest look at themselves. It then becomes hard for them to accept criticism, which would help them do a better job next time. Parents who are not getting along well together sometimes play destructive games around permission and punishment as a way of "hitting" each other. Permitting what the other parent would not allow without a discussion and an agreement beforehand can make the other parent a "meany"—or worse. Your child will know what's going on, but will play the game to get what he wants. The child will feel good about getting his or her way and guilty about it at the same time. Try to keep children out of parent or adult conflicts. Manipulating them for your purposes will encourage them to manipulate you for their purposes—with a negative effect on their development.

Again, banter and good humor about the efforts to "get by," without giving in unless it makes sense, is better than a harsh, angry response.

My wife yells at the children too much. Does it hurt to disagree with her approach in front of the children?

Disagreeing with your mate in front of your child should be a move of last resort. As mentioned earlier, a united front is extremely important. It is best to talk over your differences in private. When disagreement in front of your child is necessary, you should discuss the situation afterward. It is hard for us to look at ourselves and to be certain that we are not just claiming "necessary disagreement" as a way to put down the wife, husband, or whomever. Parents should look for ways to help each other avoid being too harsh, too punitive, unjust, and unfair toward their children before problem situations arise, and without open disagreement. Sometimes a parent who yells, scolds, beats, or is overly harsh with a child needs some assistance from the other parent, or relatives, in managing the home and the children. Sometimes this parent may need counseling or psychological treatment.

There are times when I simply can't accept my mate's treatment of our child. What should I do?

If none of the preceding measures are effective, it is important to protect the rights and needs of the child. If you feel you must disagree with your mate in front of the child, be sure to point out to your child at the same time that you do not excuse the undesirable behavior. If the child gloats because you stepped in, let him or her know that you are annoyed. Express your feelings in a calm fashion and in the spirit of helpfulness rather than as an attack. By responding to both your child's behavior and your mate's overreaction, you become the mediator of fair play rather than setting up a situation in which more manipulation can take place. Again, this is a move of last resort.

If my three-year-old hits me, should I hit back?

Until a child learns another way, he or she, when frustrated, will strike out in anger. A few parents may tolerate their children hitting them, but we do not believe it's a good idea. Hitting back, particularly with force, is not effective. Some parents hit back very lightly to make the point that if a child hits people, people will hit them back. Tapping is okay, but it is not necessary. You want your child to learn to respond to language rather than action, and even tapping is action. Sometimes saying, "I know you're angry with me, but I don't want you to hit me" relieves the child's anger and stops the hitting. Some parents prolong "fights" to get in the last lick. Why do you need it? It is helpful to direct the child's anger to a stuffed animal, a punching bag, a pounding board, and such, but not toward other people. Directing anger toward others sets the stage for using religious and racial groups that are different from your own to let out anger. Directing (or diverting) your child to another activity is a helpful way to ease frustration and anger. Often a young child given a favorite toy or offered a desired activity will forget all about his "mad." Your child's play is a place where he can deal with a great deal of fear, frustration, and anger. A word of caution: Don't offer him food every time he is frustrated or angry. Many adults eat when frustrated, leading to overeating and weight gain. This habit can start at a very early age—even when your baby is still in the crib.

When my three-year-old can't have his own way, he has a temper tantrum. How can I prevent this?

If you can alleviate the causes of his frustration and anger, and when your child learns other ways to express anger, he will have fewer temper tantrums. You also should avoid confining him within unreasonable limits.

It's natural for a child of this age to have some temper tantrums. You can't and should not attempt to eliminate all frustration and anger. It is important for children to learn to tolerate disappointment and frustration, because they will have to face many disappointments in life. You just want to avoid the unnecessary disappointments, and resulting frustration and temper tantrums. A child who does not learn to cope with disappointment and frustration is more likely to become depressed or to "drop out" as an adult.

How should I handle tantrums when they occur?

The best way to deal with a tantrum is not to pay too much attention to it. If you look out of the corner of your eye, you may catch your little angel watching to see what kind of "rise" he is getting out of you. When that happens, a little smile or a friendly wink will help. Preaching, lecturing, spanking, and too much soothing all focus attention on the child, which will only encourage the tantrum. Why should he give up the tantrum when it is a good tool to get what he wants? Continue with your usual activities. If the tantrum continues, it's sometimes helpful to make the child go to another room. Tell your child that he may play or talk to you or return to whatever he was doing when he calms down and gets himself together. Rather than fight over this, you might leave the room yourself.

Children often paint themselves into a corner in a tantrum situation. If you give in, they feel they can control you, but that leaves them without anyone to protect them from their own unreasonable demands. If they give in, they have failed and you have won. Therefore it is important that a tantrum situation not become a battle of wills. You want to make certain that what you are asking is fair. Then it is easier to be sympathetic, hold your ground, and yet let your little one out of his corner. How?

During the tantrum, you might say, for example, "I know that you're mad, but if you eat more candy you won't want your dinner." A reason for your action expressed calmly but without apology indicates that you are helping rather than controlling. You might say, "I know that you would always like to have what you want, but sometimes you can't." This is a message about how the world works. You might later say, "I think you'll be able to stop crying pretty soon." This can make stopping an achievement and lets him off the failure hook. Timing, calmness, and the amount of talking is important here. Your several comments should be far enough apart and said with a confidence that implies all will soon be well. After the tantrum you might say, "I'm glad you were able to stop all by yourself." This gives your child a feeling of control, and will make him want to help control himself next time. If you don't know what the fuss was all about, it's helpful to find out the cause of the upset. You might then want to talk to him about a better way to handle his feelings. Talk is important, but you don't want to talk too much. It comes across as nagging or lecturing, and that often causes more acting-up behavior.

Good humor brings results. Naturally there will be times when he or she will take the humor out of you. But when you can, it helps to be light of spirit, without laughing at your child. If you view yourself as helping your child learn to handle normal, lively, and healthy feelings, you are less likely to get uptight. When you've had enough and nothing else works, you may have to act more firmly; but always give your child a chance to pull himself together first.

PLAY AND HOW TO MAKE IT "WORK"

What is a child's play all about?

Play is a child's work—and play. A child uses play to deal with her thoughts, fantasies, and feelings. Often the anger she wanted to express toward Mommy is taken out on her doggy, teddy bear, or doll. In addition, she uses it to develop body control, language, thought, and social skills. In play, she can repeat an experience she enjoyed—a trip to the store, a ride in the car. She can pretend her way through a scary event to make it less scary. For example, the four-year-old may be seen giving a shot to a doll or teddy bear before or after she goes to the doctor. A child often practices being a competent, independent person in play to make up for the times she is dependent and unable to do things in the big adult world.

What kind of play is best?

Art—drawing, painting, clay work—is a particularly useful form of play activity. At two a child loves the feel of clay or paint. He enjoys breaking up clay and putting it back together. If you have the room, or can put paper down to permit enthusiastic finger painting, this can be real fun and is good for the child's hand muscles. Such play can release angry feelings. It's best not to ask her to copy from a model or ask him what he has drawn. Your child is trying to express his world and it doesn't matter in what form he does so. The fun is in the doing and not the finished product or the name.

By three a child is beginning to pay attention to the results of his handiwork. That's when the drawings become important. Displays of your child's work promote pride and motivation for continued effort. Vertical, horizontal, and arc strokes replace simple scribbles.

The four-year-old makes snakes and cakes, people and cars, animals and everything in his world with his clay. If he makes it, he's controlling it, right? He will also make such toilet-training symbols as BMs or a penis. As long as there is no preoccupation with such creations, it's best not to overreact to them.

The four-year-old is an artist of some note. By this age you usually see pictures—not in perspective and not with detail, but pictures nonetheless. Unlike two- and three-year-olds, four figures he's doing something and wants to talk about it. If you ask him too many questions, however, he will back off. Listen, learn, and praise the wondrous creation! By doing this, you'll encourage him to keep on producing as well as giving him a sense of accomplishment.

Drawings by preschool children from various income, ethnic, and racial backgrounds are very similar. Only later do clothing, jewelry, and other items characteristic of a particular culture show up.

Very small drawings, persistently drab colors, "tight" or heavy angry overpainting can be an indication that there's a problem. If, along with the artwork, your child is generally unhappy or difficult, you might wish to seek professional help.

How can I help my child gain body control through play?

Your early preschooler's climbing on every box, chair, or bench she can find is good for muscle development and control. The child will climb in and out and over old boxes, under the stairs, and wherever else she can get to. Wheel toys with pedals, such as cars and fire engines, and rockers are good exercise for leg muscles. The two-year-old loves to kick, run after, and throw balls. Swinging on low parallel bars is great fun for the two-year-old, even though it often frightens her parents. The two-year-old loves to roughhouse with her mother and father. Swinging on a grownup's stiff, outstretched arm is a favorite activity, which is also good for muscle development.

What about play for three-year-olds?

Using scissors and building with blocks, small boxes, and other items all serve to aid small-muscle development. Working with pegboards and puzzles and stringing beads improve your child's hand–eye coordination. At three, with good previous development, he is well on his way to making his body do what he wants it to do.

You will have trouble keeping up with your three-year-old. He will want to run ahead of you on walks. He will need plenty of space indoors and outdoors to run, climb, and jump. If you live in an apartment, it is important to take your children to a playground, empty lot, or park at least once a day.

All children love to dance, and this form of body expression has long been encouraged by most black parents. Any kind of rhythmic music will get them started—records, radio, your drumbeat. This is an extremely valuable method of self-expression as well as a way of letting off steam, developing muscles, and improving coordination. Today more parents, black and white, encourage rhythmic body expression through dancing.

How does play encourage language development?

Before two years of age your child couldn't express—in words—much of what he wanted to convey. But we hope you talked to him, even when he couldn't understand. Talking prepares a child use words—to talk. Once he masters a few words, he discovers he can use them to make things happen for him. "Spoon, Mommy" and "Down, Daddy," bring results. Your child understands that language is important. But his desire to express himself can be turned off if nobody responds or listens.

If all goes well, by three, the child's vocabulary and ability to use language have greatly increased. Engaging her in "normal" conversation can now be very rewarding. Talking about the things and activities around you not only improves language but stimulates curiosity and helps the child become an observer. By four she is not only a talker but a "discusser." She will want to talk about the books you read together, and about the store she just visited. She will rush in from outside with a story about a startling new discovery she has made. It will be old hat to you but listen with interest anyway. Listening, discussing her interest, remarking about how well she has communicated her thoughts, applauding, and so on are all useful tools in encouraging language development.

What other methods can I use?

Certain toys promote language development and provide

amusement as well. Three- and four-year-olds love puppets. Using your voice to speak for the puppet is great fun. Your child can be encouraged to use his voice to speak for another puppet and carry on a conversation or put on a play. Three- and four-year-olds love funny voices and funny comments. Toy telephones are also a great favorite. Preschoolers will carry on animated pretend conversations about all the things they hear you discussing on the telephone—ordering groceries, calling baby-sitters, making plans for the weekend. These activities all aid in language development as well as social development.

You mentioned that reading to children is important. Why, and what kinds of stories are most useful at the preschool age?

Reading is a way of being close to your child while engaged in an enjoyable shared activity. Listening to the spoken language is preparation for learning to read. Aside from the words, children learn pronunciation and expression. They learn to follow a plot and comprehend a story. Slipping in a question about what's going on now and then will help you know whether they are understanding it. Remember, stories should be entertaining—even if the child doesn't understand every word.

Nursery rhymes, books with pictures, and stories with familiar sounds—"ding, ding," "honk, honk," "chug-chug"—are favorites for a two-year-old. He will want to hear them over and over. Don't stop reading a story because a child knows it word for word—it's more fun that way. The youngster can feel that he's "reading." But stop when it's no longer a fun story for your child.

The three-year-old wants the facts—information stories. When you go to the store, the zoo, or the circus, reading a book about such activities before and after will increase anticipation and encourage recall and recounting of an experience. The four-year-old is a book lover—if he's started earlier. He loves facts and fantasy. Because a preschooler is relatively powerless and has few skills, mastery, or the ability to do and accomplish things, reading is of great concern to him. The train that huffs and puffs to climb the hill, the colt that struggles to stand, and other such themes are interesting to him. Your librarian or book-store clerk can help you select appropriate books for your child's age group.

But it is best to scan them before you buy or borrow. You know your child best.

Should the books be about black children?

Many of your books should be about black children to help give your child a sense of his identity and importance in the world. The number of good books for black children is increasing. We believe that as long as a book presents blacks with dignity —whether the story is set in the suburbs, inner city, or Africa —it is satisfactory reading. Books portraying black American children as capable and competent with only average frustration and failure are preferable. We feel that presenting black children engaged in unlawful activity serves no purpose—even if it is the reality for some. We see no harm in some books using dialect, but we feel that most should utilize standard English, because your child will spend most of his life with people and in places where standard English is used.

Books about African ceremonies and customs can help your child develop a positive attitude about Africa, a concept that our generation must encourage. Stories about such activities as birthday parties and family gatherings—in an African or American setting—can be interesting to the three- and four-year-old. But we do not advise that you limit yourself to books depicting black children exclusively, unless you expect your child to spend his entire life in a totally black setting. The world of tomorrow will be even smaller than it is today. Books depicting black, brown, yellow, red, and white children are one way to prepare your child for the future. Books that present different cultures provide you with an opportunity to help your child understand that people are different—and that's fine.

What is my child's thinking like during this period?

This is the period in which the child's thinking should move from the concept that he, she, or others can control all things around them to a more realistic viewpoint. Your child should develop the ability to imagine what will happen in certain situations rather than have to act in order to find out. She will gradually learn to tell the difference between her own imagination and what is real. One of the interesting aspects of children's thinking at this stage is their feeling that wrongdoing will be punished every time. They become very responsive to rules as a result of this. Another is giving living qualities to a doll or even a tree or a door. That's why talking to a doll can be so "real."

How can I help my child in this learning process?

One necessary requirement in learning to think is the ability to concentrate on a single activity for more than a moment or two. This is done by helping your child learn to wait, by taking time to talk with him about various activities, and by listening to his conversations so that he will listen to yours. Reading to him is beneficial because he quiets down and becomes organized so that he can use his inner resources to explore, learn, and interact in the world around him. All of these activities should help your child "learn how to learn," develop strategies for learning, and apply information learned in one situation to deal with another. Many bright people do not perform as well as possible in school and elsewhere when the situation requires more than memory, because they do not have a strategy for learning.

The development of language helps you and your child share experiences. Through your involvement in play or in other activities you help your child learn many concepts, including under, over, above, and through. Explaining words or concepts that will help him understand a joke or a story is very helpful.

Are there special learning games we can play together?

You can play a number of games that will help your child learn to think. Simon Says helps a child learn to concentrate and to listen for directions. You might play your own Direction Game—"Stand up . . . go to this corner . . . that corner . . . under the table and then put your shoes behind the door." There is no end to this particular game, and the task can be as difficult or as easy as the child can handle. "What would happen if?" and "What happens next?"—games in which you set up conditions or begin a story and then let your child answer or complete the story—stimulate the child's creativity and imagination. You don't want him to lose his creative ability as he gives up fantasy for reality.

Matching "like" cards from a mixture, making and pronouncing words, making sentences, printing names—his own name in particular—reading signs, and a host of other invented games can "jog" his mind. Let your imagination run wild. Being right or winning is not important in such games—they should be fun. Don't criticize him or act disappointed if he doesn't "get" this or that. He will. Let him know that you have confidence in him. But, for the moment, enjoy, enjoy.

TELEVISION: PROS AND CONS

Does television harm development?

Most children's television programs are being severely criticized by child psychologists and others. Many could be better; most will improve. A more important concern is parents who use television as a baby-sitter. Many children are allowed to sit too long and watch anything that appears on the screen, as long as they remain quiet and stay out of trouble.

Children need a full range of activities—working on puzzles, being read to, talked to, listening to conversation and music, and playing outdoors. Some of these activities permit the young child to learn by doing; they encourage creativity and fantasy. Television is simply absorbed, often without being monitored or explained so that young children can understand it or use it to help them understand their own feelings or thoughts. For lower-income and many black children, much television fare—showing whites with nice homes, cars, jobs, and such—doesn't match their own situation. Such children may feel that television is the way the world is supposed to be, and that their own world is inferior.

In what ways is television beneficial?

Although there are still too few blacks shown on television, many shows now feature blacks, thus making it easier for black children to identify with the people, the action, and the world beyond their home and neighborhood. Television provides experiences that many children would not have otherwise. Several programs—"Sesame Street," "The Electric Company," and "Mister Rogers," in particular—help children develop thinking, reading, and social skills. The adults shown interacting with children on television shows is beneficial. You can help by watching with your child whenever possible. You will find that helping her understand words or concepts in a particular sketch will increase her interest in learning.

During this stage it is particularly important to explain the difference between make-believe and real with regard to dangerous or violent activities. This is one of the dangers of allowing young children to watch television without supervision. Daring acts, violence in the form of eye-poking or hitting people over the head should be called "make-believe" and explained as something that is not to be done in real life. More than one child has jumped from high places, imitating his television hero. We have seen disturbed children mix up events in their home with television events.

How can I prevent "too much" television or inappropriate programs?

Encouraging a full range of activities—with television as only one part—is a way of avoiding too much television. You will want to avoid letting preschool children watch certain scary shows, especially before bedtime. Even childhood favorites such as *The Wizard of Oz* can trigger bad dreams for preschoolers. Many late evening shows also contain violence that may frighten the child.

If there is something you don't want your child to see, tell him so and explain—why for example, you think he is too young, or you think he will be upset by it. With older children, you are likely to get some flak: "Sam's mother lets him see it!" You can explain that you feel differently about the matter, and you are doing what you think is best. Although your Johnny may protest violently, he is also likely to feel protected—that you are acting in his behalf . . . "My mama watches over me." But not too much, Mama.

Can my child ruin her eyes by watching too much television?

There is no evidence that this can occur. If her eyes appear bloodshot, however, it may be an indication that she is suffering from eyestrain. You would then want to reduce the time she watches television, but there is no need to stop it completely. Adults can develop eyestrain from reading a book for too long a period. Children should sit at least four feet from the screen, and there should be at least a dim light in the room. Glare from outside light being reflected off the screen should be avoided.

While we're discussing vision, it is important to be on the lookout for vision problems with your preschooler. Children, particularly the very young, won't tell you if they can't see well. They will try to compensate—hold their head very close to the printed page, very far away, or get upset when you ask them to read. Clumsiness or poor coordination in eating or learning to write may also be indications of vision problems. Turning alphabet letters the wrong way is normal for the young child, but should disappear by late five and six. If you notice these problems, it's important to have an optometrist or an ophthalmologist check your child's eyesight. Poor vision can cause poor performance, which can lead to a negative self-image and even emotional problems.

THE PRESCHOOLER AND SOCIETY

Can I aid in my child's social development?

Yes. At age three children are better able to play and interact with each other, instead of solitary play with others nearby. The favorite game is playing house. Here they practice adult roles like Mother, Father, and Worker. They learn to strike an acceptable balance between aggression and passivity, which is a very important lesson to learn. It will be needed throughout life.

Such play can be troublesome to parents. Some view the make-believe play as bizarre and even a sign of mental problems. Others view it as too real, particularly the mother–father love activities. Some worry about play in which boys are dressed as girls or girls as boys. Parents opposed to interracial dating or marriage sometimes worry about love scenes in interracial play.

There is no cause for worry; it is all quite healthy. What's important here is the social skills the child is developing in play. The sexual, racial, and religious roles and preferences involved are only incidental. Generally, anything that is undesirable or socially unacceptable you hear or see in child's play should not have been heard or seen by the child in the first place. Don't feel guilty. You can't and don't want to control everything a child sees and hears. Avoid exposing your child to undesirable behavior whenever possible, but don't discourage the fantasy play. Children need it. A child's sexual identity problem is not the result of such play. You can help by providing the clothes or equipment for fantasy play. But close observation or questioning what is going on is likely to spoil the child's fun. It's "their thing." They need some place and some time without you— indoors and outdoors.

How can I help my children to be wary of strangers without making them feel that the whole world is dangerous?

This presents a problem, especially with friendly, outgoing children. Nevertheless, as soon as they are old enough to be out of your sight for even a minute they need to be taught what situations are dangerous and which are not, how to avoid danger, and what to do in case of danger. They need to learn to protect themselves against people, places, and things.

By three years of age, children in many areas can be left outdoors unsupervised for at least a few minutes. By four years, it is for even longer periods. (Unfortunately, in some areas, even in better neighborhoods, it is unsafe to leave children outdoors unsupervised for even a minute.) You must warn your children to stay away from strangers, in cars or on foot. It's useful to point out that most people are good; that just a few people are bad and might want to hurt little boys and girls. It's also necessary to limit the distance they can wander while unsupervised. Having them repeat these boundaries to you from time to time will help them remember. Stating the way you expect your child to act in dangerous situations in a clear, concise manner is best. Again, the key is a calm approach, rather than a tense, long-winded warning. Such an approach is likely to avoid making your child think that the world is full of dangerous people.

Is sexual abuse a special problem?

Yes, because not only must your child be protected against strangers, but also from friends, baby-sitters, recreation and organization leaders, relatives and, in some cases, even the other spouse as well. Children should be told not to play secret games in which people ask them to do things that make them feel uncomfortable or touch them in private areas—vagina or penis. They should be reminded that this includes parents and other relatives. They should be told to try to get away from the situation, if someone tries to touch or fondle them, and then tell you about it as soon as possible. If your child reports some kind of sexual abuse to you, it is important to listen to the child; never refuse to believe your child. Cases of sexual abuse should be reported, and help should be sought at a local clinic or hospital. When a relative or spouse is involved, a parent must protect the child by doing whatever is necessary—counseling, separation, even legal action.

My four-year-old plays well with two other boys in our building, but they exclude another youngster in a very cruel way. Isn't that harmful both for my son and for the excluded child?
It can be if it is not managed well. Around four years of age, children develop "very favorite friends, in the whole wide world"—even though they only play with a handful of children and have only seen a very small part of the world. A new or "different" child in the neighborhood can experience rejection. In some cases he may be excluded, talked about, or made into a scapegoat. However, some four-year-olds will welcome a newcomer in as a new member of the gang. Some children are confident and aggressive and will do well in a new situation, even when there are efforts to exclude them. It is really a matter of chance. Just as with adult relationships, some personalities gel and some don't.

Should I try to step in on behalf of the rejected child?
Children have less need to get along when personality conflicts arise. They are also less likely to hold long-standing grudges against people they don't like—or are told not to like. When exclusion is taking place in play, you should be cautious about getting involved. Give the children enough time to try and handle the matter themselves. If they do not, you might suggest specific ways that they can play together. "Let's let Jimmy (the excluded

child) be the conductor" if they are playing train, copilot if they are playing plane, and so on.

If your child says, "I don't like Jimmy," it is helpful to explain why Jimmy should be allowed to enter the group and why the rejecting child should give himself a chance to know Jimmy—without being moralistic or harsh. Saying, "Oh, Jimmy wants to play. I'll bet you'll like him when you get to know him," usually works, but if your child still resists, you may want to help him explore his feelings about Jimmy. He may be afraid or jealous, for real or imagined reasons. What Jimmy has done to him, what there is about Jimmy that he dislikes, and how he can deal with his feelings should all be discussed.

If your attitude and manner indicate you're confident that your child can handle the problem, he'll eventually realize that he can work out most problems in relationships. If the problem is not handled properly, he can develop aggressive tendencies to attack and exclude outsiders, or he may become uncomfortable and withdraw from those he does not know.

What should I do if my child is the rejected one?

When your child has been fair and cooperative but Jimmy still doesn't like him, you should help him understand that that is Jimmy's problem or weakness. You should teach him not to be concerned about Jimmy; however, it is not productive to encourage your child to dislike Jimmy. That would be encouraging him to think, "I dislike you because you dislike me, and I need you to like me before I can like myself." This is the quandary faced by many black Americans with bigoted white people today. Blacks who feel that they need the approval of prejudiced whites in order to have a positive self-image, can experience feelings of rejection and self-hatred later on in life. Your child should be taught that he does not need to like or dislike anybody, that he can like or dislike a person not because of who they are but because of how they behave. Hating people is a waste of energy that could be better applied toward more productive activities.

How can I tell if my child is being rejected for racial reasons?

The natural tendency of young children to exclude or mistreat others is particularly troublesome in interracial situations. It is always difficult to know whether the exclusion occurs because two children just happen to get along well with each other but not with the third, or whether it's because the third is black and the other two are white. In this age of racial awareness, we adults are and should be, very sensitive to this problem. But we should be careful not to overreact. For example, one black mother whose daughter was playing the horse in a make-believe game, broke up the play and took her child home. She was angry because her child played the horse and the white children knew, because of her anger, that something was wrong, but they didn't know what. Where there is no derogatory feeling or intent, this reaction can create feelings of confusion and frustration in your child.

It's helpful to observe the situation for a while before acting. If your child is being asked to play the horse but never the rider, the cook but never the mother being served, the porter but never the traveler—you may want to withdraw your child from the play. The children involved have been influenced by racist stereotypes. But you can be more helpful to all if you assist them with their play. Young children often mimic without understanding and are less committed to racist attitudes. They are usually willing to play fair and share the choice roles when adults make specific suggestions: "Let's let Mary play the rider sometime and you play the horse, and then you play the rider and Mary play the horse." When discussing this matter at a later time with your child, a racial approach will have little meaning. The child's ability to understand these concepts is still very limited. It is more beneficial to encourage your child to expect her fair share of the best of everything. Today more black youngsters are doing just that.

What if my child seems overly aggressive with white children?

Black parents who live in neighborhoods where racism is not extreme are sometimes surprised by the aggressiveness and expectation of fair play and justice that their children demonstrate. Parents who were taught to be nice so that they would be accepted by whites are often uneasy when they hear their youngsters saying, "I don't want to play with you!" Or, "Go away," or "Stop that or I'll sock you" when playing with white children. It is just as harmful to overreact and squelch such responses—unless they are extreme—as it is to encourage them. It's necessary to encourage a reasonable level of assertiveness and aggressiveness without promoting rude and cruel behavior. Again, wherever possible—where children are not hurt physically, psychologically, or socially—it is best to let them work out their feelings for themselves. If they can't, then step in and suggest solutions.

When there are no black children around, and you'd like your child to have contact with blacks, you may want to arrange for him to attend nursery schools, visit relatives or friends, or attend churches and social affairs where he can interact with black children.

MORALITY AND THE PRESCHOOLER

How can I promote my preschooler's moral development?

From ages two through four your child begins to have increasing contact with other children and other adults as well. Yet the child still has trouble sharing. Early in this stage, he is still inclined to violate the rights and ignore the needs of others. A toy that he wants is a toy that he wants and it doesn't matter that it belongs to somebody else. He wants it. He needs it. He'll take it!

At the same time he is willing to go along with a "you scratch my back and I'll scratch yours" kind of arrangement with you and others. "If you will be fair to me, I will be fair to you; if you let me play with your doll, I will let you play with mine; if you don't hit me, I won't hit you." Numerous situations between your Johnny, other family members, and other children will provide opportunities to help your child learn how to be fair and to share with others. At the same time you will want to help him learn to expect, and teach him how to insist that others be fair and share with him. This can only occur, however, when you, the parent, serve as a negotiator and mediator in conflicts between your child, other family members, and other children.

But isn't Johnny still too young to understand all this?

Some parents are inclined to side with their children, right or wrong. They sometimes argue that the two-, three-, or four-year-old is young and therefore should be allowed to mistreat other people—"Oh, he's just a baby." We have seen parents scold and even spank other children for hitting their child, even though their child created the problem in the first place. The seeds of manipulation, exploitation, and poor personal control are sown right here. Such children may become corrupt later on in life—in business, in government, even in their personal lives. Parents who take their child's side whether the child is right or wrong do a disservice to their children.

Obviously you want to support and encourage your children. But you do so by helping them understand their role in creating or perpetuating any conflict, and by pointing out how they can avoid the conflict in the first place. "You don't have to take Johnny's car. If you want to play with it, ask him. I'm sure that he'll share it. Maybe you can let him play with your bicycle." Or, "If you take his car without asking him, he will be mad at you." Your involvement at this stage sets the tone for future moral reasoning by your child without your help.

But blacks are often treated in an immoral fashion. Shouldn't we side with our children, right or wrong?

Defining what is "moral" becomes more difficult later on, particularly when your group is the victim of racial discrimination within the society, as is the case for many blacks in America. Parents who feel pressured by a spouse, by schools, welfare workers, or by society-at-large are likely to have difficulty recognizing the troublesome behavior of their child in a conflict. But you can damage your child's personal development at this stage if you permit him to be unfair and unjust in his relationships with others because "we have it hard." When he is right he is right and when he is wrong he is wrong. This attitude is most beneficial to your child. It puts him and other blacks in the best position to demand fair treatment from others.

You said that a child may take something because he doesn't have much of a conscience. How does he develop a conscience if he is not born with it?

Because your child is strongly attached to you, what you think, feel, or say is good or bad becomes pretty much what he thinks is good or bad. Your praise, your reward and approval for certain kinds of behavior establish what is good, and your punishment and disapproval for certain other types of behavior establish what is bad. Before the age of four, your child will avoid behaving in certain undesirable ways because he or she doesn't want to suffer the consequences—your anger and resulting punishment, or abandonment. Around the age of four, your child has absorbed your feelings and made them his own, and will experience his own guilt for acts he considers forbidden. He now has a conscience. At this point most children will experience some guilt about taking something that doesn't belong to them, even when a parent or an adult is not around.

Can guilt be harmful?

Too much guilt can be paralyzing; too little guilt is harmful as well. Most people try to behave within the rules of acceptable social conduct because of prior training, and in order to avoid feelings of guilt. Some people are able to commit brutal crimes without any guilt because their ability to feel guilt was never adequately developed. Without guilt and the need to achieve social approval, there would be little reason not to try to get all that you can get for yourself without being concerned about the rights and needs of others. Without guilt there could be no trust among individuals and there could not be a society.

But can't an emphasis on morality and guilt interfere with racial progress?

As blacks, we need not be afraid that encouraging moral development, a conscience, and guilt will prevent social action. Black children without the ability to feel a normal amount of guilt will victimize their parents, relatives, and community first. They are unlikely to be involved in social action to improve the black community. Their self-centered personalities will cause them to look out for themselves without concern for others, black or white. Guilt need not be involved when blacks, or anyone else, act against injustice. Dr. Martin Luther King, Jr., and the church members who broke the back of segregation without a gun, probably had the best developed consciences—and the ability to feel guilt—of any group in the country.

How can a child develop too much guilt?

Much is going on between the ages of three and six which can easily lead to guilt. Boys have romantic feelings toward their mothers and girls toward their fathers. They are jealous of the relationship between the parents. They will sometimes insist that they are going to marry the parent of the opposite sex when they grow up. They will wish that their rival parent would go away or sometimes even be destroyed. At the same time they fear that their rival parent has the same jealous feelings toward them as they have toward the parent, and they fear that the parent will harm them in some way. This is thought to be the cause of bad dreams in which children are chased by frightening figures such as bears and giants.

These are very powerful guilt-producing forces. Parents who "shame" their children at this age as a way of getting them to behave increase the guilt problem. If you tease your preschooler or flaunt his helplessness or your adult love relationship in his face—showing how much more power you have—you can increase the problem. Kissing your wife or husband probably calls for a kiss for daughter or son in this age range—when they are nearby. Some children will insist on it—a kissing trio, even. That's fine as long as it's not carried too far. There is no need for parents to avoid showing displays of affection. It is not necessary for a mother to try to "make it up" to her son or a father to try to "make it up" to his daughter by being permissive, or by pretending that the child is a real competitor.

But isn't it "wrong" for children to feel this way about their parents?

It is best not to respond in a shocked or angry way when you realize that your child is concerned about your marital relationship. That just increases guilt. Love of boy for mother and girl for father is normal and healthy. When a boy indicates that he is going to marry his mother, or a girl claims that she is going to marry her father, it's helpful to explain that you are already married; that someday they're going to grow up and fall in love with and maybe marry a nice girl or boy of their own age. This will reduce the frustration, anger, fantasy, and guilt.

We have described the most common and usual relationships.

Children have many different affectionate attachments to adults—to older brothers or sisters, grandparents, neighbors, and others. They have jealousies and rivalrous feelings of different degrees toward their competitors for the affection, time, and attention of the adult they "love." The closer the relationship, the greater the jealousy and rivalrous feelings—greater with parents than neighbors, for example. At this age, these are feelings of affection and not true sexual feelings.

Our son walked in on us having sexual intercourse. We were so stunned we didn't know what to say. How would you handle this?

Sexual intercourse, as mentioned earlier, should take place in private. Parents sometimes have sexual intercourse in front of very young children or fail to close the door on older children because "they don't know what's going on." This is troublesome precisely because they don't know what's going on. At this age, they will make up their own explanations. Usually they think that it is a violent act, which increases their fears, fantasies, and guilt. Even if they got over their fear, the stimulation they would receive from watching could make it hard for them to develop certain necessary inner controls.

You might have said to your son, "Edward, Mommy and Daddy are making love. Go back to your room [or wherever] and I'll talk to you later." If necessary, it's better to stop and take him back rather than get into a struggle here. You are already irritated by the interruption and not likely to handle a struggle well. Later, one of you—or both—in a casual way should explain that parents show their love for each other in a different way than children love each other or love their parents. (Otherwise you may see him "playing house" in a way that upsets the parents of the little girl upstairs.) You might also explain that when they grow up they will make love like Mommy and Daddy.

My three-year-old is a liar. How can I break the habit early?

At three, it is not a habit. It is not even really a lie. The desires, wishes, and imagination of a young child can get in the way of what is real. Sometimes a three-year-old will start to tell a story and you will hear it get out of hand as he adds bits and

pieces to fit the wishes and ideas in his head. Left with a baby-
sitter, he will point out with solemn expression and hopeful eyes
that his mother said that he could have all the cake that he
wanted. It's not helpful to say, "You are a liar." But, saying "I'm
sure you like cake but your mother would not like it if I gave
you all that you want. You may have a piece," in a firm but
good natured way with an understanding smile, will be more
effective.

What about fibbing among slightly older children?

Around four or five years, children are more aware of what
is truth and what is made up to achieve a particular end. Even
here you may or may not get the truth if you ask for it directly.
It still doesn't help to be outraged about less than the truth. It
is not a crisis of morality that is involved here. It's the child's
way of getting what he wants, which is normal and healthy at
this age. It doesn't help to investigate his story like a detective.
This makes your child feel that he can't be trusted, is devious,
that the act is most serious! Your child loses face. You may get
"the truth," but you made him tell. After he admits that he
licked the chocolate off your cake, what have you gained? You
did not encourage or help him take responsibility for his own
behavior. In fact, your pressure can cause him to tell less than
the truth next time . . . and the next. Doing the opposite of what
parents want is a strong tendency at this age. This situation can
lead to a "lying" problem.

How can I help my child to be truthful?

Some parents say, "It is not important whether you tell me
the truth or not. It is important that you tell the truth to yourself."
Most children don't want this burden and eventually "tell it like
it is." You might point out that you will not know what to believe
if she does not tell the truth. Children "distorting the truth" are
very interested in the story of the boy who cried "wolf" so often
that nobody paid any attention when the wolf really appeared,
and the boy needed help. When your child is able to change her
story and tell you the truth, it is helpful to say that you are glad
that she was able to do so. This will make it easier to tell the
truth next time.

Remember that children are great imitators. If you lie—even tell little lies—the child this age will know. You are likely to hear your child doing the same thing. We know one youngster who was told to tell bill collectors and others in search of his mother that she was not at home while she hid in the house. This caused confusion, insecurity, and anger in the child. As could be expected, by nine years old, his schoolmates knew him as a liar and a cheat. In a group, his friends said, "Man, that dude lies! You can't pay no attention to what he says!" Thus a problem that began in the home eventually led to problems with other youngsters and adults.

My three-year-old stole a toy car from the child upstairs. Does that mean he's going to be a thief?

The whole world belongs to the three-year-old. Taking the toy, the candy bar from the store, or any other item at this age is no indication that a child will become a thief. Stealing is not inborn. Even when a child under five has been told that he should not take an item, he may still take it quite innocently. Desires and wishes are stronger than his restraint. He does not yet have a fully developed conscience and does not feel guilty about it. He should be taught, however, that taking the belongings of others is not acceptable. Mild punishment may serve as a reminder that he must not act this way. Returning an item and apologizing also helps the child remember that the behavior is unacceptable. Scolding, spanking, and making a fuss are not helpful. Taking time to talk calmly to your child about the matter is much more effective.

Children who must ask before they take things that belong to others in their own home are less likely to take things outside the home. Also, in homes where others must ask before they take the possessions of a child, the child is more likely to respect the rules of ownership and borrowing.

Again, outrage and harsh punishment in such situations are destructive. We sometimes overreact to lying or stealing because we fear these impulses in ourselves. If we have a relative or friend who has a real problem or is in jail, we are particularly anxious to destroy such habits in our children. But calm, ongoing help in the development of inner control is more effective than outrage and harsh punishment.

FATHER-ORIENTED PROBLEMS

I am very busy. Can I still be a good father?

Dr. Martin Luther King, Jr., is quoted as having said, "It is not the quantity of time you spend with children that's important, it is the quality." We agree. Truly listening to your children, being reliable, warm and friendly, firm but flexible, predictable, calm, confident, reasonable, and mature makes for good quality. You should try to be present during important occasions, such as birthdays, holidays, and meetings with the teacher. Setting aside certain times for doing things together, such as attending ballgames or picnics is important . . . more important than being an ever-present "dud." Your work can wait during that special moment when your daughter must tell you that she won the special prize at Centra's birthday party. If you are busy saving the world, making money, or doing good deeds, a brief interruption won't stop you. But several rebuffs will make your daughter feel that you don't care. After a few minutes or a few interruptions you should point out in a friendly way that you are busy. Let her know when you will be finished and ready to play or listen.

Don't fool yourself about the quality of your relationship. It is important to be present and positively involved with your family. One mother said of her husband, "He always points out that Dr. King said it's not the quantity but the quality, but he's so bad that when he's there my kids ain't gettin' quantity or quality."

I do all the work and my four-year-old prefers her father. Does it mean she doesn't love me?

It is easy to feel unloved or less loved in this situation. Frequently this occurs when fathers must be away a great deal. It becomes a very serious problem when parents are separated or divorced. It also occurs when one parent is the sole "disciplinarian" and the other is the "good guy." One cause for these feelings at this age is the "love affair" between your child and the parent of the opposite sex.

As long as you are not too harsh, too punitive, or unfair and unjust, you have no reason for concern. The love affair will give way to less possessive attachment to her father. If you are the sole disciplinarian or more often present, and therefore the usual source of control, protection, and security, your child will seek you out in times of real trouble rather than the parent he or she seems to prefer in "good times." Don't take it personally or try to make your child or your mate feel guilty about it. Your child may sense your disappointment or sense a rejection and use this as a way to "fix" you for what you didn't let him have or do. Be cool. It will all balance out in time.

If you are separated or divorced there will be a great temptation to "put down" your mate when your child appears to like him or her a little too much. Try not to do this. You don't want to build a false good guy either. It is best to answer questions about your situation in ways that are not harmful to your former mate or spoil your child's chance of having a good relationship with both parents. We will say more about this when we discuss divorce (pp. 112–114).

RAISING A FATHERLESS CHILD

Can a child grow up to be healthy without a father?

Yes. But whether a fatherless child grows up to be healthy or not depends a great deal on the mother's ability to handle the problems that arise when a male partner is not present. Most mothers who work barely make enough money to support their families. Women who do not work and must depend on public support do not receive enough money to adequately care for their families. As a result, mothers who care for children without working males in the home spend a lot of time and energy worrying, whether they are working or not. This makes it difficult to maintain a calm and confident attitude, which is so important in bringing up children. Support and help from family and friends can be helpful. State and federal programs that offer improved health care, day care, and income benefits are needed.

Boys who grow up in fatherless families often turn to other boys for advice and information that they would ordinarily receive from their father. Often the advice is not good or the price is high. Because they receive attention, advice, and a sense of belonging from other boys, they are more pressured to do what the group does, right or wrong.

Some mothers, in the absence of fathers, work too hard to make their sons masculine. At other times some "cut their sons down" because of negative feelings they have toward men who deserted or abused them. They sometimes use their male children as "little husbands"—without sex, but pretty close. And in some rare cases, probably related to anger toward men, they make them "little girls." We know of one mother who wrestled with her son to make him tough. She was also sexy and seductive— voice, manner, body exposure, "accidental" breast contact—toward him. This overstimulated the youngster, making it difficult for him to develop inner controls. This, and other factors, led to learning difficulties and juvenile delinquency. On the other hand, a mother without a husband should show her normal level of affection toward her son.

How can I help my son accept a new man in my life?

Children who are made "little husbands" become very jealous and angry when a boyfriend or a new husband is brought into the picture. The rage and anger, particularly in the three to seven age range, can be very intense when the child has had Mommy alone for a long while. A child usually feels guilty and anxious about these emotions. We know of mothers who think it is cute and are very proud when their "little husbands" angrily attack a new boyfriend. It is important for the boyfriend and the mother to help the child handle his anger and jealousy. Teasing and acting as if it is a real man-against-man competition for Mommy can be very harmful. The child should be taught that there's a difference between the parent-child and man-woman relationship.

It helps when the boyfriend does things for and with the child in a responsible way. Your youngster is likely to resist and test the patience and commitment of your friend for a while. But children want helpers and protectors, and if your friend understands this, and the fact that the difficult behavior is jealousy, and persists in his efforts to be helpful to your child, he will gradually gain respect and acceptance. But neither he nor you should permit unacceptable behavior, nor should you be too harsh. A lot of talking and patience is required.

When there are many males in the neighborhood, there will be many models of masculinity and fewer problems for a male child in a fatherless family. Where this is not the case, male relatives who are mature and responsible can be helpful if they are willing to spend some time with the male child. "Big brothers," male teachers, and other males willing to pitch in can also be helpful. In all cases, reliable, predictable, and mature persons are best. People who promise to visit and then don't appear, come one time but not the next, or take advantage of your child in one way or another are more trouble, and can be more harmful, than no one at all.

I am often told that I should get a husband for my child's sake. Do you agree with that?

No. We don't believe that a man (or a woman) "at any price" is helpful. This can lead to an unhappy relationship that would be harmful to your child's development. Irresponsible, immature fathers add little to the development of their children, even when they are present. Fathers who spend all their time watching television, reading, or engaged in personal activities provide very little guidance for their children. Even worse, a weak father who will not stand up for his rights in relationships with you and others is not a good model. A father who is a tyrant and abuses the rights and ignores the needs of others is also not a good model. One reasonable choice when you can't find "Mr. Right" is to do without—a husband, that is.

PARENTAL ROLES AND ATTITUDES

We argue in front of our child. Is that harmful?

When occasional arguments occur in a home in which the atmosphere is usually one of affection and positive feelings, there is little problem. The children learn that the expression of anger is normal and will not destroy people. They learn to express their anger verbally rather than by hitting or acting in extreme, angry ways. If adult arguments lead to physical violence, slammed doors or thrown furniture, children will learn to express their anger in the same way, which is undesirable.

Very often children will not want their parents to argue. They are afraid that they may harm each other or leave and abandon them. You can reassure them by pointing out that mommies and daddies sometimes get angry with each other just like brothers and sisters. When they have brothers and sisters they will know exactly what you're talking about! If they don't, remind them of an argument or angry feelings and words they had with a neighborhood child.

When two parents are present, is it important for the male to be in control?

No. Some people feel that the decline of the strong father-controlled family has led to difficulty in child development and family life. We disagree. We believe that the increased difficulty for families—black or white—is due to the increased complexity of society. The only real benefit of a father-controlled family is that the source of authority, and therefore expectations, is clear. The problem with this in the past, however, has been that this male authority was achieved at the expense of women and children. It created a great deal of rage and anger on the part of wives and youngsters. To "get back" they often acted in a way to frustrate the male—no sex, poor grades in school, doing the opposite of what he wanted.

This family arrangement also creates a rigidity of personality and thinking. From the notion that some single person in the home has the right to absolute authority, right or wrong, comes the notion that somebody in the school, in the city, and in the nation is entitled to exercise authority and make decisions regarding your life, right or wrong.

That's the way minorities got hurt, women got hurt, children got hurt, and in the end, males get hurt. The feeling that the male should not fail, should never be sick, and cannot show weakness on occasion is created by this "all-authority," all-powerful notion. These are superhuman demands, which no one can meet. Male frustration and disappointment often leads to the scapegoating of wives and children. It can destroy the assertiveness and aggressiveness in a female child. It can lead to tremendous father and son conflict. As mentioned, it often leads to women "getting back" at their husbands in subtle, but very effective ways.

If it's not by having the father all-supreme, how should a family be run?

It is important to make it possible for all members of the family to experience respect for their rights and concern for their needs; to expect each to show that same concern for others; to expect each to accept his responsibility by contributing to the well-being of the family. These expectations and ways of relating should be discussed around various incidents and worked out in boyfriend-girlfriend, husband-wife, parent-child relationships.

One child should be asked to wait until the one who spoke first has had his say. In this way children (and parents) learn to listen to each other. We remember a two-and-a-half-year-old who was ignored by her mother, her father, and her four-year-old brother, until she pounded on the table saying, "Listen to me!" Everybody listened. Right on for her. But her parents also insisted that she listen to others. In that same house the TV channel can't be changed without mutual agreement—be it mother, father, or children who would like to change it. There is, however, an unwritten law that certain programs—football, news reports, cartoon specials, and certain variety specials—take precedence.

Children in a home that operates in this way learn how to work out ways to have their rights and needs met. They also learn fair play, to accept responsibility, cooperation, and to compromise when necessary. Children who grow up in such settings will be less rigid as adults, have less anger and rage, have less need to dominate or exploit others, and will not stand for the abuse of their rights and neglect of their needs. Vigorous discussions can and should follow the violation of house rules. But extreme abuse, verbal or otherwise, should not be tolerated.

We tend to favor our two-year-old boy over our four-year-old. Why? What can we do about it?

The "favorite age" and "favorite child" situation is a very real problem. Some parents like children best when they're babies, others when they are three- or four-year-olds, others when they are seven or eight, and so on. Some favor the first child and others, the last. Some favor one child for a particular characteristic—aggressiveness, sweetness, strength, or physical ability; it is often a characteristic that the parent wanted but feels that he or she did not have in adequate supply. It can be a characteristic that a parent has and feels is very valuable.

In this case, comparing one child with another, "Susie is more aggressive than Billy," or "John is smarter than Diane," can cause trouble between the children and between the children and you. The favored child may seek even greater favor at the expense of a brother or sister. This is harmful to the social development of both. It often makes it easy for a favored child to "get by" or develop a false picture of his or her worth and unrealistic expectations from others. The world doesn't care whether a child was Mommy's or Daddy's A-plus, number-one son or daughter. A child so misled is likely to have problems. Your awareness of your feelings is the first step toward preventing such problems. Try to understand why you feel as you do, be fair in managing conflict, in giving each child time, attention, reward, and privilege. When you tend to favor one child for whatever reason, you should make a conscious effort to control your behavior. This doesn't mean to "treat them all the same." Children have different needs. For example, one may not need as much help in going to bed as the other. He won't object to the time you spend helping the other as long as he is getting a little extra time with his own problem area.

SPECIAL PROBLEMS

I am expecting a new baby. How should I prepare my two-year-old?

It is important to talk about the coming of the new baby. It is best to use the correct words about where the baby is located and where it will come out, even though your child may not be able to pronounce "uterus" or "vagina." Do not say that the baby is in the stomach; children can get confused about eating food and having babies.

Helping your young child look forward to the new baby will reduce the jealousy. Let him feel that he will have a new, grownup role; that he will share in the pleasure of a new baby. At the birth of the new baby, it is important to involve the older child. If relatives and friends pay great attention to the new baby and forget about your two-year-old, it is important for you to bring her into the act by praising her and her new role. When younger children can do helpful things for the baby, this should be encouraged. But keep relationships clear. Telling the child it's his baby can cause confusion. It is the baby of Mommy and Daddy and the sister or brother of your child.

Don't feel hurt or guilty if your two-year-old is angry, demanding, or unruly around the time of the new baby's arrival. This may happen even if you try hard to prevent it. Even when your child tries hard to "be good about it," the jealousy and anger may arise every now and then. Here it is important to be understanding, to talk to him about his feelings, to reassure him that you still love him, to assure him that he is going to like and have fun with the baby.

An angry, harsh response at this time proves his fear that he will lose your love to the baby. Tolerating extreme acting-up because "I know he's upset about the baby" proves that you are going to neglect him for the baby. If you have a nine- or ten-month-old, don't make the mistake of believing that he is too young, that you don't have to prepare him. Talk to your infant about the coming event; let him feel your "bulge" and otherwise be involved in the excitement.

I plan to stay at home until my children are school age. Is it important to send them to nursery school anyway?

Nursery school helps a child learn to leave his parents and begin to relate to others. It can help teach your child how to get along with other adults, how to function as a group member, how to deal with how others feel about him and how he feels about others. In nursery school he will have an opportunity to play games that require sharing and playing by the rules; these activities help him to think and learn.

A good nursery school experience paves the way for smooth entry to school. It also provides parents and younger children in the family with an important reprieve. With fewer children around, the younger ones get more attention and parents get a bit more necessary rest. Children are best able to handle the nursery school experience after two and a half years of age. Two or three half-days a week are sufficient.

Many parents cannot afford nursery school programs. Nonetheless, children can still have planned interactions with caretakers and other children. These social experiences will prepare them for the social aspects of entering school.

I must work. Is it harmful to send my two-year-old to a day-care center?

Again, we believe that it is not advisable to send a child to nursery or day care until after two and a half years, and even then on a part-time basis. But what you must do, you must do. Do your best to find a good program and send your child without feeling that you are not being a good parent.

What makes a good program? Good people. Enough space, toys that encourage play, a safe and interesting place are all important, but, we repeat . . . look for good people. By good people we mean people who want to work, who like children, and who truly understand them. Good people are more interested in helping children gain controls than punishing them for things they did because of underdeveloped controls. Look for people who respect the rights and needs of children without letting them do whatever they please. Good people know how to make nursery school a fun place and yet provide reasonable rules and expectations. In short, look for a program that can help your child continue growing in the same healthy way he has begun at home.

With infants we hope there will be enough warm, friendly, capable caretakers who will stimulate motor, language, learning, social development, and all the things we pointed out as being so important in Chapter 3.

My girlfriend works on the same job but she always appears less tired and has more time for her family. Does she know something that I don't?

Some people simply have more energy than others. On the other hand, the key to success as a working parent—and in almost every other complex operation—is organization, planning, and good use of available help. If you plan your meals in advance, even cook in advance, or plan how you and your husband or wife or children will share the cooking, cleaning, and such, you will feel less pressured. If you talk with your children about the importance of their chipping in and plan their tasks with them, they can be a big help. You want to let everybody help in one way or another and let everybody know what you need in order to succeed. Let them know that you appreciate their help; they will feel like they are doing something of value and will want to keep helping.

Some people have very real trouble organizing. A list of "things to do" that you cross off as you do them is very useful. If you make a practice of doing the things you "must do"—high priority—first, you won't be too upset if less important things don't get done. The more you keep on top of things, the better you will feel and the more you and your family will benefit.

DEALING WITH ADOPTION

When should we tell our child that he is adopted?

Child-care specialists disagree about this matter. It was formerly felt that the child should be told around two or three years of age. Recently it has been suggested that children this young do not understand the meaning of adoption and can develop fears about the "solidness" of their place in the family. Some people believe that they should be told at about seven or eight years of age when they can better understand.

Our feeling is that the matter should be handled like all complicated concepts and possible anxiety-causing topics such as race or sex . . . gradually, in the ways a child can understand at a particular age. The only difference here is that there is usually nothing to cause a child to ask the question, and so it's likely that you will have to bring up the subject. Choose an appropriate a time as possible. A neighbor, a friend, or a relative who is adopting a child could be an opening. We feel that no potentially serious harm is done when you talk about adoption or tell your two-and-one-half- to three-year-old child that he or she is adopted, if your manner conveys acceptance. A simple comment, free of long-winded discussions that convey anxiety, is best. A warm, relaxed manner as you discuss the matter is helpful.

At a later period, you will want to point out that it is the love, care, and concern that makes a mother a mother and a father a father and all of them a family, and not the fact that a child came from the father's "seeds" or the mother's body. That is only a biological technicality. In many traditional African cultures, a child is not considered "born" until a ritual designed to strengthen parent-child relationships has taken place . . . sometime after birth.

We think that having a child find out from someone else later on that he is adopted can be much more harmful than when the child is told by his or her adoptive parents in a warm, accepting setting, over a period of time. If he learns from the outside, the child can't help but wonder: "What was all the hiding and secrecy all about if you love and accept me?" It is best not to tell an adopted child that he was a "special child"; that he stood out among all the others, or that he is better than a natural child because you had a choice and could have picked others. Such a statement can create more doubt than reassurance.

What is the best age for a child to be at the time of adoption?
It is best to adopt a child as soon after birth as possible. A number of problems are avoided when the child is yours from the beginning. On the other hand, there are many older children who could get along well in adoptive homes. There are many people who are very good with children and can handle even very serious psychological and social problems—more common with older, neglected, and abused children. Know yourself and your motives, and adopt the child you want.

What should I tell my adopted child about his natural parents?
It is best to tell your child that his mother and father were

not able to care for him properly and gave him up so that someone in a better position to care for him could do so. You can point out that you wanted a child and were able to care for him. You should tell your child how the adoption was arranged in language understandable at his or her age. It is best to avoid saying anything that suggests that the child was unwanted or rejected.

After your child fully understands the concept of adoption, he is likely to question whether his parents are still living. There is disagreement on the best way to handle this, but we believe that you should give an honest answer . . . to the best of your knowledge. The question indicates a youngster's need to discuss his feelings about being adopted, about being given away, about what kind of person he is, about what kind of people his parents were. All of this should be done in a very calm, matter-of-fact way. Don't act as if you are hiding something from him. Don't put down the natural parents, but don't build them up, either. We believe that there should be no contact between the natural parents and the adopted child and his family. Where a relationship must exist, however, there should be clear understandings between the adults involved so that the child cannot manipulate them.

Older adopted youngsters sometimes want to find their natural parents. If they do, don't take it personally and don't stand in their way. It is a search for roots, for full identity. The quality of the relationship will be different. Your relationship with your adopted child is not likely to be harmed unless it was very poor in the first place.

Is there such a thing as a "bad seed"?

Some people believe that a child of troubled parents is from a "bad seed" and, therefore, means trouble in turn. What an adopted child becomes, except where severe psychological damage has occurred, depends on relationships in your family, in your community and school, and—as with all children—a number of chance factors. The "seed," or his genetic makeup, has very little to do with it. It simply sets the boundaries, the limits of talent, temperament, and intelligence. But the "bad seed" notion is a handy excuse. When we see behavior that reflects badly on us, some of us don't want to take the responsibility for it. It is very easy to blame it on the natural parent—the original "bad seeds."

You can create a self-fulfilling prophecy in which you help your child become the "bad seed" that you feel his mother or father was. Your expectation that he will become bad can lead to your encouraging and tolerating troublesome behavior that produces—as you expected—the "bad seed." You can go to the other extreme in trying to beat out the badness, or prevent the badness from showing up. Normal aggressiveness can be either crushed or increased in this way. When an adopted child, whatever his background, is fortunate enough to escape early damage and is reared well, he is as likely to grow and develop as well as any other child.

Aren't many black adoptions informal?

Most black adoptions are informal—without going through official agencies. A relative or even a friend will "take" or "keep" a child for weeks or throughout childhood. This is often the case with an out-of-wedlock child, with a young or sick parent, or parents who are unable to care for all their children. The caretaker should make the same kind of explanations as in formal adoptions. The long-range plan for the child should be known.

We have seen some of the problems of foster-home children in a few informal adoption situations. The children often test the caretakers to see how much they will tolerate, but are then afraid that the testing behavior will get them sent away. This is particularly troublesome if their guardians threaten to send them away in order to make them behave. If they live near their parents, they may feel that one day they may get snatched away. They may wonder, "Why was I sent away—and not my brother Norman?" These circumstances, without explanations, can cause anxiety and behavior problems.

We are white and we have just adopted a black child. Are there some general guidelines you can suggest?

We hope that your motives were not to rescue the child from his or her blackness. Attitudes of either white superiority or pity for blacks are likely to lead to difficulties. You and your husband must discuss racial difference and adoption in a calm and reassuring way from time to time. Relatives, friends, or neighbors should not be allowed to pick on your black child, nor should other children. Conversely, you don't want to overprotect him about a difference in race any more than you want to overprotect him about anything else. See how he fights back, and help him only when he needs it. Exposure to black history, culture, and heroes (and ordinary black people of similar and different life-styles) as well as an unemotional acceptance of the child will enable your child to establish a positive identity—black and white. If you are of a middle- or upper-income lifestyle and expose your black child only to blacks of a lower-income lifestyle, troublesome identity problems, such as rejection of blackness, guilt, overidentification with the low-income style, and such can arise.

As white people, you hear and see white racist talk and acts even more than blacks do. When it touches your child you are likely to be outraged, lacking, as you do, the ongoing experience that black people have in dealing with white racism. You must make an extra effort to make your child understand the incident as the problem of the "attacker"; that your child is okay, fine, and good. You don't want to brood, complain, and overreact excessively or you will transmit anxiety, fear, lack of control, and the notion that it is bad for your child to be black. He or she needs to hear, "You can climb every mountain. . . . You must keep on keeping on . . ." in spite of racist incidents here or there or everywhere. You must provide a model of constructive ways to fight racism—ways that don't hurt you or your child. Note our suggestions to black parents. If you are having difficulty dealing with racial issues, you will find it helpful to consult a mental health professional.

My oldest child had a different father and is the only one in the family with a different name. Do you think we should have it changed?

We know this situation can cause a great deal of difficulty. The oldest child may feel rejected. In cases in which the father is dead, never lived with the family, or deserted for a long period of time, it would be advisable to have your present husband adopt your oldest child and change his name. This should be done only after a great deal of discussion with your child. Again, adoption is not recommended when the child's father is living and attentive to the child—even if he gives his permission.

We are white grandparents. Our daughter had problems and abandoned her four children, three white and the youngest, who is adopted, black. The three white children have contact with and receive support from their other grandparents. We are the only family and support our black grandchild has. Maybe because she is so vulnerable, she's "our heart" and special. How can we help her grow up to be a healthy child?

First, you will need to provide the good basic care we describe throughout this book. Second, pay particular attention to the guidelines we described earlier for the adopted black child. Be prepared for the separation and identity issues that are going to occur around adolescence. They are a challenge to all parents and can be particularly difficult where there is a racial difference that has not been discussed and managed well. (Note our discussion of adolescence.) But most important, you need to protect your black grandchild against the scapegoating, rejection, and abuse that can occur within your family and close social network in particular.

The family is a particular problem because it is the acceptance and sense of belonging here that helps us deal with all of the rejections and insecurities that exist beyond the family. Thus, you want to help the brothers and sisters develop mutual support and to reject the efforts of outsiders to play them against each other on racial grounds, or on any grounds. You must help your grandchild understand that if someone doesn't like her because of her race, the absence of her mother, not knowing her father or his family, or for whatever reason, it is their shortcoming as a human being and not hers. You want to teach her that she is the kind of person that she makes of herself; and how to develop skills and behaviors in which she can take pride. She will be viewed as a black person. She need not deny her mixed racial makeup, but she needs to feel comfortable being viewed as a black or an African-American person. If you are comfortable with her mixed racial makeup and the fact that she is considered a black child, then she has a better chance of feeling comfortable with the reality and the perception.

I have just remarried and my husband wants to adopt my children. Is this wise?

You might want to test your marriage for a year or so first. If it appears solid and the natural father has died or deserted the family for a year or more, then adoption probably makes sense. This is particularly true if the children are still very young. A child older than seven or eight is likely to have difficulty, particularly if he has strong feelings of loyalty to his natural father. This happens even when the natural father was not a good parent. Where the natural father is living and seeing his child regularly, it is probably not advisable to have the stepfather adopt the child.

I have two children by a previous marriage and my husband of one year has two children by a previous marriage. Help!

Living in a reconstituted or blended family is difficult . . . too difficult to address in a paragraph. Several good books are now available on the subject. Ask in the bookstore or the library for books about stepfamilies and blended families. There are a few guidelines, however.

Normally difficult sibling rivalries are now potentially "other family" rivalries. The young will play "loyalty and how much do you care about me as opposed to those outsiders" games with the parents. It's also easier for parents to use "your children" in disputes with each other. It's important for the parents to recognize the games and prevent them, and gradually become a new family. You must try to have as many positive experiences together as a family as possible. A constant search for what is fair to all usually makes such marriages work, like all relationships.

HELPING YOUR CHILD HANDLE ILLNESS, DIVORCE, AND DEATH

I must go into the hospital. What should I tell my child?

He will be worried about you, but he will also be worried about what's going to happen to him. When you are sure of the arrangements, you should tell him who will take care of him while you are gone and assure him that he will be okay. If possible, you should make the arrangements and discuss the matter with him about four days before you leave—no less than two days. This will give him enough time to ask questions. You will probably have to respond to a number of "why," "how," and "what" questions. It helps to answer them in an unemotional way—not too solemn or serious and not too glowing and positive. Try to explain the problem in a language he will understand without giving all of the details. You should explain that no person causes an illness; that people are well most of the time but sometimes things can break down or not work right and they have to be repaired—like his brother's car or his truck that stopped working. This explanation is important because children this age sometimes believe that they are responsible for things that happen to other people.

It will help if your child sees you making preparations to return home. You might point out, for example, that you will wear a certain dress or shirt home. You should give a rough estimate of when you will return, but don't make any definite promises. If the stay is long, your condition is not too serious, and the hospital will permit it, regular but short visits should be arranged. Again, a calm, matter-of-fact, confident attitude is the key and is even more important than what you say.

Anytime you are going to be separated from your child for more than a day, some explanation is needed. Otherwise, children will make up explanations of their own, and these can be very frightening. If you fail to tell them but they sense that you are leaving anyway, they may become restless, belligerent, and hard to manage. Even with older children, it is important to discuss any extended separation or stay away from home.

My four-year-old is going to the hospital. How can I prepare him for it?

Again, it's best to tell him about it approximately four days ahead of time and no less than two days . . . not enough time to cause excessive worry, yet time enough to ask questions. If he should find out that he is going by overhearing a conversation, don't deny it or be upset that he has heard. Your child will benefit from a simple explanation of what to expect and what not to expect. It is best to be as straightforward as possible. Some parents, in an effort to make it easier on the child (and themselves), tell the child about the wonderful things that will happen, such as ice cream after the tonsils are removed, without telling him that he will have a sore throat and it will be hard to talk. The child should be prepared to expect both situations—if that's what's going to happen. If you don't know what's going to happen, don't make promises. It is a bad idea to offer your child money or special privileges for his "hardship." Most important, don't tell him you're taking him out to buy a tricycle and wind up admitting him to the pediatric ward. We have seen this happen with a pretty nasty outcome.

Looking at pictures and reading books about hospitals can take some of the fear out of it. You can also play a hospital game with your child or he or she can play it with other children. You can tell him about the routine of the hospital—when he will eat, what kind of bed he will have, who will take care of him, what he can do in his spare time. It is not advisable to take a very young child to look at the ward before he is to be admitted. Many hospitals permit parents to board with sick children, and this is helpful, particularly at the initial stage of hospitalization. You can tell the child that he is going to miss his parents and you're going to miss him, that he may be lonely, but this will only be for a short while, that he will meet other boys and girls in the hospital. This information should be given over a period of several days and not all in one frightening conversation. Again, a positive, calm manner is most helpful.

Suppose he needs an operation? What should I tell him ahead of time?

You should explain the cause of the hospitalization in a way that your child can understand. If he is going to have anesthesia (sleeping gas or painkiller) be sure to explain that he will have a "special sleep" and wake up again after the operation is over. You can explain that the purpose is to prevent pain. When children don't understand this, they can sometimes feel that they are being attacked, even being put to death. It also helps to explain the extent of the operation. We know of a child who was terrified because he thought he was going to lose his entire leg, when only a small growth was going to be removed. You need to reassure him that you will visit and bring him home as soon as the doctor will permit. Help him pack his own bag. Most hospitals will permit children to bring their favorite stuffed animal. The animal, carrying memories of safety and security, will help your child feel more secure in the strange and frightening hospital.

If your child becomes restless or acts up before going to the hospital, don't let your anxiety and guilt about not being able to protect him prevent you from setting some limits and expectations. Tell him that you understand that he's scared and is misbehaving because of it, but you are sure that he will be able to handle the whole business like a big boy. At the same time, don't be outraged. Hospitalization is an ordeal for a little person . . . for some big people, too. It is important to explain hospitalization to older children as well.

Should a child visit a sick parent in the hospital?

It depends on the age and temperament of the child, and the condition of the parent. When the illness of the parent is not life threatening, such a visit can be helpful to parent and child alike. Children should be prepared for the visit—what to expect and how to behave. They should be given explanations that they can understand about the illness and about the time the parent will return home.

We are going to get a divorce. How should we prepare our four-year-old?

It is hard for children of this age to understand the concept of divorce. All they know is that their father and mother no longer live together. They are hurt, lonely, and confused. They wonder what's going to happen to them and to their parents. They sometimes believe that their angry and "bad" behavior caused the parent to go away. Their anger and confusion can sometimes cause them to act up even more. At other times they may try to be extra good and quiet so that their anger will not cause any more trouble.

Explanations about what is involved will be of some help, but for most children there is usually a rocky period around separation and divorce until a new adjustment can be made. You should explain that sometimes mommies and daddies just can't get along and living together is bad for Mommy, bad for Daddy, and sometimes bad for the child. Explain that there are a lot of reasons that you and your mate don't get along, but they are not the fault of the child. Whoever is going to care for the child should explain that they will be there to take care of him or her. If a mother goes to work after the divorce and has not worked before, she should assure the child that she will be coming home every day. When this is not the case, the child should be told in advance. If your child acts up during this period, you should let her know that you understand why she is angry, but don't allow yourself to tolerate excessive misbehavior because of your guilt. The child may understand this as "neglecting her already."

The important people in your child's life, and even her way of life, often change after a divorce. Grandmother, a babysitter, or a housekeeper often come into the picture. Sometimes the child must go to a day-care center. It is important to explain to all of these caretakers that they must help the child to understand that she was not the cause of the parents' separation or divorce. They should also understand that the child may act up because of her anger about the separation and the new people in her life. They should be advised to be sympathetic and indicate that they understand the feelings, but they should not tolerate extreme misbehavior any more than you do.

Children, particularly those two or three years older, are sometimes delighted by divorce. This usually happens when the parent who leaves has been abusive or difficult. Even here it is important to explain along the lines mentioned previously. Even children who are relieved and happy can experience guilt and other mixed feelings.

What is the best way to handle "visits" to my child?

You should make arrangements to visit on a regular basis. You should not "re-fight" the marriage battle during these visits. It is also harmful to try to turn the child against the other parent or make him choose sides. Above all, a promise made must be a promise kept. Your child is already hurt. A promise to visit, send a letter, go for a walk, or whatever should be kept if at all possible. If for some absolutely unavoidable reason your promise can't be kept, you should notify the other parent or caretaker and the child as soon as possible.

Remember that separation and divorce is very difficult for a child in this age group. Only time and careful management of the situation will heal the wound. Although there is always some psychological damage, sometimes it is not as severe as that which would have occurred had unhappy parents continued to live together and hurt each other and the child.

Also, nonsupport has become a major problem—not only the financial problems but the conflict. The children can be hurt by not having adequate food, clothing, shelter, and the other necessities, and by the rejection inherent in nonsupport.

If separation and divorce is that difficult a problem, what is death like for a child at this age?

It is very much the same. Children this age don't really understand the concept of death any more than they understand the concept of divorce. Again all they know is that the parent is away. In this case the parent will not be back. Because they may feel that they caused the problem, the explanations needed here are very similar to those given in the case of divorce. A child should understand that he is not at fault. He should understand that he will be taken care of . . . by whom and how. Those who take care of your child should be made aware of what has happened and should be able to help the child deal with his or her feelings. In divorce or death you can't make a child feel better. It is not helpful to scold him for his sadness or crying. It is helpful if he can feel less powerless. Try to find meaningful things for him to do. Help him return to the activities he enjoys most as soon as possible.

The death of an animal—a bird, a cat, a gerbil—is good preparation in the handling of feelings of anger and sadness that occur around death. It is a good way to understand death . . . how it is different from sleep and that the dead do not return. Helping the child find a box or container in which to bury the animal and having some kind of ritual over the grave such as saying loving things about the animal can be useful.

You must be careful about what you say happens to the body

of the dead—animals or people. One youngster who lost two grandparents and a favorite aunt all within a year's time was told that they all went to heaven to live in God's garden. The youngster was furious with God for taking his loved ones away. Some religious people tell their children that the spirit of goodness in the dead ones goes to heaven but the body remains in the earth. They also explain that there is no pain and the body will change and become like the earth. People who don't want their children to believe in God and heaven generally give only the last part of this explanation.

Some kind of explanation is important. Many children have sleeping problems associated with death, particularly where there has been more than one instance, coupled with illnesses of parents and relatives. Young children often confuse death with sleep and will be afraid to go to sleep. Some will want to return to their parents' bedroom even though they had been able to sleep alone before this time. When they are extremely fearful, you may want to permit this for a very brief period, indicating that they will soon be able to return to their own beds. Be sure to help them do so within a short period of time—two or three days.

Should a child visit a hospitalized parent who might die?

When it is not certain whether a parent will survive, a child should be prepared for the fact that the parent might not return. Trusted loved ones should explain the circumstances, using the level of language the child can understand. It is equally important to explain how a child will be cared for should a parent not return. Children between the ages of two and seven or eight probably should not visit if the parent is comatose, or has a number of support systems—tubes, machinery, and the like. But for children seven or eight and older, you must consider the fact that they may be angry with you and the parent who "deserts them" through death without their ever having a chance to see them a last time. If there is a good chance that the parent will die, you might want to ask the child whether he or she wants to remember the parent when they were in good health or whether they want a chance to see them for what might be a last time. If they want to see them it is particularly important to explain what they can expect to see and how to understand it.

It is also important for children to realize that all the tubes and machines and people are there to try and help rather than harm the parent; and that the parent or relative is making every effort to survive. You should call on the child to hope or pray for the parent, in keeping with your belief, so that the child will feel less helpless. The child might even want to write down his or her wishes or prayer. And finally, if the parent does die you want to help them with their grief. Too often adults grieve, but children do not have an adequate chance to do so, because adults think they don't understand. Children need explanations and an opportunity to feel sad and eventually get over their loss.

How should death be explained to the older child?

Children are better able to understand the concept of death at around seven, eight, or nine years of age. Even here it is important to explain how the death occurred and reassure the child that she is not at fault. But don't overdo the explanations. Children are frightened by all of the sadness in the house, the coming and going of relatives, the funeral parlor, the rituals. Unless a child asks to do so, you should not ask him or her to give the deceased a goodbye kiss. Although you need to explain what is taking place, give them meaningful jobs to do whenever possible. You don't want to stop their normal activities if they feel like going out to play ball or visit friends. Finally, it is a matter of balance: either too much involvement or too little involvement in the whole process can be harmful.

My husband is away in the army. Is that a problem for our children?

Not necessarily. Of course the best possible situation is the one in which children can grow up in a home with two good parents present. Equally healthy children can come from many other kinds of homes when the existing parent or caretakers are able to do a good job. Regular visits, telephone calls, and letters help. Preparing things for and sending things to "away" relatives is also helpful. Separation because of military service, college, or training or work programs is less of a problem than separation caused by imprisonment or even hospitalization for mental illness. What you tell your child about an "away" parent—particularly if the child is slightly older, say five to twelve—is crucial.

Jail and mental hospitals have a stigma attached to them. Yet you want your children to know and respect their father or mother or other friends and relatives even if other people do not. At the same time you don't want a child to feel that he or she must follow the same path. When you believe that the imprisonment is unjust, you must be very careful that your feelings do not tell your child that crime is okay.

Many children (over five years of age is best) visit relatives in prison. Such contact keeps the relationship alive. Your child should be prepared beforehand for the visit, which will involve locked doors, guards, and even searches. Explain why this is necessary. Some children will feel some sadness and guilt when leaving the relative in jail. The sadness is understandable, but the guilt may be harmful. A simple explanation can be: "Jim broke the law and must stay in jail for now." You can be supportive of Jim while making it clear that you and your child are not to blame for his incarceration. A mother should not bring her child to visit a jailed boyfriend unless the child has had a substantial relationship with him.

You can explain mental illness as a problem in which the patient does not always know or cannot always control his or her behavior at the present time. You can give more specific explanations as your child is able to understand them. In the very rare case of danger to children on home visits, you must take reasonable precautions—for the good of both patient and child. In the case of hospitalization and imprisonment, you need to help the child get a fairly realistic picture of the "away" person as a person. No "all roses" or "all devil" is a good rule. This will leave the child free to form his or her own opinion through experience in the future. You can explain crime as a mistake and prison as the penalty and a chance to change. When others tease, you should repeat your explanations; assure your child that the parent is or wants to be a good person; that the child is a good person and that the teasing child is unfair and wrong. Most of all, children should not carry shame or guilt for a problem not of their making.

You and your mate should discuss how you want to explain

imprisonment, particularly when you feel an injustice has been done or that it is for a cause. In general, when this is the case, we think that you should say just that. You should also explain how you are working to bring about change and why. We think that it is unwise to force your cause on your child. It may be rejected or it may not be relevant when he or she is older. Besides, if your relationship is a good one, your children are likely to take it on anyway. Some of these suggestions apply largely to older children, although some kind of explanation should be given to a younger child. We have discussed the matter here as an issue of separation.

CHAPTER 5

The School-Age Child: Ages Five to Eight

IMPORTANCE OF THIS PERIOD

I have been told that this is one of the less crucial stages in my child's development. Do you agree?

No. It has been said in the past that basic development is completed by the end of two years, and certainly by the end of five years—except for a later period involving a certain amount of teenage turmoil and adjustment. Today most people realize that some very significant things happen between the ages of five through eight. This is a time of important changes (maturation and growth) in thinking, understanding, feeling, and social relating.

THE YOUNG SCHOOL-AGER AND RACE

Is the five- through eight-year period an important time with regard to race?

Yes, it is perhaps the most important period in your child's development. During this period children become sharply aware of the fact that they are separate and distinct from their parents. They become more aware of differences. At the same time they are moving beyond the family and into the world. This arouses self-doubt and fear. As a result, around six or seven they develop a great passion to belong. To meet this need and to feel important and competent, children of this age group develop groups of favorite people. They often close other children "out" so that they can feel "in." It is a much more conscious and more serious business than the excluding of others that we discussed in regard to the preschooler.

The average four-year-old barely understands racial difference and it is rarely the basis for group exclusion. The seven- or eight-year-old does understand. Some will express angry, hostile racial feelings to deal with the fact that they actually feel small, fearful, uncertain, rejected, or insecure themselves. They learn to use race as a way to deal with their feelings in homes where family members do the same or are constantly putting each other down.

Five through eight is an important period with regard to race for another reason. This is the period during which the child does or does not "sign a contract" with society. The society expects parents, teachers, and other caretakers to help children accommodate themselves (adapt to) and "swear allegiance" to the desirable attitudes, values, and ways of the society. This is done by introducing youngsters to books, information, religious and political ritual, and other experiences that convey these attitudes, values, and ways. The process is called socialization. In return for their accommodation and allegiance, the society should provide the children and their families with a strong sense of belonging to a concerned, more powerful whole. This sense of belonging reduces a great deal of life's insecurity for individuals—whether this is a rational response or not.

The problem is that black parents have been forced to "swear allegiance" to and accommodate themselves to society without receiving in return the same sense of belonging and security that white families do. Furthermore they are expected to teach their children to do the same. There are too many ways—economic, social, and psychological—in which our society indicates that it values black children and families less than whites. As a result, many questions are now being raised about how much accommodation and how much allegiance to the rules, attitudes, values, and ways of the larger society are in the best interests of black children. Your child is now mature enough to sense these feelings of conflict in his parents, and this affects his own attitudes toward society.

What are some of the questions parents ask that show their inner conflict regarding the society?

Should my child pledge allegiance to the flag of a country in which blacks are the victims of unfair competition? Should I teach my child to play the competition game even better than whites? Should I teach my child not to play the competition game? Should black children study American history with all its distortions? Isn't it better for black children to learn about African history and culture? Should black children learn ballet and classical music? Shouldn't I expose my child to black culture only? Should I teach my child to support a governmental system that allows racism? How can I counteract what my child learns in school every day in support of that system? Should young blacks join the police force or the army?

These are important questions. The answers you establish for yourself will affect the way you teach your child to relate to the black community and to the larger society. What a child learns and accepts now becomes his or her platform and will be difficult for your child or others to change ten, twenty, and fifty years from now. We will not try to answer these questions in the abstract. We will try to answer them in relationship to questions about what children are like and how you can help them grow.

Shouldn't black children learn the realities of life rather than be indoctrinated by "white" ritual and fairy tales?

Let's separate the issue of ritual from that of fantasy and fairy tales. The latter help give your child a sense of security in an often dangerous world. They help a child handle failure and help him dream and plan success. They aid learning. They are fun. If common "fantasy figures" (e.g., Santa Claus) are "too white," turn them black, as we discuss later. Fantasy and fairy tales will fade away or change to adult forms as your child grows. Don't worry about them. Ritual, including saying the Pledge of Allegiance to the flag, is a more complicated matter.

The purpose of ritual is to give a person or group a sense of belonging, purpose, and value in the larger society . . . "with liberty and justice for all . . ." and thereby a sense of security. It is part of the contract a society makes with an individual: "You develop, take care of yourself, and meet your responsibilities as a citizen and human being and I, the society, will protect your rights and work to give you reasonable opportunities." In many ways the society has not lived up to its part of the contract with black people. Some blacks consider the contract null and void and will not participate in related rituals such as the pledge. Even worse, they fear that participation will blind children to the reality. If your child does not say the pledge in school, be prepared for some hostile reaction from teachers and students. Your child will need extra support.

We understand the feeling and in this case you should involve your children in some kind of humane ritual—a pledge to humanity, community, and so on. You also have an obligation to help them develop realistic ways to bring about a better society—their own personal skill development being the first. In other words, you don't want them to be only against something and without obligation.

We want our children to say the pledge. Is that wrong as black people?

No. Some black Americans see change, want to keep pushing toward a better America for blacks, and do not want to express rejection by not saying the pledge or not permitting their children to say it. You must make your own decision, and institutions should abide by the position of the majority. Some black parents handle this matter by permitting their children to say the pledge but explain that it is a statement of an ideal. (The wording probably should be changed to acknowledge this.) In addition, they explain the strengths and shortcomings of the nation. Here too you want to help your children understand that their own personal development is the first thing they can do to help bring about desired change.

Black people have many silent private protest rituals. Some will stand respectfully for the national anthem but won't sing, some won't stand, and so on. In all cases, you should give your child an explanation for your action suitable to his or her level of understanding: " 'Liberty and justice for all' should mean you but it doesn't," and so on. You should be involved in civil rights and other change activities when you feel so strongly—otherwise you teach protest without teaching constructive ways to bring about change, which is the cause of trouble for some black teens today.

In the preceding ways, black parents help their children recognize racist acts and help them learn how to deal with them. That is why thoughtful blacks can often see injustice and imagine people in high and responsible jobs cheating, lying, and stealing when some middle-class white children, who are unable to see and talk about things the way they really are, cannot. (This is also the reason some blacks fear that black children who grow up in white homes will not be prepared to handle the realities of living black in a white-controlled America.) Helping your children see and understand the reality as they come in contact with it, incident by incident, gradually puts all these matters in proper focus.

A white child recently bullied my seven-year-old son with racial slurs. I won't tell you what I told my son to do. But how would you suggest handling the situation?

You probably told him to knock his block off. Sometimes that's the only thing that gets a desired response. If the other child is too big or too strong, you may have to talk with the bully, his teacher, or his parents. But fighting is not the best solution to the problem—even if your child wins the fight. Win or lose, nothing has happened to change the other child's attitude about using racial slurs.

If you're opposed to solving such problems with your fists, what do you suggest?

The problem can usually be dealt with in a way that helps the other child handle his feelings in a more appropriate way and helps your child better understand what prejudice and racism are all about—and how to deal with it without fighting on a daily basis. If he must fight physically every time an act of racism occurs in America, he could become too busy to do anything else. Something similar happens to a lot of us.

Remember that most seven-year-old white children are not diehard racists. They are often repeating what they have heard —sometimes from people other than their parents. They are usually trying to handle their own troublesome feelings as best they can. Without help in coping with their feelings, it is easier to become a diehard. Understanding this, one black father used this approach: "Look, Joe, the next time Billy calls you a 'nigger top,' you tell him that he must have some problems if he has to call you names."

Joe did so. Billy was so confused and stunned that he just walked away. The next day he brought Joe some candy and never bothered him again; in fact, they became friends.

Joe learned to deal with the real problem (Billy's insecurity). And Billy learned something about himself. Joe, with his parents' help, learned how to cope with a difficult situation without his parents, teachers, or friends getting involved. This gave him a greater sense of control and self-confidence.

Is my young school-ager being exposed to attack only because he is black? Wouldn't there be problems between people of different lifestyles even if race were not an issue?

There would be some problems, but not as serious as the problem of racial prejudice. Because the American system has not made it possible for most people to experience equal opportunity and acceptance, groups have scapegoated each other to gain opportunities and to promote their own self-esteem. Too many leaders have encouraged such behavior for economic and political gain. Blacks have been the most vulnerable and have been scapegoated most. This creates a climate of suspicion and an intolerance for difference, rather than an appreciation of the richness that difference gives the country.

America has more different races, ethnic groups, and lifestyles than most countries, which means Americans have a greater need for a tolerance and appreciation of difference than people of other countries. In addition, change has been rapid in America, creating differences in lifestyles between people of the same group. Change is so rapid that nobody can really say what life will be like in the year 2010 or how best to rear children to be prepared for it. The only thing certain about tomorrow's world is that it will require a better ability to tolerate differences in others than most of us now have.

Tolerance is all well and good, but won't I be preparing my child to "sell out" our group if I teach him the ways of the outside . . . say, like taking his hat off in school?

This is an important question. Although it sounds unimportant, it gets right down to the nitty-gritty of the problem of different lifestyles. Such seemingly trivial issues may determine whether your child will do well or poorly in the society of tomorrow. Many upper-income youngsters too, black and white, are rejecting such customs as taking off hats indoors. We want to point out that they can afford to because they know enough to take off their hats in certain places and to keep them on in others when they must; they know how to act at college teas; how to handle a job interview; how to conduct themselves in a business office. We have seen youngsters wear beards and jeans and flout laws or customs during their teens and even twenties, and then conform to the requirements of the larger society when they must earn a living for themselves. They can do so because they learn the rules and styles of the larger society somewhere between the ages of five and ten. This is not the case for many youngsters from low-income backgrounds.

We don't think it's terribly important to make a child take his hat off. We do think that it is important for all children to learn how to conduct themselves in situations that demand different behavior than that required in their home, community, or subculture. If the school expects a child to take his hat off, why not? Parents have a right to socialize a child as they see fit, as long as their way is humane. But if you socialize your child in a way that results in his or her being unable to tolerate the just ways of other people, to live by reasonably fair rules, or to tolerate people other than those in his or her group, then you will limit your child to successful functioning only within your group. Many people change their dress, speech patterns, and mannerisms daily in order to function successfully in different situations.

GETTING ALONG WITH OTHERS

How can I socialize my child in the ways of my group and yet be comfortable with difference and change?

In all our suggestions, we have been, and will be, talking about ways that you can help your child grow up to be a person able to cope with life, difference, and change better than people of past generations. Let's take a specific example to illustrate what we mean.

We know of one set of parents who do not accept religious explanations about the world, but were told by their seven-year-old that God puts stars in the sky. The child heard this from children in school. The parents pointed out that some people believe that that is how the stars got there but others do not, that they (the parents) did not. They explained that they believed that an act of Nature beyond human control put the stars in the sky. (A more detailed explanation, or giving your child a book that explains your point of view, can be useful at a later date. This is enough for a child in this age group.)

A child is likely to accept the explanation or belief of his or her parents. Yet, this explanation leaves the issue open enough so that the child can remain curious and perhaps search for a better explanation in the future. The parents' willingness to accept somebody else's explanations and beliefs as okay for that person, although they disagree with them, leaves their child free to do the same without a need to reject, put down, or refuse to associate with someone who thinks differently. Because the parents were not upset by the fact that nobody knew the answer for certain makes it possible for children to accept the fact that there are unknowns in life and that's okay; that you can live without "the answer" to everything. You can see how a tolerant response, telling it like it is as you know it but being open to a position different from your own—over and over, incident after incident—can help your child become an open-minded, flexible person with his or her own beliefs, understandings, and ways, yet able to relate to different people and different ideas. Such an approach will make it easier for people of different lifestyles to get along together in school, at work, and at play.

I am trying to teach our five-year-old good manners. My teen-age son tells me that manners are a "middle-class thing." What do you think about this?

Many young people feel that good manners—good morning, thank you, please, and such—have been a way for many people to cover up bad motives and unfair and unjust behavior. But bad manners and bad behavior are just as undesirable as good manners and bad behavior. A different style is one thing and bad manners are something else. Nothing is gained by being rude and ill-mannered. In fact, much can be lost. As mentioned earlier, if your child doesn't learn to express respect to people around her—and respect is what manners are all about—your family and your child's future family are more likely to suffer than anybody else. Also, good manners are a part of something larger—good social skills. Good social skills (the way you relate) will help your child at school, at work, and at play.

We have found that children who do not have good social skills receive a less positive response from important people they must relate to, such as teachers and employers, than those who do. In fact, if an employer has to choose between two people of equal ability, he or she is most likely to hire the person with the best manners and/or social skills. A person with average intelligence can handle many jobs in this and future societies. Whether a person will function well depends a great deal on his or her social skills.

An urban school superintendent met with a group of high school students regularly, and eventually helped them understand the importance of good social skills. But one young woman questioned the value of taking a hat off indoors. When the superintendent pointed out that it could cost someone $250,000 or more in their lifetime, because not taking a cap off would deny them a better job opportunity, she understood.

Again, the way you raise your child is up to you. But we can tell you that her chances of succeeding are best when she can interrelate with others on the street corner, playground, the board room of Johnson Publications or IBM, and in the halls of Congress. Helping your child to be comfortable with people of different styles and free to have her own preferences will help her function in the complex modern world. There may be greater tolerance for all lifestyles if people are comfortable and confident with themselves.

There is a growing friction among black children and foreign-born Asian children. What can be done about it?

Immigrants often move into low-income neighborhoods until they can get established and then move to better locations. Until recently, many Asian immigrants were better educated than black children and were members of the middle class in their own countries. Even when this is not the case, they are often from stable, well-functioning social systems. They hold attitudes, values, and customs that are more likely to lead to success wherever they are. In the United States they often live initially in areas where there are large numbers of blacks, Latinos, and poor whites, who are living under economic and social stress and are less likely to succeed than the immigrants. This causes resentment and anger among the Americans, and often conflict with the immigrants—among the adults first, and eventually the children.

The situation is made worse by politicians and other social policymakers who play groups against each other rather than develop the programs and practices that would enable most families and individuals to succeed. The problem appears to be greatest with the Asians because they are more visible, and people seeking to deny the fact that racism adversely affects blacks and Latinos often point to Asians as "the perfect minorities." Most of the Asians we know resent this and point out that it is harmful to members of their groups who have had difficult prior experiences and are in need of various support programs, and because it pits them against other minorities. But some advantaged Europeans are also coming into the country and facing none of the obstacles that continue to confront black young people, even when the black youngsters are members of some of the most successful families in the country.

Political action is needed to improve opportunities for all black children. Black leaders need to interact with leaders of various immigrant groups to promote understanding and to prevent mutually harmful interactions. There is a need to help blacks of all ages understand how and why some immigrant groups get ahead quickly, and thereby make it possible for more black children to succeed.

COMPETITION: PROS AND CONS

Traditional African culture valued cooperation and opposed competition for individual gain. Shouldn't we teach young black school-agers to be less competitive and more cooperative?

There is nothing wrong with competition or being a good competitor. There is nothing wrong with reasonable personal gain. Every social system promotes personal excellence through some form of competition and personal gain for individuals, even if it's the competition to be the most giving. The important thing is that competition not be angry, hostile, destructive, or primarily selfish. It is also important that children learn to value cooperation, fair play, and respect for the rights and needs of all people. We suggest that black children learn to be good competitors as well as be cooperative and respectful of the rights and needs of others. Even in Africa, traditional values are breaking down as people move out of villages, thereby changing an agricultural economy into a cash economy—paying for what they need.

It is important to help your young school-ager appreciate the importance of cooperating with others, blacks and whites alike, in order to improve conditions for all people. Obviously you will have a particular interest in blacks. But again, example and not words alone establish this attitude. If you belong to a particular black liberation organization—whether it be a black college alumnae, black militant group, Urban League, or NAACP—and you donate your time, money, and talents, your seven- or eight-year-old child will realize that this is important.

The reason that blacks don't adequately support black organizations as adults is that they don't establish the necessary value and habits as children often enough. We would like to see a United Black Appeal where each black child in America gave at least one penny once a year as a way of understanding that he and she can and should play a cooperative and constructive role in the liberation of all black people.

Because blacks have been the victims of unfair competition and exploitation, shouldn't black children learn to be more competitive and better exploiters than anybody else?

We have observed eight-year-olds allowed to fight to the point of seriously hurting each other in order to learn to be tough enough for the cruel world they will have to face. We know parents who refuse to tell their children stories in which "everybody lives happily ever after." We also know parents who teach their children to cheat and beat the system (e.g., use the bus ticket both ways) before the system beats them through such means as low-paying jobs and inadequate housing.

We understand parents' concerns and motives. But this practice is dangerous. As we pointed out earlier, such children are more likely to develop destructive habits that make it difficult to form positive relationships with their families and their peers, rather than develop habits that enable them to try to improve conditions for blacks in America. In the real world one can't always play by the rules, but it's important to help children learn to try to be fair whenever possible.

HELPING YOUR CHILD TO THINK

What is a child's thinking like at the ages of five and six?

The minds of five- and six-year-olds are still controlled very much by their desires, fears, and fantasies. Dreams are real, Santa Claus, Easter Bunny, and the Tooth Fairy live. Make-believe play is almost real. Rules and "the way" to behave are still absolute and given from some supreme but vague authority out there somewhere. You are in trouble with your child if you step into the street before the light is green. On the other hand, you will catch your five-year-old daughter with her hand in the forbidden cookie jar because her desire overwhelmed her ability to obey the rule. Children in this age group do not appear to understand the contradiction in what they say or do, or what they tell you to do and what they do themselves. This, of course, makes it difficult for them to reason logically at this stage in their development.

Their important play during the first four years has given them concrete experiences on which to build some abstract concepts. Your command, "Jump down," your warning, "Watch the door above your head," and other such clues should have given them more than fifty basic concepts, such as "above," "below," "open," "stop," and "start." The five- and six-year-old still likes to imitate adults, and this remains an important way of learning to think and understand. Five- and six-year-olds are still learning through "touch" investigations—picking up, pulling out, and checking out whatever they can get their hands on that's new or different.

In what ways will my child's thinking develop between the ages of six and eight?

By six or seven, your calling peaches, pears, and pineapples "fruit," and a hammer, saw, and screwdriver "tools," has helped your child learn to classify objects. Your six-year-old may be able to count, "one, two, three, four, five" dolls, pointing to each, but if you then ask her how many dolls are there altogether, she may not be able to tell you. She can count, but she may not yet understand the meaning of numbers. Before eight a child will usually tell you that a tall, slender glass holds more water than a short, wide one. What comes before "twenty-two" and after when counting by twos (20-22-24) may be a stopper for a six- or a seven-year-old.

By seven or eight, even six, some dramatic things have happened. Dreams are no longer real. Santa Claus, Easter Bunny, and the Tooth Fairy are dead . . . or live for suspect reasons. (We know of one little girl who "knew" by six but kept them alive until nine because she loved fantasy, make-believe, and presents.) By six, with good training, most children know that Batman can jump off a roof without risk of injury, but they can't. Your child's wishes and desires about all things slowly yield to reality. "The ball I want belongs to Mary and I must ask to play with it, not take it."

What other advances in thinking will my child have made by the age of eight?

By seven or eight, youngsters begin to understand that rules exist to keep order, protect people, and to permit certain things to be accomplished; that rules can be changed through discussion and mutual agreement. Children of this age become greatly interested in rules—in games, at home, school, and everywhere. "Why?" or "Why do I have to?" becomes very important. Challenging and debating the rules is now a way of life. Yet in the interest of getting along well, they are generally willing to abide by rules.

The memory of the six- and seven-year-old is better. His ability to sit and involve himself in something of interest—or something he must do even when he has little interest—is better. But time is relative. A short time is three hours in the swimming pool when she likes it and five minutes at the piano when she doesn't like it. Time is now; the past and the future are only beginning to have meaning. The same is true for space. You will have a hard time explaining that you are in Chicago and Illinois at the same time until your child is around seven. Even when he can repeat what you explain at an earlier age, he really doesn't quite understand it. Probe a bit more and you'll see.

We want to repeat a point made earlier. Your child's ability to think can be improved or hindered by what you and others do. What he or she inherits only limits thinking ability at both extremes. A child may have a natural ability to become a very good thinker but may not do so if this talent is not developed.

How can I help my child learn to think well?

You will want to continue doing much of what you've been doing—helping your child learn the names of things, talking about them, and generally understanding the world around him. More complex learning is possible now because your child has a better memory, can put events together to explain or understand things, and maintain interest in an activity or a thought for more than a few seconds.

Now when you are going to take a trip, your five-year-old can really participate fully. He can anticipate the trip, enjoy the experience, and think back on it in ways that younger children cannot do. On a trip to the zoo, for example, you can help your youngster learn to learn and enjoy both the trip and the learning experience by what you do. It's helpful to talk about what your child will see, describing it as clearly as possible before the trip. A book with pictures of the animals will whet his "seeing and learning" appetite.

Being somewhat familiar with the animals will make it all the more fun to see them, hear them, and imitate their sounds. Asking your child questions about the animals that cause him to think is helpful. Answering his questions and clearing up confusion, such as, "Where is the grass?"—when reading him a book that shows the animal in a natural environment but not in a cage—is also very helpful. The same is true of follow-up discussions.

We heard a prekindergarten teacher say that there was nothing gained by discussing a visit to a park after the trip, because most of the children would never go there again. Whether they will go again or not is unimportant. Forming the habit of anticipating an experience, having the experience, thinking back or reflecting on that experience is a vital part of learning. An important integration of knowledge takes place.

Will it hurt my child's way of thinking if I "invent" from time to time to get him to obey me?

It is very important at this stage in your child's development to give logical reasons for rules or actions of any kind. Let's say you are at the zoo and your six-year-old wants to walk far ahead of you in a crowd. One mother, when asked "Why not?" by her six-year-old, said, "Because there are tigers in the zoo and they can get out and eat you up." Another said, "Because you can get lost in the crowd and I don't want that to happen." The latter approach does not create unnecessary fears, but helps your child learn to size up a situation and respond favorably to reason and logic, and does not insult your child's intelligence. Unlike the "Santa Claus" situation, where you were protecting a pleasure, a child will resent your lying to maintain control.

While we're speaking of getting lost, will your five-year-old know what to do if he does get lost? Should he just stand there and cry? Go to any stranger? Go to the park policeman? Anticipating problems and suggesting ways to handle them can help your child learn how to think in a problem-solving way, to consider the possible approaches and act appropriately. Explaining why certain things happen will help your child learn to think in a cause-and-effect way. Helping her decide what she wants to see at the zoo out of all the many possibilities—because you have only an hour to stay there and it would take three days to see everything—helps your child learn to establish priorities.

My child is constantly asking questions. Is he trying to get my goat?

The seven- or eight-year-old loves to show off his knowledge and understanding. He loves to quiz parents about interesting things he has just learned himself. Such questions make learning fun when you treat it as fun. It helps to take an interest, take his question seriously, and not be a know-it-all. You can make your child feel inadequate if you make him think you know everything. Besides, learning how to find information or investigate a problem is as important as having the information. Encouraging your youngster look up the answers to questions he doesn't know, with your help and assistance, can be more helpful than constantly telling him the answer. It also helps for a child to learn early in life that nobody knows everything.

My husband turns every experience into a "lesson." Is this good for our child?

Some parents go too far with their quizzing and teaching. We watched a parent at a concert explaining every move of the musicians to her youngster—asking one question after another as if the child was on a quiz show—becoming frustrated and angry when the child didn't understand and didn't show sufficient interest. We wanted to say, "Leave that kid alone and let him enjoy the show!" There is a happy medium. Too much teaching and questioning can turn a child off or make thinking and learning a chore, and too little can lead to an inability to think about and understand the things around him.

Providing toys and materials that stimulate thought and learning is necessary. Building blocks for the five- and six-year-old, soft wood for cutting, model planes, rockets, and boats for the seven- or eight-year-old, mixes for easy-to-make cakes, are all very useful in helping children learn to learn. These activities also permit them to have a finished product quickly. "Look what

I made!" The sense of accomplishment is motivation to achieve more. A toy microscope or an inexpensive magnifying glass will enable children to play "scientists," "hospital," "detectives," or other make-believe games.

That's all well and good. But what about those of us who can't afford such toys?

You can! Popsicle sticks, packing material, string, paper cartons, you name it, can become anything you want them to be with scissors and paste. Toys are just props or things to encourage the imagination. If the object you or your child cut out is called an airplane, it will fly to Nigeria or China just as well as one that costs ten dollars or more. It'll crash on takeoff or landing, and your child can do the whole rescue scene at a bargain price. (Just be careful of pins and sharp edges and other hazards with the toys you make—just as with many store-bought toys.)

Such play deepens understanding of the words, concepts, and roles involved. Don't ignore a little milkman or doctor, or allow your older children to discourage your five- or six-year-old by calling the way he plays stupid or dumb. Detective-like games—involving such things as unscrambling letters, words, and sentences, following clues, and correcting errors—are interesting and helpful to the seven- and eight-year-old. They help develop reasoning powers.

Won't letting my child indulge in "make-believe" delay his ability to learn reality?

Some parents feel that learning is helped by speeding up reality training. Such parents tell their three-, four-, or five-year-old children that there is no such thing as Santa Claus, the Easter Bunny, or the Tooth Fairy. There is no need to do this. Fantasy is fun. Having fun or being happy is as important to learning as having information or knowing the difference between reality and fantasies six months earlier than the kid next door. If you don't like the fact that these symbols of goodness and good fortune are represented as white, make them black. Magazines, newspaper, and television ads as well as stores now use both a black and a white Santa Claus. This can be confusing. But it can be handled easily:

"But Daddy, how can Santa Claus be black and white?"

"Santa Claus is the spirit of goodness and giving and can be either black or white."

You have given an answer a young child will accept without destroying the fun. You have laid the groundwork for understanding the real meaning of Christmas.

Isn't it true that some people believe that black children have trouble with abstract (nonconcrete) thinking?

This has been said, but we do not think there is a racial factor here. Abstract thinking grows out of concrete experiences that are given meaning and understanding by parents, teachers, and others. For example, when your child picked up your Michael Jackson record and asked what it was, you said, "record." Later, through your input, the record was recognized as a "record by Michael Jackson." Eventually it became—in the black vernacular—"a 'bad' record by Michael Jackson." This includes an understanding of the abstract concepts of a group, music, a quality of music—all given meaning to a child by others. Whenever parents or others, black or white, for whatever reason, are not present or cannot provide meaning and understanding of this kind, a child remains a concrete thinker.

Again, we stress it is important to talk, talk, talk, explain, explain, explain to your child—especially at times other than when you are scolding or punishing. Encourage your child to talk, talk, talk, question, question, question things with you.

THE IMPORTANCE OF CREATIVITY

I believe that black people are especially creative. This is a trait I don't want my five-year-old to lose. Can too much emphasis on logical thinking, cause-and-effect thinking, and priority-setting destroy her creativity?

We see no conflict. Creativity is the quality of being able to produce something original. But creative people are usually quite logical and well disciplined. Helping a child become a logical, disciplined thinker need not dampen creativity. Forcing a child into rigid thought, belief, and behavior patterns can dampen creative thinking. Modern child-care approaches—the methods and attitudes we are describing—support creative thinking and activity as well as the development of logical, disciplined thinking.

Your concern may be with the claim that black culture supports creativity and Western (largely white culture) does not, or less so. It has also been suggested that Western culture promotes problem-solving thinking more than other cultures. Such notions are dangerous generalizations. Children have been forced into rigid thought and behavior patterns everywhere. All cultures appear to include some form of art, story-telling, and poetry as well as some type of problem-solving training and behavior.

How can I help my child keep his creativity and yet become a logical thinker?

Most children will come to understand what is real and not real and become logical thinkers through learning about the environment around them at home and at school. The inventive and creative side is more fragile. You can best encourage and protect creativity through showing the appropriate amount of interest and pleasure in your child's original work or ideas.

It has often been said that blacks are good dancers and singers. There may be some physical reason that many blacks are talented in these areas. But more important, singing, dancing, and other forms of creativity have been, and are now, important, expressive methods in black culture. It is not uncommon to see black parents beaming proudly as their two- or three-year-olds, barely able to control their bodies, try certain dance steps. This approval encourages children to develop these talents. The skills that a particular culture values will receive repeated encouragement, causing more members of that group to excel in that area, unless it is deliberately avoided. Unfortunately, a few black parents, more often middle-class persons with strong scholarly interests, have discouraged early body freedom, music, and dance. This is distressing. People from all groups are rediscovering the value of these activities.

My seven-year-old's drawings look so babyish. Would it help if he copied some of mine?

With regard to drawing, we suggest that you not encourage your child to copy or use other aids to get good results. Copying limits inventive or creative expression. It is also frustrating for a child who can copy somebody else's "good" work but can't produce the same himself. Letters of the alphabet or numbers are the only copying we think useful. Even then you shouldn't push a child to copy accurately until his arm and hand control is fairly good, at around seven or eight years of age.

How should we react to our children's creative work?

We do not think it is helpful to reward the creative work of children with money. If this habit is established, the creative work may not be done unless there is an outside reward. The pleasure and the reward should be in the doing.

Too much criticism, correcting, or improving your child's artwork, dancing, or singing, especially among five- or six-year-olds, can cause them to stop. A lot of questions and suggestions can be interpreted as a criticism or ridicule, and thus discourage the creative urge. Do not allow older brothers or sisters to laugh or ridicule. Your young artist may fear that her work is not "right" or not good. Some children, however, appreciate the interest. You will be able to "read" your child's reaction. Some children are inspired by and learn from parents doing their own creative thing—dancing, painting, singing. Many love to join their parents and do things together, which is highly recommended.

All this talk about creativity is well and good, but all blacks can make music and dance. There aren't enough black scientists and scholars. My seven-year-old is very bright and could become a scientist. Shouldn't I be emphasizing books and learning rather than music and play?

It is best to offer a child an opportunity to find pleasure and satisfaction in the many different areas of life. This not only helps youngsters become well-rounded, but it provides them with an opportunity to find the areas that will be most gratifying to them in later life. It is true that constantly listening to Michael Jackson or playing ball, day after day, with no interest in books or learning, is unlikely to produce a scholar. But an interest in books and learning only is not likely to produce a well-rounded scholar. A scientist who makes music and dances is a thing of beauty. Most important, your child should not have to carry the "burden of the race" or fulfill the goals of parents. As the folk song says, "Give him room and let him grow." Don't try to force your interests and goals on your child. This generation will produce large numbers of talented blacks in every area.

DEVELOPING SPEECH AND LANGUAGE SKILLS

How can I help my young school-ager improve his speaking and use of words?

At five or six years of age, your child's speaking becomes clearer, and conversing with him is easier and more fun than ever. You should continue to talk about ideas, feelings, and the things you are doing just as you did when he was very small.

The six- or seven-year-old is beginning to use speech as a way to think, plan, act, and learn the results of his actions rather than acting on every possibility. For example, a very young child viewing a wagon near the stairs might simply hop right on, take a ride, topple over, and get hurt. A child of five or six can use words and language to think through the possible results of such a move. The wagon could provide a ride, but it could cause a fall; therefore, it should be pulled away from the stairs before he tries to ride on it. Although he wouldn't use these same words, he could tell you the problem and solution.

You don't want to ridicule or discourage your child from walking around the house, talking to himself, talking to non-existent people, or making up stories and conversations. He has learned that talking is fun, that he can use it to get things done, to say how he feels, to get questions answered, to maintain contact with others. He can understand that it's a great talent to have. He has also learned that it pays to be good at it. So, like every other talent, you practice it. You don't want everybody around at your practice sessions, so you talk to yourself. Nothing unusual about that!

Hasn't it been said that blacks are nonverbal?

Yes. But those who say so obviously don't know many blacks. Most blacks are "talkers." The next time you go to a barbershop or to choir rehearsal, think about it. Many blacks turn off in nonblack, hostile, or unfamiliar situations. People who are under great stress, black or white, often are depressed and say very little. The people who say that blacks are nonverbal must have studied blacks who were living under difficult conditions.

Another point here is the fact that some people express themselves very well with few words. Joe Louis was once asked how he would handle a punch-and-run fighter. His answer, "He can run but he can't hide." A three-page answer could not have made the point better. It also points up the image-producing nature of some black language styles. Some people talk endlessly, but say very little. Some people talk continually to cover up fear and anxiety and to avoid real communication. It is true, however, that people who can express themselves well in school and in the workplace tend to do well and are considered bright even if they are no more intelligent than some less verbal people.

My five-year-old still stutters. Should I be concerned?

Many children occasionally stutter, mispronounce words, lisp, or appear to have other speech imperfections around two or three years of age. Calm, friendly correction—and help in slowing down and pronouncing clearly, not uptight and nagging help—usually solves the problem by the time your child is four or five years old. If your youngster becomes self-conscious, stop making him slow down and helping him pronounce and just listen patiently and calmly, conveying the notion that you are sure he will get it right. Hearing may be a problem where mispronunciations continue at this age. Speech therapists can help identify the problem and plan corrective training programs. If the problem is anxiety, they will advise and refer you for help.

You mentioned children talking about feelings. My eight-year-old is very closemouthed, even when he is troubled about something. Should I make him talk?

We know what you mean. After seven or eight, children want more privacy and less intrusion into their affairs. Some pre-adolescents will put a sign on their bedroom door saying "Keep Out." As they get older, it may read, "Anyone entering this room prepare to be sorry!!!" Or, in this modern day, "This room is rated X. No adults permitted!"

This is only part of the story. They also have some very troublesome emotions during this period and will want to talk about them. Language becomes even more important when it can be used to manage such feelings. If your child won't talk about his or her problems, possibly you have made it known, without realizing it, that you don't want to talk about anything "tough," matters like race, sex, anger, and conflict. We all do this from time to time, but the damage can be corrected.

What can I do to get my child to confide in me?

When your child is obviously troubled about something, you can open the door for conversation by pointing out that you can see that she is upset about something and that you will be glad to talk with her about it when she is ready. Then, give her time, hours . . . a day before repeating your offer. If you try to force your child to talk, you are likely to get nowhere. When she does agree to talk with you, it is best to be a good listener, not an alarmist or a judge. Young children are not saints or criminals.

It's rare when a small child does something that is so serious as to cause parents alarm. Even if she has been playing with matches near gasoline, for example, it's not helpful to panic. A short, clear discussion about safety and your support and understanding and belief that she'll know enough to avoid the situation next time is the most helpful approach. When your child has been able to talk about a difficult subject, let it be known that you know how difficult it was for her to talk about that, but you're glad she was able to do so. In this way, you have made her ability to discuss a difficult matter an achievement to be repeated the next time; it will be if you were helpful the first time.

MORAL DEVELOPMENT

What should I look for in the way of moral development in the five- to eight-year-old period?

Five- and six-year-olds know right from wrong. Your rules—dos and don'ts—have been taken in and are becoming their own. Their own budding conscience now guides their behavior without your constant praise or punishment. But the "goodies of the world"—things like your money, jewelry, and cookies—are sometimes just too much for the young conscience to handle. If you leave your shiny bracelet on the dresser, it may disappear. When asked about it, your son or daughter may "lie" just as he or she did at three, although the story is now more sophisticated—maybe the neighbor stole your jewelry rather than a big monster.

Because the five- and six-year-old conscience is just barely working, your child can't bear to see anybody "get away with murder." You may hear your six-year-old talking in a disapproving way about "the boys who had their names put on the board for being bad," while barely hiding his approval of their behavior—doing things he would like to do, and occasionally does. Children of this age group are beginning to develop respect for the rights and needs of others in return for respect for their own rights and needs. Acting up by other kids is a kind of violation of the contract—if you can, why can't I? He tells you about their misbehavior to get your support for his doing right. The tattletale is asking for the same help, which is why five- and six-year-olds are notorious tattlers.

What can I do to help my child's moral growth?

Beating the badness out doesn't work. Just as with your preschool child, going to great lengths to make your child confess to a crime, admit that she lied about it (and the several other lies she told while you were conducting your criminal investigation) won't help much either. In most cases you both know what happened. You are not the district attorney getting a record of convictions that will help you become governor. You simply want to help your child develop responsibility and good control of his behavior.

You might say something like this: "I can't know for sure whether you took my money or not. Only you know. It's up to you to be honest with yourself." You can point out that if she took your money, you know it was only because it was so tempting and if she decides to give it back you will be proud of her. You can point out that anything on your dresser belongs to you; that if she wants something, she should ask you. Given the responsibility of being honest with themselves and not attacked and strongly accused by the parent, many children will acknowledge their misbehavior and develop a greater commitment to self-control. The money may just reappear or be given back to you directly. When it is given back you might say, "I'm glad that you were able to give the money back to me." With this approach you have indicated that you believe in her and you expect her to be able to control herself. You have given her a chance to turn a lack of control and embarrassment into positive feelings and achievement.

By seven or eight the conscience is not only fairly strong, it is strict. Yet many children are still unable to control their desires, and therefore break the rules from time to time. They are hard on themselves and others when they do so. Adults sometimes have to help children of this age be less critical of each other when they break minor regulations. They want the rule breaker spanked and "boiled alive." A lot of arguing, hard feelings, and attacks on each other occur because of the strict conscience of the seven- and eight-year-old period. Some children, once they admit to misbehavior, will become overly apologetic.

It is important to help children learn to discuss rule-breaking and make commitments to try to live by the rules the next time, rather than calling for extreme, harsh punishment or demanding apologies. Discussions about what's fair for all are much more useful.

Isn't the strict conscience a particular problem among young black children?

The strict conscience, angry feelings toward violators, and harsh punishment are a problem wherever parents, black or white, set rigid rules and give harsh punishment. Because blacks have had to "toe the line" or face trouble, child rearing had to be more strict and rigid. Although a period of strict conscience occurs among many children, it's probably more of a problem among black children whose upbringing has been rigid, strict, and harsh. We have listened to black seven- and eight-year-old schoolchildren from such backgrounds who expect and demand harsh treatment for minor misbehavior. Yet the punishment often does not prevent the behavior, resulting in anger and negative feelings about themselves and others.

Are there ways that parents can encourage "right" and "wrong" at the same time?

Yes. We can say all the "right" things, but do just the opposite. We can say the "right" things, but our voice and manner will indicate that we're not sincere or that "these words are for the public—not for real." We can repeatedly see but not see misbehavior that we don't really object to. For example, if the lady next door doesn't want our Matthew to cut through her yard, we can say, "Matthew, don't cut through that old Battle Ax's yard." "Battle Ax" tells him what you really think and gives him permission to disregard your words. In addition, you can just see and "not see" him do it time after time.

All of these attitudes can lead to a conscience with a hole (or many holes) in it. Well-trained children of dedicated, caring parents sometimes have trouble obeying the rules because parents have unintentionally failed to enforce these rules. This behavior, if not corrected, can carry through to adulthood. We can remember a pathetic extreme in which uncontrolled aggression and conflicting attitudes toward rules and laws stood side by side. A driver mistakenly turned into a one-way street and wanted to drive into the nearby alley to turn around. But two men drinking wine in the alley—in violation of the law—threatened to break his neck for driving the wrong way.

You mentioned five and six as years when many children become tattletales. How can I help my young tattler to break the habit?

Let's take the following example as an illustration of what

you might do. Your six-year-old Thelma repeatedly tattles on her eight-year-old brother Charles. Charles gets furious. You might say something like this on an occasion where she tattles: "Thelma, I'm glad to see that you know what is right to do, but Charles is going to be mad with you if you always tattle on him. You'd better let me help Charles learn to control himself." With this approach you have praised each child for doing the acceptable thing without putting either one of them down. It is important to control your tone of voice in this case. There is a little lawlessness in all of us, and we sometimes approve of the acting-up child more than we do the tattler. Our irritation with the tattling can cause us to put the tattler down in a way that makes him or her unhappy. On the other hand, if we are particularly fearful that the acting-up child will get into trouble, we may punish him or her too severely. If we understand that our job is to help children gradually develop control—and not expect them to learn it overnight—then we can support desirable behavior without offending the tattler or the child who is acting up.

SEXUAL DEVELOPMENT OF THE YOUNG SCHOOL-AGER

When my seven-year-old was three, I was worried about his great interest in his penis, where babies come from, and so on. Now that he is seven, I'm worried because he doesn't appear to have any interest in anything related to sex. Is that normal?

The behavior you described is normal for the three-year-old as well as the seven-year-old. Children in the six to early teenage period tend to show less active interest in their bodies than at an earlier age. If development is progressing normally, they have learned to separate their sexual feelings from other bodily sensations, and there is less confusion and concern about sex. They have learned—though they usually will not discuss it openly— that parents have a private sexual life of their own.

But although there is usually less obvious interest and curiosity about sex, the seven- or eight-year-old interest does appear from time to time. You may overhear seven- or eight-year-olds telling sex jokes or using sex words. In groups they may even poke fingers at bottoms or breasts. There is often chasing and great excitement with such activity.

Unless the play goes too far, it is best to keep a watchful eye on it but not stop it immediately. It can be a kind of release of sexual energy. You must determine for yourself when it's time to call a halt to such play. When you stop the play, it is not necessary to deal with the issue of sex, because you can't always be sure that's what's going on. You can simply tell the children that they are becoming too excited by the play; that it's time to stop. Providing them with ideas for other activities is helpful. They will be relieved by your stepping in and not letting things get out of hand. Lectures at the time won't help, but keep your eyes and ears open for questions and natural opportunities to answer questions and clear up possible confusion about sex, or to clarify your child's understanding, based on these incidents.

My eight-year-old hates girls. Will he be okay?

Your son's "hate" for girls at this period (and girls for boys) is not uncommon under present conditions. It is one of the ways that children firmly establish their own sexual identity—by being with others of their own sex, by doing things that a girl or boy does, by shunning the other sex. Disliking the opposite sex is a way of protecting themselves against interests they feel they should reject as a boy or as a girl. A seven- or eight-year-old boy's dislike for a girl is a good way to protect himself from his interest in cuddling a doll. The "hate" is likely to be less "needed" as it becomes more acceptable for boys to have "girl" interests and feelings and girls to have "boy" interests and feelings. We've always had these feelings but up until now we (particularly men) have just denied them. As attitudes toward women change and women's roles change, some of the "need" to "hate" girls will be eliminated.

Won't such play lead to homosexuality?

No. It should permit men to express more real warmth and affection toward girls and women. Much male "design" on women or "super-maleness" today is to prove manhood and to disprove the lurking suspicion of softness caused by normal feelings of attraction to both men and women. What a young boy who plays with dolls or plays house can learn is that he can do that and still kick, run, fight, be aggressive and assertive—in short, be a boy and man. Girls, more and more, will learn the same. Masculinity and femininity can be maintained without the absurd extremes of the past.

There may be a problem when boys do only feminine, domestic things and girls do only aggressive, masculine things, even though it may only be a phase. The parent or adult model, or what the parent encourages, determines sexual roles most. You can encourage both warmth and affection and reasonable aggression and assertion. Actually, female parents can encourage traits thought to be male and male parents sometimes encourage traits thought to be female. The truth is that nobody really knows the causes of homosexuality.

On several occasions, I have found my eight-year-old masturbating. I spanked him and told him to stop it but it didn't seem to do any good. What should I do?

First, we hope that your concern is not because you feel that masturbating is abnormal, bad, or nasty. Masturbating, in one way or another, is normal for boys and girls. A little girl may do so by rubbing her vagina against her father's or mother's leg or by squeezing her own legs together. Boys' masturbation techniques are more detectable. Masturbating is a problem when it becomes the only way to relieve common anxieties and tension. You should make certain that your child is sufficiently occupied with various activities. You should also make certain that your child isn't burdened with disturbing or stressful concerns.

Spanking is not helpful in this situation. It is best to talk to your child about what is going on. Rather than trying to force him to stop, you might point out that you know that he has sexual feelings; that all boys and girls have sexual feelings just like grownup mothers and fathers do. You will want to remind him that it can be embarrassing for him to play with his penis in places where others will see him; that other people will not want to be around him if he has such habits. If your child appears to need to show you or others that he is masturbating—or appears to do so in preference to many other activities—you should talk with your doctor, the school nurse or social worker, or child-guidance counselors in your community.

SPECIAL DIFFICULTIES OF THE YOUNG SCHOOL-AGER

What kinds of problems am I likely to come up against with children of this age?

Let's take a hard one where the usual issues—race, sexual attraction to parents, anger, and guilt—all get tied up together. A five-year-old black girl living in a predominantly white neighborhood told her mother that she liked her (the mother) more than Daddy because he was not as light-skinned as the mother. The fact was that he was as light as or lighter than the mother. In any situation where the facts don't make sense, the question must be, "What else is going on?"

Actually the girl was angry with her father, and "downing" the father to get some emotional distance from her strong attraction to him and getting closer to her mother was part of her problem.

You do hear a negative feeling about being black in this case. But it is not fixed or unyielding. In fact, it is more of a question than a statement. The child is attracted to both parents, and feels guilty and confused about these feelings. In this predominantly white neighborhood, she wanted to be like the other children in order to feel a sense of belonging. Her question is, "How should I feel about Dad, Mom, and my skin color?" These are not complicated issues that only a psychiatrist can sort out. We have found that when parents "keep cool" and listen, most can find the real issue behind what is stated as the problem but obviously is not. In this case, grave concern about the child's feelings about being black could have made it hard to find out what else was going on.

Don't feel that if you live in an interracial neighborhood your child will not have racial pride; that you must live in a black neighborhood to appreciate blackness or that, "Oh, my goodness, I have failed my child." Such thoughts and feelings will cause you to respond anxiously to questions about race. Your uptight manner and not your words will say, "Yes, there is something wrong with being black." If this happens, you are adding your own fears, uncertainties, and confusion to those of your child.

How would you handle the preceding situation?

We'd say something like: "Honey, you must be angry with your daddy. Sometimes little girls get angry with their daddies. That's okay. And dark skin is okay, too. Some nice people have dark [or black] skin and some nice people have light [or white] skin."

It is a simple but powerful response. You identified the emotion in question (anger), which is necessary. (Helping your child identify these emotions is good training. Many adults get into trouble because they are not in touch with their feelings or emotions.) You have said with words and a calm manner that angry feelings are okay and not a cause for guilt. Your child will notice that the feelings didn't harm or destroy Daddy. That helps her understand that angry wishes and what happens in reality are not the same thing. You said that skin color does not make someone a nice person; that the way a person behaves is more important. The message over time will lead to calm, positive acceptance of skin color and race.

When you look for and understand the real issue, you are less likely to become alarmed. Growing, searching, learning children are bound to ask questions that upset us if we give them adult meaning rather than trying to figure out what is going on within the child. It is important to develop the habit: "Stop . . . think . . . identify and address the real issue." Alarm and over-reaction are our own feelings and self-doubt "talking." If you act disturbed it will also tell your child that he or she can't come to you with the tough one because you can't deal with it.

My seven-year-old son is very aggressive. He often gets in fights. I am afraid he is going to hurt himself or someone else needlessly. Is this just a stage he is going through?

Fighting at this age is not necessarily cause for concern. The seven-year-old is scrappy, and some children are more physically aggressive than others. You will just have to stick in there with your management of his aggression and fighting. You want to help him to be fair. You want to gradually help him learn to develop ways to talk and get others to be fair with him rather than fight it out all the time.

Be sure to provide other outlets for the child's energy. Running, swimming, and team sports in the community and at school can be helpful. As long as your child is a fair competitor, a good winner, and a good loser, there is nothing to be concerned about here. Children with a great deal of aggression often tend to be impulsive and do things on the spur of the moment. Some of their impulsive acts, like darting into the street, striking matches, and throwing things, can be dangerous to themselves and others. You will want to remind them again and again to think before they act, that if they throw while angry they may hurt someone and will feel guilty about it. You also want to help an impulsive child learn to enjoy himself without getting overly excited.

I caught my seven-year-old playing with matches. How would you handle this?

One father noticed his eight-year-old son hiding matches. Rather than showing alarm, he said, "I see you are interested in matches. Come here and let me tell you about them." He gave the youngster a demonstration on how to use them safely. He explained the possible danger to himself, the house, and others. He explained that because they could be dangerous, he didn't want his child to play with them. He added that if the youngster had cause to use them (barbecue fire, candles, and such), an adult would be glad to help him.

The discussion took the mystery and attraction out of fire and out of a forbidden act—using matches. Many an apartment and home in the city and suburb alike has gone up in smoke from the tiny torch of a curious, impulsive seven- or eight-year-old. Matches should be locked away from somewhat younger children. Even before you catch youngsters playing with matches, you should discuss the matter with them. A natural time—when you're using matches, for example—is best.

Are there other problem areas during the five- through eight-year period?

Yes, competition is a major problem. Your child has been in competition with you since he or she was "knee-high." Not only are you better at everything, but you have a lot of privileges and can order her around. In addition, she can now look beyond herself and can compare herself with others. She notices that in some things she's not as good as Jermaine and LaTasha. Finally, five- and six-year-olds in particular start more projects than they can successfully complete—or bite off more than they can chew. All of these situations are normal, yet they result in disappointment and failure for your child on occasion. Anger and frustration can result. When this happens, children need help in dealing with their feelings.

What can I do to help my child cope with these competitive feelings?

You can help in several ways. You can assure your child that he or she will one day be able to catch the ball or read the book as well as you do. You can point out that he's doing fine for his age and size.

It is not helpful to compare your child with other children. He is already doing that. You want to help him learn to be satisfied with his best effort; to have personal standards of excellence but not to feel that he must do something he can't do. You can help by praising your child for a good try at whatever he is doing. When there is a prize for winning, there should be some recognition for "doing your best." In this way your child learns to take pride in a job well done—win or lose, best or not. Without telling your child what to do or nagging, you can help him learn to set up work and play goals that he can bring to completion. Raising questions that will help him adjust the "job" to the time he has to do it in and helping him learn to organize his time so that he can complete the job can cut down on frustration and failure.

You might also look for an area in which your seven- or eight-year-old has knowledge or talent but you are relatively uninformed. One father noticed that his eight-year-old son was very interested in outer space. He bought the youngster a telescope and the son learned a number of things that his father knew very little about. The youngster took great pride in "laying the facts" on his old man. As a result, he felt less inadequate in relationship to his father.

Should I let my child win when we play games together so that she won't always feel so powerless?

In games of skill, you can help her plan her moves—but don't play the whole game for her. She can sometimes play with people of about her own skill. You don't always want to play as if you are playing for the world championship either. Unless your child is very unusual, she won't always be best in everything and needs to learn how to compete in work and play, do her best and learn to enjoy things without being first or winning every time. If your child can tolerate losing without extreme frustration, withdrawing from competition, or giving up, you need not let her win at all. On the other hand, if the preceding reactions do or are about to occur, you can "help" her win. It's phony. She knows it. You know it. You don't want to do it too often. Watch your child's reaction and play it by ear.

I know what you mean about competition at this age. My eight-year-old is so competitive he will cheat to win. How can I help him?

First, be certain of your own feelings about the importance of winning. Sometimes we criticize cheating in government and in business and cheating to get higher grades in school, yet, at the same time, make winning or being the best so important at home that children are encouraged to cheat. Watch parents "kill the umpire" for calling little Johnny out on strikes at the Little League game, and you will know why some children have to do anything—lie, cheat, steal—to win. Some children are made to feel that they will not be loved or valued by their parents unless they win or are the best—by any means necessary. We parents do this because our children are our last chance to live out our unfulfilled dreams—whether it's to be a major league baseball player, a singer, or a lawyer. That's unfair! Your child should have a chance to carve out and live his own life. In addition, if he senses that success means so much to you, not doing well can become an effective way to frustrate and irritate you, his powerful, controlling parents. Many teen-age dropouts or runaways are doing just that.

It helps to state very clearly that you believe that the way a person plays or competes is as important as winning. You must be satisfied when your child makes his best effort, enjoys himself, but loses. One eight-year-old cautiously told his father how he dropped a pop fly with the bases loaded. They laughed about it together. The father, in a matter-of-fact way, told the youngster that he was sure that he was embarrassed and his teammates were upset. When the youngster acknowledged that this was the case, his father went on to say something like, "Some days you win and some days you lose, but it's fun to keep trying." A few days later the boy won the ball game with a hit.

This attitude, and not "kill the umpire," helps the child become a good competitor, yet able to operate under less pressure with less need to win at all costs. Had the father gotten uptight about the error, not only would the child have been under great pressure, but he would have been less likely to talk to his father about such a situation next time.

Speaking of competition, my four-year-old tries to keep up with my eight-year-old. Isn't that bad for them both?

The eight-year-old is bigger, stronger, and knows more about the world. He will tease and attack the younger child—often verbally, but sometimes physically. At the same time he is often a teacher, helper, and a protector of the younger child. If the older child is a positive role model, trying to keep up with big brother or big sister is helpful to your younger child. Big brother or sister helps the young child with motor and physical development, language and thinking, social and moral development. It is less frustrating for your youngest to have a role model who is not as big, strong, and capable as his parents but more capable than himself. The teasing and attack is one way the eight-year-old handles his own feelings of fear, anger, and frustration. The teaching and taking care of "little brother" helps the older child feel better about himself because he's able to help somebody else.

Though it is sometimes hard to take, the teasing, competition, and fights between your children can be quite healthy. Children want your affection and attention, and they want to be successful. They compete with each other and are jealous of each other's success in their relations with you, others, and the world. They put each other down to feel good about themselves, even though most children in a reasonably well-functioning family—at this age—love each other dearly. Child-development specialists call this competitive behavior sibling rivalry.

With your help in not letting things go too far, calling for fairness, and helping them discuss and resolve their differences, your children will develop socially acceptable ways of handling conflict. In the meantime they release anger, handle frustration, and compete with people who—in the long run—will be more tolerant than parents or nonfamily members. In fact, a certain amount of sparring is exciting and fun, and they will do "little things" to each other to keep conflict going. You can clamp down and stop the arguing if you really want to, but that can create other problems. We think it is better to permit disputes within limits that you and your children can tolerate.

It is important to protect the younger child, particularly when there is a wide age difference and the children are not of the same size or strength. On the other hand, the younger child should not be allowed to get away with murder because she is younger. Teaching your younger child that she will be able to do the same things as older children when she gets to be their age will cut down on some of her frustration and disappointment, sense of failure, and inadequacy.

My children only fight when I'm around. Why is this?

It is very interesting that the same two children who argue and fight when parents are home—when things are going well overall—often turn into adorable angels and helpmates when the baby-sitter arrives. Or the oldest, when left as a sitter at twelve or thirteen years, is responsible for the younger child. The presence of the parents provides the security that allows it "to all hang out." When they are not there, it is better to band together in mutual support.

My eight-year-old son is a good reader, but he brags and calls the other kids dummies. How should I handle this?

Boasting is quite common at this age, but you should quietly but firmly discourage ridiculing losers or less able people as well as excessive bragging, although there is nothing wrong with reasonable pride. A helpful approach would be something like "Freddy, I'm glad that you are a good reader and you should be proud. But if you brag and make other people feel bad about themselves, they won't like you very much." You can remind him of the time he was irritated by Joe's bragging or his brother's teasing about things he couldn't do. You can explain that some people are good in one thing and not so good in another.

When there are physical or psychological reasons that one child will never do as well as your child or most other children, you should explain that they are different and that is okay . . . as long as they are doing the best they can. You want to help a talented and successful child develop an attitude of respect for the less able, even to assist them when it is not condescending or harmful to do so.

Let him do his bragging or talking about his success with you or other family members with whom he is not in immediate competition. He should be able to feel proud about his accomplishment. Don't deflate his pride. We have seen gifted black children hide their talents because their classmates made them feel they shouldn't have them—especially in areas as sophisticated as poetry or ballet, not to mention math and reading. Some blacks call such interests and good performance "acting white." The classmates are victims of society's brainwashing. You may have to protect your child's freedom to be good whenever and wherever possible by explaining his classmates' behavior to him in words that he will understand, for example, "Some people have made black children feel that they should not be good in math, but you have the right to do whatever you can do . . . as long as you don't hurt other people without reason."

Some "experts" have confused this issue by claiming that teaching low-income children mainstream skills and encouraging them to do well is making them middle-class, as if something is wrong with that. This is nonsense. If the experts could choose, they wouldn't be poor. And if the poor could choose, they wouldn't be poor. We are simply suggesting attitudes, values, and methods that will enable young people to succeed in school and to have a better chance to take care of themselves and their families and to become responsible adult citizens.

Won't such attitudes make my child too nice for the real world?
No, but we understand your concern. An honored professional football coach has said, "Winning isn't everything, it's the only thing." An ex-attorney general of the United States has said that winning is so important that lying, stealing, and cheating to do so is okay. People in business and government too often illustrate this point. An attitude of "They're all doing it" has developed among too many people in this country. In this climate it is understandable why a youngster rigged his soapbox derby car in order to have a better chance of winning. Such attitudes are fast destroying the country. It is in this kind of climate that the rights and needs of so many vulnerable people—minorities, women, children, the elderly—get trampled on. The political and economic practices of the 1980s have contributed greatly to this problem.

Because the scandals get the headlines we forget that most people prefer fair play—even when they become cynical about competitive excesses and even engage in them themselves. As long as you permit and encourage honest, aggressive, competitive thought and action, but discourage cheating, lying, stealing, hurting others, or looking down on the less successful, your child will become a healthy competitor and a fair person.

But it is important to help your child learn how to deal with a cheater, liar, and thief. One of the reasons that wrongdoers can get away with so much is that too many people, as children, are not allowed to see "bad" or are not taught how to handle it. A child who is not allowed to play with a child who cheats does not learn how to deal with a cheater. An adult who as a child was told that cheaters don't win or don't go to heaven can become disillusioned or can choose not to see the truth. It is particularly difficult for him when the wrongdoer turns out to be someone in a position of trust. That is why so many people can't imagine a President or a head of state lying, and are so hesitant to take action against them.

How should I teach my child to cope with wrongdoing?

It is best to wait for your child's natural response to a cheater or wrongdoer of any kind. If she tells him that she's not going to play with him if he cheats, great! But in some situations it would be to the cheater's advantage and her disadvantage if she quits. Because of this, we suggest that if the first approach doesn't work, that she deliberately cheat back with an offer to play fair if the cheater promises to play fair. And we don't tell children that only good people are successful and go to heaven! We don't know about heaven, but we do know that a great number of successful people down here are wrongdoers. In the real-life fairy tale, sometimes Cinderella is never found—her pumpkin never becomes a carriage and her clothes remain tattered.

Children have to come to understand the realities of adult life without becoming disillusioned or upset. Again, we don't need to abandon the fairy tales or fantasy, but we do need to help children learn to deal with the world the way it really is, incident by incident.

THE QUESTION OF WORK AND REWARDS

What kinds of chores are helpful for children in this age group?

Finding work for the young child in this age of automation is difficult. At one time, children helped to bring in water, took care of the chickens, and picked cotton by six or seven years of age. A few still do. Their contributions helped to keep the family going. The work of such children was necessary, and they could feel good about themselves because they were contributing to the well-being of the family. We are not suggesting that there is a need to return to picking cotton, but we are suggesting that you look very carefully for real jobs and ways that your child can contribute to the family's welfare.

Regular responsibilities such as carrying out the garbage and helping make the beds are useful but not critical, and they do provide an opportunity for the child to contribute in some way. Again, this is a place where children of working parents may have "one up" on other children. If they are not overburdened by responsibilities for younger brothers and sisters, taking care of the house and preparing meals, they can have a real sense of making a vital contribution to the welfare of the family. If you are a working parent, it helps to explain to your child why you are asking her to assume certain responsibilities that other children in the community might not have. It also helps to recognize and express your appreciation for her work and the contribution she is making.

For most children, however, their real work today is in school. We will discuss the child-school relationship in detail in Chapter 6.

Should I reward my child for his help? If so, how?

Some parents believe that paying children for good performances makes money or other material rewards too important. We agree. You want to help your child become a good performer, primarily because of his or her own personal pride. Reward from the outside should be of lesser importance. Help your child understand that he is working, writing, reading, painting for his benefit and pleasure more than yours, working to do his part, not yours. Sure you are happy about his good work, but because he is able to do it for himself, not for you. But a child should receive an occasional treat for a job well done; it won't hurt your training and it makes childhood a lot more fun. When children are able to do work that you would pay others to do, such as mowing the lawn, then paying your children for their work makes sense.

How about a regular weekly allowance?

This can be a positive way to help your children establish good savings and spending habits that can stay with them the rest of their lives. The amount you give should depend on what you can afford and what you consider a reasonable amount to spend. Even when you can afford to give your children a great deal, you should teach them that money doesn't grow on trees. We know that a number of middle- and upper-middle-income black families have trouble with allowances. Most of us in this group just made it "running scared all the way." We want our children to have all the things that money can buy, but most of us don't have the means to do so. More than providing three TV sets and three weeks in Bermuda in February, we must teach habits that will help our children succeed, just as we were fortunate enough to do.

Children must learn, like everybody else, that money doesn't grow on trees; that it is hard work that most often leads to achievement and a reasonable income. Children must be taught to "save some" and "spend some" and not to buy a toy or treat every time they go in a store. This is the time—not twelve, fifteen, or twenty-five years—these lessons must be learned. It's not easy. The children of a physician we know periodically responded to this message with a friendly "cheap, cheap" noise. Their father's friendly response back was, "That's right, I'm Mr. Cheap Cheap and I still say that 'money doesn't grow on trees!' " We are not suggesting that you be stingy—just reasonable. But it's all out the window if you are conspicuous consumers. The message is what you do more than what you say.

Don't be embarrassed if you can't give your child what the people down the street can give, or give even if they can't afford it. If you can't afford to give as much as you would like, you should explain this to your child. They may protest, but they will not love you less because of this. You can give in other ways. Special treats, favorite meals, family trips to favorite places all can be better and more important ways of telling your child "We care a great deal about you" than giving them money.

HELPING YOUR YOUNG SCHOOL-AGER MANAGE

It is a struggle to get my seven-year-old boy to do anything. He is late for the school bus. He won't do his chores without a fuss. He stays up late. Everything is a hassle. Then he complains about my picking on him. What should I do?

You are not alone in this situation. These reactions are usually a part of the independence-dependence struggle that most children go through. One part of them wants to be independent and self-reliant, and not take orders from adults. Another part of them wants to be taken care of and dependent just as when they were younger. Doing things for them that they could do for themselves makes them feel inadequate, weak, and power-less. On the other hand, it means that somebody is looking after them, giving them a sense of safety and security.

Children can't acknowledge that they are having trouble giv-ing up their dependency. They don't even realize that's what's going on. They try to have their cake and eat it too. They demand independence and less interference from adults, while at the same time do things that bring adults into their lives to guide and teach them. To avoid serious problems of this nature later on it is important not to get locked into struggles with your children about the things they should do.

The best approach here—though never instantly or perma-nently successful—is to teach your child to go to bed for his own good and not as a favor to you; to help him catch the school bus so that he will have a good attendance record at school for himself and not for you; to help him do his chores so that he can meet his responsibilities to the family and not just as a favor to you. In everything children do, you are encouraging them to establish and meet their own standards—unless these standards are un-acceptable to you, in which case you need to discuss and work out the problem with them. If you don't force your standards on your youngster, usually your child's standards are going to be very much like yours.

Now you may be saying, "That's an awful lot of work. It's easier to make him do what he's supposed to do." When a child is young, you can simply force him to do what you want him to. That is easier in the short run but more troublesome in the long run. By the time most children are ten and twelve, and certainly by fifteen or sixteen (and remember by then you are ten to twelve years older), it is very difficult to control them physically. Even when the physical problems aren't that serious, the verbal disputes can be very unpleasant. It is much better to take a little more time to help your child develop inner respon-sibility and positive habits that will carry over to adult life than it is to get instant control through "making him do things" at an earlier age.

How would you handle a child who needs to go to bed but wants to watch television?

We would suggest something like this:

"Okay, John, it's our time to turn off the television and go to bed."

"Aww, I don't want to go to bed. I want to watch television."

"We agreed that you need to be in bed by nine o clock in order to feel good enough to get up in the morning." . . . or to feel good in school, or whatever your agreement was. The tone of your voice and your manner must indicate that you expect him to do as he promised. If you are too strong, you'll sound like you're making him do it, which will not help him feel that he's taking responsibility for his own behavior.

If it turns out that there are five more minutes left on a television program, or he will finish his puzzle or model or whatever he's doing in a few more minutes, it's best to give him the extra time, then expect him to go right to bed. Agree on how much more time will be needed and set the new finishing time. If he doesn't want to go after you have been reasonable, "making him go" is now justified, but point out that you would prefer that he lived up to his agreement. When there is a special program on, you might want to extend the time and make an exception to the rule. By doing this, you help your child learn to live up to basic agreements, yet be reasonable and able to make exceptions to the rule when necessary. On occasions where your child is particularly resistant, you might want to point out that if he doesn't want you to nag him about everything, then he should do what he has agreed to do without your having to push him. Don't use this technique too often or it will lose its effectiveness.

So far I'm with you. But what if he won't settle down in his bed?

Then you've got a real procrastinator (in one way or another, he puts things off) on your hands. Children like this will move from the television to their bedroom at your insistence, but once there will start to read a book or get involved in some other activity rather than go to bed. Here it is important simply to restate the same expectation that he go to bed without getting upset, although you can be a little more firm this time. You may have to set the time that you're going to give him at this point, and turn off the light yourself if he doesn't make it in that period. Even here, it is best not to get upset, to regard it as a struggle the child is having in himself, but wants to draw you into. It helps to think, as in the spiritual, "I shall not be moved"—or in this case, be drawn into a fight. When you turn out the light you might want to indicate that you hope he'll be able to do it himself without your getting involved the next time.

On some occasions—but again, not too often—when he really tries very hard to start a fight or an argument, you might say very directly, "John, you're trying to get me into a fight, and I don't want to fight with you. I can see you're having trouble taking responsibility for going to bed on time yourself, but you'll be able to do so later on."

Frustrating. Children can make you very angry. But that's what they're trying to do, and it's best to avoid an argument whenever possible. Sometimes you won't be able to, but that's all right. Children need to know when you have reached your limit. You are a human being and not a machine, and they need to know that, too. But again, you want to try and handle touchy situations through talk that helps them develop inner control rather than use talk or actions that simply attempt to control them.

No matter how much I shout and threaten my child still won't obey. Why is this?

One parental habit that often leads to trouble is what we call "long-distance communication." Once you sense real resistance and your child has had a reasonable time to turn off the TV, yelling for him to do so from the upstairs bedroom when he is in the basement is an invitation to be ignored. If you stop and take a few minutes to talk face-to-face, it will usually be more effective than communicating "long distance." When you encounter real resistance and you must call again, it is especially important to be close up . . . still friendly . . . more firm . . . confident that you can handle the situation without dire threats . . . but close up.

Dire threats—now there is another problem. Some parents

go overboard: "I'll kill you. I'll knock your block off. I'll beat you to within one inch of your life." When these parents deny privileges they do it like this: "You won't get your allowance for three months" or "You can't go to Bob's house for three weeks." Children figure out very quickly that you can't and won't follow through on dire threats; you and your threats can be ignored. Threats of punishment should be in line with the way you actually punish. The approach to punishment we suggested in Chapter 4 is applicable to all ages.

Once you have established a pattern of expecting your child to do things and to meet his own responsibilities, he will take pride in meeting these commitments—although he won't admit it to you. From time to time he will still procrastinate and try to draw you into a fight. Sometimes you can avoid a struggle over control by doing whatever you've asked him to do yourself. Again, you don't want to do this too often, but when you really don't want a fight and he's working hard to get one, it's better to dump the garbage yourself, or turn out the cellar light, or whatever minor chore it is, than to spend hours and even days in conflict. Children who have developed pride in taking care of their own chores will usually rush to do the job before you can do it. After all, what is turning out the light or dumping the garbage yourself anyway? Your action of doing it simply says, "I'm disappointed that you weren't able to do this minor thing yourself. I'll do it." You might even want to say this. Again, don't do it too often. When it seems necessary, you will want to suggest that your child will be able to do his or her own chores without your help next time.

I'm already locked in a struggle with my son. Much of what you suggest won't work for me. What can I do?

True, where parent-child struggles have become a way of life, some of these approaches won't work. If you carry out the garbage your son was supposed to dump when he hasn't accepted responsibility, he might say, "Fine, and when you get through with that you can polish my shoes." Other children locked in a battle of wills resist parental control by not hearing. We have had parents bring children for treatment who have said, "Maybe we ought to check his ears first because I can stand right over him and yell and he won't budge. At other times his hearing is okay."

Other parents report that their children do just the opposite of what they say. "Stop running" causes more running, and "hurry up" brings a slowdown. This problem can become extreme and you may need to seek professional treatment. Doctors call it "the oppositional child syndrome."

All of these problems are a part of the independence-dependence struggle that goes on inside a child and between parent and child. You will see some of this in all children and between all parents and children. If you are caught in this struggle to the point where nothing seems to work, you need to try to correct the pattern and help your child accept independence and responsibility more gracefully.

First, you should think about how and why you are demanding certain kinds of behavior. Do they make sense? Are they really necessary? Is it really necessary to yell repeatedly to get your child to do something? Why can't you just talk to him and expect him to do it? You might then calmly discuss the situation with your child, explaining that you are unhappy about having to yell at him all the time, and that you are sure that he's unhappy about being yelled at. You might suggest that the two of you together work out some way to avoid such struggle. You are negotiating a new contract.

There are usually three or four problem times in every household (like bedtime, bath time, and taking-out-the-dog time), which repeatedly cause difficulty. When the moment comes to do these things, you might discuss them together and decide what is a reasonable time to be in bed, a reasonable time to take the dog out, and so on. Once you have made these agreements and established a kind of contract or understanding of what your child's responsibilities are and what yours are, you should then try to encourage the independent and responsible side of your child just as we suggested for the procrastinating child. This will take a great deal of time and patience because the problem is now more difficult. Your child will try to see if you are "for real" about this. If you continue to respond in the new way—calmly, firmly, with reasonable expectations—your child will gradually become less oppositional and take pride in meeting his obligations. But again, with a serious problem, you may need professional help.

Can you encourage your child to give you trouble while asking him not to?

Yes. Ranting and raving as if you are powerless, or throwing up your hands as if to say that your child is hopeless, are both good ways. Comments like, "This girl is going to drive me to drink" or "This boy is impossible!" are very encouraging to your child. Calling in your spouse for minor problems, "Paul," or "Louise," "You're going to have to do something about this child, I can't do a thing with her" is another goodie. In a struggle it means you're on the ropes and about to go down. Your child is winning and will often sit there with a pleased look on her seven-year-old "killer" face. But most important that part of you that enjoys getting beaten up—and as strange as it seems we all have a little of that—enjoys her behavior . . . and she knows it.

Back up. Admit to yourself that there is no way in the world that the vast majority of children in this age group can't be managed. Drop the dramatics. Work out clear expectations with your child. Be firm but flexible enough to make exceptions to the rules when necessary. Calmly follow through until your child completes her task. She will gradually realize that you really mean business.

THE IMPORTANCE OF GAMES, ACTIVITIES, FAMILY FUN

My seven-year-old is frequently bored. How can I help him?

First, think about whether he is actually bored and unhappy or just a loner. If a child appears to be happy while alone and is able to get along well with other children when they are around, don't worry about it. On the other hand, bored children or children who are always alone, even when they don't appear unhappy, need some help.

First you want to make certain that there is enough to do around your house—games to play, cookies to make, that kind of thing. Second, you should encourage your child to visit friends and to have friends in. Five- and six-year-olds love company. It is an opportunity to have others on their turf. If the distance to a friend's house is long or the way is dangerous—even if it's the apartment three floors down—you need to take the time, even if you are too busy, to take your child there. It is that important!

You should also think about whether your seven- or eight-year-old feels free to bring his friends home. You don't want to tolerate chaos and disorder in your house, but if you are tense, fussing, and scolding a great deal, your child might not want his friends to see you in action. It helps to have a place in your house—even a time, if it's not a big house—where your child and his friends can "mess around." Much fussing and scolding is centered around the disorder caused by active young hands. It is best to permit some disorder at some time and place. A certain amount of disorder is normal and healthy.

What can I do to make the time my child and I spend together as stimulating for her as possible?

Like all of us, children can get in a rut, do the same things, and get less pleasure from them each time. Your questions and specific suggestions about activities that would be a nice change can be useful. You may need to help the five- or six-year-old plan her day. You will also want to plan yours to permit her to engage in both outdoor and indoor activities, a little reading, a little rest, a shopping trip, a little music—at times that are convenient to your schedule. If your child appears bored all the time, and no amount of effort to get her involved with other children or different activities seems to help, you may need to seek professional help.

Finally, you might take a look at how much time you spend doing things with your child other than telling her what and what not to do. She spends a lot of time with you during which she is nothing more than an unimportant part of adult business. She needs, and you need, some time together that is playtime. Most parents are busy and often away from the home, so that many of us simply do not take the time to enjoy our families. It is important to seize the time and use the occasion to enjoy and do things together.

Boredom often leads to moodiness. I can see this all too well in the case of my child but nothing I do seems to help. What is the best way to handle this situation?

The best way to deal with this is to avoid being provoked by your youngsters' accusations and insults. (If you get angry and attack them, they will "read" this as proof of their rejection.) You can point out that you understand they're in a bad mood and you would like to help whenever they will let you. Your show of concern says, "I'm with you but I respect your feelings." Don't make jokes or try to cheer up your child. All of us get angry with the person who wants to joke when we're depressed. You are also demonstrating that you can accept their bad moods as well as their good ones. This is reassuring and part of the motivation for the return of their spirit and confidence. If you can get children into a game or similar situation that they have enjoyed and had great success with in the past, the bad mood, like a cloud, will often pass and a bright mood, like the sun, will soon appear.

We would like to spend more time with our children, but we can't stand those five- and six-year-old games. Should we play when we're bored and the children know it?

A few minutes of checkers, dominoes, or other games can be terribly important to your child. Try and play the games that you can tolerate best, but don't play to the point of total boredom. Your child may want to play until he wins, or play over and over to keep you with him. It can be helpful to set a limit on game time, without being rigid about it. Some people put aside a regular time, ten or fifteen minutes after dinner, for game playing. The regularity reduces your child's need to have you play for long periods of time.

Some parents love to play children's games and can really let go and laugh and shout and be thrilled just like the children. If this is not true in your case, it's nothing to feel guilty about. Whether or not you have the ability both to feel like a child and to be a mature adult at the appropriate times is a matter of luck. Family fun is just as important a way to provide the training, learning, and sense of security that your child needs as the information you give and the limits you set.

I have seen parents playing marbles and "street games" with their children. Isn't that a bit much?

No. To each his own—as long as parents don't force themselves on the children and their play. Many children enjoy playing a game of marbles, a little stickball, hopscotch, baseball, bike riding, and other activities with their parents. Sometimes they will want you; sometimes they won't. (Don't be upset when they don't.) You don't want to dominate the game, play too hard, or play too long. This is particularly true for older parents and with older children—twelve or so. There is a great temptation, as you approach forty and your youngster approaches the peak of physical excellence, to win at all costs. Your play should involve more fun and togetherness than competition. It is easier to play indoors together than outdoors, particularly if it means leaving an apartment on the twentieth floor. But outdoor togetherness is important and you should go out of your way to arrange it.

Why is family fun important?

Family fun is the best outlet and protection we have against everyday stressful situations: war and rumors of war, racism, trouble on the job or on the street. It can even be a good way to deal with conflict and trouble in the family. We can't really control religious, civil rights, labor, political, or government agencies that are supposed to protect us and give us a sense of well-being. However, we can work to make our family a source of fun rather than a source of conflict and trouble.

What are some important things for parents and children in the five- to eight-year-old age group to do together, other than play games?

Occasions like birthdays and holidays, and special events, including short trips and bicycle riding, are important. We were once amazed by the story of a teenager from New York City whose life took a turn for the better because of a birthday party—not one he was given, but one he gave. A mother asked him to help give a party for her seven-year-old son, whose father didn't live at home. She felt that the involvement of a male would make the event more meaningful to her son.

The importance, the pride, the sense of "I'm somebody" the

seven-year-old felt—and his appreciation to the giver—were shared by the teenager. It became an important event in shaping his own future. Parents and children feel a strengthening of the bond between them when they give and receive in this way. Holidays—particularly Mother's Day, Father's Day, and Valentine's Day—offer the same opportunity to give, receive, and strengthen the bond of affection.

An exchange of cards, making your own cards or notes, a special meal at home, dinner by candlelight, dinner out, or any other way you can think of to say, "I care, I love you, I appreciate, you are important," will help your child feel good about himself or herself. This will lead to a positive self-image as much as repeating "Black is Beautiful." When it's not his special day, the seven- or eight-year-old, even the five- or six-year-old, will still get pleasure from helping Mom or Dad pick out the cards, plan the party, or however you mark each other's birthdays. This kind of participation helps teach a child to show respect and affection in specific ways.

Suppose we don't make a big fuss about holidays in our house. What then?

Some of our fondest memories as grownups—upon which we draw for much of our sense of security and well-being in adult life—include the barbecued ribs on the Fourth of July, the New Year's Eve prayer watch at the Baptist Church, and decorating the Christmas tree. Even if you no longer choose to observe these occasions, you should give your child some memorable and emotional experiences that will remain with him throughout his life—Martin Luther King Day, African Liberation Day, Kwanzaa, and such. Pausing to mark things that we believe in, things we hope for and accomplishments that have been made, give purpose, direction, and meaning to life.

Why are family trips important?

The family trip is an important way to introduce your young child to new things, to stimulate her thinking; it's an important opportunity to be together; it's an important way to play together. It's a chance—particularly for the seven- and eight-year-old—to be useful helpers preparing for the outing. A picnic offers the best opportunity. Don't do all the planning and work and then tell your children a few minutes or even hours before that you are going on a picnic. Let them know far enough in advance so that they can help choose the time and place, and the menu. They can also help prepare the food and have a say in what games to take along. Trips to the museum, to hear Stevie Wonder, the zoo, all require this kind of planning.

We have found that including your child in the planning is important to the success of the trip. Children act up less when they are not "shuttled" from one place to another with no input about what's going on. It is difficult for them to feel positive about themselves when they are treated like baggage. This does not mean that you must do what your children say. For a number of reasons—including money and time—this may be impossible, and you will want to explain to your youngsters the whys and why nots of what you do. But we hope you are open to their suggestions. Children, particularly when they are frequently encouraged to contribute, can come up with some good ideas, remember things you forgot, and be helpful in a number of ways.

Children can learn to organize and plan if you can organize and plan and give them assignments that they can handle and that will make them truly useful to you. Make certain that you have what you need and allow yourself plenty of time so that you won't be anxious about being late and, therefore, irritable toward your children. The better you can plan ahead without being obsessed with planning, the more fun you can have together. You will be less likely to "dump" on each other. Teaching your child to plan and organize is one of the most important skills to be learned in today's world, where planning and organizing are essential. This early experience with you helps your child learn to plan and organize in school, at work, and in every situation where things are not planned and organized for him.

Do black children have greater trouble planning and organizing than children from other groups?

Many people—black, white, middle-income and low-income—have trouble planning and organizing. They find it difficult to set priorities. The homemaker who has two hours to get ready for a party and decides to clean her closets is an example.

But there does appear to be more difficulty in planning among people who have had little experience, or little reason to plan for long-range activities. Children who grow up in dysfunctional families often have trouble planning and organizing. You can see, then, that blacks, closed out of the larger society and suffering from more stress, might have more families and children with this problem. On the other hand, blacks who have been involved in church and other social programs are likely to have as much or more training in organization and planning as anyone else.

Because blacks as a group perhaps have more children with difficulties in these areas, we will discuss this matter further in Chapter 6.

We seem to do fine when planning and organizing local trips, but our vacation trips are a disaster. My husband and I argued and were unhappy most of our last vacation, and we said we'll never take the children with us again until they are teenagers. What happened?

Vacations can be more trouble than fun, but they don't have to be. All that we have said about local outings is even more important on vacations . . . regardless of how you travel. Familiar things, people, and activities give us a sense of security and well-being without our even being aware of it. When we are suddenly separated from these things and repeatedly faced with new situations, we can become upset without even knowing why. We just know that we're irritated with the children, with each other, and that the children are fussing more than usual. Some of their acting up is a response to parental anxiety and fighting, plus their own anxiety.

The first way to avoid such situations is to realize they often occur, and why. Planning and organizing your trip well in advance—especially how much money you're going to spend—can help. But the day-to-day planning of where to go and how to get there should be the subject of family conversation. Getting enough rest is also important on vacations. We generally do more than we ordinarily do in trying to "see it all." Fatigue can lead to irritation and conflict. It is also important to plan ahead so that you can see some of the things that are important to you, and your children can see things that are important to them. Vacation trips provide a good opportunity to learn to compromise in a way that's fair to all.

Vacations—wherever they may lead you—can be a source of great mental stimulation. Talking about the trip afterward, looking at your photographs, and writing stories about what happened during the vacation period can be particularly rewarding to your seven- or eight-year-old. You might suggest—but don't insist—that he or she keep a log or draw pictures during the trip itself. This is a good way to use the unplanned hours. Just as at home, your child will need some leisure time that doesn't include you.

Some of my eight-year-old's leisure-time activities seem so worthless—like reading comic books. Shouldn't I discourage this?

Comics have great appeal to children in this age group, particularly seven- and eight-year-olds, for very good reasons. Your child is having an inner struggle between good and evil—your rules and regulations are slowly becoming his against his desires to have anything he wants, do anything he wants. It certainly simplifies things to have Mr. America, Superman, the Globetrotters—all the "good guys"—triumph over evil. But evil needs its moments. Youngsters also like to see children like themselves getting away with the kind of mischievous behavior they'd like to be getting away with—thus the popularity of rebellious TV children who drive their parents up the wall. (And you must watch it with them yet!)

Superman also fills a child's inner need for success. We mentioned earlier that children in this age group often bite off more than they can chew. They are often confronted with things they are unable to do, but things that you and other grownups can do—this often makes them feel like failures. It sure is nice to have "Mr. Good" be "Mr. Bad" who can "do it all"!

Comic books won't decrease your child's interest in reading other stories. Comics take care of one set of needs; other books take care of other needs. You want to make certain that your eight-year-old gets to the library and other places where he'll be exposed to other kinds of books. Most comics are not hateful or vicious. But you should take a look at them from time to time. You don't want to let some adult "humorist" express his own anger and hateful feelings at your child's expense. Children have enough angry, hostile feelings of their own to cope with without taking on those of adults,

By the time your child becomes an adult, there will probably be more leisure time for everybody. It is important to help your youngster learn how to use his leisure now—both with others and alone. Give some thought to hobbies . . . things like model building and painting. Many adults who have never learned how to use leisure time are miserable on long weekends, fussing and fighting with relatives and friends . . . and worse.

CHAPTER 6

The Black Child in School—An Overview

Before moving on to discuss the nine- through twelve-year-old, let's pause for a moment and take a look at a very important development in your child's life. His days are no longer centered around his family and his home—by now he is deeply involved in a whole new world, the world of school. What problems does his new environment present to him? What is the most effective way for you to help him cope with them? How can his teachers best aid him in fulfilling his potential?

Many factors are involved in the all-important question of education, and one of these is the interaction between you and your youngster's teachers—between home and school. Your child's development is no longer in your hands alone, but has been entrusted in part to specialists in the field of education. It is by working together that parents and teachers alike can achieve their common goal.

With an eye toward furthering home-school interaction, we are dividing this chapter, devoted to the black child in school, into three sections. The first deals with questions parents ask, the second with questions asked by teachers, and the third with queries from parents, teachers, and friends (all those who influence black children in one way or another). We hope that by studying each other's questions, each group will gain a greater awareness of the other's problems, and opportunities, and think about ways they can address them for the good of the children involved.

For Parents

HOME-SCHOOL INTERACTION

I am busy and my child is doing well. Is it still important for me to be involved with the school program?

Many parents must work, and it is difficult to become involved with the school program at the same time. But if it is at all possible, you should do so. It is important not to let other activities—such as politics, social clubs, and volunteer work—keep you from becoming involved with your youngster's education. Your child should come first.

It is sometimes difficult for parents to understand the importance and the effect of their involvement in the school program. But an important transfer of attitudes and feelings must take place as your child moves from the home to the school. You and your family have been the important developers and motivators of your youngster up until now. Your relationship has helped your child develop a sense of security and competence. The teacher and staff of the school must now do the same thing. Your presence and interest gives a stamp of approval to the staff and the work of the school in a way that enables your child to identify with schoolwork, as well as classmates and teachers.

If a parent is not involved in the school program and shows no interest in the work and performance of a child, the school program may not be as highly valued by a child as it should be. If you are overly critical of the school program and the school staff, you can send a double message to your child: "The school is your friend and hope for the future," and, "The school is your enemy." This can cause your child to do poorly in school—in work and in relationships with staff and other children.

Suppose I disapprove strongly of something the school is doing? What then?

In cases where you disagree with the school, it is important to work this out with the staff rather than involve your child in the conflict. This problem is similar to the problem that arises when parents disagree. Children will play one adult against another—as a way of dealing with their own fears and feelings of powerlessness—if we permit them to do so. This does not mean that you should teach your child to tolerate anything the teacher "puts down." On the other hand, it's best not to believe everything your child says about a teacher or the school until you have investigated the situation with an open mind. When you have reason to think that someone has been unfair to your young child, it is up to you to act in his or her behalf. As your youngster gets older, should such situations develop, you should try to arrange for three-way discussions—you, the teacher, and the child—around any serious problem. We believe that it is as important for children to learn to work out conflicts—to know how they come across to other people and what other people expect from them—as it is for them to learn their ABC's.

Why should I bother to go to school? I asked the teacher, "How is Donald doing?" She said, "Fine." I still don't know how he's doing.

When you want to know how your child is doing in school, go armed with specific questions. Know what courses he's taking. Find out how he's doing in each. Can he concentrate? Is he able to complete assignments? Is he capable of organizing his work and developing a strategy to complete it? Does he understand concepts? This is more important than getting the correct answer. For example, we watched a bright youngster miss nine out of sixteen problems on a math test. When we took a close look at the paper we saw that he had made the same kind of subtraction error every time. Once the concept was explained to him, he answered all of the problems correctly.

Is he able to explain what he understands? Is he able to express his understanding in writing? Does he participate in class discussions? Does he appear to work up to his ability? What are the teacher's goals for the class and for your child? Is your youngster meeting these goals? If not, why not and what can be done? You can get some evidence of progress by looking at the written work, starting back at the beginning of the year and observing the changes as the year progresses. If such work is not available, you might indicate to the teacher that it would be helpful to you if he or she could find it. Finally, you should ask how you can help the school help your child.

Our daughter is unhappy in her classroom because the teacher shouts at the students all day long and we seldom shout at home. Can this be harmful, and how can I help?

Just as there are too many parents who routinely yell at their children, there are too many teachers who do the same. Younger children, and particularly sensitive children, often feel uneasy in such a situation. They frequently imagine that the teacher does not like them, even when the yelling is not directed toward them. You should make certain that the situation is not extreme and is not directed toward your child. When you have assured yourself of this, you need to make your child understand that yelling is simply the teacher's style and not to take it too seriously. Sooner or later children have to learn to deal with a wide range of personalities in a way that does not interfere with their own performance. With your help now, they will be better able to deal with such situations later.

Conversely, if you find that the situation is extreme, you should try to encourage the teacher to function in a better way. You might observe in the classroom and then discuss your child's unhappiness with the teacher. If you are tactful in pointing out the cause for your concern, the teacher may well stop yelling or try to make it clear that she does not dislike your child. If this is not successful, you may have to discuss the problem with the school principal, or someone else in authority. The more closely you are involved with the school, the easier it is to deal with such problems.

We have found it more helpful to state the problem and ask how you can help rather than to go into the classroom and verbally attack the teacher. Most teachers want to help children, not hurt them. But for many reasons—problems caused by the society, school problems, their own personal problems, the nature of the growing child—they sometimes do. If you can see their side of an issue, it will increase the chance that they will see your side and make an extra effort to make an adjustment.

In addition, it is important not to expect miracles. All schools have problems from time to time. At the same time, you don't want to tolerate unacceptable conditions without letting your dissatisfaction be known. But you are much more likely to get the desired outcome when the teacher does not feel "attacked." Try to create a situation in which you and the teacher are working together for the good of your child.

Some members of the school staff are not good role models for our children. What should we do about it?

We have heard parents who wanted their children to learn to be neat complain about a principal who threw his leather jacket on the floor in the corner of his office rather than hang it up; about messy classrooms; about teachers who left the building with the children at the end of the day without giving any time to preparation and organization for tomorrow's class. Such behavior indicates a disrespect for the community and often indicates an underlying belief that the parents don't care and the children aren't capable; that it is not worthwhile to make an extra effort. Many teachers in such situations would like to do better but are simply not allowed to by others. New teachers who are placed in such situations are often quickly brought into line.

Many parents are reluctant to do anything about these conditions, fearing that their children will suffer as a result. If this is a possibility, you should organize a number of parents to make your needs and wishes known. Ministers or other responsible community people, including your alderman, can be enlisted to change conditions in your school. But again we caution you not to go after "the enemy." Many people can be persuaded to function better if you appeal to their good side rather than forcing the issue. Some can't, so force will be necessary in such cases.

My nine-year-old told me that his white teacher slapped him and called him a nigger. After I got to school and made a screaming fool of myself, he told me it was not true. What was going on?

We must be careful that our own emotions about racism and our strong desire to protect our children and prepare them to protect themselves from racism do not get "used." The fact that there is widespread racism makes this difficult. We know children who have done similar things because they felt they weren't getting enough attention and appreciation from their teacher. They simply played adults against each other in order to get what they wanted. Young children don't know how to confront parents, teachers, or other authority figures to let them know that they feel they're not being noticed. Children often use the immature method you have described here.

Children can sense circumstances that will cause trouble or enable them to manipulate people to get their own way. In most cases they don't understand, and in some cases they don't care about, the consequences of their acts as long as they achieve their goal. This can be very troublesome for your child in the future. It can lead to serious personality problems. On the other hand, some people with such personalities become quite successful in business and government because they are manipulators. But such personalities often get involved in the kinds of "dirty tricks" in business and government that have been so troublesome in this country—recently revealed so dramatically in the Wall Street scandals. You can reduce your child's need to manipulate you and others by helping him learn more positive ways of dealing with problems.

One black parent, aware that the young mind sometimes handles problems in inappropriate ways, responded to a charge of racial injustice in this way:

"Is that right? That doesn't sound like Miss Smith."
[That's why it's important to visit the school or the adults wherever your children are involved. Then you know the likelihood of such events occurring or not occurring.] The mother went on, "That would be mean and unfair if she said that . . . of course, it would be mean and unfair of you to say that about your teacher if it's not true." [The child hesitated but did not change the story.] The mother went on, "Well, I'll just have to go to school and hear her side of the story. If she did that, she's going to have to apologize to you. If she didn't you'll have to apologize to her."

With that, the child said, "No she didn't, no she didn't!"

The mother remained calm during the discussion. She did not accuse her child of lying. She did not deny the possibility that the teacher had been unfair in a racist way. After the child acknowledged that the incident did not occur, the mother indicated that the child must be upset about something if she made up that kind of story. The child then went on to indicate that she was upset because her mother had started working recently. The child's behavior was an attempt to ask the question, "Do you still care enough for me that if I'm in trouble you would take time off to come and help me out?" The mother's response not only answered the question—that she would take time out —but it also established the fact that she was not a pushover, gave the child a lesson in fair play, and encouraged direct discussion of the matter rather than setting up a test that would have been troublesome to everybody.

The mother did go to the school shortly thereafter just to make certain that everything was A-OK. In fact that child was getting along very well in a racially integrated classroom with a white teacher.

What do you think the mother should have done if the teacher had called the child a nigger or hit her?

Even if the child provoked the teacher, such a response is malfeasance, and inexcusable. Teachers should not permit annoying situations to get out of hand, causing them to respond in a verbally or physically abusive way. Where the response is racist, black parents have a responsibility to see that such teachers do not teach their children. Even in situations where a parent doesn't have the power to make changes, a responsible confrontation with the teacher involved or his or her superior is likely to cause the teacher to be more responsible and professional in the future. Certainly the teacher—or anybody else responding in a racist way to your child—needs an experience that will change his or her racist attitude. But we know the limitations here, and all we can really do is insist that people be responsible and fair in their relationships with us and with our children—

even if they harbor racist viewpoints and attitudes. That's their problem. Our job is to make certain that their racist attitudes and behavior do not interfere with our opportunities and performance.

Such confrontations, when handled well, preserve our sense of dignity and can force racists to develop appropriate ways of responding to blacks. Angry, hostile attacks, although relieving our feelings of justified or unjustified anger, often reinforce racist attitudes and hostility toward our children.

My son's teacher says he is hyperactive and should be put on drugs. Do black children tend to be more hyperactive or is this a racial stereotype on the part of the school? What should I do?

Several school systems have used drugs to control children who were too active in school. A large number of these children were black. There is no good evidence, however, that there are more hyperactive (and hyperkinetic) black children than any other group of children. Frequently, poor conditions at school and in the home are responsible for what is thought to be hyperkinetic or hyperactive behavior. In these situations, it is better to work to improve the relationship between the child and the adults than to put the child on a drug.

On the other hand, there are some rare situations in which neurological problems make children too active. Certain kinds of medication can be helpful in these cases. You should talk this over with your doctor and with the school authorities at length before permitting anyone to use medication to control your child's behavior. Once done, there should be at least two or three evaluations a year to decide whether or not the medication is needed. Ask about these evaluations before you make a decision.

Many people now claim that the "crack" (cocaine) babies are hyperactive. There are conflicting studies about this. Some of the addicted parents have lifestyles that could contribute to hyperactivity in their children even without the effects of the drug. And some of the children of drug users function adequately. Thus, we can't jump to conclusions; we must find a way to help these children learn and function normally.

QUESTIONS OF CURRICULUM AND METHOD

My seven-year-old doesn't bring schoolwork home. Don't you think there is too little emphasis on reading, writing, and arithmetic and too much on fun—art, music, dance, and physical education—in the schools today?

School learning need not be a painful experience. We shouldn't look back to our own school experience to evaluate modern education. The test should be whether your child is learning well and is reasonably relaxed and happy with school. Art, music, dance, and physical education aid body development and expression. These areas can provide a school climate that encourages the teaching of basic educational skills. Certain organizing skills that are used in these areas are helpful in learning reading, writing, and arithmetic.

Sometimes the arts and physical education provide children with a positive experience when they are not feeling good about themselves because of difficulty with the 3 R's. We think that every teacher should be trained to use the arts to aid in the academic areas. It is a serious mistake to drop art and physical education—as is being done in many financially pressed areas—when they offer so many benefits. They are a basic part of black culture!

My son is in an open classroom. Is this kind of learning good or bad for the black child?

The open education classroom—with less rigid seating, more individualized learning programs, more student choice—can be a useful approach for black children—in fact, for most children. It can be particularly helpful for children who have not developed good organization and planning skills. It can also be a very good way to help children learn to cooperate and talk out problems that arise in work and play. The open education approach lends itself very well to helping children develop inner control, self-direction, and responsible, independent action. All of this can lead to a better-adjusted adolescence. Conversely, a poorly functioning open classroom can be more troublesome than the traditional class. We will discuss this matter in more detail later.

Is cooperative learning and the use of portfolios good or bad for black children?

We believe that cooperative learning and the use of portfolios can be very good for all children. As a country we have carried individual effort and/or independence and competition to an extreme. This has led to cutthroat competition, individualism or concern only about the self, and a lack of sharing and respect for others. In the process many children lose out and feel that they can't learn; therefore, they give up and act out in ways that are destructive to themselves and others. They often act out against the "winners." Our schools create too many losers and too few winners. Those who give up often become dependent. Cooperative learning is based on the notion that all children can learn and that all can contribute something to the learning of each other. This promotes responsible participation in group activities and more winners.

In cooperative learning, groups of children work together to achieve a learning goal. They may work as a team in competition with another team. In this way individual effort, cooperation, and competition are promoted.

Through portfolios students keep a record of their own performance in all curricular areas. They are helped to set goals for themselves, evaluate their own performance, and make the necessary adjustments. This technique encourages self-motivation, self-evaluation or assessment, and the development of success strategies.

My child is in a predominantly white school system, yet I would like him to appreciate black culture, know black history, and develop concern about the black cause. Is this possible under these circumstances?

Yes, although it may or may not require more guidance on your part than otherwise. Unfortunately even many schools serving predominantly black areas do very little to teach children about black history and culture.

Young children should understand American history as it really is, rather than believe distortions presented in many classrooms and textbooks. You should provide them with books and other materials that relate to them the black experience, achievement, and obstacles to achievement. Don't miss any opportunity to expose them to black art, literature, and cultural programs of all kinds. Your participation in and contribution to the activities of civil rights organizations will impress upon children the importance of being involved. Most important, you should help them understand that their own personal development—educational, social, and moral—is the most important contribution that they can make to the black cause. As the society becomes more complex, it will be increasingly difficult to maintain and make new black gains without the contributions of many more skilled people.

It is possible and important for predominantly white schools to do more to give all children a multicultural education. We have seen enlightened white school districts make an effort to do so. It's interesting to watch the serious attitude of eight- or nine-year-old white children putting on plays about the life of Martin Luther King, Jr., or doing research projects on Africa. These activities are important for their development. You might suggest that your child and his or her white classmates would benefit from such study and programs if they are not now available. Many school districts are making an effort to develop multicultural education programs, which makes sense in a multi-ethnic society.

Why is it important for my child to be on time and have a good attendance record?

Wherever people work together and depend on each other, being on time and being present (except when there is a good reason not to be) is very important. It is unfair to those in a classroom or in a work group when someone disrupts or slows down the progress of the group by being late or absent without good cause. Children who are frequently late and absent from school are likely to be late and absent from work as adults. Such behavior patterns often make it difficult for these people to hold a job and keep friends who cannot tolerate a disregard for punctuality.

We have heard people say that black culture is more spontaneous than some others and less time-bound, and that that's a good thing. But a person doesn't have to be late or absent, especially without advance notice, to be spontaneous. Such behavior in blacks, when it exists, is according to some, a carryover from slavery— a reaction to powerlessness and forced dependency. It was a way to "fix" the all-powerful master. Menial jobs and harsh treatment have served to reinforce such habits among many blacks. Oppressed white workers have shown the same patterns. These habits make it difficult to develop well-managed institutions. We believe that parents and schools should help children establish the habits of punctuality and good attendance. If relationships with the employer or teacher are not satisfactory, they should be talked out rather than acted out through lateness or "no show."

Again, parents are role models. If you make appointments with others, arrive late, postpone without good cause, or fail to show up without cause, your children will follow your example. Such behavior is actually a sign of disrespect for ourselves and others. It is less likely to occur where good relationships have been established.

TEACHER–PUPIL INTERACTION

My son comes from a fatherless home. Wouldn't it be better for him to have male teachers?

Maybe yes and maybe no. The quality of the relationship between a child and an adult, parent or teacher, is more important than the sex of the adult. When good male teachers are available in the community or in school, it is helpful if boys from fatherless families can be exposed to them. Ineffective male role models, as fathers or teachers, may do more harm than good. Where good role models are not available, it is important for mothers and female teachers to permit boys to identify with and play male roles—which should not encourage sexist attitudes toward women. For example, there is no reason that they should not play with dolls, as male children preparing to become good fathers. But we would not suggest sacrificing quality for sex any more than we would suggest sacrificing quality for race—black teachers for the sake of blackness, male teachers for the sake of maleness.

Be cautious about making assumptions about the reason for

fatherless families in black communities. Whitney Young, the late executive director of the National Urban League, once told the story of the teacher who pointed out to a youngster that he did not give his father's name on a questionnaire. When the youngster said, "I don't have a father," the teacher apologized and said knowingly, "Oh, yes, I understand." She understood that it was one of those fatherless black families, but in fact, the youngster's father was killed in a car accident when the child was three years of age. The point here is that although we talk and think from time to time in terms of groups, we must always remember that children—people, for that matter—are individuals and should be treated as such.

I feel that white teachers don't have high enough expectations for black children. What's your impression about this?

We must be careful not to generalize here. We know many white teachers who have had reasonable expectations and have had a good deal of success with black children. On the other hand, when white teachers have outright racist assumptions—that blacks are lazy, unruly, dangerous, and dumb—they are likely to have lower expectations and achieve less. Such teachers should not be allowed to work with black children. It is the responsibility of administrators to help these teachers adjust their attitudes and behavior, or to transfer them to another setting.

The other side of the coin is that some white teachers feel that some black teachers concentrate too much on manners, dress, and behavior. We have seen such concerns as "shirttails tucked in," "hats off" in the building, and "gum out" considered major problems. Again it is dangerous to generalize. We have seen these kinds of concerns voiced by teachers in both racial groups, but it is more pronounced among blacks.

A difference in background and age group leads to these differences in concern. Many black teachers had to overcome great hardships to get an education. They know that certain kinds of behavior and performance that will be destructive to a black child may not be destructive for a white child. They also know that some black children, because of harsh social conditions, do not receive the necessary support and guidance of parents that is so vital to their education and to their adult life. They are acquainted with the pitfalls and temptations in the community that may lure a youngster from the educational pathway. As a result there is often passionate concern and strong demands to "straighten up and fly right."

Questions of dress and behavior should be worked out by teachers and parents (and children when they are old enough) and reviewed from time to time. The decisions should be based on what will help youngsters function well as adults rather than what was taught thirty years ago or what somebody is rebelling against as a young adult today. Children function best when they know the time and place for everything—to laugh, to cry, to compromise, to rebel, to run, to fight, to hold their ground, to be neat, to be casual, to use street language, to use black English, to use standard English or whatever. Children who know what behavior is appropriate will function best in our multistyled, fast-changing society.

In a school where the rules are worked out by both students and teachers, there is less likelihood of mixed feelings, disruptive arguments, and fights over any particular rule.

PROBLEMS OF PUBLIC EDUCATION

As the mother of school-age children I get terribly upset when I hear people say there is no hope for the public schools. What do you think?

It's easy to give up on the public schools, but we see no alternative to public education. It's very costly to operate private schools. Even the Catholic Church is having difficulty supporting its school system. Private schools can educate only a few children. In our opinion, the only solution is to help public school systems become more effective; this can be done. There are many public schools that do function well. In our opinion it's largely dependent on the quality of the leadership—parents and school staff.

We are in agreement with those who say that social change is necessary to dramatically improve conditions in the society and in school. But in the meantime the school is shaping the lives of the people who must bring about the social change. Therefore, we must help the public school systems do a more effective job now. You should become involved with your child's school.

Can the policy of "school choice" improve the situation?

Magnet schools emphasizing areas such as the arts, language, science and mathematics, and the like are not harmful. But they are probably not as beneficial as many people think. A system of choice that allows parents to place their children in schools they believe to be the best is controversial. Such programs are based on a survival of the fittest notion that has already gotten us into trouble as a country by creating too few winners and too many losers. And just as poor blacks have often lost out in the political and economic system, poor black children will often lose out in a system of school choice. You must make the choice to do what is best for your child and society.

There is little reason to believe that the promised "scholarships" for poor children will be provided at the necessary level. The decision will be left up to the states, and some areas have already passed legislation that permits choice without the financial support necessary for poor children to actually attend the alleged better schools. Some blacks have supported the choice program in the belief that funds will be made available for Afrocentric schools. Don't you believe it. Even if it's true in the short run, it won't be available for long. In some areas, white parents in predominantly black school districts are using the choice policy to allow their children to attend schools in predominantly white districts, and expect to use public money to do so.

And finally, choice is not about children and learning. Some of the alleged better schools are good simply because the children are from families that have prepared them to meet the expectations of school, whether the program is good or not. If these schools had to educate large numbers of children from disadvantaged circumstances, they would not be good schools. And we know of schools that have been very successful in educating children from difficult circumstances, because the staff and the parents work together to support the development of the children, and in turn, learning. The goal of education should be learning, choice or no choice. Focusing on choice prevents us from doing what is necessary to help all children learn.

Do you think that "slow" children in the public school will hurt the education of my child?

We believe that children of different levels of ability can be taught together without hindering anyone's progress. We don't believe that rigid grouping of children by ability (tracking) is necessary. This appears to be a phony issue used to avoid facing the real issue. Children from different backgrounds often don't get along well unless the school staff actively teaches all children to develop adequate social skills and helps them deal with their feelings about difference. Ability tracking frequently separates children according to their social development and, sometimes, just race.

Such tracking often means that if a child in the lower-ability track shows promise, he must "leave his own." It also means that children in the higher tracks are denied the opportunity to get to know and learn to respect different people. In addition, it has been shown that you can affect the quality and level of a child's work by giving him or her a label. Children quickly learn whether they are in the smart, "dumb," or average tracks.

Increasing numbers of school programs are being designed to allow children to move at their own rate of speed. Flexible groupings can be used where skills must be taught at different levels—particularly with young children—without separating children of different abilities for all activities. A wise teacher will encourage children to help other children. When working with young children this way, the teacher can help them learn to accept differences in ability levels without ridiculing each other or feeling inferior about not being the best. This can decrease hostilities between different groups. It is also a way to promote cooperation and fair play as important values. It is in disruptive schools and classrooms that mixed-ability groupings don't work. But in such schools children are unlikely to do well under any circumstances.

How can I help at home?

You can help most by making schoolwork interesting and

challenging to your child. Your interest in projects and papers, and questions such as "How did it go in reading today?" can be helpful. It is best not to be too eager to help your child with homework. If your child is having specific problems and wants your help, give it. "Let me know if I can help" is supportive without interfering. Praise for your child's interest in doing the work, at an early age, is an excellent incentive for young children. Don't criticize the teacher for assigning too much work, too little work: "Why did he tell you to do it this stupid way?" This makes the work seem less worthwhile, and the teacher less credible. Talk to the teacher if you have a disagreement, not to your child.

Protect your child from too much MTV, too much basketball, too much television and too much fun, games, and noise from brothers, sisters, and others in the household. Some of all of this is normal. But you should give "doing your schoolwork" top priority and consideration. Have your child or children plan their schedules so that they can do their activities without interfering with each other. You may have to help them work it out in the beginning, but they can learn to budget their time and do their work so as not to interfere with each other, and in time they won't need you to police them. We know parents of well-rounded teenagers who have never had to make them do their homework. Such acceptance of responsibility, planning, and organization is important preparation for the future.

Noise? Find or make a quiet room or a quiet corner for a child who needs it in order to work. You should skip your favorite TV show if that's the only room available. What better way to say schoolwork is most important?

For Teachers

TEACHER-PARENT INTERACTION

If black parents are really interested in education why aren't more of my students' parents involved in the school program?
It will surprise even black professionals to find out how many black parents feel uncomfortable and intimidated with professional people. Many parents are intimidated by the jargon and

mannerisms of middle-class teachers. This is true in spite of the fact that many of the professionals have come from backgrounds similar to those of the parents. In some cases parents feel that they have very little to offer the professional school staff. In others, they feel inferior because they did not achieve professional status. In some cases, they have somehow received a message from the staff that they are unimportant and are not wanted in the school. Finally, many black parents work two jobs. Often they are too tired or too busy to get involved in the school program unless it is particularly inviting, although, as we have mentioned, it is very important that they try to make the time.

I have noticed that whenever there is a problem in my classroom, many black parents automatically assume that the school is against their child. Why is this the case?

Blacks experience antagonism at the hands of so many service agencies, in their dealings with welfare workers, police, and clerks at the license bureau, to name a few, that it is natural to assume antagonism in the case of the school. Differences in income and training between the staff and the community can also lead to a feeling of alienation. In this case, it is the responsibility of the staff, as individuals and as a group, to make adequate efforts to eliminate distrust between the parents and the staff.

You as a teacher, particularly if you are involved with early elementary school children, should make an effort to get to know the parents of the youngsters you teach in situations other than conferences about a child's problems. This can be done through communication by notes, telephone, and face-to-face conversations at home and at school. The school should develop programs that reduce the social distance between home and school. These programs—whether they are banquets, parties, the church choir singing at a school program, or workshops about the school programs—would enable parents and teachers to get to know each other as people. Parents and staff could then respond to actual human beings rather than stereotypes. When this happens, parents are less likely to assume that the teacher and the staff are against their child, and more likely to be helpful in managing problems, or they may even be willing to help out in the school.

As a teacher I get the runaround about home visits. I am not sure that parents want me in their homes. What is your thought about this?

For reasons mentioned earlier, some parents assume that teachers will think badly of them if they see their homes and living conditions. If you go into a home, you should be very careful not to pass judgment on the lifestyle of the family in question. Negative attitudes, facial expressions, and comments will be picked up in one way or another, and you'll defeat your purpose for going to a child's home.

It may be easier all around, under some circumstances, to invite parents to the school. Again, your attitude is very important. Parents who have experienced discrimination or abuse of one kind or another are particularly perceptive. If they feel that you don't respect them as people, they are likely to stay away from school, or be critical or abusive toward you when a problem develops.

I have invited parents to school, but they don't come or they break appointments. What else can I do?

First, you should explain why an appointment is important even when there is no problem. When a parent does not show up for an appointment, don't take it personally. You should make a follow-up effort to have the parents make a visit. If "no show" becomes a chronic problem, you might want to send reminders the day before or the same day by telephone or by letter. Most important, you should have something to say when you invite parents to the school—such as explaining the school program to them, explaining your goals for the class and for their child, how they can be helpful at home, explaining how you motivate children. Otherwise it is not worth their taking the time out to come to see you. In the case of parents who simply refuse to come or make appointments and fail to show, don't assume that they are simply irresponsible. Because of various insecurities discussed earlier, some parents will test your interest through a "no show."

Certain parents, fearing bad news about their children, use avoidance of the teacher and school as a way of dealing with their fear. Some simply lack the confidence to sit down and talk with a teacher. In these cases you must reassure parents of your interest and concern and, at the same time, particularly when the problem is chronic, you can point out in a friendly way how disappointed you are by "no shows" and how you lose time in preparing to help their children and other children when appointments are missed. In short, without using these words, you will be saying, "I will respect you and treat you fairly if you will respect me and treat me fairly."

Why are homework and the report card so important to black parents?

This is really not a racial issue. Most of us were educated in traditional and competitive school programs. In addition, blacks from the traditional culture believe that hard work is the key to success. Homework and hard work are almost the same thing. Some parents forget that the same "seat work" and homework that turned them off as kids is what they are asking their children to accept. Report cards enable parents to know at a glance where their children stand, largely in relationship to other children. As we pointed out, such information is not very helpful. But if a school or the educational establishment, in general, wants to reduce this tendency to compare, then we must put less stress on being number one and more on doing your best. In addition, the goal of development in the social, emotional, and psychological areas should be made as clear to parents as those involved in the academic skill achievement area. The objectives and the specific school program should be clearly spelled out to parents. Some statement of achievement in these areas should be given.

More and more teachers are now evaluating children in this way rather than giving report cards, or in addition to giving report cards. We hope that many more will do so. Report cards tell one very little. What does an "A" mean in a school where children are two years behind in grade level? A "C" means one thing when a child is working at the top of his or her ability and something else when a child is capable of making an "A." Letter grades are quick and easy, but they reveal very little about the objectives of the classroom or course and often reveal little about a child's performance. Letter grades give parents little indication of how they can help. Unfortunately, some teachers do not evaluate children along the lines we have mentioned. But if you raise questions in these areas with your colleagues, this may help them to do so.

I am a white teacher in a predominantly black school. I want to be fair, but some black parents doubt my intentions without giving me a chance. What can I do?

You must first examine your own feelings and actions to be certain that you are not doing something that causes the parents to distrust you. Racist comments should obviously be avoided by a teacher who wants to survive in a predominantly black school. More often, problems are created in indirect ways—by frequently proclaiming that you are free of prejudice, by proclaiming a love for all blacks, by leaning over backwards to please everybody, by excusing shortcomings of a youngster because he is black, by expecting too much or too little from black youngsters. Teachers should try to be fair and respectful and expect the same in return.

We have found that, except in areas of extreme racial antagonism, black parents and children are fair with white teachers when they feel that the teachers are respectful and fair with them. Close contact can destroy stereotypes. In one instance, during the 1968 riots in Washington, D.C., black children escorted their white teachers out of the danger area and returned to throw rocks at cars of whites whom they did not know. A number of educators have pointed out that white teachers who claim to have problems with black children are often the same people who have problems with all children, but are less aware of their difficulty with white children.

Incidentally, you might also point out to the college where you trained that not all people are going to teach in middle-class white schools. It is their responsibility to prepare people to teach anywhere. One black history course won't do it. Child development dealing with social problems, teaching by objectives, using school-based management, mental health teams to improve the school climate, and a host of other things that are not yet being widely taught are sorely needed.

I have different ideas and approaches to discipline and motivation than my students' parents do. Won't this confuse the youngsters in my class?

Not necessarily. Children, particularly young children, are very good at adjusting to the demands of a given situation. This is particularly true if they feel respected and comfortable in these situations. But, here is a situation in which a child can play teacher against parent, and vice versa, if he or she so desires. It is very helpful—even in cases where problems are unlikely—to discuss your differences of ideas and approaches to discipline and motivation with parents. It also helps to share ideas with other teachers. Most of us would prefer not to shout at and punish our children, yet we often feel it's the only solution. But when we are mature and self-confident enough to look at how someone else does it, we may find another way.

QUESTIONS OF DISCIPLINE

I'm in my first year of teaching and I have a great deal of trouble setting limits. I don't want to be a harsh, mean person. What can I do?

Setting limits need not make you a harsh, mean person. You are probably suffering from the problem of many young people—mixed feelings about having authority. When you are just out of adolescence and young adulthood—and for some of us, even as adults—having authority is a real problem. We sometimes still have trouble dealing with people who have greater authority than we do.

Authority in itself is not bad; it is the misuse of authority that is troublesome. Your authority helps you set the mood and the tone for your classroom. It helps you demonstrate to your students, through your own behavior, that cooperation, fair play, and good work efforts are desirable. Your authority brings order and safety to the classroom. It helps you protect the withdrawn and frightened child. It permits you to help the aggressive child bring his aggression under his own control so that he is not the victim of it—acting up, being punished, and then, feeling bad about himself. When you don't exert authority, chaos and confusion are likely to develop.

We knew one teacher, like the one who asked the preceding question, who was having some difficulty in this regard. She had real trouble saying no. She wanted to be a friend to the children. A youngster walked into her classroom after school and asked if he could play her violin. She wanted to say no because she was busy talking with someone. Her voice said, "No, not now, I'm busy talking to someone." But her face, her eyes, her manner, all said, "If you bother me enough, I'll let you do it." The child continued to ask and then demand and finally acted up. He had to be physically forced from the room.

Because of her reluctance to be friendly but firm, exercise her authority, and indicate that the youngster could come and play some other time, she created a problem. She finally had to deal with it in the very way she had tried to avoid in the first place. We have seen this happen many times with young people who talk about all of the right things to do with children, then fail to set limits and eventually end up yelling, screaming, hitting, and becoming angry with children in inappropriate ways. As a result they are not only furious but extremely annoyed and disappointed in themselves.

The trick is to be fair, warm, firm but flexible without being a "patsy." You have rights and you don't want the children to forget it, or you'll be trampled on. Part of your job is to help children learn to respect the rights of other people. They learn, in part, from the way they interact with you. In the same breath, we want to say again that children have rights. One of the ways that they learn to respect and stand up for their rights and respect the rights of others is to have a teacher who respects their rights.

How can we control the classroom when there are rules that will not allow us to spank bad children, people frown on our yelling at them, and we have no authority in the eyes of children?

Children sometimes misbehave in disturbing ways because they are fearful, frustrated, angry, and abused. But children are not naturally bad—or good. It helps to think of discipline not as a punishment or a means of control, but as a way to help a child solve a problem, develop inner controls, and learn better ways of expressing his feelings. Teaching children to work out problems between themselves, with your help as needed, is a good approach. We know one teacher who handles conflict in her first-grade class like this:

"Henry hit me." "She tore up my paper first." "No I didn't." "That was because . . ."

The teacher's response was "Okay, I can see that you and Henry have something going. I don't want to hear what he did and she did. Why don't you go to the back of the room and talk things out quietly. I expect you to have everything settled in five minutes."

In the beginning you may have to help children learn how to talk things out and arrive at a solution that is fair for everyone concerned. But even then you want to let them try to settle it on their own first. Even very young children are amazingly good at the art of compromise. This approach helps them learn to negotiate, to stand up for their rights, and to communicate. It helps them learn a way other than fighting. Learning to solve a problem in a way that allows a child to maintain his or her rights and dignity but still get along with others is one of the most valuable skills to be learned in today's world.

Sometimes I feel a child really must be punished. What should I do?

When punishment is necessary, it should not be harsh and traumatic for minor incidents. For example, you don't want to keep a child who has been looking forward to going on the class outing to the zoo from doing so because he got into a fight. It is the quality of your response that has an effect, not the severity.

In a case where it is clear that one child is responsible for the trouble, it is best to find out what is upsetting him. Even if you can't find out exactly what is wrong, indicating that you know by his behavior that something is troubling him will help the child feel understood and will also indicate that you know he is capable of a more desirable kind of behavior. You should then let him know what he can do when he feels angry or disappointed. Some teachers encourage children to use pounding boards, painting corners, and other frustration- and anger-handling equipment and methods.

Even when a problem must go beyond the classroom and be referred to a parent, counselor, or principal, it should still be handled in the spirit of problem-solving rather than punishment. You may have to help others, including parents, develop this attitude. We know of situations in which parents have come into classrooms and whipped children, or done so at home when they were told that there was a problem at school. This either destroys a child's spirit, has no effect at all, worsens the problem, or makes it more difficult for you to work with the child in school—he or she no longer trusts you.

Everyone involved with an acting-up child should find ways to help him or her develop the kinds of controls necessary to function in the classroom. When parents, teachers, principals, and others convey to the child that we want you, like you, and would like to have you in this school and this classroom, but there are certain things we expect of you, the response is often miraculous. The provocative and troublesome behavior is sometimes a way of testing whether you care, whether you really want this child in the classroom.

My students keep saying I'm not fair. How should I handle this?

Asking a child to be fair and responsible is going to be effective only when you are fair and don't play favorites. Incidentally, what do you do when you are wrong? Secure teachers permit children to correct them when they make an error in classroom work, conversation, or other areas. For example, a child returns late from the playground and you reprimand him. Then you find out that he was stopped by the principal, or had some other good reason for being late. We believe that it is best to apologize in this kind of situation.

One of the major concerns of the young children we deal with is the issue of fairness of parents and teachers. Six- and seven-year-olds in particular are "sticklers" about fairness, and this is understandable. They are developing a conscience, trying to learn and understand rules that will help them govern their own lives. The teacher provides a poor model if he cannot admit he was wrong and apologize for his mistake. There will be no loss of authority and control because you apologize. Children will simply appreciate the fact that you have been fair with them, and they are much more likely to be fair with you. Your fair behavior strengthens their developing inner controls.

What should I do when I have tried, nothing works, and my patience is growing thin?

If you can make a prior arrangement for handling difficult situations before you lose control, you can often avoid a lot of trouble. Many schools are geared to help you out in such cases. The principal, an aide, volunteer, or someone is prepared to work with the child during this period. When you maintain good control but the child is out of control, you can handle the situation in a way that will help the youngster improve his or her self-control. We have seen this work very successfully.

One third-grade teacher, after other efforts failed, said to a youngster, "Hugh, you are having a real problem handling yourself today. Let's give you a chance to pull yourself together. I want you to take this material and work on it in the principal's office. Let's see, it's one-fifteen now. I want you to get yourself together by two o'clock and then you can come back to the classroom." At two, Hugh was back, without being called for, ready to work, and he did so without further difficulty. If he had stayed in the classroom, he would have acted up to the point where he embarrassed himself and received punishment that would embarrass him more and possibly encourage more acting-up behavior. By giving him room, but at the same time setting definite limits, the teacher was able to allow him to save face, and feel good about himself for his ability to bring things under control on his own. Similarly, when you lose your cool, leaving the situation temporarily gives you a chance to calm down without a head-on collision. This is not running away; it is a strategic retreat that allows you to deal with the situation more effectively. After all, it isn't war—or at least it shouldn't be.

A final word here. We must all handle behavior problems or disorder on occasion, but the majority of these difficult situations can be avoided by a good instructional program and careful classroom management.

My second-graders talk all the time when they are supposed to be doing their work. Should they be punished?

Friendship and conversation are very important. Children develop communication skills and enjoyment from being with and talking to each other. Much schoolwork can be done while children talk at a reasonable noise level. No talking—at any time—is an outdated rule. There is a classroom noise level that brings chaos and confusion. There is another noise level that is the sound of production and satisfaction. It has a hum and a ring of warmth and enthusiasm. You can hear the difference between the two.

You want to help keep your children at this latter level of conversation, understanding that going beyond it will interfere with work—their own and that of others. There are times and places in which silence is necessary, and you should help children understand why this is necessary during a particular period. The same is true of order and neatness. Too much disorder is chaotic; too little usually indicates that the classroom is oppressive and that the spontaneity and creativity of the children are being smothered. Some children who talk a lot need more physical activity. We are distressed that some schools do not have a physical education program, and that some teachers punish children for talking by not letting them go to physical education classes.

How would you handle fighting in school when children have been told to fight by their parents?

Parents teach their children to fight in neighborhoods where they must do so to keep from being constant victims. Some children are told that, "If he beats you up, you are going to get another beating when you get home!" But when the school is safe and the classroom is calm, most parents are happy to have their children solve problems in a peaceful way.

At PTA meetings, during home visits, or whenever you meet and talk with parents, you should tell them what you and the school are trying to do to prevent fighting. You should let them know that you understand that sometimes their children may have to fight, that fighting to solve a problem occurs frequently among young children. At the same time, point out that your job is to try to help children learn ways to work out their problems through talk and compromise rather than beating up on each other. You can explain that an offer not to fight but a willingness to fight if you must can "save face" and cut down on the number of black children who victimize each other.

If you point out that young children who learn a better way to handle disagreements are less likely to fight with each other as teenagers and adults—in gangs, with knives and other weapons—most parents will agree with your approach. The majority of people in troubled black communities are tired of assaults and living in constant fear. We all know that making our neighborhoods safe is going to take more than the way we teach our children to handle conflict, but that's one part of it.

Sometimes I feel as if I spend so much time struggling with a few disruptive students that there's no time left to teach. How can I cut down on these battles?

It is important to help the youngsters understand that you do not want to struggle or fight. If you need to fight—verbally or physically—with a young school-age child, you are in the wrong business. In your own way, you will want to direct a student's provocative, challenging behavior into classroom achievement, success on the athletic field, in art or in music, or into improving his or her relationships with other children. You should let it be known that that is what wins points with you. But you can't do it by saying, "Look, Billy, if you keep fooling around you're going to grow up to be as dumb as your mama." (We have actually heard this approach used.) Again, you help best by praising the positive, the constructive, the direction that you would like the child to go, or the direction that will bring him success in his relationships with others without a loss of dignity and self-respect. Your response to negative behavior should be to try to direct it into a positive area, ignore it when it is minor, and stop it head-on when other approaches don't work—enough is enough.

Often the disruptive child has not thought about the needs of others and how his or her behavior interferes with these needs. A screaming child prevents another from reading or concentrating. A strong, aggressive child can intimidate the other children and prevent them from wanting to associate with him—unless he forces them. A provocative child can make you so angry that you won't want to have anything to do with him. Pointing these things out from time to time will help a youngster understand what he must do to get along in the classroom and elsewhere. When he begins to change for the better, it helps to tell him that you're pleased that he is able to do this or that; don't do this too often or it becomes phony. When other children respond to him more positively because he is handling himself better, you can point out what is happening, but again, not too often.

This approach is more effective than it seems on the surface, particularly with young children before they've given up on the human race. Most people, particularly children, want to belong, to be accepted and respected. Your responses help the child learn how to achieve these goals. He appreciates your help and this gives you a better chance of influencing his behavior in a positive manner. Getting along better with others will give the child a greater chance to succeed at his schoolwork. Scholastic success can change a troubled child. In fact, your classroom and school can become an oasis of security and good feelings in the overall insecure and difficult life of a child.

Be careful not to expect too much too soon. A child in trouble at five has usually had four and even five difficult years. (But it is also important not to rationalize that he's only in your classroom three to six hours a day.) We have seen children, and even their families, change dramatically because of breakthroughs made in the classroom during those few hours. But it takes time. There are those few unfortunate cases where little will happen regardless of what you do. But even here, sometimes way down the road—in prison, after a few failures at work and in marriage—people pull themselves together thanks to the advice, values, or training they received from a handful of teachers or people they "heard" but couldn't respond to at the time.

CREATING EFFECTIVE CLASSROOMS

What kind of a classroom atmosphere should I try to provide for children who come from a home environment very different from that of their school?

It is important for the teacher to make his or her expectations for the classroom known in a friendly, calm, and confident way. Most of us, without even thinking much about it, make the assumption that children know why they come to school and know what they are supposed to do. But usually children are there because they are brought or told to go. Often there has been no prior discussion about learning, how they will learn or what to expect. If they have been told anything, they have probably been told, "Mind the teacher." If children are used to doing the opposite of what their parents want them to do, an order to "mind the teacher" can be a challenge to do the opposite.

We believe that in areas where the rules of the home and the rules of the school are different, it is important for children entering school for the first time to move into a highly structured setting—whether it's a traditional or an open classroom. By structured, we mean that the children are told where to sit, how they are expected to line up for the bell, how to go to the washroom without running. Schedules and ritual also give structure and order—an opening classroom exercise at the same time every morning, a specific time for reading, a set period for artwork, and so on. All of this can be accomplished in a warm, friendly manner. As the children begin to understand what is expected of them, they can start to work toward these expectations. By learning to work together without hurting each other, being destructive or disruptive, they make it possible to move gradually to a more open classroom, with more choices, more free time, more self-direction. Often this can be done in a few weeks.

Both children of authoritarian (all-powerful) parents and neglected children function better in a more structured situation than an immediate open classroom.

Why do so many black educators raise questions about open education classrooms?

Unfortunately, the open education classroom approach was promoted as a cure-all much in the fashion of many patent medicines. It became a sign and symbol of "progressive education." Teaching in such classrooms was thought of as a "happening" by too many teachers. It is just the opposite. Open classrooms require more planning and constant evaluation of progress than traditional classrooms. "Happenings" occur without chaos because there is solid planning and management underneath. We recall an open education classroom in England, where the idea was developed, in which children were all over the room, apparently "doing their own thing." The teacher then showed us a massive record book in which she kept track of the academic skill and social progress of every child.

A retired district superintendent in London told us that he was afraid Americans would adopt the system without fully understanding it or preparing teachers for it. He was right! Inadequate planning and too many inexperienced teachers can be found in open classroom situations today. In addition, in adopting the open classroom, Americans failed to consider very important differences between British and American culture and social conditions; there is less sense of alienation from the larger society among most Britons than is the case in the United States.

Black educators and parents, perhaps more than white, have raised serious questions about indiscriminate, unmodified use of the open classroom approach. Because of difficult social conditions, too many black children grow up in homes and communities where they must struggle for survival by any means necessary. Sometimes the ways of the school are different than the ways of the home and community. There is sometimes open or unspoken alienation and conflict between parents and school staff. Moving directly into an open classroom before these relationships are improved and before children understand the expectation of the school can lead to chaos. This is even more likely to occur when teachers are inexperienced and have not planned adequately.

Many black educators have cause for concern. Too many black children go through the educational system without developing the discipline necessary to achieve in school, at work, and even at play. Moreover, a number of successful parents, teachers, and black school programs are highly authoritarian and structured—but not oppressive. Some of the Muslim schools, black nationalist schools, the Summer Study-Skills Program, and some public schools are cases in point. We suspect that any approach or method that gives children a sense of belonging, worth, comfort, direction, and purpose—and includes good instruction—will be effective. Although we favor an approach that gives children more responsibility, we are not against any approach that produces the results mentioned earlier.

What kind of classroom provides the best climate for learning?

The best climate for learning is one in which children get along with each other and with their teacher. That is not to say that differences of opinion or disagreements will not arise in such situations. But it does mean that such problems can be worked out in a way that is not too disruptive. Some people look at this kind of classroom and imagine that it is the charisma of the teacher, the background or the intelligence of the children, or just plain magic that makes it work. But organization is the key.

When we're working in a group, and nobody knows exactly what to do, how to do it, or when to do it, we tend to get restless, irritated, and even angry, sometimes striking out at others in the group. That is exactly what happens with young children, who have even less control and less experience in handling such situations. That is why it is important for teachers to have classroom goals and well thought-out ways for children to accomplish these goals. It is even better when a teacher helps the children establish goals themselves. Children should know exactly what you and they are trying to accomplish during your lesson period—for a morning, for a day, for tomorrow, for the week.

What classroom techniques can I use to help my students work toward goals?

It is helpful for children to keep a record in their notebooks of their individual progress toward goals that have been established for them or by them. This helps a child learn to think in terms of long-range achievement instead of only in terms of the here and now. It helps the child begin to see the connection between yesterday's work, today's work, and tomorrow's work. It creates a kind of relationship and a connection between things that many children from "here and now" homes do not automatically bring to school. Yet understanding the relationship of yesterday's work to today's and how the work leads toward a goal is what helps a child become goal-oriented and motivated.

As children learn to work toward goals, they discover that there is more fun in achievement than there is in acting up and other disruptive activities, such as "punching George" or "controlling teacher."

With young children, two elements of organization are particularly important. The first is movement from one activity to the next, and the second is providing activities that are within the child's ability range. For example, we have seen teachers present lessons that were interesting and helpful, but watched the classroom fall apart after the lesson because they did not give clear instructions or establish routine ways to help the children move on to the next activity.

We watched a group of children play a new game designed to improve their arithmetic skills. Unfortunately the teacher did not look at the game in advance and thus did not realize that it was beyond the ability of his class. The children tried very hard to play the game, but were unable to do so. They knew they were supposed to be quiet because other children were working. But they were unsuccessful at the game and eventually became bored. They became talkative and the teacher yelled across the room several times without asking about the cause of the problem. Finally, Ernie hit Maggie and a full-scale disruption began. Such problems will occur from time to time among all children. They are even more likely to occur with children who are unfamiliar with the rules and expectations of the school and among those who lack inner control.

EDUCATING THE VERY YOUNG

I believe that it's important for black children to learn to read, and I work on reading more than anything else in my first-grade class. What are your thoughts about this approach?

Reading is important. But there is a near hysteria about reading that can be harmful. We have seen teachers work on boring drills in barren, drab rooms because, "They must learn to read!" Most children will learn to read if we don't overreact. In fact, we have seen children who could not read learn to do so during the summer vacation, without their teacher. It's not that prior help is not important, but a relaxed atmosphere probably does more to help children learn to read than a rigid, uninteresting approach.

Of course, good instruction is the key, relaxed or rigid. It is not enough for children to read more. A careful evaluation of specific reading skill weaknesses and training and practice in these areas is needed.

What kind of prekindergarten and early elementary experiences are the best for my black students?

All children should have a curriculum program that enables them to prepare to learn the basic skills of reading, arithmetic, spelling, and writing. But even at this early age, attention can be paid to providing black children with materials that will give them a sense of self and racial pride. Books, magazines, films, and other materials showing black children and adults having successful experiences in all walks of life should be available in classrooms. Successful experiences should run the gamut from rock singers to athletes to professional people and families.

All children are not at the same stage of development when they enter school. Children from backgrounds where talking was not as much for conversation or sharing information and experiences as it was for control—"sit down," "shut up," "don't bother your brother," and so on—have had less experience in hearing language used for conversations. Hearing conversational language is good preparation for learning to read. It can be very useful to set up classroom situations in which such children can use language for conversation and hear it used in that way by others. Talking to each other, reporting on personal experiences or television programs, play-acting as newscasters, playing house, store, town, and a host of other experiences provide this opportunity. You as teacher might also want to lead conversations with groups of children so that they can hear and use language for sharing information and feelings.

It is also helpful to read to children who have not been read to in the home. They will need a familiarity with words and the rhythm of words, sentences, and paragraphs to learn to read. When you go on school outings, discussions before, during, and after the trip help children learn to use language in a conversational way, and help them learn to organize, rethink, and reorganize their thoughts and expressions. Once they learn to write, having them write about a trip before and after helps them learn to anticipate, observe, and recall—all important skills to develop. Making drawings and later making cutouts and reconstructing certain scenes helps to do the same thing.

An additional advantage of observing and describing things in the child's school and community is that it indicates that such things are worth observing. Children learn best in the early school period from the things around them, just as they first began to learn by exploring their own bodies. Once they are "hung up on" or addicted to learning, more distant and less immediately stimulating things will turn them on.

What other experiences besides book learning are good for this age group?

We hope that every teacher of young children will use the arts and physical education to provide additional ways for children to learn. Through such means as painting, model-making, and drama, children can express their feelings about things they are doing and things they have observed. The arts, movement, and physical education help children channel energies into activities that help them learn. These activities promote rhythm and body control. Some children who are slow learners or "late bloomers" are more successful in the arts and physical education. Sometimes they lose interest in learning—and we suspect some never regain interest—if they are unable to succeed as well as some other children. The arts and physical education sometimes make it possible for them to achieve this success.

The arts and physical education can be used to take advantage of the physical and rhythmic ability of some black children. As we said earlier, some middle-income black parents favor "head" things over "body" things; for example, learning to read, write, and do arithmetic as opposed to clapping, dancing, and singing. Such parents may be cutting off important ways of learning and expression. One is as valuable as the other, and physical and body expression can aid learning and written expression. Certainly no harm is done if both receive sufficient attention.

Another useful experience is community service. Young people who are developing well have a strong desire to be helpful to others. It enables them to feel good about themselves and to feel useful to others. Successful community service programs—helping the elderly, helping younger children, volunteering in a hospital, and other activities—can provide an outlet for this desire to be helpful, which carries over into adult life. It can reduce selfishness, scapegoating, and other negative behaviors. Many middle and high schools across the country have or are now developing such programs.

Should children in this age group be "graded"?

We believe that careful and consistent study or assessment of the work of children is very important at this age. What reading skills has Martha mastered? What does she need to work on? We feel that this is particularly important in cases where parents, for whatever reason, do not follow the progress of their children. Not only does your assessing the work give it added value, but it should enable you to do educational programming that identifies obstacles to skill development and permits you to develop exercises that will enable children to overcome these obstacles. Without such programming you may not recognize confusion in a child's mind, which can lead to an unnecessary feeling of failure that can cause the child to lose confidence and lose interest in learning.

We observed a youngster doing addition problems. He had missed nine out of twelve problems. A big "X" marked each wrong answer. He added 12 and 4 and got an answer of 56; 10 and 7 and got an answer of 87; 11 and 3 and an answer of 44. He was extremely discouraged and hid his paper from his classmates. Once the conceptual error was pointed out to him, he answered all the problems correctly. The moral of this story is that it is not how many answers are right or wrong but how much is understood that counts. Teachers should look for this understanding rather than simply "grade" papers. Understanding and learning to learn are far more important at this stage than the number right or wrong. The best way to keep up with a child's level of understanding and level of skills is to make some kind of consistent, periodic assessment of skill development.

RACISM AND RACIAL PRIDE

I am a teacher in a predominantly white school. I sometimes have a lot of trouble handling my anger when white parents, teachers, and children say and do racist things. Is it best to try to control myself, or should I let it all hang out?

Such a decision must be up to you. But as we pointed out earlier, you can spend all of your time responding to racism without necessarily decreasing your frustration and anger. If you can keep your cool and deal with racial incidents without losing your self-respect, you may be able to help whites, particularly children, become less racist, or at least more responsible in their behavior toward others. Your question brings to mind an incident told to us by a black teacher in a similar situation.

A ten-year-old white youngster who was quite insecure frequently bullied a black youngster on the school bus. The black youngster finally reported the situation to the black teacher. She promptly put a stop to the bullying without getting overly upset or putting the white youngster down for his "racist views." Several months later, after two other teachers had given up on him, the black teacher was asked to accept the white child in her class. They got along fine. On the last day of school, she asked the youngster to remain after class for just a minute.

She said, "Michael, I am glad we were able to make it together. I wondered whether we could. You remember the incident with Bobby Jones?" He indicated that he did remember, and took pride in being able to do well in the class. Although his emotional problems might not be solved, his black teacher had helped him achieve two successes—one in school and one in race relations. The chances of his using racism as a way of dealing with his own insecurities were lessened by his experience with his black teacher. As we indicated earlier, children of this age group understand the concept of race but are still learning how to handle their feelings about it. If you can set a good example, you can be more effective in helping your students.

The same is true in dealing with parents and your colleagues. We sometimes resent being "teachers" in predominantly white settings. But many white people have severe misconceptions about blacks. Some can directly, and many can indirectly, affect the lives of black children and people in general. We think it's necessary to clear up some of these misconceptions both through what you say and through your performance. When you find whites who are truly interested, you might recommend literature and other information that will help them understand and interpret the black experience.

In some situations, you simply won't be able to contain your anger—and that's all right too. This response will say, "Enough is enough."

As a white teacher, I worry about putting children down when I correct their errors, particularly their English when it is the style of their community. Won't they take it as a racial slur?

It is not so much that you correct, but how you correct that is important. It's your voice, facial and body expressions, and attitudes that count. If a child says, "That's number fo'," and you respond, "The word is not fo'! It is four!" you have sent a message. You have said that the child is wrong. The language of her community is wrong. You have shown disdain for her way of speaking. But if you explain that that's one way of saying it, or that may be the way she's heard it pronounced, but at school the word is pronounced "four," you will be giving her information without putting her down. The words "at school" really mean standard English. The tone of voice, choice of words, and attitude do not convey error, disdain, or a racial put-down. You now have a child learning standard English without having to reject her dialect. Eventually you will be able to give the standard English form without giving an "at school" explanation.

There are formal and informal school papers, and some of the unimportant practice work of children need not be corrected. But when youngsters are doing serious assignments it is necessary to correct spelling and grammar. How else will they learn the standard form? It is important to praise what is praiseworthy while pointing out the errors here and there. It pays to do this in the spirit of helping rather than finding fault. Again, it is the way you do it and not what you do that counts.

Some of the children in my first-grade class call each other names when they are angry—"black nigger," "black pig," and so on. How should I handle this?

In young children such expressions are not always an indication of a deep-seated negative feeling about being black. Sometimes the children have simply heard the words used elsewhere and are just repeating them. You can often end such name-calling by saying something like this, "Black people who feel good about themselves do not call each other names." The major task is to reduce the cause of anger and help youngsters learn to handle it in a better way. You should think about whether the youngsters are having success in class—and ways to help them if they are not. Hostile and aggressive anger toward each other is often related to failure and frustration in learning. Helping them learn to talk out their differences is the best way to reduce anger, but there are other ways—from writing to running to pounding on a bag made for such purposes.

A black seven-year-old and one of his white classmates called each other racial names in my schoolroom. I stopped them and made them apologize to each other. Do you think I should have punished them as well?

Punishment is usually not effective. Racial attacks by young children are simply the repeating of expressions that they have heard used in anger or fear or at a time of conflict. Stopping the name-calling and making the youngsters apologize is okay, but a discussion can be even more useful here. You will probably find that the real issue is that Coretta had a ball Joan wanted to play with, or Peter wanted Paul to be in his group. By the second or third grade the problem probably goes deeper. At this age it is important to indicate that racial attacks will not be tolerated. An eight- or nine-year-old who repeatedly makes racial attacks is usually a frustrated and insecure child—except when he has been deliberately taught to act this way by older people. You will want to help such a child with the underlying problem.

As a white teacher in a predominantly black school, how can I help black children develop racial pride?

Some people claim that it is not possible for a white teacher to help black children establish a positive black identity. We do not think this is true. For example, we remember one situation in which a white teacher left her predominantly black class at the end of the year to get married. The children drew a picture of the teacher and her husband-to-be as a going-away present for her. The color of the teacher was brown and her groom was white. This was an indication that they recognized the difference but accepted her. It also indicated that they valued brown or dark skin.

We have heard white teachers express concern just as we have heard black parents express concern when their four-year-olds try to wash away their skin color or indicate that they want to be white. Again, this is not always an indication that children of this age dislike being black. Children want to be like the people around them. A white physician, whose child went to a predominantly black school, told us of visiting the school and seeing his child's self-portrait on the bulletin board. The skin was colored brown like that of the children around her. We have worked with white children who color their drawings brown as an indication that they like their therapist or want to be like the therapist.

There is cause for concern in such cases only where this incident is not isolated or limited to a three- or four-month period. When your child repeatedly makes negative statements about being black or makes extreme efforts to be white, there is a problem. Remember, you can be the one to create it by overreacting to his race statements rather than discussing the matter in a calm, confident way. Efforts should be made to expose such a child, in a relaxed and natural way, to successful black role models and to black culture and experiences.

As we indicated earlier, a sense of worth and value and pride arises first from the way one is treated by adults. If a white teacher is fair, respectful and, at the same time, has reasonable expectations for learning and behavior, black students will succeed and feel good about themselves. Using materials that show blacks having successful experiences can also be helpful. Your respect for black art, literature, dance, and music will be observed by the children. Your interaction with black staff members and black parents will also be observed by the children. Your respect for blacks will prevent the child from having any doubt about the value of his blackness. At the same time, it is important for black children to see blacks in positions of authority, upon whom they can model themselves. A school with a significant number of black children should employ some black teachers and administrators.

A black youngster in my nursery school class slapped her black doll, and said, "Shut up, you black bitch." I know I should have said something, but I was horrified and turned away. How would you have handled this?

Brutality both fascinates and horrifies most people. This is particularly true of the majority of people in the "helping" professions—teachers, doctors, social workers. It is even more horrifying when you realize that the child was probably repeating an act that she learned at home. In fact, she was just "playing house." As a white teacher this could easily have caused you to feel guilty. But the child doesn't need your guilt. She needs your help in learning how to handle a frustrating situation. The baby was crying and frustrating her. In a case like this you could say, "Nadine, I'm sure the baby will stop crying if you hold her [or give her milk, or whatever you do to comfort her] rather than hit her or call her names." At the same time you might want to put your arm around Nadine (if you feel real compassion).

A lecture or discussion about black pride would mean almost nothing in this situation. That is too "intellectual" at this point. The issue is "feelings." You can help best by providing her with a positive model of behavior and a little understanding. It is hoped that children from abusive homes can learn to respond in school and other places in ways that will enable them to receive nonabusive, considerate treatment from others. This, in time, could make it possible for them to respond in nonabusive ways. At some appropriate time—story time, when cutting out pictures, on a trip, when asking a spontaneous question about blacks—you should help the child experience her blackness in a proud way.

VIOLENCE AND OTHER PROBLEM AREAS

I work in a school where you lock the doors or risk attack from somebody off the street, and there is a buzzer to call for help if you are attacked by the students. The kind of control measures you have mentioned so far are not going to help me. What can I do?

Most elementary schools are manageable, but unfortunately many junior high schools and high schools, both black and white, are chaotic and dangerous. The solution to the problems within these schools often goes beyond the individual classroom or school, beyond change through management, instructional, and relationship improvements. Troubled homes and troubled communities—a product of inadequate social policies and negative attitudes toward the poor and minority groups—are the real problems. Social change is needed to improve the quality of community and home life in such cases.

But let's be careful here. We are all too quick to place the blame outside of ourselves. We have seen good leadership "turn around" some extremely tough schools.

One teacher, in response to an article about how teachers fail in inner city schools, wrote, "No teacher has ever failed in an inner city school!" She went on to point out that City Hall fails, the City Council fails, administrators fail, but not the teachers.

Nonsense!

It is interesting that some teachers are successful even in some of the most troubled schools. We have seen chaotic schools become safe and successful through the cooperation of parents, teachers, students, and administrators. Yes, there are dangerous schools. Much needs to be done outside these schools. But many of the problems in these schools can be resolved, even in the high schools.

That's all well and good, but in the meantime how do I cope with a child who's about to knife another child or me?

You should do your best to see that nobody, including yourself, gets hurt and to prevent a youngster from hurting himself and his own future. Calmness—to the extent possible under the circumstances—and allowing the two combatants to save face and maintain their self-respect is the best way to survive in such a case.

We recall a situation in which a young black man attempted to stop a fight between two snarling, angry eleven-year-old black youngsters at a shopping center. He parted them only to find himself, a second later, between two cocked arms holding bricks. A crowd of amused white adults had gathered. The black man pointed out that the crowd was thinking, "See, that's the way 'they' are." He also pointed out that if the kids threw those bricks they were going to hurt him and themselves—when they had previously been and could again be friends. He also indicated that the problem could be solved without hurting each other. The arms slowly dropped. If you are a fair and respectful teacher, you have the leverage of being someone the youngster really doesn't want to hurt.

Although the preceding approach is the best way to handle an extreme and dangerous situation in principle, in reality it doesn't always work. You are the expert when such situations arise, because only you can "read" the intensity of rage. You must decide what to do. Again, don't get yourself hurt.

When your school is in chaos—whether it has experienced dangerous fights, drugs, or other difficulties—the staff must look for new approaches. Have you involved and given support to the parents who want more for their children? Even troubled parents want more. Does your staff treat each other in a way that is a good example to the students? Does the staff treat the youngsters in a fair, firm, yet reasonable way? Have you developed programs and activities that teach the youngsters skills they did not receive at home, which focus on problems around them, which give them direction, purpose, and hope for the future?

Easier said than done? Right on! Teachers in such situations have the toughest jobs in this country. You also have the best chance to "turn around" confused black youngsters, and we need all the "turnarounds" we can get—if our communities are ever to be safe places to live and good places to rear children. We know it will take more than better schools—but better schools are an important part of what is needed. Better schools can produce more people capable of taking effective political and social action . . . to the degree and in any way necessary.

Let us say once more, loud and clear: if it's going to take a militant struggle, remember that it's the disciplined, dedicated and, in today's world, well-trained people who can bring off a militant struggle, not irresponsible thugs exploiting other people for self-gain in the name of some greater cause. We are highly suspicious of proclaimed revolutionaries wearing expensive clothes, driving flashy cars, "digging" jazz on expensive stereos. We suspect inner trouble—even suicidal intent—when a person's acts appear designed more to bring the roof down on his head than to bring about lasting improvement.

A six-year-old threw our classroom pet, a gerbil, against the wall. Is that an indication of a serious psychological problem?

Not necessarily. Children who have been neglected, rejected, or brutalized in one way or another often show a brutality and harshness that is beyond the ordinary. Sometimes this is a sign that psychological problems exist which will require professional help. On the other hand, if teachers understand that there are reasons for this behavior and do not simply consider the child "bad," they can be very helpful, although you must not tolerate such behavior.

Youngsters who are cruel or rough usually have had difficult experiences with powerful adults. Their reaction is to try and control adults through provocative, negative, even threatening behavior—or to take their anger out on a building, animals, or children who don't fight as well as they do. They often are distrustful of adults and need evidence that they can trust you. Such trust comes through your being fair and respectful to everyone in the classroom. This includes the teacher aide, parents, and the custodian who comes into the classroom from time to time. A distrustful child will often provoke and test you to see if you are for real—whether you honestly care and are really concerned about him and others. If you make an effort to help the youngster but become provoked by his behavior, shout, and punish, your response will enable him to think, "See, I knew it all the time," even though he will probably not say so out loud.

If you do lose control, it's not the end of the world. Calm down and say that you're sorry. But then calmly but firmly point out that there are certain things you expect in the classroom. You can also use a situation like this to help the youngster see

that what he does to you and others causes what he considers
mistreatment to himself. Such incidents provide the opportunity
for "verbal contracts"—you play fair with me and I'll play fair
with you; you abide by the reasonable rules of this classroom
and I will be able to be fair with you.

*Some black children seem to have a chip on their shoulders.
One of my students rolls her eyes at me whenever I ask her to
do something. What does this mean and what can I do about
it?*

Abused children, black or white, are likely to have a chip on
their shoulders. Such a child expects you to be unfair and unreasonable like the other adults she has come in contact with at
home and in the community, or like the society at large that is
wary of blacks. Don't let the rolling eyes throw you. It is the
expression of the questions, "Who are you? Where do you stand?
What right do you have to tell me what to do?"

Distrust, testing, and questioning will disappear as you demonstrate, time and time again, that you are fair and working in
the best interest of each child. Directly challenging the eye-rolling
or the hostility generally gets you nowhere. Banter or joking,
rolling your eyes back—after you have established a fair relationship and if you are comfortable doing it—generally lessens
the tension, but still doesn't answer the child's unspoken question. The important thing is to be able to tolerate a certain amount
of hostility without using your power and authority to crush it.
"Stop rolling your eyes at me" may stop the eye-rolling, but not
the "mind-rolling"—anger and hostility.

Most of us have our own ways of handling hostility. If you
do not overreact because the hostility is coming from a black
child, your usual methods will probably work. If there is an
irrational feeling that blacks are dangerous and the hostility and
anger may get out of hand, you may be fearful and ineffective
in handling a hostile response. There are some dangerous black
children just as there are some dangerous white children. But
most young children can't do much harm, and you must learn
how to separate the real danger from irrational fear.

*I have the impression that many black children lack confidence
and avoid difficult academic work. Is this true?*

The problem is not race but the preparation for learning and the quality of instruction. We have seen children who were not adequately prepared to learn use all kinds of avoidance methods. We have observed this most in relation to beginning reading, where children have not heard the language used much in the giving, receiving, and sharing of information; have not been read to; and are unable to appreciate reading as an enjoyable experience.

It can also be a question of comfort—is it safe to risk trying to solve a problem and perhaps be wrong? A sharp word, a facial expression, a body movement, may tell a child that he's "a dummy" for missing a problem or answering a question incorrectly. A classroom where children are permitted to tease each other for making errors can be an uncomfortable place to make a mistake. Where teasing has been permitted at home, some children have learned to avoid any situation in which they can make an error. We indicated earlier that because of difficult social circumstances, too many black children are "put down" by too many people, at home and away from home. We recall black children in a hostile, predominantly white classroom setting who did not respond to classroom questions at all. However, at church and on the playground, they were quite expressive and obviously bright.

Avoidance occurs less frequently when children feel secure and accepted enough to make an error, try again, and eventually learn. Teachers of young children, particularly those who have been put down and made to feel stupid, inferior, or unwanted, should be especially supportive. Such children tend to put each other down, and teachers should discourage this. But be careful not to be supportive to the point of producing dependency—a need for your presence in order to do anything.

My problem is that I favor bright children although I know this is harmful. How can I handle this?

We are less than professional if we favor any child, and it is our responsibility to police ourselves. It helps to think consciously from time to time about the way we treat children from different backgrounds, of different ability levels, of different sex and personality. Do we limit girls to passive play and encourage boys to be self-assertive and aggressive? Do we expect more from white children from middle-income backgrounds (or black children from middle-income backgrounds for that matter) than we do from black or white children from low-income backgrounds?

It is important to remember that all children are valuable and must be helped to develop, regardless of their IQ level or their achievement test scores. It is also helpful not to think of children as naturally good or bad. We have pointed out in previous chapters that many factors can cause troublesome behavior. Yet the behavior of children, particularly young children, can be modified. If we do not assume that a child behaves according to racial and class stereotypes, we have a better chance to modify the child's behavior in a more positive direction.

As professional educators, we tend to favor children who are bright. On top of this, those of us who feel that the future of black America depends on the development of bright, aggressive blacks are likely to favor "the brightest and the best." We must be particularly careful to recognize and deal with this tendency, for only in a climate where all children feel valued can they achieve at their highest level.

Some of my students are terribly withdrawn and timid. Why is this?

Children are withdrawn and timid for different reasons. But most children who are timid generally lack confidence and are fearful of rejection and abuse—harsh criticism from adults or other children and occasional physical abuse. Sometimes children are timid simply because they've been cautioned to "be good" in school and are uncertain about what they can and can't do. The latter group becomes more outgoing when they understand the rules of the classroom and school. The problem is more complicated for other children. In some cases black children are quiet and withdrawn in settings where white adults are in control. The children may be unsure of where you stand on race or of whether a white teacher or principal will be fair. Home or school visits by parents on enjoyable occasions—parties, special programs, and such—can be helpful, if you are a fair person.

This group generally fares very badly in chaotic classrooms with a great deal of confusion, scapegoating, and mutual abuse. These children do best when a teacher is able to create an environment in which each child feels safe, believes that his rights and needs will be respected, and feels that he will not be ridiculed and put down. In such an environment you can work to help timid children develop more self-confidence and personal pride. When you are dealing with severely withdrawn and timid children (usually psychologically traumatized), do not move too quickly or expect too much too soon. We know of one situation where a child did not smile or show trust in her teacher for an entire year. But most withdrawn children will come around after a month or so—when they feel safe and secure.

How can I best work with timid children to help them become more assertive?

You might start out by encouraging them to participate in classroom discussions or activities, without waiting so long for them to answer a question or join in a game that you embarrass them. After extending an invitation and waiting a reasonable length of time, indicate that you know that they will be able to join in later on. You might say very directly, particularly if you can say it in private, that you can see that the child is a little embarrassed and uncomfortable, but that he will be all right . . . he'll come through . . . she'll gain her confidence, or whatever your way of soothing and reassuring happens to be. When they begin to participate, it's helpful to express your pleasure and delight that they are able to do so, again, without overpraising and embarrassing the child.

Withdrawn children often become the victims of more aggressive (but often just as insecure) children. You must protect the effort of the withdrawn child to come out of his shell just as you would protect a budding plant from too much sunlight, too much water, or whatever will kill it. For example, if you see a withdrawn child suddenly rise to defend himself from a bully or from some kind of attack from others, you don't want to stop the fight too soon—unless there is a possibility of injury or it looks like the withdrawn child is going to get the kind of beating that will humiliate him.

There are two problems to watch for here. Sometimes the withdrawn child will overshoot the mark and become overly aggressive. Sometimes he or she will become overdependent on you. We remember one situation in which a teacher placed a withdrawn child next to an aggressive, acting-up child, and within a short period of time you could not tell the difference between the two. A child who is functioning well—aggressive and assertive but not acting up—is the best model for a withdrawn child. You can avoid the overdependence situation by encouraging and protecting the withdrawn child without smothering him or her. In other words, as he gains confidence you will want to encourage him to stand on his own and fend for himself, just as you would any other child.

Some children will need professional help. When this is necessary and services are available, think of the withdrawn child as much as you do the acting-up child. The misbehaving child is more troublesome and disruptive in a classroom, and therefore is the first to get help. But the withdrawn child has a problem that is equally serious (for him or her, if not for you) as the problem of the acting-up child.

What can I do when there are so many children who need help and so few psychologists and social workers in our schools?

It is unfortunate and risky that schools having financial problems cut back on social work and other support services, psychologists, counselors, and such, first. But it is also unfortunate that support service people stick so closely to a costly and less effective casework model, geared more toward sick people than toward basically healthy children and families. More personnel will be available when parents, teachers, and support personnel work together to change the atmosphere of a particular school rather than try to "fix" each child and family. Many of the conflicts between teachers and people outside the classroom will be reduced when this happens.

Take a closer look at both your school and your classroom. Children who are ordinarily well-adjusted often have problems in chaotic, disruptive schools and classrooms. Often the individual teacher cannot do much about changing the school, but he or she may be able to do something in the classroom. But we have also seen chaotic schools brought under control and the number of children needing help for behavior problems cut by almost eighty percent. Good classroom organization, careful management, and praise for good performance (accentuating the positive while ignoring the negative whenever possible) usually bring this about. But, as we have said, there are times when you must deal directly with misbehavior. It is easier to deal with when not everybody is misbehaving.

For Parents, Teachers, and Friends

THE ROLE OF EDUCATION IN THE BLACK COMMUNITY

Many studies show that black parents from the low-income group, more than parents from other low-income groups, indicate that they want their children to get a college education. Why is this so?

Actually blacks from all income groups show a great interest in higher education. This is true for two reasons. First, high-paying, high-prestige blue-collar jobs that do not require college training—electrician, bricklayer, and such—have been less available to blacks than to other low-income groups. Second, just as the Israelis have found that Jews from countries with oppressive conditions are less willing to work as waiters, delivery persons, or in any other service capacity, the same is true of blacks. A college education provides the best opportunities for a high-prestige, white-collar job.

While everybody who can go to college and successfully compete should do so, the high-paying, high-prestige blue-collar jobs should not be ignored. It is unfortunate that some people "put down" any training but college training. Some people are not cut out for college, can't hack it, and won't make it. Yet they might do very well from a financial standpoint and from the standpoint of their own personal satisfaction if they became TV repairmen, mechanics, health-care workers or technicians of one kind or another.

You have indicated that learning and education has its roots in the early childhood experience. Isn't the black community antiintellectual, and doesn't that hurt the black child in school?

The black community, like most communities, is a combination of many different groups. Some segments of it are antiintellectual. In some segments, people read and debate the Bible as the scholars at Spelman and Howard debate the meaning of the works of great philosophers. In the poolrooms and barbershops, people debate and discuss the important issues of life—war, love, and the like—as thoughtful people throughout history have done. There is a long-standing tradition of scholarship and intellectual endeavor among some blacks. But there is a problem.

From the beginning, all elements of organization and control among the slaves were destroyed—families, government, business, traditional religion, and work. The only elements of traditional African cultures that were permitted were those that provided pleasure and prevented depression—music, dance, games, and other physical activities. But it is the need to establish understanding, order, and control in the environment—with the help of business organizations and governmental programs—which stimulates the kind of intellectual activity most useful in school and certain occupations. Until very recently, blacks were closed out of such roles almost entirely, and many still are today.

Although we have great appreciation for music, dance, and all the other spiritual and social aspects of black culture, it is unfortunate that too many blacks devote more attention to these activities than to the pursuit and application of knowledge. You don't believe it? One look at any black newspaper or magazine will tell you that this is true. It is not surprising, therefore, that black children aspire to be athletes, entertainers, or civil rights leaders more than college professors, bankers, and business executives. But it is the latter who are involved in the pursuit and application of knowledge, organization, and control. Schools, as well as other institutions in the black community, should work to balance this situation. After all, only a handful of people can play professional football.

Concern about knowledge and control of the environment is a white middle-class thing. The application of knowledge has been used to exploit people. Why would you urge that the black community go in that direction?

The fact that learning, schooling, and control through the

political and economic institutions is even considered a "white middle-class thing" is part of the problem. These skills are necessary in every social system. Blacks had them prior to coming to America, and many have them now. Schooling and knowledge have been used positively to improve medical care, reduce hunger, and in many other ways. We should encourage black children to gain knowledge and develop their skills, and to use them humanely.

Middle-income people sometimes expect too much in the way of academic achievement from their children. I have seen caring black parents in our community who expect very little from their children, and the children are much less frustrated and anxious. Why would you urge otherwise?

We must train and encourage young people to be leaders so that we will be able to develop the kind of social policy that will not victimize so many black people. Leaders of business, industry, and educational institutions make decisions that influence and shape our lives and the lives of our children and their children. For every mother who is caring and accepting of children, because she is not involved in competitive education or in the process of trying to find a job, there is another who is frustrated, depressed, powerless, and abusive because she is unable to provide for the needs of her children. (The same is true for fathers.) All parents must be careful not to push children or anyone else beyond their capabilities. It is possible to be warm and accepting as well as competitive and achieving.

CURRICULUM AND SKILL DEVELOPMENT

Do you think that black English should be used in any black schools?

Black English has enriched our language in many ways, but we believe that standard English should be used in all schools. Black English appears to be a combination of African language forms and Euro-American language forms, brought together through the contact of slaves with whites in the Deep South.

The fact that black English contains elements of legitimate language forms is not a reasonable justification for the routine use of this form in the classroom, except as an aid in learning standard English. On the other hand, we should not be disrespectful of black English, or dismiss it without trying to learn something from it. In fact, the more a teacher understands black English, the more effective he or she will be in helping a student make the transition to standard English.

We believe that black English should be studied by scholars for academic and practical purposes—for example, to determine whether there is anything in this language form that could help black children learn standard English and foreign languages. One of the strange paradoxes of the language-reading problem is the fact that black African children often speak two and three languages or more, whereas some black American children have trouble learning to speak and read standard English. Perhaps the study of black English and African languages will shed some light on this paradox.

But the purpose of education is to help children function well in the society in which they live. Children from many ethnic groups enter school with language forms or dialects different from that of standard English. As we mentioned earlier, teachers should respect the language of the home or community, but should help children learn the language that will help them function at the bank, at the university, at the computer training program. If they learn standard English at school, they have a choice. If they use only black English or the language of their home, they will only be able to function successfully where that language is accepted.

How can the curriculum of the upper-elementary and middle-school child help give a youngster a positive feeling of racial identity?

Biographies, filmstrips, and other material dealing with successful blacks are particularly interesting to youngsters in the nine- through twelve-year-old age group, because this is a period of identifying with important role models. It is particularly important for children living under difficult circumstances to know about and be able to identify with blacks who can help them feel good about being members of the same group.

School projects that require research into traditional African village life or study the contributions of black Americans or black American organizations can also be helpful. These programs should be made a part of reading, social science, science, and other curricula. Skits and plays developed around black contributions to America and struggles against obstacles will sensitize children to the black experience. They can give youngsters a sense of blackness that goes beyond their immediate family, ties into the past, and helps point them toward a direction for the future. This is very necessary.

We recall a black child who, in 1966, looking at pictures of famous black Americans, did not know who Jackie Robinson was or what his contribution had been to his country and to black Americans in particular. Not one black American over the age of thirty at that time would not have known the story. It is a story that has both a far-reaching symbolic meaning and a direct impact on the lives of all blacks. It is a tragedy that every black child does not know the story of Jackie Robinson and many other blacks whose important contributions have made life somewhat more tolerable for all blacks.

Without such teaching, the works and contributions of each generation are lost, and each begins anew as if there were no past. In fact, the young are more critical of older blacks than they would be if they fully understood. More young people could respect and learn from the older generation—and vice versa. Young people could build on the past and learn from it as a way of gaining direction and purpose. Schools serving black children should dramatize these experiences and serve to link the past with the present and point toward the future.

Can a child's immediate community contribute anything in this regard?

Yes. In reality, Jackie Robinson, Dorothy Height, Malcolm X, John B. Johnson, George Washington Carver, Frederick Douglass, and others are far removed from the lives of many black children. In fact, their lifestyles are and were often quite different. It is important to get people within the community—who are talented and skilled, and who are making important contributions now—recognized and involved in the school program. We have often felt that one of the problems of public schools in inner-city communities is that the culture of the school is so very different from the culture of the community. This problem can be solved by involving parents or people from the community who paint, do needlework, sing (choirs, musicians), are computer operators, and are involved in other activities—in the school program. Such people, when they are good examples and support the goals of the school, can bridge the gap between the community and the school for many youngsters.

What kinds of skills should schools help black children develop?

The schools must do more than teach basic educational skills. Black people have been consistently closed out of the political, economic, and educational mainstream of this country. As a result, many of the skills that white children (and a few black children) learn because their families are involved in banking, education, administration, and politics are not automatically passed on to most black children. This could be done through classroom projects and programs.

It is absurd to have fourth- and fifth-grade students plodding through the "curriculum as usual" when a political campaign is going on—with black candidates yet! English, social science, math, and other courses could relate to the campaign. Essays, stories in the class newspaper, percentage of votes, a study of the campaign issues, student polls, and a thousand other things could be made relevant. A visit to a polling place would make the campaign even more significant.

Candidates, and others, could be invited to the school. Teachers could teach their students how to invite guests, prepare programs, and send thank-you notes. In make-believe projects, youngsters would learn to make the arrangements to purchase land, save money, contribute to drives, and serve on boards. The need to be punctual, efficient, and organized in our modern world should be stressed. Such activities should help to teach children how our social system works, who makes the decisions that determine whether their parents work or not, and what kinds of organizational and work skills they will need to influence or control their lives and the society around them. Such programs could teach black youngsters greater personal skills, direction, and purpose.

As things now stand, we generally tell black youth that it's a racist society, sometimes tell them they will need an education to correct it, but rarely direct their attention to the machinery of change—the operations of political and economic institutions. Can these institutions work for us? We don't know. But before anyone talks of overthrowing them, we had better help our youngsters thoroughly understand them. The same skills required to understand and oversee institutions would also be required to change them. In fact, these same skills are needed to function successfully in a family.

THE PROS AND CONS OF BUSING

We find that we have more problems with the children who are bused into our school district than with the black children who live here already. Is that true because of the socioeconomic level?

Most children can get along well when a school enables them to feel important, comfortable, and capable. There are many subtle ways in which the opposite attitudes can be conveyed. We were told of a situation in which a black child from the middle-income neighborhood gave a sophisticated explanation for the cause of war. A passing teacher said to the youngster's teacher in a knowing fashion, "She must be one of ours." The point was that the bused-in black children would not be that intelligent. (The fact is that many of the children, black or white, who lived in the neighborhood could not have given the same explanation, but that wouldn't be held against them.) Such attitudes will be noticed by children.

The exposure, experience, and educational development of middle-income children are likely to be more sophisticated than that of the lower-income children, regardless of race. Again, the important point is not to make assumptions about the intelligence or motivation of the bused-in children. It is important to provide the opportunity for growth in the classroom. This is most likely to happen when you reach a child at his level, demonstrate concern and respect for him as a person and not as an IQ score, and guide him toward his highest capability without comparing him with or judging him against others. Children from outside a school district are less likely to be troublesome when this is done.

It is unfortunate that so many school busing programs have been the subject of so much negative feeling. The success of such programs depends on children feeling wanted and valued and capable. Teachers and parents in the receiving school district are less likely to be able to create this climate after being involved in bitter opposition struggles.

Is school busing desirable?

Let's answer another question first. Was school integration desirable? We feel that school integration was necessary because school segregation was the sign and symbol of black inferiority. Education, after defense, is the single biggest business in America. In addition, it feeds people into the most powerful positions in other businesses—industry, government, medicine, and so on. The isolation of blacks in schools made it difficult for them to gain knowledge and experience in these areas. This, in turn, made it easier to limit black opportunities. School desegregation destroyed the argument for limiting black participation anywhere.

Inadequate economic opportunities for blacks has always been the basic problem, not busing. With adequate income African-Americans could live almost anywhere and go to school almost everywhere. This would have led to a spectrum of income, racial, ethnic, and religious groups in many communities, and we would not have the serious racial problems that arise in many schools today. At the same time we would have retained and upgraded many of the black schools that are the foundations of black culture, particularly at the college level.

We do not believe that busing is undesirable where it is possible. A mixture of people from different income groups and cultural backgrounds—when properly organized—can reduce the stereotypes they hold about each other and permit a sharing of values. In addition the victims of poverty and extreme racism will not all attend the same school or live in the same area. The danger here, of course, is that the problems of the victims can become the culture and climate of the school. The same is true with regard to affluence. This does not mean that there are no problems in schools that are integrated, through busing or otherwise, but we have seen these problems greatly reduced with enlightened school leadership.

The reality of today, however, is that many schools simply can't and won't be integrated. It is important here to make certain that the youngsters receive the best education possible. We have seen Black Muslim schools, schools operated by civil rights activists and black nationalists, as well as some public schools in which the climate for learning is highly favorable. The principles used in these institutions can be used in other places as well.

INTELLIGENCE AND TESTING

It seems to me that black children are very verbal and physically active in creative ways indicative of intelligence. But some are less skilled at written expression and analysis. Has this been your observation?

Again, it is dangerous to make generalizations. There are wide differences of ability and style within the black community just as there are wide differences in the white community. The differences within groups are greater than the differences between groups. This is an area that deserves greater attention and research. Ability in analysis and written expression is more a matter of experience and training than it is an indication of intelligence. Yet intelligence and achievement tests require these skills. If what you have observed is true—and we think we see the same things—many blacks are being unfairly judged and often barred from academic and work programs that evaluate people largely on their analysis and writing abilities.

We must remember that traditional black culture was an oral culture. In addition, large numbers of blacks were denied opportunities in a society that required the development of analytical thinking, planning, organizing, and written expression. Finally, because of difficult social conditions, some black families developed a "control" language: "sit down," "shut up," "mind your business," "be nice." Language used to explain and share information and ideas helps children to develop verbal and written expression, the understanding of concepts, and analytical thinking. At this point, we really don't know how these factors affected the black child's abilities, but they should be studied.

We do know that certain programs have helped black children learn through rhythmic exercises. We know of black students who have been judged as bright as or brighter than their black and white peers on verbal examinations, who do far less well on written examinations. These observations suggest that there is much that we don't understand in this area; that there is a real need for more research in the learning style of some black children. We suspect that it would be very easy to improve analysis and written expression in cases where it is simply underdeveloped in otherwise bright youngsters.

Aren't there some culture-free tests?

No, and even if there were, cultural difference is only one part of the problem. Most cultures in America are not that different, and tests could be made that canceled out the middle-class white advantage if that was the only problem. (This should be done if we continue to use such tests to measure potential.) The real problem is that blacks and other minorities are thought to be inferior and often despised groups confronted with deliberate obstacles. These factors—past and present—affect black performance on achievement and intelligence tests.

Deliberate segregation and inadequate educational and economic opportunities implied inferior ability when it was not stated directly. Exclusion from important decision making and social roles created real knowledge deficiencies in certain areas. Limited future opportunities lessened the motivation to develop some skills measured on so-called intelligence tests; for example, the collection and storage of nonessential information. Underachievement by too many blacks as a result of these circumstances has been used as "evidence" of limited intelligence.

In subtle and not so subtle ways, by omission and commission, the mass media—print (books, newspapers, and magazines) and electronic (TV and radio)—have advanced the idea that blacks are less intelligent than others. Many whites are all too willing to accept this idea in order to justify their "right" to hold more than their share of the better jobs. Direct and indirect individual and institutional claims to this effect are widespread. As a result, self-doubt becomes a tremendous problem and plays an even bigger role in affecting intelligence and achievement scores than cultural difference.

The scores of both black and white children under eight or nine years on IQ tests are unreliable. They are particularly so for children from families who are under stress and unable to provide positive early developmental experiences.

The casual use of psychological, achievement, and intelligence tests to judge and place black children is unfair and dangerous. The case of the boxer Muhammad Ali is a case in point. He was ridiculed by many sports writers for his "low intelligence" as shown by Army entrance examinations. But anybody who listened to him field questions and give bright and clever answers was aware that he was a very intelligent person. False stereotypes of this kind are made every day in this country because of our overreliance on tests and figures that often don't tell the real story. We have seen Irish, Italian, Hispanic, and other foreign-speaking youngsters judged "not too bright" because of their performance on intelligence and achievement tests when they couldn't even understand the language. Many suffer serious consequences!

You're not suggesting that all black children could do better on IQ and achievement tests. Wouldn't that be a dangerous assumption?

We are not suggesting that all black children can do better on intelligence and achievement tests. Some black children, like some white children, cannot achieve at high academic and intellectual levels because they do not have the intelligence to do so. But they shouldn't have to. The fact that they cannot should not make them less important as human beings. Our job as educators is to help these children develop to their highest potential, but not to frustrate them by trying to push them beyond their potential. Our concern is that existing tests and attitudes may cause some people to assume that black children can't achieve, when they can.

A black youngster from Harlem was scoring very low on an IQ test. During a break in the testing he observed his white tester warmly greeting a black colleague. This made him feel like he belonged, which made him more motivated. When he began testing again he scored in the very bright range. A black youngster in the Midwest was considered a smart aleck and a problem child. His family was poor- to working-class and his mother had had difficulty in school. He was curious about his own intelligence, so a school official arranged to have him tested. He had an IQ of 165! Beware of IQ tests for black children.

Indeed, beware of the meaning of achievement test scores among blacks until we know more. A white college professor in California noted that his black math students appeared to be as bright as everybody else, but they didn't achieve as well as the Asian and white students. He arranged to have them study together, and eventually they performed just as well as the other students. What does this mean? We don't know—different learning styles, relationship issues—we don't know. But we do know that black kids are bright and capable, and we must find a way to help them achieve to the best of their ability.

CHAPTER 7

The Elementary-School-Age Child: Ages Nine to Twelve

IMPORTANCE OF THIS PERIOD

Is it true that the personality of a nine-year-old is the same one she'll have at ninety?

There is some truth in this, but the notion is misleading. Certain basic attitudes, values, and strategies for handling problems in life, ways of working and relaxing gel (become the usual way of responding) during this period. But important events in people's lives after this period—in college or at work, in marriage and in the family—can and do modify a person's personality. Let's put it this way: generally, the basic personality does not change much from this point on. Yet a great deal of personality development takes place during this period and in adolescence.

DEALING WITH RACIAL ATTITUDES

Are racial attitudes among those that gel during this period?

Yes. Children understand the concept of race quite well by this age. Attitudes about their race and other races are fast becoming a permanent part of their personality. But changes in attitude can still take place. The kinds of experiences children have and the kinds of persons they become will determine the racial attitudes they develop. Again, fear and frustration are the underlying causes of racist attitudes in individuals. Children of this age group who have positive feelings about themselves, who are successfully coping with life—and do not have the racist attitudes of their parents forced on them—have no need to repeatedly put down other groups in order to build up their own self-esteem. This is true of all children, regardless of race.

What can happen if parents express strong racist feelings during this period?

A problem is created even when parents do this at an earlier age. But nine through twelve years, for most children, is in a sense their last chance to develop healthy ways to handle their fears, frustrations, and disappointments. Brian can still learn to accept the fact that he is not as good in spelling as Debra, and that's okay. Joe can learn that he isn't liked by the boys because he brags too much, but that he can change. Matthew can learn that his family is on public welfare, but that's no mark on him as long as he is working and preparing himself to be able to contribute his fair share. But if children in this age group are "given" blacks, Jews, homeless people, white people, or any other group to hate—by adult instruction or example—in order to make them feel better about themselves, we are cutting off their opportunity to develop more healthy and more useful ways of gaining a positive self-image. They can easily develop a negative way of trying to "be somebody." Racist attitudes will ultimately limit the success of most people in later life.

Since children are so sensitive to racial issues at this stage I realize that my child will watch closely to see how I deal with problems in this area. What's a general approach for handling racial incidents in a way that will be helpful to him?

The important thing is to handle the incident in a way that does not consume too much of your energy. Otherwise such occurrences can prevent you and your child from functioning well. There is no such thing as a "best" way. It is really very much an individual approach. Your temperament, situation, mood at the time, and a number of other factors will determine how you respond. The blatant incidents are easier to deal with.

The subtle incidents are more difficult to deal with and are probably the most troublesome in the long run.

Two examples of the latter type should be helpful here:

CASE A: One black father, accompanied by his son, entered a store and asked to look at an expensive piece of camera equipment. He was not wearing his business suit and was not carrying his attache case, but he did have his black skin with him. The white clerk responded, "But that costs three hundred dollars!" With a steely voice, the man replied, "I didn't ask you the price, I said that I would like to see it." The clerk got the point and apologized. It is important here not to feel obliged to buy the equipment after such an incident . . . unless you want it. Some middle-class blacks overtip and overbuy under such circumstances just to prove that "We ain't all poor." Your child should learn from you that you don't have to prove anything.

Shouldn't you educate the clerk? You can, but it's usually a waste of time. He was displaying a stereotyped attitude that said, "All blacks are poor." The incident—his response and your response—does more to change his way of thinking than any amount of words could ever do.

CASE B: On this occasion, a black family was driving to the airport and went through an intersection on a "late yellow" stoplight signal. A white policeman stopped them. It was truly a judgment call; that is, it could have been called either way. The driver explained that the light was still yellow when he entered the intersection, but acknowledged that he was rushing to the airport because they were late. The policeman indicated that it could have been yellow, but it appeared red to him. The policeman considered the situation for a few seconds and then told them to go ahead but to be careful.

This simple little incident is just loaded with all of the "stuff" that leads to black and white conflict: the issues of manhood, "Establishment power," and whether the policeman represents a just or unjust authority system. The father could have reacted in a way that might have caused the child to feel that every white person is constantly out to get "us"; that *every* authority figure is constantly out to get us. When a police officer, or any other authority figure, has a valid question and is treating you fairly, it is important to respond in a fair way, and in a way that allows you to maintain your sense of dignity or self-respect. It does not help your cause to become unjustifiably belligerent.

We recognize all of the forces that might cause a belligerent reaction. But such a reaction is likely to cause you to lose your dignity. We have seen an awful lot of "bad talk"—"what I'm gonna do"—followed by meekness and powerlessness. Nothing is a more negative model to your child. In this case, the father was "cool," lost no dignity in the eyes of his wife or son, and successfully resolved a problem.

Was the child watching and learning? While father and son were on the way home, after putting mother on the airplane, out of the blue came, "Black people don't like policemen, do they?" The father replied, sensing what the child was asking, "Some black people don't like policemen." That kind of answer gave the child permission to go ahead, and he asked, "That's because of the way policemen have treated black people, right?" The father answered, "Yes, some policemen, but I'll bet you're thinking about that policeman that stopped us on the way to the airport." The son replied, "Yes, he was nice, right?" The father replied, "Yes. I spoke nicely to him and he spoke nicely to me." A smile of relief spread across the child's face, probably for a couple of reasons.

First, the father's response permitted the child to validate what he saw and heard rather than be bound to a stereotyped response, "Black people don't like policemen. All policemen mistreat black people." Seeing and hearing what isn't there in a specific case, because that is the group response one is supposed to have, is the way a generalized paranoia develops. This is troublesome, because a great deal of our sense of security comes from a feeling that authority figures or people with power will be fair with us if we are fair with them, or can be made to treat us fairly by higher authorities. Of course, you do just as much damage when you pretend that all is well when it is not. In short, we are not saying that you should never see a race problem when one exists. We are saying that you should call it like it is.

Even if the child had not asked about this incident, as it was handled, it would have been a helpful experience for him.

Suppose the policeman had said, "What's your hurry, nigger?"

As we all know, this has happened. Most of us cannot (and should not) walk away from such an incident without a confrontation. On the other hand, it is important to maintain your self-respect without paying a high price—physical and psychological harm, and social consequences—loss of a job, a possible fine or imprisonment. A police officer is an authority figure with a loaded gun. If you assault him or her, call him a bunch of dirty names, and you happen to be in an isolated location, he can beat or kill you and give false justification for his malevolent behavior. Incidents of this type have occurred with police officers despite there having been little or no provocation from the black victim.

Before suggesting a response, let us tell the "little girl and the cookie jar" story to show how people in the wrong react to protect themselves. A cookie jar was placed out of the reach of a daring two-year-old. She stacked books and chairs in a precarious fashion to reach it. Just as she stuck her hand in the jar, her father walked in. Frightened that she would fall, he yelled at her. With no excuse for her disobedience, she paused for a moment and said, "I'm mad at you, you yelled at me!" She cleverly shifted her wrongdoing and any fault from herself to her father.

A police officer who calls you a nigger in a community with even marginal black political and social power can be subject to punishment. But if you punch or abuse him, he can justify whatever he does to you. With this in mind, we believe that it is better to take neither a "Tom" stance nor a "crazy nigger" stance (an aggressive response without fear or concern about consequences) in such situations. Don't take any risks to your well-being by getting in an argument or a fight. Later, report the incident and take action through black civil rights groups, white civil rights groups—or your alderman, councilman, or mayor if they are concerned about the rights of blacks. The important thing here is to follow through. It is too easy to "forget it" after a time or in the face of obstacles put in your way.

Today, in most parts of the country, you can do something effective in such situations. It is important to explain to a youngster involved exactly what you are doing and how. When more effective complaints are made and actions taken, police—and other authorities—will think twice before they show racial abuse. We don't deny that black anger and violence have already caused authority figures to be more cautious and respectful. On the other hand, abuse and violence in a specific, isolated situation are likely to result in abuse, violence, and other serious harm. Such action and outcome are not positive models for youngsters.

When the authority figure is not a policeman, such caution is not necessary, although physical attack and extreme abusiveness are possible. Even here—with supervisors, public service workers, teachers—the most effective action is to bring pressure on the perpetrator through civil rights groups.

The problem of racial abuse from people in authority is a greater problem than most of us realize. Authority figures—political leaders, police, public service workers—should provide us with protection and opportunities. Their lack of fairness creates much of the rage, anger, and ambivalence we often feel toward our country.

Can you make your child overreact to racism?

Yes. There is no need to go around looking for racism everywhere. Every black child in America today knows that racism exists. Again, the important thing is to help youngsters learn to deal with it in a calm, effective way which permits them to maintain a sense of dignity and well-being. At the same time, black parents must not deny disrespect that stems from racial bias. But we must be careful not to call disrespect based on other factors—religion, income, occupation, lifestyle—racial prejudice. (We are opposed to all disrespect.) Calling it all racism can make your child feel that he is drowning in a sea of ill-feeling with no allies or potential allies anywhere. It can cause black children to be fearful and uncomfortable, except in the company of a black group . . . and friction within black groups suggests that even here they will not always be comfortable. Although it is important for blacks to be able to get along with each other, it is also important to be able to function effectively in important situations where there are few blacks, but where more are needed in order to protect the rights of the group—such as on school boards, financial boards, and bank boards.

If you call everyone a racist and every injustice racism, your child will soon learn to do the same. Your child may want to fight all injustices but should be aware that not everything is an issue of race. It pays to study an incident or a situation before jumping to a conclusion and reacting. Is the store clerk cold and aloof because you're black or because that's his personality? Look around. How does he treat white people? Very often what you think is a racial response turns out to be something quite different.

But what if the white museum guide talks only to the whites in the tour group, and demonstrates a conscious act of racism? You can leave, but you've paid your money like everybody else. You can leave any situation where you feel slighted or rejected, but why? You have the same right to enjoy every benefit in the country as anybody else. When you feel certain that the unfair response is due to your race, rather than calling the offending person a racist, a string of other names, or leaving in a huff, you can often gain your rights and due respect by calling the behavior in question to his or her attention. Such a confrontation, when handled properly, will preserve your sense of dignity and force racists to develop more effective, less racist ways of responding to blacks.

But don't you have to be more aggressive about putting a racist down?

Why? You're already operating from the morally superior or "right" position. Because racism is widespread, it makes no more sense to spend all your time and energy putting racists down than it does to keep stomping out rain on a rainy day. It makes more sense to help your child learn to survive and thrive in a "race storm" in the same way you teach him not to get too wet in a rainstorm. If you develop methods to get your rights respected and your dignity preserved without always fighting with bigots, you and your child will have more time and energy to devote to fulfilling your personal goals and aspirations. This is the age when black children will either learn how to do this and thrive, in spite of racism, or feel a growing insecurity that often impairs their future ability to function.

Many blacks get trapped into asking and demanding that whites prove that they're not racists. So what if they are? That's their problem. All Americans are racist at some level, including some blacks who are antiblack or anti-other ethnic groups. The important thing is not to allow racism to interfere with your life aspirations and to force racists to legally respect your rights and the rights of your children. This is part of their responsibility as citizens. Many whites don't want their deep-seated prejudice known. Most large companies and government agencies won't tolerate an open display of racism. Your reasonable demand for respect will be heard in many instances.

Of course, when people ignore the reasonable approach, you will have to be more forceful. But the forceful approach should be an approach of last resort. If you go that route, you are likely to pay a high price in terms of personal and psychological trauma.

Is there any danger of children misusing the issue of racism?

Yes. At this age children will hide behind "stuff"—race or anything else—to excuse poor performance. It is just as important to help your child learn not to use race—or any other jive excuse—to get his own way when he doesn't deserve it as it is to teach him to fight for respect as a black person. Some success in this life comes from luck, but most is a result of good effort and performance. Your child must learn before he gets beyond this age that, cute as he is, aggressive as you are, as unfair as the society is, a good effort and a good performance are still his best chance to succeed. The job of blacks as a group is to remember that they can achieve success by changing the society, rather than using society's faults to excuse poor performance.

A great many parents inadvertently help their children become mediocre, irresponsible, dependent, and even criminal by allowing them to "get away with murder." In fact we heard a mother plead for her son, convicted of murder, saying, "But he's my baby!"—and he was twenty-seven years old! Racism is racism, and jive is jive, and it's up to you to help your child learn the difference; otherwise, you, your child, and his children may be the victims down the line.

Black parents, and particularly black writers and social service people concerned about racial problems, must be particularly careful here. Because we are outraged—about the opportunities we are denied, about harmful myths still being developed, about the fact that the government has gone back on its promise of the 1960s, about the fact that the press and government seem more concerned about the deaths of whites at the hands of blacks than about the deaths of blacks at the hands of whites, about the fact that big business and industry are moving to the suburbs, leaving city blacks jobless, about so many other things—it is sometimes easy to excuse black mistreatment of whites or "foolin' the man" when there is no just cause for doing so.

What can happen to a child who is allowed to "hide" behind race issues?

Such children may find it difficult to be honest with themselves about the quality of their own performances. They may not develop the ability to respond in a responsible and fair way toward other people, including blacks. We recall the black youngster who justified ripping off the stereo components from a white student because, "He's just a rich white kid." When questioned further he admitted that he stole money from his father's wallet regularly. He also made a practice of exploiting his girlfriend and other friends.

A young black man who was in jail, when asked about the cause for his imprisonment, indicated that he was a political prisoner. Asked the specifics, he acknowledged that he'd killed his mother and father. But his dead parents—and the imprisoned son—did not and will not benefit from being allowed to hide behind the racial issue.

Parents have the right to raise their children as they desire, as long as they are not inhumane. That may be the most important good thing left about this country. But, we must remember that in spite of the fact that the society created most of the problems confronting blacks, it is mainly blacks—organizations, professionals, and the community at large—who can "save the children." Helping a child learn to take responsibility for his or her own behavior while working toward the development of effective ways to fight injustice is more helpful to a youngster than allowing him to take out his anger on "whitey" or anybody else without specific justification. Children who are permitted to "take it out on somebody else" are the very ones who make many black communities unsafe and unhappy places to live.

HOW THE NINE- TO TWELVE-YEAR-OLD THINKS

What is the thinking ability of children in this age group like?

As we mentioned in Chapter 5, the seven- and eight-year-old is just beginning to understand that rules are made by people and not enforced from on high. Nine-, ten-, and eleven-year-olds fully understand this concept. They may spend as much time discussing—arguing, changing, and agreeing on—the rules of a game as they spend playing it. While it may wear on your nerves, it is good practice in establishing orderly and organized thinking. Help them move on to the game only when they are hopelessly bogged down in "rules."

Youngsters will improve their ability with math concepts during this period. Your child's memory will continue to improve as will her ability to observe and remember. Her reasoning and general information will sometimes amaze you. Late in this age period and in early teens is the period in which batting averages, rock group membership, the number of bolts in the Eiffel Tower—and 1001 other bits of "important" information—will be "laid" on you, if being knowledgeable is encouraged in your household.

How can I help my child improve his thinking ability?

Much will be learned in school and from books, and much can be learned from games. Naming singing groups, cities, famous people, the streets in town, and any "brain game" you want to make up is good training. Observing the contents of a room for two minutes, leaving, and trying to recall what you have seen is helpful and fun. Puzzles, checkers, chess, and many other games can sharpen your child's ability to think, reason, plan, organize, and develop strategies.

Most important, around eleven years of age, your child will begin a lot of "if . . . then" thinking. This makes it increasingly possible to understand "cause and effect" twice, thrice, and more removed from what is obvious. The good thinker is now full of questions, possibilities, and theories about the world. Again, raising questions that will help your child figure out how to solve a problem is helpful. Uncovering "frauds" in TV commercials is very helpful. For example, "if" the stomach is designed to handle acid, "then" the acid in the soda is not the problem the antacid manufacturers claim it to be. Stimulating your child's interest and enjoyment in thinking through a problem is more important than helping him acquire information. Information is in books and is available.

ASPECTS OF EMOTIONAL GROWTH

My nine-year-old daughter acts twenty-seven one day and three the next . . . even sometimes within the same few minutes. What causes this?

This is not unusual for a nine-year-old. Don't let the looks and sounds of maturity fool you. Children today know more words, hear more complex and interesting things than we heard at nine years of age. But they still have the same nine-year-old emotions and limits of understanding that we had. Children need a great deal of guidance in handling their feelings and emotions.

We as adults sometimes feel we have bitten off more than we can chew, that we're in over our heads. We despair and we're afraid that we are going to fail. The same is true for your nine-year-old. Because she is trying to demonstrate her capabilities to you and to herself, failure at something she considers important can be humiliating and cause her to feel bad about herself and react immaturely. Children often set their own standards for success, so that although you may think they've made a good effort, they may feel they have failed.

Nine-year-olds are often still quite fearful, and too often we tell them they must be fearless. Bad dreams and fear of the dark can be a problem at this age. Squeaking floors and doors and rustling trees can mean danger at night. Illness, death, or violence involving friends can increase their fear. All you can do is hang in there. Point out that, as real as it seems, the dream is not real. The "prowler" is just the sound of the wind against the window—when that's the case. See Chapter 4 for more about death and sleep problems.

When a child acts twenty-seven one minute and three the next, it's easy to become disgusted and angry that she can't act twenty-seven all the time . . . or at least nine. Shaming your child because she's acting like a baby is a great temptation, but it's not helpful. It's best to try and find out what she's concerned about, be supportive, and help her learn to accept a failure and work toward success next time. If your child bites off more than she can chew, help her chew it. Praise her for her efforts, but at the same time, help her to learn to establish realistic goals— or at least to ask for help when the task is beyond her ability.

One little girl we know arranged a surprise birthday party for her mother. She invited guests, ordered the food, and made most of the arrangements before her father knew about it. When faced with the question of who was going to pay for it all and how to get the mother away from home in order to prepare for the festivities, she became frightened, moody, and irritable. Sensing a problem, the father inquired and was told about her plans. He helped her with the party, praised her for her efforts and accomplishments, but at the same time he indicated that next time it would be a good idea to let him in on her plans from the beginning. It is important to encourage and help children achieve things, but it is also important to teach them to be realistic.

My nine-year-old has a fit when I say "no," and then he cools down quickly. Why?

The nine-year-old is on the verge of bringing his unreasonable desires and demands under control, but he hasn't quite made it yet. He needs help from time to time. Outrageous demands are meant to test your concern and ability. Even though he may put up a fuss, he respects a strong hand when it is reasonable and fair. This makes him feel protected from his own inner desires and demands, which he knows are unreasonable but can't control. Your ability to say no indicates that you can protect him from threats from other people and other dangers in the world.

When you feel you must disapprove of some of his behavior—for example, riding his bicycle on busy streets—think carefully about the position you are taking. Are you being overprotective? Is the street really that busy? Is there a time when it's not busy and safe for riding? Is your child safety-conscious enough to handle at least the nonbusy hours? It's helpful to give your reasons for taking a certain position, without preaching and without being defensive. Discussions concerning such issues help your child become a logical thinker, a safety-conscious person who can learn to anticipate and solve problems, plan and organize in advance.

Regardless of the issue involved, don't take a stand because of "what the neighbors will think" or "my reputation." This can make your child feel that you care more about your reputation than about him. Most of all, don't take a stand because "I'm your father," which means "I have the power to make you do whatever I want you to do whether it's right or wrong." You should take a stand because you believe that the action your child wants to take is in some way harmful to him and to others. The more you are seen as a reasonable and responsible being with the power of parenthood, able to listen and change your position when convinced that your child is right or not change it when not so convinced, the more likely your child is to accept your decision without extreme protest. "I'm your father (or mother)" is like waving a red flag at a bull.

My nine-year-old son frequently has "stomach trouble." The doctor says that he hasn't been able to find anything wrong with him . . . that the problem is psychosomatic. How can I help?

Most doctors are very careful before they suggest that problems such as asthma, diarrhea, vomiting, excessive perspiration, and allergies are psychosomatic. Other diseases can cause these problems, and they do not want to overlook them. On the other hand, they can be caused by emotional tension alone, in which case they are called psychosomatic illnesses.

Doctors are not in complete agreement about the cause of psychosomatic illness, but it is generally agreed that a combination of a person's physical makeup and certain stressful or difficult situations cause emotional tension and lead to psychosomatic illness. It is a very individual thing in that the kind of stress that may cause one child to develop an illness will not affect another. Some children will be bothered with a psychosomatic illness for perhaps one or two years and will never be bothered again. Others will have the problem for a while, with a long free period, only to fall ill again at a time of stress later in life.

The problem usually starts with a crisis in your child's life, such as starting school, trouble in the family, a problem with a teacher or relative.

It is not helpful to tell a child who develops a stomachache, diarrhea, or another problem that it is "all in the head." It is best to look for and deal with the cause of the stress rather than pay a lot of attention to the symptoms. Problems at school or at home that could be the cause of the illness should be talked about and resolved by whatever means possible. As we mentioned earlier, where there is severe conflict between parents, children sometimes react in ways that force their parents to focus on them instead of on their marital difficulties. In such a case you should try to help keep your child away from the situation, and you and your spouse should attempt to improve your relationship. If the health problem persists, you may want to get professional help from mental health workers. They will want to make certain that there is no underlying physical problem.

My eleven-year-old son was a fighter and a half at seven. But now he rarely fights. What's the change all about?

Seven-year-olds fight largely because they are out in the world of competition but have not yet learned the fine art of negotiation and compromise. The only way they know to handle problems and their feelings is to battle it out. If all disagreement and opposition from others had to be fought over, children would have time to do little else but fight—little time to accomplish a goal. In situations where others are unreasonable or unfair, your child may have to fight—and should. But the child who is fighting repeatedly at this age generally has some kind of problem —feels insecure, has been excluded from the group, has poor inner control, or has a need to "bully."

In communities where there are large numbers of children with these problems, fighting at the "drop of a hat" or the "cross of an eye" becomes a way of life. This is the case with street gangs. Even here, community workers and others working with problem children have been able to turn these tendencies into constructive work and play efforts.

Less fighting generally does not represent a loss of healthy aggressiveness. The aggressiveness is simply no longer physical, but now often shows itself in the desire and effort to learn, and in play. You need to be concerned about this change only if the child will not stand up for his rights and permits himself to be pushed around. Even when this happens, it is best not to encourage your child to fight but to encourage him to speak up for his rights. If we don't encourage our children to be willing to fight if necessary, but to be more willing to talk it out first when possible, we may never see a decrease in black against black attacks. It takes more courage to talk and work out a problem peacefully than it does to fight it out. Anybody can fight.

Youngsters at this age should also be encouraged to develop other ways to work off their angry feelings. These might include shadowboxing, "big" and "bad" talk that comes to nothing, and teasing. But most important children need to develop the skill to "talk it out" and compromise so that both parties can feel that a fair solution was reached . . . and save face. If children are constantly fighting, they have less chance to develop this most important art.

My eleven-year-old was very fearful at four, wild at seven, and now at eleven is calm and confident. What happened?

Your eleven-year-old now has a lot more information about the world than he had at four. Because you helped him think and talk about sex, violence, racial discrimination, death, and other troublesome subjects, he now has resolved a number of issues that were once frightening. He'll still ask questions about these subjects, but they simply will no longer be as pressing, urgent, and ever-present. In addition, his inner controls are now stronger than his desires and impulses to act to get what he wants, when he wants it, regardless of the consequences. As a result, he is not always an inch away from trouble and punishment the way he was a few years ago.

Much of the energy that once went into "mischief" now goes into doing things that represent achievement of one kind or another. If development is going well, achievement has become pleasurable and important to your child—not in order to please you, but to meet his own developing standards. Again, because of this, he is less likely to do things for which he'll be punished. At the same time he now fully understands that the punishment you give him cannot hurt him; that in fact it is a reminder and not designed to hurt. Also, he now knows that his angry feelings toward you will not actually hurt you. All of these developments decrease fear and testing, acting-up behavior. But before you figure you have it made, remember that the relative calm of eleven- and twelve-year-olds usually gives way to fear, confusion, and much testing and troublesome behavior in the early teens.

WAYS AND MEANS OF DISCIPLINE

Will spanking be effective during this period?
From this age on, it's important to be able to encourage and work with your child through talk alone. As we pointed out earlier, it is absolutely clear to children by this point that your spanking or hitting can't hurt them. We have seen children with poor relationships with parents who just laughed when their parents spanked them. Certainly this situation is not good for the child or the parents. Where the relationship between the parent and child is not good, spanking as a method of discipline can lead to actual physical violence between parents and children.

We recall an incident that reinforced one father's idea that it was more sensible to talk to his son than to use physical force. From the time the boy was a tot, his father threw a football to the youngster and the boy ran directly toward his father and the goal and was playfully tackled. When the youngster was eleven, he grabbed the ball, put his head down, and drove toward the goal. The old man looked at that "husky" and decided that it made more sense for the youngster to score. In short, children grow bigger and stronger at a time when most parents are past the peak of their physical excellence. By this age the quality of your relationship and respect for you as a protector, provider, guidance counselor and, most of all, friend, must be working for you rather than your physical strength or title of "parent."

If I don't use physical force, what kind of discipline is best?

Again, we are not the masters or the servants of our children. We are not here to rule and control them or let them rule or control us. We want to help them learn to control themselves so that they can accomplish their goals and accept their responsibilities. We want to help them learn to behave in a cooperative, fair, and just way. We do this best not through punishment, but by praising and encouraging the child who wants to be cooperative, responsible, and accomplished; by being interested and involved in our children's activities; by doing things with them.

Your child, under the best of circumstances, will not always live up to your expectations and her expectations. You must deal with this. But you want to do so with as little outright punishment as possible—spanking, yelling, or denying privileges. When your child doesn't do what she is expected to do, then it's helpful to tell her about your disappointment that she wasn't able to do what she agreed to do or was expected to do. If you have established this pattern over time, this in itself will be enough to make most children more responsible in the future. Only with persistent misbehavior or failure to accept responsibility do you have to move to more direct forms of punishment, primarily denial of privileges. The denial should be reasonable in time and severity.

You won't always be perfect at this. Your child is going to "get your goat" and you're going to "explode" from time to time.

DEALING WITH PROFANITY

My nine-year-old comes out with the most horrible words. But there are those who say that profanity is part of the black language style.

Profanity is profanity, period, and not a part of the black language style. On the other hand, you should not let words like fuck, shit, ass, and motherfucker cause you to have seizures, see red, or run for the Bible. These and other words are used in "vigorous expression" by paupers and presidents, black and white—but in the appropriate place and at the appropriate time . . . in the poolroom, on the street corner, on the ballfield, in the locker room. They are usually used in anger—when a team loses, when a statement in the press hurts one's image, that kind of thing. They should not be used in anger against someone— a teacher, parent, or another child. When improperly used—in the classroom, in the hallway, among strangers in public places—swearing is usually a sign of disrespect for others and the self.

True, some people never use profanity. We should respect and try not to offend them. On the other hand, these people should not consider others "bad" because they cuss. A youngster who says, "I don't like this fucking sandwich" or "That son-of-a'bitchin' Jimmy Jones hit me!" is not a menace to society, to be drummed out of the human race. What he needs to hear from a "cool" adult is how when and where such language may be acceptable—if he needs to use it—and where it's not okay. When you forbid angry profanity, you can help by saying "I know you're angry, but . . ."

Are you saying that it is all right for a youngster to swear?

Some parents permit their children to use cuss words directed toward them as a way to release anger. This is not harmful when it is controlled anger and the parents point out that such words should not be used against other people, in the classroom, store, or church. If you don't approve and don't swear at your children, point out this fact and ask them to treat you in the same way. When parents talk to their children about their feelings and the reasons for certain actions, the need to "cuss the parents out" is not there. When a youngster is using cuss words to try and shock you, a calm smile or the comment, "I'll bet you thought I never heard such words before" or a similar response will usually make the "bad words" disappear. Direct disapproval in a calm fashion will usually work also: "Come on now, you know I don't like that . . . ," and such.

If you forbid swearing completely, you won't do a child any great harm. That's your way. You should not think of yourself as a "square." You are not denying your child a basic right, and you are being friendly and respectful. The child should learn to adjust to your wishes. We will discuss profanity further in Chapter 8.

FAMILY FUN AGAIN

Is family fun still an important factor in this age range?

Yes, it is. Now, more than at earlier ages, friendship and mutual respect are necessary to help you influence your child's behavior in a desirable way. As mentioned earlier, physical control is less possible and the denial of privilege can create bitterness. Family fun provides the storehouse of good feeling that makes the setting of limits less difficult.

Your daughter will want to sleep over at Dawn's house more often and your boy at Martin's. They will have more opportunities to go on trips or to places without you—school trips, outings with friends and the parents of friends. They will roam on their own more. Toward the end of this period they will not want to visit the Johnsons with you, as they have done since they were very young. But home and family, in a friendly atmosphere that tries to give children all the independence they can handle in a responsible way, is still important.

Including your youngsters' friends in trips, games, and other family fun is beneficial. Don't insist that your children come with you to the Johnsons' when they can be under responsible supervision elsewhere. When you really want the Johnsons to see how much your children have grown and what fine young people you have, tell your children that. They are often not "above" a few cheers, but don't do this too often.

Special dinner treats, homemade ice cream, popcorn, malted milks, and a number of other inexpensive snacks can make home a relatively "hip" place to be. If you can tolerate the exuberance of eleven and twelve—loud yeahs, dig that blue racer! whoee! and so on—you are even more likely to provide a happy home. Don't let them overdo it, but appeal to reason rather than threatening to knock somebody's block off or close down the record playing, dancing, and car racing altogether. Enjoy it. You may never feel or be close to such exuberance again.

"WORK" AND THE NINE- TO TWELVE-YEAR-OLD

Some people call this period the "age of industry." What do they mean?

Children of this age are workers . . . even at play. They are no longer the uncoordinated, uninformed tots of two and three, struggling with strange body feelings and an unfamiliar world. They are more than the fairly well-coordinated and learning little people of six and seven years of age. At nine and twelve, they are ready! They are usually healthy and full of energy and are well-informed about the immediate world around them. They will be paying more and more attention to the world beyond their home, family, and school during this period.

Although they are still great explorers, satisfaction appears to come more now from finishing things than starting things . . . doing a job . . . bringing an assignment or a project they start themselves, to completion. (They still often resist the things you tell them to do.) They want to do real things, like the things they see the adults around them doing. If not real, they want to do things as close to real as possible. They enjoy race cars, trucks, model making, and teaching school and detective play . . . because the play can be so much like the real thing. They want to test and demonstrate their abilities during this period. It is the proving ground for adulthood.

My ten-year-old is involved in so many things. How can I help him get everything done?

This is usually the period when the amount of school homework increases. It is the time when organized sports and recreation present more of a challenge. If you have been successful in helping your child understand that achievement is for himself or herself and not for you, your child is likely to approach homework, sixth-grade basketball practice, and movement lessons with a dedication that amazes you. Now you only need to help your children learn to set priorities and to schedule their time in such a way that they can do the things they must or want to do. You might suggest a written schedule until they have scheduling down pat. Some people are never able to achieve at their true level of ability because they never learn how to organize and schedule their time properly.

My eleven-year-old always has her nose in a book. Isn't this harmful?

If you feel that your youngster spends too much time on her schoolwork, don't say so or imply it. Provide other exposure and activity opportunities. Help her gradually work out a balance of activities. But if children prefer the books, it's okay—as long as they're not withdrawing from people. If they are, help them learn what to say and how to be comfortable in social situations. In the generation to come, there are going to be more black "eggheads"—students first and foremost—and that's fine. We'll still have a lot of linebackers and singers.

What benefit do youngsters this age receive from good work? How can I help?

Children who learn deep within "I can" from their work and play during this period develop a deep sense of adequacy, of being okay. Children who learn deep within that "I can't" can develop a great sense of inferiority.

You can help your child during this period by not expecting performances far above her ability, and not accepting performances far below her ability. Gentle encouragement, "Oh, come on, you can do better than that!" is needed when your child's effort is below par. Your interest and praise for good effort remains important during this period.

Talking about workers, I have just the opposite problem. My eleven-year-old son is lazy. How is he going to make it as an adult?

Laziness is not a simple problem. It can be due to boredom, apathy, and depression. It can be caused by a lack of direction, purpose, and inner discipline. It can be a way to "fix" you because you want your child to be active. It can be a way to remain dependent on you when your child is fearful of failure. In most cases, however, it occurs because taking responsibility for doing his or her part in work and play has not become, over time, your child's way, style, or habit.

Calling him lazy, telling him that he will come to no good end, pointing out "lazy people" and telling him he'll have the same problems generally aren't effective. Help, rather than criticism, is what he needs. First you need to identify the problem. Is he locked in a struggle with you? Is he afraid of failure? Is he afraid of taking responsibility for his own behavior and standing on his own two feet? Have you set routine chores and expectations?

There is another problem to watch for here. Sometimes adults fight each other in a way that can unintentionally hurt a child. This can be a mother and father, a mother and grandmother, or any two people deeply involved in the care of a child. They can undercut each other by providing the child with excuses for not performing well or working hard when the other person expects him to do so and the expectations are reasonable. "You're too tired to rake the leaves today, aren't you?" "You had a hard day today, why don't you let your homework go tonight?" When this happens, the two adults involved need to talk about what they are doing to each other . . . and reach an agreement that will benefit the child.

We have already discussed approaches for handling the preceding problems. Again, when you attempt to break a long-standing but harmful pattern, you are going to meet great resistance. Your child has become comfortable in handling things in this way. He, like we, will feel threatened by the possibility of change. It is important, however, to patiently, persistently but firmly establish chores, responsibilities, and expectations for your child. This is a critical age; if not doing becomes your child's style, it will be more difficult to change from this point on.

I have chores and expectations for my child, but in school they let him do whatever he wants to do. Isn't that harmful?

If that's true, it is. But in some modern schools, as we pointed out in Chapter 6, it may seem as though they're doing whatever they want to do, when that is not the case. But we do know of instances where some whites and some blacks—such as school-teachers, boy scout leaders, and coaches—do not expect or require good work performance and responsible behavior from black children. This is one of the most troublesome kinds of racism and classism.

Children will often regard the permissive person—the one who does not expect them to do their schoolwork, who expects them to be late and disruptive—as easy, their friend. They may regard people who expect a good effort as harsh and mean. Years later, after they've missed an opportunity to enjoy a sense of achievement during this critical age period, they often realize that they were "had." But for some it will be too late. The same "friend" who had no expectations for them because they were black, poor, or on public welfare will often criticize them later on because they are "lazy" and unable to work or perform well.

This is another reason that you should get to know the teacher or the adults, wherever your child is involved. You should make your expectations known and insist that other adults working with your child have appropriate expectations for him or her. Remember, however, to keep an open mind. If the other adults working with your child are not doing exactly what you do and working as you work, you must be receptive and listen to their explanation of what their methods are all about. After all, achieving the goals is more important than the method—unless the method is unfair or unethical.

What's the point of encouraging my child to work and "be something" when I hear people say that black children lack confidence, are easily discouraged, and discourage each other?

This is not as much of a problem today than it has been in the past. Less than forty years ago, the role model of a black child portrayed by society was "Little Eight Ball" or "Little Black Sambo." The message: stupid, incapable, inferior. Today there are many role models of bright, successful, capable black children—we see many of them on television. This is valuable, but we must remember that for most children, how the important people around them behave—parents, teachers, friends—has more effect than the behavior of distant strangers; even if they are celebrities.

Too many black children are made to feel that they are worthless and unable to accomplish anything of value by their parents, teachers, and friends. Self-doubt causes too many children to avoid making efforts to develop their abilities. Where this negative feeling is widespread, any child who attempts to achieve is a threat, and he must be ridiculed or discouraged to the point that he gives up believing that "I can."

Many successful blacks indicate that their parents encouraged them to keep on trying despite efforts to discourage them by "friends." We recall the twelve-year-old who was told by classmates that he needn't bother trying out for the choral club in his predominantly white school because the director was prejudiced and freshmen rarely made it anyway. His parents encouraged him to keep on singing, and said that if he was unfairly judged, they would speak to the director. He did—and he made it.

If you live in a community where blacks have been "beaten down," it is very important to stand strong behind your child in just this way. Most of all you must be sure that your own comments generally support the notion "you can" rather than "you can't." On the other hand, "you can" when, at the moment, the child "can't" can be a damaging suggestion. Again, you must study the situation carefully and respond in the most reasonable way.

You talk about workers. I think today's kids are quitters. What do you think?

"Hanging in there"—undergoing struggle, sacrifice, and hardship, even hard work—is a major problem in this high-tech, push-button day and age. Too many children are given so much with so little effort that if things don't come easily they will quit. They receive little in the way of struggle and hard work as a way of making things pay off. This is less true in the case of lower-income black families working toward a goal. It is a very real problem for middle-income black families, and creates a dilemma for families on public welfare.

Because many middle-income parents had to struggle so hard, they are too willing to give their children too much for too little effort. This practice has been harmful to many middle-income white children, and blacks can make the same mistake. Parents on public welfare have an even more complicated problem. It is important that they are not made to feel ashamed of being on public welfare and that they do not pass these feelings of shame on to their children. At the same time it is important not to cripple their children by making them feel they will be taken care of, regardless of whether they make their best effort. Once a child begins to think like this, there is no longer any need to compete, struggle, face hardship, or develop personal discipline. Youngsters are thus denied the sense of well-being that comes from achievement and the competence that grows out of sustained efforts or work.

Both welfare parents and middle-income parents, from the start, must set expectations for performance and give rewards and approval for a good, hard try even more than for success. Many parents do this, and many young people have fight and determination. Unfortunately there are still too many youngsters who are ready to quit when they trip over the first hurdle. Well-coached athletic teams, wilderness programs, and similar activities can provide young people with demanding experiences that help them develop "strength," determination, and stick-to-itness.

Aren't black parents accused of overburdening their children with work during this period?

It is often said that some black parents deny their children their childhood by loading them with too many "adult responsibilities." It is interesting to note that young children, seven and eight years of age, begin to take major responsibility for their brothers and sisters in many traditional cultures of Africa. Often young children carry younger children on their backs. It is impossible to say whether or not this is a carryover.

When parents force their children to do house and child-care work that they could and should do themselves, in order to have more social time, this is neglect and exploitation. When the whole family must work together to survive, with children helping to take care of the other children and pitching in to cook, wash, iron, and keep house, a valuable lesson is learned. When parents are working or ill or unable to get along without the help of the child, there is a special reward for the child—he or she is a valued and necessary contributor to the welfare of the household. When children feel "used," they often act up and act out against their parents by doing just the opposite of what their parents want them to do. Parents who are neglectful or exploit their children cannot expect to win their child's respect. Without respect, it is very difficult to get a child to behave in ways you consider desirable. The influence of the street, or any other outside influence—which is strong at this age, anyway—becomes even stronger. Frequently boys and girls in this situation act up in aggressive ways, with destruction of property and fighting. Later, sexual acting up often occurs.

Neglect and exploitation of children are usually not typical of the great majority of black families. Because of limited opportunities in the past, many black families have low expectations, and little demand for performance, whereas many other black families' expectations are too demanding.

SPORTS VERSUS SCHOOLWORK

My son is crazy about sports but has no time for his studies. What can I do to get him to buckle down?

Organized play or sports are tough competition for anything. It requires thinking, judgment, and planning. It is a test for physical fitness, it provides competition, the thrill of victory, and the agony of defeat—thus touching and moving emotions in many directions. Much of what is important or meaningful in life is found in athletics. Unless your child has been exposed to music and painting or had the opportunity to be stimulated by science, reading, or other kinds of learning, these areas will usually be unable to compete with organized athletics—that is, unless athletics is an area in which your child constantly experiences failure. In that case you need to help him develop athletic skills.

You can force him to spend more time doing his schoolwork and less time on the sports field, or even forbid athletics. This, however, is an ineffective, even harmful, way of handling the matter. This is another case when your best weapon is not the force or authority you can bring to bear, but the strength of your relationship and your willingness to talk directly to your child about the problem. You can explain why he enjoys athletics, but at the same time point out the importance of learning and developing skills in other areas. You might also point to the many people who enjoy athletics but have other interests and talents as well. You can explain the relationship between learning and getting a job in the future, but this is less meaningful to your child than most of us imagine. The future seems so far off to children in this age group, even though we know it is right around the corner.

We know parents who constantly argue with their children about this issue:

"You're not going to be anything but a basketball bum!"

"Yeah, well only a handful of people make the pros and you're not big enough anyway."

"You play ball from sunup to sundown and you're not interested in anything else!"

"Why don't you do something cultural or intelligent for a change!"

"I don't like that gang you play ball with anyway." And on and on and on.

These responses are irrational and harmful. A parent who says these things is putting down the activity that brings the child enjoyment, satisfaction, and a feeling of accomplishment and well-being. It is better for a youngster to be involved in athletics than getting into trouble on the street—although it's possible to do both. Whether the interest in athletics pays off financially or not is unimportant. The discipline, the learning, the joy of achievement in athletics can be transferred to learning and even to a greater appreciation of music, art, and dramatics. Think of how many professional athletes are also musicians, artists, and actors!

How can I get my child to appreciate these other things?

It is often possible to help your child transfer his enthusiasm for athletics into enthusiasm for accomplishment in other areas. Begin by asking your child to give himself a chance to enjoy other areas. Then look carefully to see if there is some area of schoolwork that is interesting to him—for example, reading books about athletes or athletics. Fulfilling school requirements by doing research projects or writing about athletics is a good way to get his interest transferred and associated with the skills of reading, writing, or some form of expression.

Think back. Have you really made an effort for your child to develop other interests? Have you gone to the museums, libraries, zoos, planetariums, art shows, drama presentations, or concerts? If not, now is the time—better late than never. Your presence and your interest in these other areas are needed to "turn a child on." The feedback or reward in athletics is so immediate and strong that frequently an adult is not required to get a child interested. Thus you must work harder to expose and involve your child in areas outside of athletics. Finally, try to help your child organize his time so that he'll have plenty of time for athletics and sufficient time for his schoolwork and other activities.

Don't be discouraged if gentle persuasion and more exposure to other activities don't spark his interest. Many a parent has lost the battle of the piano versus the football. You want to help your child give himself a chance with the piano, but if it doesn't work, no big deal. You want to be more insistent when it comes to schoolwork. You may have to insist that he play ball only after he does his schoolwork. When this is necessary, it is best to discuss the matter with your child in advance and come to an agreement about the time and place for schoolwork and the time and place for athletics. You will want to try to avoid the role of enforcer. Encourage your youngster to set up a schedule and make him responsible for sticking to it. When he does this successfully, praise for his achievement goes a long way toward getting him in the habit of scheduling his time.

THE QUESTION OF IDENTITY

You said earlier that the nine-year-old's personality is pretty well framed. What about her sense of identity at this stage?

A child establishes an identity by becoming like a particular person or group of people—mother, father, teacher, women, men, blacks, middle-income people, and so on. This process begins with the infant. Love and respect from the person or group being imitated enables the child to become like that person or group, and feel positive about it. Sometimes a child must identify with rejecting persons, in which case there are often mixed (positive and negative) feelings about becoming like that person or group. In addition, a child accepts the cause, problems, aspirations, and privileges of the group she identifies with.

Identification as a male or female, black person or white person, rich person or poor person, gives a child a sense of "I am." Such identification can provide direction, limits, and motivation to think and act in particular ways. People respond to her behavior in spoken and unspoken ways. They say, "You are smart, black, friendly, outspoken, tall, shrewd," or whatever the case may be. Attitudes and feelings about whether these qualities are desirable are also passed on to the child. Through a complicated process a child accepts and rejects some of the outside feedback, includes her own impressions, and the mixture is her self-concept.

How does self-esteem and the self-concept affect achievement?

When children develop an overall positive self-concept, they become free and confident enough to go where their skills, desires, and opportunities will take them. Success improves self-esteem and, eventually, the self-concept, thus making it easier to take on the next challenge or tolerate the occasional failure. On the other hand, people with low self-concepts may never fully develop their talents or pursue opportunities because of self-doubt and the fear and pain of failure.

Although a child's identification process occurs and the self-concept develops at a very early age, the self-concept does not really gel until the approximate ages of nine through twelve. "Who am I?" is the question teenagers raise in many different ways. They wear different clothes, follow different fads, swear off fish or meat because killing is involved, and do a number of things to say "I am" or "This is me." But it is all a rearrangement of what became fairly firmly established during the ages of nine through twelve. A child's self-concept and identity are simply moved to a higher level of consciousness during the adolescent period.

An established self-concept can create a sense of well-being within a person, even when it is not a desirable self-image from the standpoint of other people. That is why there is so much resistance to change, even among people not faring well. Change means uncertainty, readjustment, usually a temporary sense of helplessness, and establishing new identities with no guarantees that conditions will improve. The suggestions we have made to help your children become more flexible will also make them better able to handle change.

There is good evidence that children who have a positive self-concept and are accepting of themselves are more tolerant and accepting of others and of change. You can see then that a positive, personal and/or racial identity is a must in order for your child to deal more effectively with other blacks and whites.

My twelve-year-old son says his hairstyle is important to his racial identity. Does the hairstyle help?

For some reason all young people are concerned about hair; it's an important part of their identity. During the period in which blacks were aggressively asserting their rights in the 1970s, the Afro haircut was an important part of the identity. The accepted style has now changed, but it means the same: "I'm black and that's a positive thing."

But don't encourage your child to think that having an accepted black haircut is enough to establish his identity. The good feeling that comes from accepting black as beautiful or even identifying with successful blacks or the beauty of the black culture or the importance of the black cause cannot be sustained in the face of individual failure. We are sure that you're aware that some of the same people who yell, "I'm black and I'm proud" often do destructive things to themselves, their families, and the black cause. And we have seen people who wore Afros in the 1970s who are now wearing geri curls, hair weaves to give them Caucasian-like hair, and blue-eyed contact lenses. This is because they are really "using" blackness to try to feel good about themselves when their overall self-concept is low. An individual's overall self-concept usually is low because of the way he is treated by important people around him—parents, teachers, and others. It is low when poor treatment leads to poor performance. Blacks who have been well treated at home, at church, or in school have often been protected from the negative or racist message about blacks in the larger society. In fact, the notion of black self-hatred is an overstatement. People who have studied the problem and made such claims generally studied people who did not have this kind of protection. That does not mean that all blacks have not been affected to some degree by the racist message sent out by the society.

It would be helpful to explain to your child at an appropriate time that lasting pride is a product of performance; that black talk without a determined effort to develop one's self, one's skills, and one's sense of responsibility is doubletalk and nonsense. Then go on to warn him about what we call the "crabs in a basket" problem.

People at the bottom of a system that permits and encourages the exploitation of others will be the most destructive to each other—regardless of race, religion, or anything else. They will be jealous and try to pull back anyone who tries to climb out of the basket—in this case, achieve or simply be different. Starved for success and attention, every crab will want to lead or be seen and will unfairly criticize and ridicule anybody who appears to be "getting ahead." Such behavior has destroyed many black groups. We can't even begin to talk about blacks working together until we help enough children—who learned from adults, or were not helped to correct immature behavior—overcome such tendencies.

Can black children who did not have a positive experience at home or in their communities develop a positive self-concept by identifying with successful blacks and the black movement?

Many black children have gained direction and purpose by identifying with blacks in important positions and with the black cause. A youngster from a fatherless family drew a picture of a man and called him her father. When asked what kind of person she would like her father to be, she replied, "Like Mayor Washington" (then mayor of Chicago). But whether a child like this can use the mayor or the black movement as a source of strength will depend on a number of things—how harmful or supportive her family and early upbringing was and is, the kinds of people and conditions she is exposed to in her neighborhood or community, whether she is able to reach out and identify beyond harmful things in her immediate environment, and what aspects of the black movement she identifies with. If she is able to identify with excellence, fair play, and personal development, her chance of performing in a way that will result in positive feedback is increased, which will in turn increase her chance of developing a positive self-concept. But often this is not enough.

The ways to achieve success—in society, at school, on the job—are learned through contact with successful people. Children from troubled backgrounds lack ongoing and close contact with success models. These children often feel that they are destined to be like the people around them, or feel that it is "selling out" not to be. They often sense the rejection of outsiders.

In trying to help a youngster talk about his feelings about his father, a therapist said, "I'm sure it must be difficult for you to see your father drunk on the street corner as you go to school every day." The youngster exploded, slamming his hand against a wall. As troublesome as he was, the father was all this child had. Such children often need professional help. In many cases you can help youngsters from troubled backgrounds understand that they are not destined to become like the adults around them, that they can take a different direction. At the same time, it is important to help them understand the problems of these adults—to accept them as relatives and friends, while following a path that will lead the child to greater success. In some cases, it will be too difficult for such youngsters to reach out, but even when they can, the "how to achieve" and the reward for trying will not be evident on a daily basis.

THE QUESTION OF SEX EDUCATION

What kind of information does a child need about sex during this period?

At the most natural time possible, when your child is ten or eleven years of age, you should discuss menstruation or ejaculation or discharge in a simple and straightforward way. Bleeding is associated with an accident, pain, or an unhappy experience. If your child is prepared in advance, she can think of menstruation as an important growth landmark. You should explain to your girl that fully developed girls and women have two ovaries in the lower part of their abdomen. The abdomen is the chamber or "big room" that holds many of the internal body parts. Every month an egg is freed from one of the ovaries and passes through tubes into the uterus. The uterus (usually called the womb) is like a small, oval room. It, too, lies in the abdomen. Because many people refer to the abdomen as the stomach, young children often become confused and think that a baby can come out of the stomach and can result from overeating. To prevent confusion, you should explain that the womb and ovaries are separate from the stomach, which also lies in the abdomen.

If a man and woman have sexual intercourse during the time that the egg is released, the egg can join with the sperm from the man. The joined egg and sperm attaches itself to the wall of the uterus and begins to grow. It is then called a fetus. A cord develops between the fetus and the wall of the uterus. Nourishment passes from the mother to the baby by way of the blood vessels inside the cord. As the baby grows, the uterus expands to make room for it. After about nine months the baby is fully developed and is pushed out of the uterus through the vagina.

If the egg does not become fertilized (joined with the sperm of a man) the egg and the lining or wall of the uterus peels off and passes through the vagina out of the body. This lining is a bloody, meshy mucus and does not contain any body tissue that is needed. This material is the blood of the monthly period.

The lining of the wall of the uterus is needed when a woman is going to have a baby. It does not peel off during pregnancy and that's why there is no menstrual period when a woman is expecting. Instead, the lining expands and becomes a solid disc-like form called the placenta (or "afterbirth"), which nourishes the growing fetus. It is expelled at the time of birth.

Explain it in words your child will understand. Don't go on and on to the point that your youngster is made uneasy. It may help—as with all complicated or potentially touchy discussions —to talk about the matter at different times and in different ways and not "snow" your youngster all at once.

There are many false explanations given about how a woman has a baby. For this reason, you should explain that it only occurs when a woman has sexual intercourse with a mature boy or man.

Explain, but don't overexplain, that menstruation is normal and desirable. As with everything else, children will have doubts when you overexplain. Be sure to tell your child that being able to grow and possibly have children is something that a girl should be proud and happy about. On the other hand, you don't want to indicate that it's her duty or her responsibility to have children when she grows up. You also don't want to suggest that a woman's role is to have babies and rear children while their husbands follow careers. It is around the discussion of these issues that boys and girls begin to firmly establish their identities, and any harmful or negative suggestions that you make during this period can be very difficult for them to overcome later on.

Some parents talk about menstruation as if it's a woman's burden—unpleasant, indecent, and unnatural. Such attitudes can increase a child's likelihood of having problems about menstruation throughout life. Also, a mother complaining loudly and demanding sympathy at the time of her own menstruation can also have a harmful effect on a young girl. Negative feelings about menstruation can negatively affect one's attitude about sex or the sex act. Menstruation should be regarded as a normal, healthy body function. See Chapter 8 for additional discussion about menstruation.

Should I discuss sexual intercourse?

You mentioned it when you discussed how the sexual organs work. Generally it is best not to flood children with information or tell all at the same time. Discussions about sex should be ongoing, and different aspects should be discussed at different and natural times. A book explaining sex, a pet having sex, or a television comment about sex may spark a question from your child that leads to a discussion about sexual intercourse.

You can acknowledge in a natural way that adults—young and old—have a sex life; that people have sex in order to have children and for pleasure, out of a closeness and good feeling for each other. You need not give the details or you may want to give them a book that explains. Most children won't ask for details, but it's normal to explain that the male penis is placed in the female vagina. You can point out that one day when they are young adults, they may feel very strongly toward someone with whom they may have sex.

You should point out that sex is a private matter, so that you don't ask people about their sex life. You should point out that youngsters are not ready to have sex until they have given themselves a chance to grow up some, to have good control over their feelings, and to be able to make good judgments about what they want in life.

In the past many of us didn't tell children about diseases that can be contacted through sexual intercourse. Because AIDS (Acquired Immunodeficiency Syndrome) can cause death, it is necessary to discuss sex-related diseases. We shouldn't use the threat of AIDS or any other disease to convince them to delay sex. But the disease problem should be discussed in terms of self-protection and responsibility to others. Everyone knows that people are being urged to use condoms for protection. But even condoms are not 100 percent safe. Intravenous drug users and people who have sex with strangers or many different partners, and practice anal sex, are at highest risk themselves, and are most likely to pass AIDS on to others.

I can't talk to my child about sex. What should I do?

You should try again. It is preferable that parents themselves discuss sex with their children. This takes the mystery, intrigue, and unnaturalness out of the whole matter. But if you can't, you can't. Most of us were reared to think of and treat sex in a hush-hush way. One thing you can do in this case is provide your children with books that discuss sex in a clear, nonstimulating but straightforward manner. Even when you are able to talk to your children about sex, it's helpful to provide them with a well-written book explaining the essential facts. There are many helpful pamphlets and books available about AIDS and the other venereal diseases. We advise you to read the book first, to make certain that it is helpful but does not try to excite or stimulate your child.

Some mothers can't talk to their sons and some fathers can't talk to their daughters about sex. If you can't and there is only one parent, again a book can be helpful. Or you might call upon close relatives or friends to help you out. Be careful here. You should have a talk beforehand with the person who discusses sex with your child, to agree on how the matter should be handled. Make certain that the person you ask will not take advantage of your child—stimulating or even assaulting him or her. Even you, yourself, must be careful not to overstimulate your child. But don't worry about the fleeting sexual thought or feeling you have about your child. We all have them. The mature adult does not act on them, although frequent, extreme, harsh physical punishment is sometimes a parent's way to avoid facing these feelings or acting on them. For more information on sexual development, see Chapter 8 on adolescence and young adulthood.

MORALITY AND RELIGION

Where is moral development during this period?

For many children of this age, good behavior still means being fair so that others will be fair with you. For many others, "right" is that which pleases or helps other people. For still others, doing right comes out of a respect for authority and a sense of a need to maintain law and the social order—whether that order is the school, the home, or the society. Some children—capable of and allowed to develop theories about themselves, life, and society

—begin to think of right in terms of personal values and opinions. This latter group, around eleven and twelve years of age, will generally go along with authority figures—you, the teacher, the president—but they will begin to consider and raise challenging questions about the way the society is run, the way they are treated, and the way others are treated. Some of this is a challenge of your right to authority. Some of it is an effort to be less dependent and beholden to you. Some of it is a real search for a code of ethics or a way to behave that makes sense to them. Many, if not most, people operate at the "I'll be good if you'll be good" and the "law and order" stages throughout life.

Children who grow up in a climate of fairness but who are permitted to challenge and question the rules and the rule-makers of society, and are encouraged to work out the best ways of handling or solving problems with you, with teachers, and with other children, are most likely to learn ethical values that are personal and flexible, yet generally in keeping with the rules of the society. Such children, as adults, do not say, "My country, right or wrong." They are more likely to say, "My country, and if it's wrong, I'm going to try to help make it right." Children who are forced to do what you or other authority figures tell them to do are more likely to become strong believers in law and order, even when the laws are unjust and the order is through force.

Bucking the law or rebelling against honest authority figures without a cause can also be damaging to your child's development and can lead to future problems.

We are a religious family. Won't that take care of moral development in our children?

There is nothing wrong with going to church or being religious. Any method that a person can use to find dignity and respect and receive encouragement for treating others the same way is fine. But just going to church alone won't do the job. Some people attend church regularly and still behave in an immoral way—inside and outside the place of worship. It is possible to be a moral, fair, or just person without religious training. A child's deepest sense of morality comes from the way he or she is treated—whether or not concern is given to the child's rights and needs. In fact, going to church and talking Christianity and mistreating your husband or wife, children, and other people in one way or another can confuse or anger your children. They may see you as a hypocrite. This can make the usual teen rebellion against your beliefs and teachings more extreme and difficult.

We send our children to church so they'll have good moral training, but we don't go anymore. Does this do any harm?

If we were your children, we'd probably ask, "If going to church is so important, why don't you go?" On the other hand, if your children want to go because other children in the neighborhood do so, there is no reason why they should not. But they are more likely to value and learn the teaching of the church when they see that it is important to you.

My eleven-year-old daughter was listening to television reports of government scandal in Washington and out of the clear blue sky said, "I hate the government." What was that all about?

Most children this age are still very interested in the things that happen to people and in places close to them. Conversely, when parents take a great interest in outside events, youngsters are likely to develop a similar interest. But they tend to see the outside world in a very personal way. Who can they count on if they can't trust and gain strength from parents, teachers, ministers, and presidents? Many children in this age group are very aware of a contradiction when you tell them to be fair and honest and some public leaders are shown to be crooks.

The reporting of crime and wrongdoing by high government officials and other important authority figures can be confusing and frightening to children. Your child's statement, "I hate the government," was probably an expression of disappointment and anger in having the bargain broken ("I'll be good if you'll be good"). Television, more than the newspapers and radio, has given public officials a kind of presence and importance as models of morality that did not exist before. But again, you are your child's most important model of morality. You will have much more influence on the kind of person your child is than dishonest stockbrokers or any other scandalous behavior that is so prevalent in this society.

But you must be careful how you respond to such situations. You don't want your child to be naive, but you don't want her to become cynical and have a sense of hopelessness about the future of blacks, the country, or the world. Such feelings often lead to apathy, depression, and "dropping out." There have always been hypocrites, thieves, and liars in the world, and there always will be. You want to help your child understand that the vast majority of people wish to be good and honest; that many people in important positions are responsible, fair, and just. Besides, the only protection against "Doomsday"—black genocide or the use of the bomb—is the contribution of people who have the spirit and determination necessary to keep fighting for fair play and justice.

How can I help my child understand adult shortcomings?

You don't want to justify undesirable behavior. But you can help your child learn that people aren't simply good or bad, that they are subject to certain temptations to deceive, cheat, and lie. Reminding your youngster of some of the things he has done to get his own way—half-truths and manipulations (such as telling your husband that you said he could buy a game when you didn't)—is a good way to help your child understand why adults lie and steal to get money and power. You want to point out how this kind of behavior hurts people and is damaging to country. You might want to talk about how you spot and deal with the con man whether he is your neighbor, a businessman, or a politician. This is a good opportunity to point out the importance of using your vote and how to write letters to consumer protection agencies, legislators, and other groups working to promote fair and honest government and business. Such discussions will give your child an early understanding of how his country works. Most important, a discussion of this kind about what can be done prevents your child from feeling powerless.

It doesn't do any good to "lip" about the world unless you are doing something to make it a better place. Aside from spreading depression and a feeling of hopelessness, your child may decide that you are all mouth and no substance. What great "ammunition" for the teenage put-down of parents which is coming up next.

THE ROLE OF "OUTSIDE ACTIVITIES" AND HOBBIES

My eleven-year-old daughter is in school clubs, on the girls' basketball team, loves games, dancing, reading, and is ready to go whenever we propose a trip anywhere. How much is too much?

This is really a very individual thing. Children in this age group seem to have more energy than the law allows. They are joiners. They are goers, and they like to make and do things. If your daughter is not worn out, I would not worry about it, just enjoy her enthusiasm . . . if you're not too worn out to keep up with her.

If she does overschedule herself to the point of exhaustion, help her learn to limit her activities and do the things she wants most without "overdo." If necessary, step in and rule out certain activities yourself. Simply make certain that the reasons you give make sense. Aside from being overtired, an overscheduled child may become irritable, anxious, and troublesome.

The opposite of your situation also presents a problem. Some parents push their youngsters into more activities than the child wants. These parents often expect too much. We know youngsters who were forced into Little League baseball to live out their parents' dreams, and they tired of baseball and quit as soon as they could. On the other hand, we know of parents who were very interested in their son's playing sports, but they did not push him because he appeared more interested in his schoolwork and other hobbies. Without participating in organized sports, we have seen such youngsters later become very well-coordinated, fine athletes, through an interest that developed largely on their own. Certainly, the parents' interest had some influence, but when parents don't force their interests on their children, the children are more likely to develop a lasting interest with less need to rebel against the parents.

My daughter develops one interest after another. We bought her an expensive piano, and she started piano lessons. Two months later, she stopped. How can I help her stick to one thing?

Every parent is familiar with this problem in one form or another. If it's not piano lessons, it's bicycle riding, photography, or dancing lessons. This is normal for this period. Before you spend a lot of money on something your child swears on a stack of Bibles he or she will be interested in forever and ever, you should make sure that the child shows a sustained interest . . . even if you can afford it.

First, you want to make certain that you are not strongly suggesting that your child develop a hobby or activity area that you want for him or her. This does not mean that you should not discuss the relative advantages of one activity over another. Don't buy a piano or push football in the hope that you will someday see your youngster's name in lights or that he will be receiving a fat bonus contract. As we have said before, children should not have to live out the dreams of parents. If your child has unusual talent, you will know it without pushing. Even if he does turn out to be very gifted, you can destroy the motivation by pushing too hard. Only if your child shows continued interest should you try and help him get the lessons necessary to develop a talent.

If your child has given something a fair try but then lost interest, it's better to let her drop out for a while. There is a good chance that she will want to return to the activity later on. Before she drops out, however, you might ask that she give herself a final chance to enjoy it, perhaps setting a time limit. You might also discuss the problem with the teacher and your child, and see whether there is any specific problem that can be worked out to improve the situation. Sometimes, for example, children think teachers are too demanding. If this can be resolved, they often can learn to enjoy themselves. It helps to find a teacher who stresses playing the piano, dancing, taking photographs, or whatever, simply for enjoyment, and transmits that feeling to the child. At the same time, the teacher should emphasize the need to develop basic skills.

It is important to avoid struggles with children about taking lessons. You want to encourage them, praise their success, remind them that if they weren't successful with this lesson, they can be with the next. But remember that you can't make them learn. Struggles will make both you and your child unhappy. In this case, after a reasonable try, it is better to quit than fight.

My eleven-year-old son is interested in photography, and sometimes wants me to help him develop pictures. I don't want to get in the way of "his thing." What do you think about it?

If your child asks you for help, you are not invading his privacy. If you can help without taking over and doing things your way, you will not make him dependent on you. He may simply want to spend some time with you or show you how competent he is. On the other hand, he may feel that he is a little over his head, and may need some help in order to do a good job.

If he is asking for help, you can help best by raising questions that will enable him to see the problem involved. Have him explain how he would solve a particular problem. Very often when children are involved in complicated activities, they need help with organization. Developing pictures is a good case in point. Here you have to get your solutions prepared and lined up to meet time and lighting schedules. If a child needs and receives help, this can become a useful lesson in organization. Without help he might drop the hobby and experience an unnecessary failure.

But isn't it best to let children learn by trial and error?

Some people feel that you should let children this age explore, make mistakes, and develop their own interests. We believe that that's appropriate before they have found an interest they would really like to develop. Once they have focused on an activity, however, it is important to try and help them achieve competence. We remember a situation in which youngsters took cameras without instructions, then went out and took pictures with a great deal of excitement. They came back and developed their work only to find that they had made a great many errors. They were turned off and "through" with picture taking. We observed another situation in which the teacher gave the youngsters a great deal of instruction in the use of cameras, how to identify a good shot and how to take it, before they went out to take their first picture. Some of the youngsters got very good shots, and it was a rewarding experience—not only in learning how to take pictures but in learning how to approach a problem and achieve a goal.

We can't afford an expensive hobby like photography. Do you have any other suggestions?

Children don't need brand-new materials or kits to develop a hobby. Most of us feel that we are fortunate that we can afford to buy manufactured items. We might actually be better off if we knew how to make our own furniture and repair our cars. By the time our children are adults, people will probably be working fewer hours with more free time. If they know how to work with tools, there is no end to what they can do . . . as a hobby or in providing goods and services necessary to the maintenance of their homes. Old and damaged materials like used motors, wires, and broken utensils can provide much of what is needed for an inexpensive hobby. We hope you have helped your child learn to think and work safely by now!

Collecting anything from old Christmas cards and postcards to baseball cards can also make an interesting hobby. Weaving, needlepoint, making model cities out of cardboard, leatherwork, and a whole host of inexpensive leisure-time activities can be enjoyable. There are some good books on leisure-time activities for children. You might want to check them out at your library before you buy them.

FILMS, BOOKS, AND OUTINGS

I went with my twelve-year-old son to one of the black movies for what I thought would be good shared recreation. But I was horrified by the message of the film. What are your thoughts about the black film?

Several have been quite good. But we are as concerned as you are about most of them. If more films depicted the full spectrum of black life, the films that glorify poverty, pimps, prostitutes, drug addicts, con men, and sexual exploitation of women would be less troublesome. Unfortunately, that is not the case. Many black children from troubled communities don't even know the full spectrum of black life.

One black youngster from such a background got up and left after a tender, powerful love scene in the film *Sounder*, commenting, "That ain't black!" We know too many black youngsters whose notion of blackness is the chaos within their home, housing project, and neighborhood. Most of the black films confirm their impression. This is the message that the white media—movies, newspapers, magazines, radio—have long conveyed. The images of blacks on the screen still reflect the six "S" syndrome—slavery, sin, sorrow, savagery, silly, and sorry (irresponsible) . . . never the seventh—successful. As a group, we have complained that they were not presenting us with desirable models and good representation. In recent years, there has been a renaissance of high-quality black films, many of which were written and directed by African-Americans. A number of these films have been powerful and honest portrayals of different aspects of the black experience. We hope this positive trend continues.

My twelve-year-old son likes to read. Are there any books that might be particularly helpful for a black youngster of this age?

First, let's pause for a moment to say that reading is a great leisure-time activity. Second, we don't believe that black families read enough. Usually this is true of poorly educated families, but too many middle-income, educated blacks don't read either. As blacks, we have an urgent need to change this society, and reading can be valuable in this regard.

The biographies of successful blacks—King, Carver, DuBois, Robinson, and such—can be very inspirational to youngsters in this age group. Books provide a child with an opportunity to read about some of the factors that lead to success without having a parent constantly "pounding them into his head." Books can also provide much more information than any other medium about complex problems and the way that one must organize and plan to solve them. Books are less likely to be as one-sided when dealing with blacks than are films, television, and radio.

Finally, we encourage you to have your child read a wide range of material. It's not helpful to read only books written by people with whom you agree. There is much to learn from people with an opposing viewpoint. You are limiting yourself if you read about your culture only. Much can be learned by reading about other cultures and other groups. Children this age enjoy reading about children their age in other places and cultures. The time has come (young though he is) for your child to be exposed to a variety of reading matter that will open his mind to new possibilities, prepare the way for future interests, and perhaps eventually guide him toward a career.

When a child does not show an interest in reading, it is important to try to find an area of interest that might attract him or her. Look for books about the things your child likes to do— train books for the avid subway rider, sports for your athlete, detective books for your young sleuth or detective comics reader. Reading is a valuable skill—for pleasure and for learning. Encourage it. Books on your shelves and in your hands speak louder than a thousand words.

What are some good trips for children this age?

You've been to museums, zoos, art exhibitions, and dance exhibitions. Keep right on going. But also, think about taking your nine- or ten-year-old youngster with you when you go to vote. This is a meaningful experience for a child. Youngsters have a pretty good idea of what's going on at this point. If they are introduced to the practice of voting by their parents at this age, they are much more likely to attach an importance to such things than other children. After all, we need all the informed voters we can get . . . and then some.

The same is true when going to the bank, when shopping for furniture, when doing any number of things that involve "taking care of business." You might want to take your twelve-year-old to an Urban League fashion show or to a fund-raising banquet for black colleges, explaining the underlying objectives. Children should have plenty of fun but they should also be introduced to the decision-making, problem-solving organizations in society. This is where white children from upper-middle-income families have a tremendous advantage over black and other white youngsters. Their interests in the stock market, board decisions, and government action that affect our lives as much as theirs, are developed early by listening to and being with their parents who are the decision makers. Because of this, they have a greater understanding of the importance of developing certain kinds of skills—leadership and social graces, for example—than many other children.

My twelve-year-old daughter's idea of a trip is to hitchhike around town, although I have told her it is dangerous and have forbidden her to do so. What more can I do? Why do children sometimes do obviously dangerous things?

Some of a child's attraction to danger is related to the struggle for independence. Some of it reflects a child's effort to demonstrate to himself or herself that he or she is not vulnerable. Or it can be a statement of both concerns: "See, I am apart from and independent of you and I cannot be melted down or destroyed." Sometimes it is an effort to prove that the world is not dangerous so that children don't have to be afraid of moving out into it. You can't be with your child every minute, so forbidding him to do dangerous things often doesn't work. If he's in the business of defying you, he will do exactly what you forbid him to do because you forbade him to do it.

If you have had good communication all along, your child is much more likely to stop doing extremely dangerous things when you discuss the matter in a concerned and reasonable way. You can let it be known that you consider hitchhiking dangerous, that you are concerned about your daughter's safety, and that you don't want her to do it. Point out that some hitchhikers have been abducted and murdered. The important thing is to help her understand that doing dangerous things is no indication that she is stronger or better than people who are more cautious. Help her learn that there are real dangers in the world; that she and others risk harm from these dangers; that she should take reasonable precautions to avoid danger, without stopping her normal activities because of these dangers. You can point out that looking out for the self, or learning how to avoid unnecessary danger is a true sign of being an adult. In other words, you want to help her learn to live with the reality of her vulnerability. Of course, if you are a risk-taker or do things that you know are dangerous—such as driving fast—your child is likely to do the same thing.

While we're on the subject of hitchhiking, my twelve-year-old daughter says that it's all right to hitchhike in our neighborhood because it's black and blacks will do her no harm. I want her to have racial pride, but . . . ! How should I handle this?

Late in this age period and in adolescence, young people establishing their own identity identify strongly with causes—in this case, the black cause and the need for black unity and trust. They go all out and everything black becomes good. You should help your daughter understand that there are individuals within all groups who are capable of doing harm. There is little reason to believe that blacks who have lived under extremely difficult circumstances would produce fewer people capable of doing harm than whites who have lived under less difficult circumstances. We have seen young people be harmed believing that black is beautiful and all blacks are capable of only beautiful deeds . . . ignoring and denying the reality of the "not so beautiful" deeds they observe.

FRIENDS AND FRIENDSHIPS

My ten-year-old spends a lot of time at the home of a friend. Could there be something wrong with our house?

Friendships are very important to children of this age group. As a rule boys associate with boys and girls associate with girls. Their favorite friends are usually children who are very much like themselves in interest and personality . . . though "odd couples" do occur.

With friends who are more or less equal, they can share hobbies and play games without the threat to their self-image and self-concept that a parent's ability constantly presents. Until around ten or twelve, you can usually beat them at everything. They develop ways of handling competitive feelings and jealousies with "their own." They argue, tease, support, and put each other down in an important give-and-take way. Sometimes they fall out, starting off friends in the morning, enemies by noon, and friends again after dinner. They bounce off each other and get to know and feel themselves as people in these close relationships. They begin to understand a lot about themselves as they notice what they like and dislike in others.

At this stage youngsters develop their ability to "read" or understand people and situations. You may hear a nine-year-old say, "Well, you can't always pay attention to what Ben says," or, "That Jimmy is some character, anything I have, he claims he has a better one. He sure has a problem." They remain friends in spite of these and other observations because of certain positive attractions. Learning to understand and tolerate shortcomings in others, and having others understand and tolerate your own shortcomings, is an important skill. It prepares a child for close relationships later on in life.

Being away from you, yet being in the home of someone much like you, the buddy's parents, enables your child to feel some independence and freedom while still feeling protected. When they're not at the house of another friend or at best buddy's, they are often traveling around the neighborhood together. Together they are braver and can go places and do things they might not do if they were alone.

Chances are there's nothing wrong with your house. If you stop to think about it, you'll probably realize that the buddy spends a great deal of time at your house as well. But you might want to think about whether you're doing something that makes them uncomfortable at your house. Again, setting limits—even if it makes children unhappy temporarily—is important and should not be abandoned just to get them to come to your house. If there is a problem, it may be the way you're setting limits rather than the fact that you're setting them.

My child often talks about what goes on in his friend's house as if it's better than ours. I probably shouldn't feel jealous, but I do. Why?

You're probably concerned about whether you are a good parent or not, whether your house is as good a home for your child as someone else's. You shouldn't feel jealous. What your child says about someone else's house is not a good test of your parenting. The test is how your child functions. He talks about what goes on in other homes because he is dealing with difference. The way things are done in another household—the time for meals, who cleans off the table, the way the house is arranged—all of this is quite an eye-opener for your child, who has only had your home and your way of doing things as a model. The enthusiasm with which your child makes certain reports—Al's father washed the dishes! or Tiffany's mother painted the hallway!—is usually a statement of surprise and not a judgment one way or the other.

You can help your child learn to appreciate and be comfortable with differences by accepting them without condemnation or ridicule, by explaining that there are other ways of doing things—unless, of course, they are unreasonable or inhumane. If your child insists that something is wrong because it's different from the way you do it at home, you can point out that people have a right to do things in different ways, as long as it is not unfair or harmful. On the other hand, don't apologize for your own way. But remember that reports from the outside world, if heard with an open mind, can sometimes help us to change for the better.

If you are tolerant of differences during this period, your child is less likely to angrily attack your ways of life during his own adolescence. He will not feel trapped into a mold or a rigid way of life from which he can't deviate because you have said it's "the only way." By noticing differences and talking about them you are saying that it's okay to be different, and that your child has the right to make his own decisions.

But what if I really disapprove of how the friend's family does things?

We are not saying that you should approve of everything that goes on in the homes of others. Where others are dishonest or unfair or extremely permissive, you need to point out in a tactful way where and why your family disagrees with these approaches—without putting the other family down, and without having your child going back and repeating your opinion.

Making it known that you don't want your opinion repeated can be a little lesson in diplomacy your child needs to learn. Dishonest? . . . no. Tactful? . . . yes. We will never forget the "honest" young teacher who, when asked by a troublesome eight-year-old child whether she liked her or not, told the truth, "I don't like you." The child was crushed and the teacher was devastated in turn by the child's reaction. There are times to speak up, regardless of the consequences, but never when it serves no useful purpose and only hurts someone.

My daughter seems to be as friendly toward grownups as she is toward children her own age. Should I be concerned about this?

If she likes grownups because she has difficulty getting along with groups of children her own age, this is a reason for concern. In a case like this you need to help her learn how to relate to children her own age without discouraging adult friends. But relatives and neighborhood friends can be good "other parents" for a child. The "other parents" can be friends without having the major responsibility for the child's behavior. This can make visits with such friends quite enjoyable. After all, children have enough places where they must "measure up."

What should I do about bad company?

When you must talk to your child about the behavior of another child, be careful not to simply call the other child "bad." Nor should you blame all the problems on the other child. All of us have a little lawlessness and mischief in our hearts, and so does your youngster. You will want to teach your child that a child who repeatedly does undesirable things has problems, and can create bigger problems for himself and for your child. It is probably not advisable to try and force your child to stay away from a child you don't approve of. Except in extreme cases, the "bad influence child" is not likely to do great harm to your child's development. One benefit of such a relationship is that, if you talk with your child from time to time about the problem, you can help him or her learn to deal with undesirable influences . . . observe undesirable behavior but not put down the person displaying it and yet not get involved in it. This is an extremely important lesson to learn during this age period, and children who learn will be better able to resist peer pressures to act up during the teens and throughout life.

Why would my child, who is doing well, get tied up with a troublemaker?

Sometimes it's because there aren't many other children around to choose from. But most of the time, it's because your child is attracted to some aspect of the other child. If your child is a little on the timid and goody-goody side, a more aggressive, acting-up youngster, with your supervision, may bring your child out to the point of being aggressive enough but not overly aggressive. Children from troubled homes or who feel neglected often seek out the parents of friends for the guidance, praise, and attention they do not receive at home. If you give them respect and establish positive expectations of behavior in your home, some children with problems can learn to change unwanted behavior and develop well.

If you try to break up the friendship, you may have two children acting up against you—your child and the troublesome child—when you might have been able to help them both. When you are concerned about your child's friend, it helps to have the child around your house fairly often, and do things with him or her as much as possible. In this way you can build a relationship that will enable you to influence the friend . . . and to keep an eye on their activities. In cases where the development of your child is going well and the development of the other child worsens, the friendship is not likely to last. There is the rare case where nothing works and you must help your child break the tie. "Friends" who are engaged in illicit drug activities or involved in crime should not be tolerated. Your child may end up in jail, or worse, murdered, under such circumstances. You must take a strong stand in this case and seek the help of a therapist for your child and for the family, if necessary. In some cases, if he breaks the ties after you talk to him about why and how, you may be surprised to find out that he was ready to do so, but needed your help.

COPING WITH PEER PRESSURE

My son stopped playing tennis because his friends told him that it was a white man's game. I think he should be able to play whatever he likes. What do you think?

We're with you. But the pressure of peers is great. You might point out to your son that there were and are many great black tennis players . . . Althea Gibson, Arthur Ashe, Zena Garrison. (The same is true of golf, hockey, skating, gymnastics, swimming, and other sports where there are few visible blacks.) Many blacks are not in these sports because of the expense—they require costly equipment, facilities, and coaching personnel. If you can afford to pay for your child's participation in any of these areas, by all means encourage his or her interest. We believe that black children should have the freedom to go in any direction their intelligence and skills will take them. They must be taught that there is no such thing as a white man's sport or a black man's sport. You can also point out that their friends may be jealous that they are doing something different, or that perhaps they simply do not know any blacks who participate in these sports and therefore cannot identify with them.

Maybe it has nothing to do with tennis. Could it be that they are asking my youngster to apologize because he is from a middle-income family?

Yes, and just as we don't want our children to apologize or feel bad about being black or different from the majority, we don't want them to apologize or feel guilty about being from a middle-income family. Both the black and white media have equated blackness with poverty and romanticized the black poor. This has put a number of black teenagers from middle-income black families under a great deal of unnecessary and harmful stress—being middle-income is "not black," less black, or even "Uncle Tom." This is the age period during which you need to help your child prepare to handle the pressure he or she will feel more intensely as a teen.

It is important that your youngster understand that as long as he is fair in his relationships with all people, he has no reason to feel guilty. It's helpful to point out how you are supporting improved conditions for all people. You should teach your youngster that much of the pressure he feels is due to jealousy and is often defensive behavior on the part of the attacker.

On the other hand, some middle-income youngsters may invite attack because they openly snub and look down on black kids who are poor. Some affluent youngsters may flaunt their expensive clothes and circumstances to build their own egos. Such behavior usually indicates insecurities that need to be resolved. You must be certain that your child is not acting out snobbery that he may have picked up from his parents' attitudes.

PARENT-CHILD INTERACTION

I feel jealous when my child talks about other adults as if they're perfect and I am his enemy . . . when I do all the work! Should I have such feelings?

We all do. Your child will talk about other adults as if they're perfect, but he will come to you when he needs help. This means that he has confidence and trust in you. Children often express angry feelings toward parents and positive feelings toward other adults as a way of showing some sense of independence from you. The angry feelings, while often exaggerated for dramatic effect, are real, and understandably so. You must set limits, express disapproval, and deny your child things that are not in his best interest. But as long as you are fair and understanding, you need not worry . . . you're the one, the one most loved and respected.

Is there a way to avoid some of the problems and difficulties of the teenage years by the way I respond to my child during this age period?

Yes. All of childhood is movement from complete dependence toward a condition in which a person can care for the self— independence. The effort reaches its peak during the teenage years. The severity of the problems you and your child will face during these years can be reduced through the approach you use right now. In fact, as we have recommended all along, we hope that you have been giving your child as much opportunity for independent action and expression from the beginning as he or she was able to handle in a responsible way. This is the last age—before children are fully caught up in a more open struggle for independence—for them to realize that you are pleased about and support their striving for responsible independence. This can reduce but will not eliminate the turmoil of the teenage years.

There are many ways to offer your child a chance to make independent but reasonable decisions, without giving up your responsibilities. She can work out the time to do her chores. He can select his own school clothes. She can decide what she will do with the part of her allowance that she is not required to save. You will be able to think of many other ways for your child to learn to think for herself, if you are truly prepared to help her achieve responsible independence. But don't just "go away" or dump all the decisions into her lap.

It is very important to help your son remember that if all of his allowance is spent on rockets, he will not be able to go to "the show" this weekend. You can help your daughter understand that certain clothing or fads are commercial rip-offs—maybe okay after you have what you need, but not before. It's helpful to do this by asking matter-of-fact questions that help youngsters establish priorities and to think things out, rather than through criticism and ridicule. Too often we don't teach children how to reason and achieve their goals, and then criticize them when they make "dumb decisions" or "get taken."

Not all fads and frills should be considered unreasonable. Funny-looking little hats, shoes, insignias, and so on may be important to your child, because they are forms of self-expression. The same is true of your youngster's tastes in things like music. Where you disapprove, say so. At the same time help your child to see that he will have to live with any undesirable outcome of his choice. You can and should reserve the right to veto a choice when it can be dangerous or harmful or just too extreme. But try, try, try to help him and let him become a good thinker and doer, making decisions that are in his best interest and not against you. When it is made clear during this period that you support your child's strivings for independence, the teenage years are likely to be less stormy.

I have been told it is important for my child to see me actively handling problems in the society during this age period. Why?
In the four- to eight-year-old period, your child was a passive learner about the ways of our society or your culture—going to church, celebrating Christmas—with you and in your way. He was also busy trying to get control over himself, learning how to handle his feelings and getting along in his group. With much of this under his belt and a greater ability to understand and learn, he can now turn away from personal concerns on occasion and look at the larger society.

Hearing you talk about the issues—the need for clean streets, honest government, better schools, less crime, and better jobs for blacks—helps your child identify with these causes. But, more important, watching you helps him learn how he can do something to solve these problems. You are the model on which your child's response pattern will be built.

If you insist on seeing the airlines manager when your flight is oversold, instead of verbally abusing the clerk, your child will learn an effective way of handling the problem. If you write a letter to the company that failed to deliver your couch in good condition and send a copy to the State Commissioner of Consumer Affairs or to your congressional representative, again, your child will learn an effective way of solving a problem rather than just feeling "had" and powerless. When you vote, or if you don't vote, it is observed. If you contribute to your favorite civil rights group or if you don't contribute, this is likely to be noticed during this period when we actively socialize our children through what we say and do. If you don't talk to children about these actions, they will miss an important part of their education.

Sometimes I'm so discouraged by personal problems and racial conditions I find it difficult to be optimistic and encouraging. Can this be harmful to my child?
All of us have varying degrees of hope and confidence in ourselves, our family and friends, our people and our country. Moderate changes in mood from time to time are not harmful.

But persistent and unrealistic optimism or persistent and un-realistic negative feelings can be harmful. This is the age when a child should learn to reach for the stars. Through your de-spairing words and your actions, you can say, "There ain't no stars and there's no need to reach."

We hear many young black parents repeatedly despairing about the condition of blacks in America. Although there are many very real problems and dangers, if you overstate the case or despair beyond reason, your child can develop a crippling cynicism and hopelessness about people, the country, and the world. This can lead to apathy, depression, and "dropping out" by the middle or late teens. The ugliness of the world, racism being of particular concern to us, can become an excuse for not going out and facing life. A sense of hopelessness can also cause your child to remain dependent on you. This will lead him to attack your ideas, your way of life, and even your personality, in a way that a child who is trying to become less dependent on his parents during the late teens would not. It can also cause children to isolate themselves from all but those who think and feel exactly as they do. Youngsters who do this often argue that they are "getting themselves together" or "preserving their cul-ture." In these cases, they should eventually be able to associate fairly comfortably with people who are not the same or who do not think the same. When they can't, they are, in fact, hiding from the problems of the world.

Are you trying to say that I shouldn't face the facts?

No, we don't mean that you should deny reality. You should identify and discuss injustice, on racial grounds or any other grounds. But you can help your child by discussing with him ways to overcome injustice—to keep on keeping on. This has been the approach that has sustained black Americans against overwhelming obstacles throughout our history. If we give up the fight now—because the preacher is no longer reminding us every Sunday—we and our children are going to be in for a lot of trouble.

My twelve-year-old wanted to go to camp and I didn't want him to go. I realized later that I was really trying to hold on to my last "baby." I won't know what to do without children to raise. What can I do about this?

This is a very common problem. Many parents, particularly mothers, devote some of their most vigorous and healthy years, between twenty and forty, to bringing up their children. As the children become increasingly independent, the parents begin to feel cheated. This can be even more of a problem when parents do not have a good relationship, and the wife does not have a career or friends and social activities independent of those of her husband.

It is no longer necessary or desirable for parents to put all of their time and energy into rearing their children. It is best for both children and parents that, as the development of the child proceeds, parents enjoy a healthy mixture of activities, with and without their children. Clubs, hobbies, volunteer work, and part-time jobs all permit parents to have interests that are not related to rearing children. Parents who are not otherwise occupied may, in conscious and unconscious ways, try to keep their children from leaving home or becoming independent. This interferes with a child's normal growth and can lead to real problems in adolescence. It can also lead to boredom and depression for parents who no longer see themselves as valuable people with an important task—rearing children.

CHAPTER 8

Adolescence

DEFINITION AND CHARACTERISTICS OF ADOLESCENCE

What is adolescence?

Adolescence is the time of life between puberty (ages ten to thirteen) and young adulthood (ages eighteen to twenty-one), but there is much individual variation. It is a period in which critical sexual development and social and emotional growth take place. Puberty is the beginning of biological adulthood, marked by the ability to reproduce. The appearance of secondary sexual characteristics—pubic and underarm hair, increased size of penis and testicles, growth of breasts in girls, beard and deep voice in boys—is followed by a spurt in growth. Girls may begin to menstruate—as early as age ten or as late as age fifteen—and boys usually begin to ejaculate—in the early teens or later. These variations are normal. Because their bodily changes occur rapidly, teenagers go through a period of physical awkwardness that in most instances eventually disappears. Early and late adolescence are quite different.

What is the difference between early and late adolescence?

Early adolescence, generally the period from puberty to age fifteen or sixteen, gives way to late adolescence and continues to young adulthood. The beginning of puberty is marked by a rapid growth spurt and sex hormone changes, and is frequently accompanied by psychological turmoil and a periodic return to immature behavior and awkwardness. Adolescents in the early stages are particularly drawn to same-sex group activities. Later, most develop strong attractions to the opposite sex.

After about sixteen years of age, adolescents may feel more secure and self-confident. They tend to be less self-concerned and are willing to devote more time to vocational planning and social and philosophical issues. Parental influence is greatest in early adolescence. As teenagers mature the influence of parents decreases and that of peers increases.

Do girls attain puberty earlier than boys?

Yes. Girls usually go through the changes of puberty two years earlier than boys, but boys catch up by age twenty-one. Remember, however, that there are many individual differences. Some fourteen-year-old girls are fully developed physically, whereas others of the same age are just starting to develop.

Is it true that black children reach adolescence earlier than white children?

No, not physically. Sexual development and growth begin at similar times among blacks and whites. Occasionally puberty is delayed in youngsters who have suffered from chronically poor nutrition or physical disorders. However, black children who are reared in an environment of poverty and are forced to assume adult responsibilities at an inappropriately early age may be socially advanced for their years. Burdening children with adult tasks may inhibit their passing through the usual stages of childhood. Such children may revert to the type of behavior that they did not have an opportunity to experience at the usual time.

Why is adolescence a problem period for parent-child relations?

Adolescence is not necessarily a problem period. Many children and parents actually thrive during this time. Adolescents can be exciting and challenging individuals who add excitement and interest to a household.

However, a very important struggle is going on during adolescence. Most youngsters seek to lessen their reliance on parents and become more independent. Although they usually maintain close emotional family attachments, they gravitate toward establishing closer ties with people outside the home, because they are spurred on by social and sexual needs. But this reaching out is accompanied by much fear. Teens ask themselves a number of questions about their capabilities: "Can I be as competent a person as my parents?" "Will I be able to succeed in further education and training?" "Look at me: Joe is taller and better-looking; Mary is smarter and her father is an engineer. How can I possibly compete with them?" "Will I be able to get a job, a husband—or wife—take care of a family?" "How should I handle my sexual feelings?" "What does it mean to be an African-American?"

Although we should be prepared to help our teens deal with these questions and issues, we often botch the opportunity. At the peak of our own achievement and success, we are therefore threatening to adolescents, or, floundering and frightened ourselves, we may feel threatened by teenagers. We may be past the peak of our physical excellence. We can be jealous of and frightened by the energy, beauty, and opportunity of adolescents. We fear losing control over our youngsters' views and behavior. We see in them *our* last chance to achieve spectacular success, to see *our* names in lights. We can visualize our children missing out, just as we did, in their every uncertainty or questionable move. As a result, we are frequently inclined to push and nag them on the one hand, and throw up our hands or moan in despair on the other.

Most important, we are prone to misread tactics teens design to feel more independent when they are accused of lacking appreciation for "all that we've done" for them. Because adolescence is a time of self-assertion and concern about personal rights, many teens turn on their parents. They become critical of and hostile toward parents—rejecting their views, goals, and so on. Teens say, by their actions and words, "Get away from me." But parents who listen closely will also hear, "Don't get mad and go too far. Who else would tolerate all my 'stuff'?" "Who else can I count on to help me answer all my questions?" Thus, our problems and reactions and our childrens' problems and reactions interact to create the conflicts of adolescence.

How can parents be most helpful?

As we pointed out earlier, adolescence is a less troublesome

stage if parents gradually grant their children as much independence as they can handle; help them learn to be realistic and to
plan, organize, and follow various activities to completion; and
make it possible for them to call for help verbally rather than by
acting up as a cry for rescue. Youngsters who are secure in the
knowledge that their parents support their independence and
accept their limitations do not feel it necessary to test their elders
to find out how far they can go. There is less chance that such
children will disguise their fears by claiming that parents are
deliberately trying to block their freedom, make them slaves, or
whatever their rhetoric.

Be aware that as a parent you represent a threat. Respect
your child's right to independent thoughts and actions, and raise
questions only to provide useful information or challenge actions
you consider improper or unjust. Be aware that your fears, arising from your experiences and aspirations, strengths and shortcomings, may be your problem and not relevant to your child's
situation. Remind yourself, and continue to inform your child,
as we trust you have been doing since he was old enough to
understand, that he is going to school, working, loving, and so
on, for *himself* and not for *you*; that you can try to help him, to
protect him, but you can't and don't want to live his life for him.
Be mindful that teens want to participate in decisions that affect
their lives. They also want to be given "reasons" for what they
must do. Commands that work with younger children, such as
"Do it because I told you to!" are not likely to be effective with
teenagers. Discussion and compromise, which help children
learn from their own mistakes, are a better approach to disci-
plining teens.

Adolescents often pick quarrels and fights. Be aware that a
teen who snaps off a television program in your face may be
crying the old blues song, "Help me, somebody," not attacking
your parenthood. If this happens, one way to help is to say,
"Joan, it's obvious that you want to get my attention. Let's talk
about whatever is bothering you. But you should know that it's
going to be easier for me to talk if I'm not angry because you
turned off the program I was watching." Then be cool. Don't
expect an immediate apology or a sincere effort to identify and
discuss the problem—though you may get both. Watch for an
opening and a cue that says, "Now I can talk."

Be especially aware that you can crush aggression, anger, and self-assertion. Instead of rebelling, an apparently compliant child may turn her aggression inward and against herself. Her silent anger may erupt into highly rebellious behavior later on. Some youngsters become self-destructive, exhibiting their anger through poor learning and work habits, using drugs and alcohol, sexual promiscuity, dating people you don't approve of, or becoming pregnant just to hurt you.

I know that I'm at fault, but the approach you have described won't work with my youngster. We've been at war too long. What can I do?

Make peace. We mentioned earlier that the longer a pattern of relationship exists, the more difficult it is to change. But nothing beats a failure like a try. If things are really bad, you have nothing to lose. Indicate your unhappiness with the relationship, acknowledge your part in the difficulties, and point out your child's contribution to the conflict. Suggest an approach to improve the situation and spell out how you propose to improve it. Discuss ways in which both you and your youngster can be more cooperative. If it works, you will have reached a new contract.

The contract will surely be tested. Are you really going to relate differently? You have to hold up your end of the bargain and make sure your child holds up hers. It is a fragile, but very powerful connection. The glue is the fact that you need and receive so much from each other.

Sadly, some parents not only don't care but also display their lack of concern in destructive ways—through neglect and abuse. Youngsters subjected to such treatment may develop serious social and psychological problems during adolescence. Unfortunately, because of fate and unforseen circumstances, it is possible for youngsters from the best social background—in which they receive love, guidance, and support—to have psychological and social problems. Such young people will need your guidance more than ever.

Are there other causes for the turmoil of adolescence?

Yes. Adolescents are searching for their identity. Sexual, religious, and racial issues, fairly settled for eleven- and twelve-year-olds, are subject to reevaluation, new understanding, and revision. In this regard, adolescents ask themselves, again without being fully aware they are doing it, several critical questions: "Who am I?" "What do I believe in?" "When should I stand up for what I believe in?" Where am I going?" "How am I going to get there . . . and with whom?" They ask and answer these questions through the clothes they wear; their hairstyles; the heroes, friends, and enemies they select; the cliques they form; the fads they follow; and the causes they support.

Could this be why teens are so concerned with where they sit in the school cafeteria?

It is a major part of the reason. Even in situations where youngsters belong to the same racial and religious groups, certain similarities and differences cause the formation of in-groups and out-groups and for-and-against attitudes. "My group" is a way of narrowing the possibilities of who they are and what they stand for. Because adolescence is also a period of proving their adequacy, it can be a time of scapegoating or putting down the most vulnerable out-group, which can lead to serious racial and religious conflict. It is a time when young people ask each other to prove their loyalty to their group by living up to group norms—moral or immoral, reasonable or unreasonable, humane or inhumane.

There are groups and groups and groups. We know black and white youngsters who are friendly in their neighborhoods, interact and play together on school teams, but do not associate with one another in the school cafeteria, where black-white group membership is the dominant issue. Some youngsters successfully defy such group-prescribed arrangements. These kids usually have parents who have supported their independence from the beginning. They clearly measure up to important standards—good students, good athletes, personable—and persons whose self-esteem comes from within rather than from what others think or say.

The community climate with regard to race or religion is also important. Minority-majority ratios can have an important influence on the prevailing social atmosphere of a school.

Is fighting a big problem in adolescence?

Yes and no, depending on conditions. Most adolescents who function well have channeled their aggressive energy into satisfying work and play—academic studies, hobbies, sports. They feel adequate enough, view themselves as improving in many areas, and receive good vibes about who they are. They have learned to tolerate average frustrations and release anger through joking, teasing, physical activities, and so on. Such youngsters are likely to fight only if attacked or in the extreme heat of competitive athletics. But youngsters who are not succeeding, particularly in an environment of strangers or "vulnerable others," without mature adult supervision, are more inclined to fight. They often band together as belligerent out-groups, intimidating, disrupting, and fighting with individuals and groups they believe are successful and deliberately rejecting them. Their path to making their mark may include such antisocial behavior as purse snatching and even fighting.

In many cities, some youths form gangs that engage in violent criminal acts, including drug dealing and armed robberies. Murder has become commonplace in many inner cities and is a scourge on the community. Black-on-black homicide is the leading cause of death among young black men. The easy availability of guns and drugs compounds the problem. Parents must make every effort to stop the random violence in their communities and to prevent young people from killing each other. Violent acts, including murder, must be strongly condemned. Parents who look the other way or otherwise rationalize destructive and criminal behavior are not worthy of the name *parent*.

Parents, teachers, friends, youth workers: do your best to help angry youngsters learn to channel their frustration and threats to their macho image or womanhood (adequacy) into some constructive behavior. Teach such youngsters what they should have learned earlier—that it is okay to talk or negotiate, that manhood and fighting are not the same. This is the last chance for many of these kids. Many violent acts and homicides in the black community arise from insignificant issues—for example, "He stepped on my shoes."

How do the forces you described interact?

The hostile climate of the 1980s and continuing into the 1990s has served to attract adolescents to racial causes. Hundreds of racial incidents have occurred on predominantly white campuses. Racist graffiti and attacks on black students have been recorded. Other nationally publicized racially motivated murders of blacks by whites, and attacks by black youth on whites have occurred. This atmosphere has led to increased polarization of whites and African-Americans on college campuses and in urban centers.

The progress that blacks expected to realize in the 1980s was diminished by continued discrimination and a depressed economy that kept about one-third of the black population mired in poverty.

African-American children are still mainly confined in de facto segregated school systems that often lack quality programs and teachers.

Black adolescents in particular may succumb to despair, and many give up—victims of a negative environment. Others, however, are fired up, in spite of their poor heritage, to search for identity and equity.

Don't identity and adequacy struggles sometimes lead to more troublesome outcomes?

Yes. We are particularly concerned about the difficult racial identity problems we are seeing in black youngsters who are completely isolated from whites, and in those who are taught that it is acceptable to hate whites. At the other extreme, black youngsters of mixed racial parentage who have inherited white features, those living in predominantly white or other ethnic communities, or those who live with nonblack families can experience difficult identity problems. The same is true of those youngsters whose lifestyles are comparable with that of middle- and upper-income groups.

In adolescence, suburban youngsters may blame their parents for raising them in a white environment; for the fact that the only people with whom they can have close relationships or date (if they date at all) are white; for the fact that blacks say, "You are not black." We have seen school failure, criminal behavior, extreme militant behavior, depression, and even outright mental breakdown result from such identity confusion. We have even seen black teens from supportive, upper-income families become hustlers and drug addicts in a misguided effort to be black or identify with their less-affluent brothers and sisters. We have seen blacks who blame whites and racism as the root of all their problems focus only on hating whites, at the expense of their own personal development.

Whites have similar problems. Do blacks have special problems?

Yes, several. The uncertainty and confusion of adolescence usually decrease once young people test their abilities and find themselves adequate; once they discover what their past moral training, beliefs, and ideas will and will not permit them to do and believe in; and once they have identified future roles that are acceptable to them and possible for them to achieve. Once they feel sufficiently independent and adequate, adolescents are able to identify with and adopt their parents as models for their acceptable future selves. That is why, once past adolescence, most young people closely resemble their parents in values and actions, although sometimes exactly the reverse results and specific differences occur.

Parents who are insecure about their own identities have to fight to control their adolescents, which encourages the teens to concentrate on fighting rather than on the real issues of adolescence. Parents who are comfortable with their identity and roles as blacks, whites, doctors, lawyers, African chiefs, butchers, bakers, and automobile makers are living proof to adolescents that they, too, can become secure in their identities.

As black adults we know that much remains to be done to free society of prejudice. As a result, we are still in the process of rejecting long-standing negative racial identities and limited and undesirable social roles, and searching for positive and acceptable ones. This is similar to what is happening with young people, therefore they sometimes display the same confusion, fear, bravado, and uncertainty concerning racial issues.

Our problem is still one of redefining blackness. In 1988, many blacks chose African-American as their preferred designation. Some black parents are not sure how far to push black identity and Afrocentrism or how strongly to encourage their children to assimilate into the mainstream. Most black parents support a pluralism that does not diminish the richness of African-

American identity. We must learn—and teach our children—to be black without being self-defeating or consumed by antagonism toward whites and white-controlled America.

How does this affect black teens?

Adolescents are best helped by parents who understand their feelings or problems and, seeing the situation, call it "like it is." Because we, as an out-group, are angry about conditions for blacks in America, angry with white America, it is sometimes possible for black teens to persuade adults to go along with actions that are alleged to be against the "enemy" even when they are not in the best interest of the youngsters. Blacks who won't compromise are called Toms. This is a very real problem in a setting where guilty or manipulative whites permit black teens to do whatever they want, even when it is clearly against their best interest.

For example, in one predominantly white high school, the white staff put a jukebox in the study hall "because blacks wanted it." We know black parents and teachers who "use" black youngsters to express their own anger toward whites, only to have the youngsters become antagonistic toward their black mentors unless the adults agree to go along with whatever the young people propose. Where such relationships exist, adults can't be trusted to help young people deal with real issues realistically.

We have seen a number of black youngsters hide behind race—intimidate with attacks on whites and Toms—only to have to face their real fears and problems later on, often too late.

How can I discourage my teen from using race to avoid his problems?

Again, you can be most effective by teaching your adolescent to "see it like it is." One eighteen-year-old college freshman complained that he was given a "D" because he was black. His roommate said, "Oh, I thought you got it because you had your behind in the sack during the man's class." If you have acknowledged racial injustice—without seeing it where it doesn't exist —and taught your youngster to keep working toward his goals in spite of it, to fight it in an effective but non-self-destructive way, your adolescent is more likely to be like the latter roommate.

Educate your teen to beware of people who talk "angry black" to cover up personal hostility, petty jealousy, and greed. Too many black youngsters have been led astray by ego-trippers long on talk, but short on commitment to blacks—and to the youth they lead out on a limb. It is important to recognize, however, that many militants are deeply sincere in their commitment to blacks and are not attempting to be exploitive.

Why is the racial identity problem more difficult for black teens who have little or no contact with whites? I would think that it would be easier.

The distortions of reality so common in adolescence are best brought into line by exposure to reality. Many blacks have never met a reasonably fair white person who displays all the strengths and weaknesses of all other human beings. Thus, it is possible to endow whites with imaginary strengths, weaknesses, and negative intents toward blacks. It is easier to punch a stereotype to help establish one's own identity than it is to attack a real person, but positive blackness based on anti-whiteness is as hollow as the reverse. When a stereotype is all an adolescent has to go on, she can get hung up on that view, reduce the problems of her life by blaming them on "the man," and not move beyond this simplistic level of identity and adaptation.

What causes special identity problems for black youngsters who are considered to be out of the black community mainstream?

For different and complex reasons many whites and a few misled blacks have defined blackness in America in terms of poverty, broken homes, troubled communities; ability in athletics; singing, dancing, pimping, and mugging; hating whites; and not being intelligent enough to pursue academic subjects. White racists trying to keep blacks from moving into positions of power by improving our lot would like to convince us that to be truly black we must meet the stated definition of blackness.

Unless you and your youngster fit this definition, you may be categorized as "white," "not black," or "not black enough." This false stereotype is the cause of the absolute terror and psychosocial paralysis we see in some black students from low-income families whose status as students means passage out of this black stereotype. It is a source of great conflict for black teens who would like to maintain friendships with blacks and whites, who enjoy Beethoven as much as Stevie Wonder, who prefer algebra to football, and so on. This confusion reaches its extreme when black students accuse other black students of "acting white" because they work hard and achieve academic success.

Black parents who have mixed feelings about being black can create severe identity problems for their youngsters. We know several youngsters who were reared in mostly white communities by parents who preferred to mingle with whites. When the youngsters reached dating age, however, the black side of their identity suddenly emerged. Parents who had encouraged their children to associate only with whites then expressed strong disapproval of interracial dating. The youngsters, uncomfortable with blacks, tried to repress interest in the opposite sex, which led them to doubt their sexual adequacy and, in several instances, resulted in serious psychological problems.

What steps can I, a white parent, take to help my black youngster accept her identity?

We have known teens of interracial marriages or adoptions who have only the usual racial identity problems and others who have more serious problems. If you have talked candidly all along about your interracial relationship, others' attitudes toward it, and the quality of black-white relationships in general, your teen is less likely to be plagued by identity problems. If overall development has taken place within a positive family relationship, the likelihood of such problems is small. We hope that you have helped your youngster to appreciate the full range of her black heritage rather than trying to compensate for your relationship by being blacker than blacks.

Children of mixed blood are labeled black by a society that defines anyone with African ancestry as black. We trust you have not asked your child to reject the black or white part of herself or encouraged her to wear her white heritage as a badge to compensate for being black. Your teen may accuse you of making her abnormal. Recognize it for what it is—the adolescent-attack-in-the-service-of-independence ploy. Guilt and fighting back only make matters worse. If your daughter, like many mixed children, looks almost entirely Caucasian, she may encounter special difficulties. Again, help her deal with the real fear, by assuring her that it's possible to be black and white and okay, and that you will continue to love her whatever her future choices of friends, goals, and causes.

Teenagers may turn on their parents after being rebuffed in mixed dating efforts or similar rejections. That is why it is important for your child to understand her role as a black and society's response to blackness. It is also the reason your teen should have contact with blacks of similar background and interests—to appreciate the fact that she is not a racial nonperson, without a racial identity. If you have not talked out these issues previously, it may not be too late to do so.

How can I support a positive black identity during my son's adolescence?

Your ongoing interest and support will give your youngster a positive sense of himself as a person. This makes it possible for him to achieve many of his goals and to view himself as competent and worthwhile. Talk about, have him read about, and expose him to African-American culture and black achievement within the total culture. "Shoot down" negative and racist attitudes about blacks, and offer logical explanations for problems within the black community. Most important, help him understand that white racist attitudes and behavior are the problems of white racists, and are no measure of his value and worth as a person. Continue this guidance and support as long as your son is in your care.

Idealistic, action-oriented adolescents who want to make their mark will want to work toward abolishing racial injustices. We must help them find constructive ways to accomplish their objective. The first and most important is their own personal development. We will discuss others. All of these efforts can produce black, proud, and capable young adults.

My son, who is about to graduate from high school, already has plenty of freedom, but he often talks of his need for freedom. What does he mean?

Most teens are tired of being in an obviously dependent situation, even when they are allowed to make some responsible decisions. That is why, after high school, it is best for them to leave their parents' homes to attend college, enter the military or other training programs, or get a job and live in an apartment. If your son appears obsessed by the notion of freedom, take a closer look and listen.

This is often the cry of a teen in conflict who is unable to make a wise career decision or love choice or break away from the comfort of the parental nest. Recall that these and other issues are related to adequacy and identity concerns. Try to avoid conflict around the "freedom" issue in order to help your son see what is really going on. True freedom is an inner quality—an ability to observe, feel, and act independently in line with personal needs, beliefs, and humane goals. Independent people are free to live with their parents but don't *have* to; they can wear jeans to church but don't *have* to; they can disagree with a friend but don't *have* to; and so on.

Point out that minor rules and restrictions for individuals protect the major rights and freedoms of all. Cite as an example that household rules alleviate a great deal of worry, confusion, and general difficulty for your entire family.

VALUES, MORALS AND ATTITUDES

Do most black youths distrust whites?

No one knows for sure to what extent black youths distrust whites. It certainly depends on their individual experiences with white people and the degree of racial discrimination they have experienced.

Is it true that black youths are anti-Semitic?

No. Some black teenagers are hostile toward some whites, including Jews, whom they identify primarily as white people. Black youths are probably less anti-Semitic than antiwhite, perhaps because many Jews have been involved in the civil rights movement and other liberal causes. But some black teens may express displeasure with Jewish groups they believe are not supportive enough of affirmative action. Young blacks are occasionally involved in anti-Semitic incidents.

How can I help my teenager acquire a fair attitude toward whites? Would an integrated school help?

Emotionally stable youngsters who have had positive experiences with whites—relationships of fairness and mutual respect—have no reason to stereotype an entire race. However, inner-city black children who are forced to attend segregated schools, and have little opportunity to interact positively with whites may have a different attitude. It is therefore not surprising that many of them resent the entire white community. When discussing this issue with teens, don't preach or try to make them admit that they are being unfair. Raising questions about the charges they make about whites helps them see that they are generalizing unfairly. Examine your own opinions before you make generalizations. If you have a firm commitment to fairness, your youngster will probably adopt a similar attitude.

Sending your youngster to an integrated school might help, but it could have the opposite effect if the school is one in which racial conflict is common. In addition, adolescence is a difficult time and a period when racial differences are likely to flare. Feelings of adequacy are so necessary that youngsters who feel negative about themselves are likely to try to put down members of another race to make themselves feel superior. Some youngsters in all-white, middle-income areas, who have been taught not to put down blacks openly, belittle the most vulnerable white groups in their community instead.

Standards have changed so quickly that I am confused. Sometimes I think our teens are in real trouble and at other times I think they are great. What do you think?

It is confusing, because so much has changed so fast. Youngsters are disenchanted with adults' management of society; they deplore racism, war, political corruption, and persistent poverty. Adolescents reject these problems, but they certainly don't have solutions. They are going through a period of trial and error, grappling with issues as minor as appropriate dress through larger issues such as trial marriage and relationship with authority.

The best approach is for parents to be receptive to new ideas and practices and not try to impose the standards of our childhood on our children. *The test to apply to a youthful idea, attitude, or behavior is whether it is humane or not.* Parents who want to maintain their standards will find that teens who are well adjusted will respect these practices—if you respect theirs.

Isn't it true that most teenagers adopt the values of their friends rather than those of their parents?

Only in some areas. Music and entertainment, fashion and clothes, and language styles are the fields in which peer group influence is strongest. However, the basic moral and social values that teenagers adhere to are most likely to be those they learned at home. These are absorbed through the years, particularly in the late preteens, but what you say and do in their early teens has great impact.

Teens are fairly closemouthed about their activities—at school, on teams, at parties. But they raise many questions when they try to organize their thoughts about work, competition, race, class, and so on. Preteens want to know why they live in certain neighborhoods, why they can't vacation in Nigeria, why the houses in certain neighborhoods are run down. Early teens may ask the same questions but generally in a more philosophical context. For example: Why are there wars? Why do some people have more money than others?

Don't dismiss these serious and personal questions. "Who am I? What should I believe? What should I stand for?" Your answers can persuade your youngster to become fair or unfair in his assessment of other people, or to become satisfied or dissatisfied with his status. Your casual words of encouragement or comments on life can become powerful organizing forces, values, and attitudes: "Nothing beats a failure but a try." "A man's word is his bond." "The world loves a gracious winner." And so on.

Thus, talks with your teen should be fun, but keep an ear open for the questions. Remember that your attitude and how you express it can help your child learn to "keep on keeping on" or give up, respect or abuse people, and so on. The basic attitudes, values, and morals have been forming all along, but youngsters in their teens are building from their learning a code of ethics that will probably remain with them for the rest of their lives.

COPING WITH TEENAGERS

Are the problems of teenagers today greater than those young people faced a few decades ago?

They very well may be. The issues that confront today's teenagers are profound—sexual emancipation, feminism, rapidly expanding communications and technology, a diverse multicultural population, environmental concerns, and serious weaknesses in the American economy. With a rapidly changing society and family structure, the transition from youth to adulthood presents a difficult and unfamiliar challenge.

Our children accuse us of not taking their ideas seriously. But some of their opinions do seem silly, don't they?

That can be a problem. Some of the opinions teenagers express do appear foolish to adults. However, many adults have far-fetched ideas, too. Try to take your children's opinions seriously and express your differences in the same tactful way you would use with an adult. Remember that teens are exploring and will eventually reject many far-out ideas themselves. But excessive teasing and ridicule can cause them to cling to ideas they would otherwise discard.

My thirteen-year-old has become a real show-off, especially around girls. How can I stop this behavior?

Many early adolescents go through a period of exhibitionism as a means of convincing themselves of their adequacy. Showing off is also a first awkward attempt to attract the attention of girls. Anything more active—holding hands or dating—is too threatening for most youngsters at this stage. A show-off will gradually discover more mature ways to establish relationships; he will not necessarily become a conceited adult. You can handle particularly outrageous exhibitions with a little good-natured bantering—"The macho act again, huh?" or a similar quip. But do not put him down—and don't use the tactic too often. Saying, "Okay, that's enough," without anger or agitation, can usually control excessively undesirable behavior, provided your parent-child relationship is basically good.

Our thirteen-year-old daughter seems to challenge everything as if to show us up. How should I handle this?

Playful banter can also be useful in this situation—for example, "Here comes the Supreme Court again." A backdrop of good family interaction permits this sort of humor, but refrain if it seems to damage your daughter's spirit or leads to more than a smile and checking of an extreme statement. Sometimes you can simply point out that she doesn't have to dispute everything, that you are glad she has her own opinion, that you respect it; but encourage her to be objective and accurate in presenting challenging viewpoints. Your failure to offer a positive alternative can contribute to the development of negative thinking on her part. If, however, she is backed against a wall and is made to feel embarrassed, drop it. Who needs a victory at that price?

The slightest teasing hurts the feelings of our fourteen-year-old daughter. Is something wrong with her?

As we indicated, teenagers who are trying on new identities, are sometimes quite sensitive to critical remarks about their various fads, fashions, and customs. Harsh teasing makes a teenager feel that she is not respected. Teasing and sarcasm often disguise thinly veiled hostility and rejection and should therefore be avoided, unless you have a very close relationship with your teenager. Because advertising pressures girls to be physically desirable, any slight criticism or teasing about their appearance may cause them to feel unattractive. You must therefore teach your daughter that beauty is achieved by developing inner standards, not by pleasing her peers. When she shows you something of which you approve, adding, "How do *you* like it?" can be a boost to her ego.

My fourteen-year-old, who used to be quiet and calm, has lately begun to have temper outbursts at the slightest provocation. Is this to be expected?

Teenagers undergo many frustrations because of sexual and psychological changes and new social roles. It is not uncommon for them to have periods of sensitivity and tantrums. Although parents should try to understand this behavior, they must not permit abuse of themselves or other family members.

My fourteen-year-old daughter has recently begun to act very flirtatious toward her father. Is that normal?

It is not unusual for early adolescents to show renewed interest in the parent of the opposite sex. The teenager will later transfer such feelings to an unrelated member of the opposite sex. Parents must be careful not to respond to teenage interest with fear, rejection, or overseductiveness. Try to take her behavior in stride, but take pains *not* to encourage it.

My fifteen-year-old son seems to develop crushes on older women: last year a neighbor, this year another friend. Should I consider this a problem?

Many teenage boys develop crushes on older women. These are usually short-lived and do not lead to anything more serious, especially if the women don't encourage your son's attentions.

My fifteen-year-old daughter objects to everything I say. Sometimes she says she hates me. How can a mother cope with this?

Adolescents, in the process of asserting their independence, may become quite angry at parents whom they view as too controlling. Parents should expect such outbursts from time to time; these hostile feelings seldom last long. Nonetheless, if particular issues arouse conflict between the two of you, try to work them out. Stop to listen and talk with your daughter. Not everything is "just a teenage stage." We can frequently bring about positive changes in our relationship with our teens by demonstrating a willingness to be fair without letting them do whatever they desire.

Our two teenage girls call us and older blacks "Uncle Toms."
How can we best handle this?

Many young blacks lack a historical perspective. They view the necessary adaptations of African-Americans to white oppression as selling out. The risk in being outspoken about racial matters is far less today than it once was. Your daughters' reaction is similar to that of Monday-morning quarterbacks. Your childrens' opinions should be respected, but the youngsters in turn should be taught to respect the opinions and behavior of older adult blacks who struggled in their own way to survive and bring about the improved conditions we now experience. But some blacks, young and old, still express antiblack feelings and accommodate white racism to achieve some type of gain.

Encourage your daughters to read about the work of dedicated black people of the past, who did the best they could as they understood it, in addition to the glib rhetoric of today. If they are clearly using "holier than thous" to get by, point it out to them. If you are involved in civil rights efforts or contributing time or money to community improvement programs, your case will be stronger. But if you are smugly enjoying cars, a nice home, vacations, and other luxuries without contributing to the betterment of the total black community—and rationalizing it—your youngsters have a good point.

Most important, don't take it too personally. We know militant leaders who have also been called Toms by their teens.

Do black teenagers generally show less respect for their parents than adolescents in other groups do?

No. In fact, respect for authority and parents remains very strong among black youngsters. Sometimes, however, depending on where they live and the social class of the family, black children may see their parents as weak and helpless, particularly if they are very poor. Thus, such children's sense of protection and security from their parents might be diminished. Currently, one-third of black families fall below the poverty level, so this is a significant issue. Nevertheless, parents who have self-respect, even under conditions of hardship, usually gain the respect of their children.

Why don't teenagers listen? I'm constantly saying, "I told you so!" But it doesn't sink in.

Adolescents often insist on doing it "their way" in a search for independence. They need to find out for themselves. It's not helpful to say "I told you so!" because it usually makes people resentful and even more determined not to listen in the future. Your child may be making mistakes because he is doing the opposite of what you say rather than what makes sense to him. You can sometimes raise questions that will help him see the logic—What would happen if you did . . . ?—rather than constantly telling him what and how.

Could I communicate better with my teenagers if I used the latest "hip" language?

Teenagers usually resent or are amused by a parent's attempt to talk their lingo. Their language style is part of their identity, which is separate from that of adults, and they wish to preserve this separation. It is better for parents to be themselves rather than awkwardly try to imitate adolescent colloquialisms. It's okay to use the hip words and mannerisms of your own rebellious period to prove that you are not an uptight square. But being a so-called square is all right too, if you are comfortable with more conservative styles.

Is it right for teenagers to criticize their parents to their faces?

Why not? Parents will never be perfect and should expect occasional criticism from their children. Too many parents take their children's criticism as a sign of disrespect and become enraged. Such a reaction is uncalled for if the criticism is made in a respectful way. If they forget how to be respectfully critical (you taught them earlier, right?), remind them. Don't use their bad manners as an excuse to ignore the criticism. Don't accept the criticism just because your child is being "beautifully aggressive and assertive!" If it is unfair criticism, point out why and help your child listen, learn, and grow. It is a valuable lesson in give-and-take that they will use throughout life.

When is it right to beat a teenager?

Beating does nothing to aid a teen's development. A big,

strong, and impulsive teenager can inflict physical damage on you. However, parents are human, and they occasionally explode with hurt or rage. If this happens, you owe your child an apology after you calm down. Teenagers in particular react with extreme bitterness and indignation when they are physically assaulted. Beatings make them feel immature and diminish their sense of autonomy and independence. Youngsters inwardly lose respect for parents who beat them, though outwardly they may appear compliant. It is best to try to reason with all persons rather than use brute force. See our discussion on spanking in Chapter 4.

What shall I do if my teenager hits me?

Make it very clear that you find such behavior unacceptable and will not tolerate it. You must also defend yourself physically or obtain necessary help. If your child repeatedly assaults you, request police intervention and then seek professional help to try to eliminate the underlying problem and to avoid future physical violence. But before a problem reaches this stage you should have tried to develop a "new contract," which we described earlier in this chapter.

Because I am more experienced, doesn't it make sense for me to control my teen's thoughts and actions to keep him from making mistakes?

Young people need experience in making many decisions, having much success, and making some mistakes. Paying the price for their mistake can teach them to make a better decision next time. Certainly when a possible mistake is too costly—in terms of money, esteem, future opportunities—you must try to prevent it. The younger the teen, the more necessary your intervention. If you have allowed your youngsters to make many minor decisions on their own, they are less likely to resent and resist you on the major ones.

The important thing to remember is that parents who repeatedly try to control their teenagers are asking for trouble. Such parents tend to suffer mild to severe instances of alienation from their children. The more controlled and dependent the child, the greater the likelihood of an explosive break and permanent alienation. Where the march toward self-assertion and independence has been gradual but continuous from infancy, children are able to seek their parents' help more easily, gain self-confidence, and relate to adults as equals—or respected superiors—more quickly.

My friends tell me I shouldn't try to get my child to do what I ask by saying, "If you loved me, you'd do so-and-so." Isn't it okay to make such an appeal?

No. Such comments sound like bribery to children and may make your child feel unnecessarily guilty about refusing to carry out your every wish. Your attempts to control your child in this way arouse strong resentment and are likely to cause rebellion at some point. On the other hand, children should not be allowed to neglect chores or do whatever they want, because that would be permissiveness. Permissive parents neglect and hurt their children by failing to set limits that give them a sense of direction and guidance.

We have been trying to increase the freedom we give our fifteen-year-old, but he "goofs" every time. What can we do?

Youngsters who have not been encouraged to be independent or do not have the knowledge, skill, or confidence to handle freedom sometimes play a funny little game called "Free me, don't you dare." In this game they demand to be free and independent, "goof" in a way that forces you to step in, then point to your interference as evidence that you don't want them to be free and independent.

What can you do? Call the game in a straightforward but friendly way; point out what is going on. Indicate your willingness to support freedom and independence when your teenager can handle it responsibly. Children need help in developing the skills necessary to deal with particular situations.

The question of curfew is a good specific example. It is best for parents and teenagers to reach an agreement together. Ask what they feel is a reasonable time to be home, or suggest what you consider reasonable, giving choices—10:00, 10:30, 11:00 P.M., or whatever. Your suggestion should be based on the amount of rest they need in order to function well the next day and also on the safety of your neighborhood. When you consider your child's idea of a reasonable hour to be unreasonable, insist on your time. Even when you arrive at an agreement together, infractions may occur. You can help your youngster live up to his agreement. He may want to know how to pull away from his gang at a reasonable time. Tell him to try "See you later, man." How should he handle teasing? "My old man is a mean dude." Teens know the ropes. They may need your positive or bantering support only as reinforcement.

When a youngster breaks an agreement—by coming home at 2:00 A.M. when he agreed to 11:00 P.M.—you have to think about what he is trying to tell you by his violation rather than what he is doing to you. He may be angry and want to hurt you, but he may be saying, "I'm on drugs, help me." Attempting to define and work out a problem is better than laying down the law—though you may have to do both.

How should a parent deal with "But Roz is allowed to do it!"?

Teens gain strength for their own independent positions by listening to and watching their parents take independent positions. Your attitude should be fair and reasonable based on thoughtful consideration. Feel free to change your mind if *good* reasons or changed conditions suggest that you should. Your decision should be in keeping with the goals you have set for yourself and for your family. You must help your teens make decisions to smoke or not to smoke, to avoid alcohol, when to date, whom to associate with, and so on, the same way.

The formula, stated in a positive way and in your own words, could be: "I am not Roz's father. Her parents may think or operate differently. This is what I want—for me, for you," and say why. If Roz's parents approve of such behavior as smoking or drinking, which are dangerous to their child's health, do not hesitate to say that you feel they are acting irresponsibly.

Young people with a future goal and the confidence that they can reach it survive the perils of adolescence better than those without goals. People who have goals and self-confidence can base decisions on their probable contribution to the achievement of those goals. People who have no goals, or doubt their ability to reach a goal, make reckless decisions, which prevents them from dealing effectively with freedom, independence, and failure. That's frequently the cause of teenage pregnancies, substance abuse, destructive marriages, and even crime and violence.

THE QUESTION OF PRIVILEGES

How long should we let our children talk on the telephone?
This depends on the other family members and their need both to make and receive calls. As part of developing a sense of responsibility, teens should have some limits, preferably self-imposed. A family discussion should resolve most problems. Teens must not be allowed to spend hours talking on the phone when they have homework or other chores to complete. Also, you might wish to preserve the family dinner and discussion hour by prohibiting phone conversations during that time.

If you have a talkative teenager and can afford to do so, providing your teen with a private phone could be a solution to family conflict. However, be sure to inform him or her that it is important to share facilities and personal items with other family members when appropriate.

Is it all right for me to listen in on phone calls occasionally to make sure my daughter is not up to anything that will get her in trouble?
It is never proper to listen in on teenagers' calls without their permission. Adolescents usually become quite angry about such an invasion of privacy, viewing it as a lack of trust in them and a lack of respect for their independence. Avoid reading children's mail or going through their belongings unless invited. A breakdown of trust resulting from such behavior may be disastrous to parent-teen relations. You must make it clear, however, that you will not tolerate their bringing illicit drugs or contraband into your home.

Under extreme conditions (threatening letters, their own suicidal thoughts, and such) children may leave mail or open diaries lying around in the hope that you will read them and come to their aid. Even in such situations, point out before reading their papers that you feel they are asking for help and that you would like to find the reason. They will probably tell you their concerns, but press them if they don't confide in you at this point.

At what age should teenagers be allowed to drive a car?

In most states, teenagers sixteen or older may drive a car, and eighteen-year-olds may own one. We think these are reasonable limits. It is advisable to have youngsters provide maintenance for their cars out of their own earnings and take full responsibility for them, if possible. If they are able, teenagers should pay some share of the higher insurance premiums that parents must pay for a young driver. Generally it is better for teens to take an approved driver education course rather than learn from a powerful, competent parent who owns the car! This represents a "loaded" situation—other types of parent-child conflict can disrupt driving lessons. First and foremost, you want your child to be a safe and careful driver.

Even though the laws of some states permit sixteen-year-olds to get a driver's license, what should a parent do if he feels his child is not mature enough to drive?

It is hard to tell when sixteen-year-olds are mature enough to drive until they have had an opportunity to demonstrate their sense of responsibility. Many youngsters who appear to be irresponsible suddenly get their act together when evidence of mature behavior becomes a requirement for driving. If your child is careless, negligent, or takes unnecessary risks after using the family car for a trial period, withdraw car privileges until the youngster demonstrates better judgment. Teenagers should pay traffic fines and fees for other violations out of their own pockets whenever possible. Those who receive more than one or two moving violations can probably be classified as "not yet ready."

My husband takes away car privileges from our son whenever he receives a poor grade in school. Is that a good way to keep him in line?

Not usually. Car privileges and school performance are separate entities. Such awkward attempts to reward and punish your son may backfire. A better method would be to investigate the real causes of his poor performance at school and provide any necessary help.

My husband has worked hard all of his life to buy a car and simply refuses to allow any of the children to drive it. Is this bad?

Not necessarily. It sounds like a situation your family may just have to learn to live with. If the family income is marginal, auto upkeep, high insurance premiums, or accidents are a real consideration when deciding whether children may use the family car.

Should teenagers be given an allowance?

Yes, but try to keep them from being completely dependent on you. Whenever possible, they should earn their own spending money. A teenager who is away at school and unable to find a job should receive money from the family, if possible. Even if they do not receive an allowance, teenagers should be expected to assume responsibilities around the house.

How much weekly allowance should teenagers be given?

The amount should be based on the costs of routine and reasonable weekly activities, such as movies, athletic events, snacks, and toiletries. It's appropriate to provide extra money for special events. Again, the value of an allowance is to help a youngster learn to manage money. Spend a little, save a little, is as good advice for your teen as it was for your eight-year-old. Allowances should be adjusted upward as the child grows older. It is also a good idea to canvass parents in the community who have children the same age as yours to learn the general range of their allowances. Once you've settled on an amount this way, your youngster can't complain that "Jim gets such-and-such" because you will know better.

Should parents who can afford to still give allowances to children who work?

Sometimes. You may want to reward the motivation of a child who works by continuing her allowance. On the other hand, you may want to offer other forms of reward for effort—a trip, special athletic equipment, or a contribution to her college savings. If your family needs that money for other purposes, however, you may want to reduce or discontinue the allowance of a working adolescent. If you explain your rationale, your child will usually understand.

Should children who work be expected to contribute part of their earnings to the home?

Parents should not demand control of a child's earnings or even insist that a certain percentage be turned over to them. If you need the financial assistance, however, remind the child that he or she has the same responsibility to contribute as other workers in the family. Let your teenager know how her share is spent—for example, to purchase necessities for the home or to supply a younger sibling's weekly allowance. Parents should also encourage young workers to save some of their earnings. If you have not already done so, accompany your child to a bank and assist her in establishing a savings account. Even if you don't need the money but your teenager can't establish a saving habit, accept a share of her earnings and save it for her. Under no circumstances should you use money you don't need to buy extras for yourself. Avoid borrowing money from your child unless it is absolutely necessary. In such cases, a parent must be especially diligent in repaying the amount borrowed.

Should teenagers have checking accounts?

Where banks and credit laws allow minors to have checking accounts, teens should be encouraged to learn to manage such accounts. Older teens with jobs should establish checking accounts to help them plan and oversee their use of money. Well-managed accounts allow youngsters to establish a good credit rating early in life, but poorly managed ones can be troublesome for you and your child. Help your teen form responsible habits—preparing a budget, knowing her balance, entering each withdrawal and deposit, and avoiding sprees of check writing or credit-card use. Parents should not act out their own conflicts about money by encouraging their teens to handle checkbooks and credit cards irresponsibly. Be careful.

Should boys be given larger allowances than girls?

No. The traditional notion that boys need more money because they must pay for escorting girls is outdated. First, even when girls are the guests of their dates, they require money for clothes, cosmetics, hair preparations, and other necessities. Second, many girls now pay their share of expenses. We think it's a good idea for girls to learn not to become dependent on boys, and to realize that they owe them nothing. In addition, many teenage girls spend a good deal of their leisure time with female friends in activities for which they themselves pay.

How much influence should parents have over what teenagers buy with their allowances or personal funds?

Little. Of course you have a right and responsibility to object to purchases of illegal items and goods. We hope you have already taught your youngster to be cautious and to avoid being a sucker for every gimmick that comes along. You may want to warn your child to be wary of being victimized. But for the most part a youngster's choices should be accepted. Remember, the purpose of an allowance is to give your child an opportunity to learn how to use money. If he wastes it, he'll have to live with that. Parents should also refrain from giving advances on allowance for this reason.

Interfere as little as possible in the area of dress styles, a common point of contention between teens and parents. It is prudent to express your preferences and opinions, but not to insist that they be accepted. Although they are greatly influenced by their friends, teens express their own individuality through their clothes. Unless their dress is extremely inappropriate or injurious to health, it really can't hurt. Even when you must intervene, do your best to be helpful rather than critical.

What should we do if we can't afford to give our children allowances?

Most families, even those on public assistance, can afford to give their children some sort of token allowance. Do not feel guilty about the amount. Your love and care are more important than the amount of money you can give. Never apologize for your income level. If you discuss your situation and what you are trying to do, most youngsters will understand and even want to help. In this case, it is a good idea to strongly encourage both boys and girls to seek and find jobs. Employment is a constructive use of a teenager's time and provides needed income.

If you have a relative who has no children and earns a good income, encourage her to "adopt" one of your children by supplying him with a weekly or monthly allowance. Don't be embarrassed to ask. Such relationships are in keeping with the extended family concept and should be encouraged among black families. This concept recognizes a number of adults as interested in and responsible for a child's development rather than one mother and one father. Your youngster should convey his or her appreciation and offer to be helpful when possible. The notion that "I deserve something for nothing, not even a thank-you" should never be encouraged.

PERSONAL HABITS AND APPEARANCE

My sloppy fourteen-year-old never wants to bathe. Is this normal for teenagers?

Some teenagers are slow to accept responsibility for self-care, often as part of an unconscious desire to return to early childhood when mother and father watched over them. Don't nag your child about cleanliness, but do not permit him to offend others with sloppy personal habits and bad odors. Calm reminders and requests for him to take responsibility for his personal hygiene is the most effective approach. Pressure from his friends and interest in the opposite sex will usually prod a teenager to adopt cleaner habits. If the behavior is extreme, however, watch for signs of depression and seek help if other unusual symptoms develop.

Is it proper for my adolescent daughter to walk around the house, in front of her father or brothers, wearing only a bra and panties?

Generally, both teenage boys and girls should be appropri-

ately covered—to avoid unnecessary sexual arousal or entice-
ment of others.

My fifteen-year-old daughter is overweight. How can I help her reduce?

Teasing an overweight teen is cruel and generally does more
harm than good. Obesity usually results from hereditary predisposition and overeating, which *may* in turn be due to anxiety,
depression, or just plain lack of self-discipline. Don't nag your
daughter, but encourage and support her efforts to lose weight.
Stock your cupboard with low-calorie foods and snacks. Eliminate junk foods from your family's diet, and serve low-fat,
low-calorie meals. Nutritionists, health clinics, and physicians
can provide practical information about dieting. Any weight-
reduction plan should include a program of regular exercise to
increase strength and muscle tone. And make your child aware
that overweight predisposes a person to diabetes, hypertension,
heart disease, and other serious ailments.

Can obesity signal a fear of sex?

In some instances. Teenage girls and boys may try to appear
unattractive to discourage romantic-sexual approaches from the
opposite sex. Occasionally, young people who think they are
unattractive adopt an I-don't-care attitude and overeat. Such
youngsters need praise and support from their parents for their
good points. Children who eat when they are tense or emotionally upset should be discouraged in a friendly but firm way.

Her friends constantly tease my teenage daughter because she wears glasses and has braces on her teeth. How will this affect her?

Your daughter should let her friends know that she resents
their teasing. After she has made her feelings clear, she should
ignore their taunts. The teasing is then no fun for the tormentors
and usually stops. Help your daughter learn to see it as *her friends'*
problem, to minimize the damage to her self-esteem.

What should parents do about the hairstyles and personal grooming habits of teenagers?

Nothing, probably. Encourage your children to be clean for reasons of good health. Unusual styles of youthful dress are popular in every generation. They proclaim, "I am unique and different from you but very much like my gang." Make grooming aids available in your home, but as long as your youngster is neat and clean, do not insist on their use or nag about appearance. Today, nearly every variety of attire except bare feet is acceptable in most public places. However, many schools establish minimum dress codes that must be adhered to. In addition, youngsters should be advised of the disadvantages of not dressing properly when they apply for employment; many people are denied jobs solely on the basis of their sloppy or unusual appearance.

When should I allow my daughter to wear lipstick and use eye makeup?

Wearing lipstick and eye makeup does not imply, as it did in the past, that a girl has loose morals. Battling over makeup is unnecessary. Teach your daughter how to apply it properly and to use it at appropriate times. Find out at what age the teenagers in your community begin to wear makeup by observation or by talking with teachers and other parents. But don't allow your daughter to be pressured into wearing makeup just to please her peers or to attract the opposite sex. Some females feel that makeup projects them as sex objects and refuse to participate in what they believe are sexist traditions. If your daughter rejects makeup, that is just fine. More and more young women now prefer the completely natural look.

Should I allow my daughter to straighten her hair?

You should allow your daughter to wear her hair any way she chooses—except if it's unkempt. Don't pressure her to keep her "natural" if she doesn't want to or to straighten it if she prefers an Afro. Encourage your daughter to wear her hair in whatever fashion is most becoming and makes her feel most comfortable. Even African women arrange their hair in different ways. If your daughter is otherwise comfortable about being black, straightening her hair has little significance—it need not mean she's trying to be "white." If she isn't comfortable being black, making her "go natural" won't help. You and she must discuss and try to find the reasons for her discomfort.

How should I react if my son wants a "process"?

It's your son's choice. Some young males still have their hair relaxed with permanent straighteners. Most, however, have adopted more natural styles. In the 1970s, young people wore large Afros. Today, the style for men and women who keep their au naturel look is to have it closely cropped. In some cities, young men have adopted geri curls, which project a very greasy look. Girls and boys who regularly receive approval and compliments from parents and others on their natural look are unlikely to straighten their hair or wear geri curls. It is becoming increasingly clear that hairstyles are just that—hairstyles—and not a true indication of one's blackness.

My young teenage girls, who have long braids, want to have their hair cut and wear it close. I object. What should I do?

Long hair is one of the standards of beauty admired by some blacks. Many black parents fear that cutting a girl's hair keeps it from growing, which is not true. On the contrary, well-groomed, clean, and trimmed hair grows well. There is no reason why a girl should not have her hair cut if she prefers a short style. Hair grows back under normal circumstances. A strong preference for long hair can be interpreted as rejection by black girls whose hair does not grow long. It's also hurtful to them when only blacks with long hair are considered beautiful, a preference more in keeping with white standards of beauty. In the last analysis, adolescents should make their own decisions about hairstyles and grooming.

My daughter has bought skin bleaching cream. Should I say anything?

Perhaps your daughter has discovered minor discolorations and blemishes that she hopes to clear up. But if she is trying to lighten her skin because she is ashamed of being dark, she has a problem. Even youths whose parents teach black pride in the home become unhappy about their skin color in school or through wider social contact. Talk to her about it. Assure your daughter that her skin color is fine just as it is. Help her to deal with her concern about being black without criticizing her lack of black pride. In any case, most commercial bleaching creams cannot lighten the skin to any significant degree. Such creams may also damage skin and should be avoided.

What can I do when children in the neighborhood call her black and ugly?

It's a pity that some blacks still behave this way. Such vicious and cruel remarks are usually made by people who have a negative self-image. Children who develop self-respect at an early age are able to handle name-calling with self-assurance. Racial slurs have a minimum effect on them. Your child might try talking directly with black children who make racist remarks, calling on them to respect her as she respects them, pointing out that they can't be black and proud while attacking blacks for being black. You can sometimes help your child by contacting the parents of the name-callers. When nothing else can be done, help your child understand that it is the name-callers' problem, not hers.

My teenagers won't go to the beach because they're afraid of getting too dark. How can I handle this situation?

They may have a problem about being black. On the other hand, they may just prefer their particular shade and be perfectly comfortable with their race. Too much sunbathing—on the beach or elsewhere—can be damaging to the skin, causing premature thickening and wrinkles. Although they are less vulnerable to sun-induced skin cancer than whites, blacks who overexpose themselves to the sun tend to develop such cancers as well. In general, outdoor activities are important for all teenagers. The outdoors contributes to their total development and gives them a sense of harmony with nature, which is so important for the spirit. Camping out, biking, and swimming are enjoyable, healthy activities that should be encouraged, accompanied by a warning about the hazards of too much sun. And remind your teens that each skin shade has its own special allure.

Our very light-skinned daughter is ashamed because she isn't darker. Sometimes the blacks in school tease her about having too much "white" blood. What do you advise?

Black people come in all shades. Point out that "black is beautiful" means the group, not any particular color. Brown, yellow, and white blacks are also beautiful. Blacks who attack other blacks on the basis of their skin color are ignorant. If your daughter tells her tormenters just that, they may well stop. Letting them know that she is upset by the teasing only encourages it.

PROFANITY AND THE TEENAGER

My teenage girl uses a lot of foul language around the house, like "fuck you" and "kiss my ass." What should I do about it?

If your daughter is using such language, it may be because you previously ignored it or did not make it clear which expletives should be deleted and which are acceptable. It is not too late to insist that she not use such language in your presence. Whether or not she feels it is acceptable to use profanity is irrelevant; she should respect your wishes. Perhaps you can remind her of a habit of yours that annoys her, which you have given up out of respect for her feelings. If you yourself curse, however, it will be difficult for you to justify a demand that your daughter refrain from using profanity.

Point out that excessive bad language is an immature way of handling an uncomfortable and disturbing situation. Cursing that is directed at objects or unfamiliar situations is a form of emotional release that can be healthy. Again, you might remind your youngster that there is a time and place for everything; that unacceptable language in an inappropriate setting is disrespectful and can cause her to lose both respect and opportunities. For example, swearing at strangers can incite physical attacks and worse. (See Chapter 7 for more on profanity.)

What is the significance of black youth using the word "motherfucker"?

In the past, that term expressed great hostility and disrespect. It was a way of putting a person down by suggesting that he was violating the universal incest taboo (mother-child sexual intercourse). The use of this term has often led to physical violence and sometimes killings, because young blacks took this epithet as a profound assault on their honor and manhood, and on their mothers. Today the use of "motherfucker" has so changed that some young blacks use it as a term of endearment and respect. The terms "shit," "bitch," and "nigger" also serve as both epithets and expressions of endearment within sections of the black community. However, in many black communities, use of this language pattern is frowned upon. But remember that use of these terms in verbal abuse can be extremely provocative and can lead to physical violence.

What is the "dozens"?

The dozens is a word game played by some young blacks in which they tease and irritate one another by composing profane, often sexualized, jingles. It's usually a put-down of "ya mama" or other family members. An example: "I fucked ya mama from roof to roof. She swore to God she was bullet-proof." Each person tries to outdo the other. It has been suggested that playing the dozens helps to toughen black youths for survival in a harsh environment. We see it as a mechanism for discharging anger and tension.

"Rapping" is a cultural form that is partially derived from the dozens. Rap music, which can be socially uplifting or profane, raises the verbal skills of the dozens to higher and more poetic levels. Rap, in fact, has entered the mainstream of American music and has crossed over into the white, Latino, and Asian communities.

FRIENDSHIPS AND SOCIAL RELATIONS

How should we react if our teenager starts hanging out with people we don't approve of?

Teenagers are particularly sensitive about being allowed to

choose their own friends. In learning about life, they will explore relationships with many different types of people. Parents should be concerned with the character and values of their teenagers' friends, but avoid rejection on the grounds of social class. It is important for blacks to feel a sense of brotherhood across class lines. Take the time and express an interest in getting to know your child's friends.

Encourage those friends to come into your home. That will give you opportunities to meet them and avoid forcing your child into socializing with them in less favorable surroundings. You may, however, want to limit certain friends to visiting only when adults are present. Again, should a friend appear to be "undesirable," parents can exert positive influences on the friend—and on their own child—by showing interest and understanding. Express your objections about any friends to your teenager. But here, unlike the preteen stage, it is important to actively discourage relationships with youngsters who persistently display unacceptable behavior. Troubled teenagers can present problems for you and your youngster. With a little help from parents, teens who are generally doing well will usually part company with a troubled soul who abuses helpers and refuses their assistance.

Can I help in such a situation?

Intervene in a calm but firm way. Advise your daughter of the possible risks to her well-being and to her future. However, your child should not reject anyone merely because she was once in trouble with the law. Many inner-city black youths are arrested because of supervigilance and harassment from police officers. But many teenagers do commit criminal acts, and you want to prevent your daughter from becoming involved with such persons.

We realize that in some areas youngsters must belong to a gang "or else." Parents must do whatever is necessary to expose young people to healthy and constructive activities inside and outside the community. Become involved in their schools and churches. Seek out community youth groups involved in mentoring youths or job training. Part-time after-school jobs offer paid learning experiences. Help teenagers find a summer job, or investigate ways to make it possible to offer them an away-from-home summer camp experience. Such exposure often gives them a broader and more mature slant on life.

In the meantime, support the activities of civic groups and law enforcement agencies working to diminish the violent and criminal behavior of youth gangs.

Should we allow our child to invite a drug addict or a criminal into our home?

Each case must be evaluated individually. Friendships with "straight" people are important to addicts who are rehabilitated. But there is always the risk that some may abuse or steal from the family. Your teenager must not expect his family to tolerate mistreatment from any of his friends.

Your youngsters may taunt you by saying, "You think we're better than he is." In reply, point out that black people who repeatedly exhibit criminal behavior in spite of efforts to help them are self-serving and antisocial. Encourage your child to befriend persons who are trying to better themselves and the community. Should a "friend" steal from the family, report the theft to the police. A person who has proven to be untrustworthy should be barred from your home—unless he or she successfully embarks on a rehabilitation program.

Some black children at school criticized my daughter for associating with whites. Is it wrong for blacks to have white friends?

Our best hope for black survival lies in our support of rights. You should uphold the right of your daughter to have friends of all races and religions. If your daughter seeks out only white friends, however, she may have a problem. You need to help her sort out feelings about being black. Although some black youngsters may be afflicted with racial self-hatred and reject friendships with other blacks, this is not likely to be a problem for those who have been raised with a healthy degree of racial pride and self-respect.

I have a sixteen-year-old who is militantly antiwhite, yet dates only white girls. Isn't this hypocritical? What does it mean?

Your son "doth protest too much." Deep down, he is probably not really secure about his identity and may be going to extremes of "blackness" to hide his negative feelings about blacks and his racial self-negation. His attraction to whiteness is evident in his compulsive pursuit of white girls to the exclusion of blacks. Such love-hate reactions toward whites are not uncommon among blacks. Try to help your son face his true feelings. He may use the excuse that he is "punishing the white male power structure." Your reaction—something on the order of "bullshit"—should lay that one to rest and make it possible to talk about the real causes. If he wants to date white girls, that's his business, but let him know that you don't want him to hide behind "stuff."

LEISURE

How can parents influence teenagers to use their time constructively?

Adolescence is essentially a period of leisure in many respects. Many teenagers are present-oriented, and are very focused on activities that affect their daily functioning. They are also involved in an adolescent subculture, in which primary importance is given to interaction with their peers. They become more deeply preoccupied with the concerns of their immediate friends than with those of family members. Much of the so-called idleness among teenagers is devoted to deep contemplation. They explore issues that may seem trivial to adults but are important to them.

By giving adolescents too little responsibility and respect, however, we encourage their idleness and isolation. Teenagers require an environment in which their serious participation in the affairs of the home and community makes a positive contribution to that home and community. Such participation in turn reinforces their sense of worth and personal value. Activities in which teenagers can become involved are suggested later.

To what extent should teenagers be allowed to plan their own time at home and away?

The more a young person thinks, plans, and takes responsibility for himself, the sooner he or she becomes self-reliant. Teenagers should be allowed to plan their days in much the same way that adults do. Yet it is important for family members to coordinate plans so that they can share rides, attend to errands without duplication of effort, and so on. This is good training in cooperation and coordination. You can help young adolescents by raising questions and offering suggestions to aid in their planning without being critical or controlling.

Should teenagers inform parents of their whereabouts at all times?

It is common courtesy for all family members to let someone at home know their whereabouts. Safety is the important factor here. Someone who plans to stay away longer than intended should be required to phone and let other members of the family know that she is okay. Young people can become so wrapped up in their activities that they fail to notify parents of their whereabouts. However, parents may complicate this problem by chastising children when they do call and probing too insistently into the identity of their companions and their activities. Such nagging makes young people feel inadequate and dependent and discourages them from calling their parents; they prefer to take the flack when they get home. When your child knows that your primary concern is her safety, it becomes easier for her to keep in touch.

Stress safety without paralyzing your teens. State your requirements firmly but calmly: proper habits in the car, wearing batting and bicycling helmets, and such. You need not pry into their every move, but remind them to use sound judgment about whether the places they visit and the friends who accompany them meet your moral standards. For safety's sake and not for control—particularly with young teens—you have to have some idea of where they are and when to expect them.

It is reasonable to probe only when you feel that a youngster is in immediate danger. If you are concerned about the person your youngster is with and what they are doing, it's better to discuss it quietly and constructively, at an appropriate time.

What are important points to consider in planning teenage recreation?

We hope that you have been exposing your youngsters to a wide range of activities, and that they have been finding many of their own. If a special talent or interest emerges, nurture it without developing unrealistic expectations. An average piano player is not likely to become a virtuoso, nor is a sandlot home-run hitter likely to be a major league home-run king. But fully developing an interest is fun and will give your teen an area of mastery, a sense of competence. This is one of the reasons many city youngsters spend so much time on basketball courts and football fields.

Teens, like younger children, can fall into a rut—all music, all dances, all baseball, nothing. You want to help "nothing" get going again and acquaint your teens with a variety of recreational interests, although satisfaction and preoccupation with one should not cause great concern. For the most part, older teens do their own thing.

Is it valuable for teenagers to attend summer camp?

It is especially helpful for young city people to get away to the country to enjoy activities that are not available in urban areas. Camp teaches new skills and gives children a chance to make new friends from different backgrounds. It is an opportunity to learn how to relate without leaning on parents, and it's good preparation for college or the working world. Older teenagers can find jobs as work-campers or counselors. Local churches, Girl Scouts, Boy Scouts, and the YMCA, YWCA, and other social service agencies can supply information about summer camps. But don't send a child away just to get rid of him or her. Don't feel that you have failed your child if you can't afford to provide or otherwise arrange for a camping experience.

How should we proceed if we cannot find a summer camp or if our children do not want to go?

Encourage your teenagers to join local sports groups or clubs, or to find jobs so that they don't waste their summer hanging out on the corner—although corners without drugs or dangerous gangs with guns, are not bad locations if they're not the *only* places your teen goes. Many libraries, museums, churches, and other service groups provide worthwhile free programs in which you should try to interest your teens.

Are teenagers better off being excluded from family outings?
Not at all. Teenagers need to be part of the family. Trips to the beach, family vacations, and visits to relatives should include the youngsters. The notion that adolescents are too "grown up" to participate in family recreation is unfounded. However, refrain from forcing them to participate in family functions. Encouraging them to bring friends along can increase their enthusiasm. They are more likely to want to participate if you ask for and follow up on their suggestions for outings and vacations.

BOY-GIRL RELATIONS

At what age should we allow our son or daughter to date?
The age at which parents allow their children to date varies with community standards. You can usually get a cue from what most of the other parents allow, although you should not necessarily accept others' standards for dating if they do not meet your criteria. In some areas, parents permit their twelve-year-olds to date. In others, parents do not sanction formal dating until sixteen or older. The dating age should be based on the maturity of your teenager. When your child is capable of good judgment, and understands how to maintain respect in relationships, dating is reasonable. Many young teens prefer group dating in which they are not required to pair off. This protects them from going too far too soon or simply getting "too close." This form of dating is appropriate at a reasonably early age.

What do we tell our daughter if she does not want to date interracially and many black boys are dating white girls?
Most black boys are *not* dating white girls. Only a minority are. Thus, your daughter will probably meet someone she can date. It is important to boost her self-esteem without causing her to be intimidated by white girls or become excessively compet-

itive with them. You may have to help her to be physically and socially attractive without compromising her rights or reputation. We have seen hostile, selfish, abusive people who place the blame for their dating problems on the interracial dating of the opposite sex. You might also want to help your daughter reconsider her attitudes toward interracial dating. It can certainly be an option for her, as it should be for anybody.

Isn't it damaging to black girls' egos for black boys to pursue white girls?

It shouldn't be. Blacks are slowly learning that black is beautiful, too. Parents should not condemn black men who marry white women—or black women who marry white men. All men and women have the right to date and marry whomever they choose, and this right should be respected.

My thirteen-year-old daughter is not dating but has a crush on a white boy. She doesn't like the two black boys in school. How can I prepare her for the pain of possible rejection?

This is one of the very real problems of living in a predominantly white community. If this is your situation, and you want your child to associate with both blacks and whites, you should arrange for natural contacts with other blacks long before adolescence. It helps to discuss black and white attitudes toward interracial dating well before children reach dating age. Make your own attitude known, but it is probably wise not to tell a youngster who she must or must not like or date. Adolescents often do the opposite of what parents advise in this situation as a rebellious statement of their independence.

Most teens handle this dilemma by directing their interest toward people of their own race or religious group. Some black parents tackle the problem by forming clubs for travel, study, and general socialization, so that widely scattered black youngsters can get together, experience themselves as blacks, and form boy-girl relationships free of racial rebuff. Even so, be prepared for the normal heartaches of "I like him but he likes her and she likes somebody else".

Suppose your youngster does date her white friend, the fellows rebuff him, and he drops her. Don't say, "I told you so!"

Just help her to understand racial reality: that the problem is theirs; that she is a good and worthy person; and that she will find a steady—either black or a member of another group.

Suppose my teenager is willing to date only light-skinned members of the opposite sex?

Because teenagers may harbor color prejudices learned in the home or elsewhere, black parents should guard against instilling such prejudices. For example, the parents of one girl rejected a dark-skinned boyfriend, regardless of his background or achievements. Her mother insisted that she date light-skinned boys because "You must think of your children. You're too brown to marry any dark fellow." Her parents' attitude caused the girl to dislike light-skinned men and view them all as arrogant, conceited, and selfish, even though she had discovered similar traits in the brown-skinned boyfriends she preferred. By overreacting to her parents' prejudices, she lost her own sense of priorities. There are indications that the pursuit of black pride has not eliminated this problem entirely, especially among the over-forty generation.

I want my youngsters to date, but I'm afraid that dating leads to sex too soon. How can I advise my youngsters?

In the past, girls about to date were told, "Keep your dress down and your pants up, and boys were told, "Don't you bring nothing home." Not only was this advice often ignored, it created discomfort and contributed to unhealthy attitudes toward sex. It portrayed sex as a forbidden and dirty activity. Many people develop feelings of excessive shame and guilt that inhibit a happy, healthy sex life, which can lead to marital problems and divorce.

In the first place, dating and boy-girl friendships are not usually about sex. They frequently take the form of talking, laughing, studying, going places together, and sharing experiences. Most early teens want no part of sex. We mentioned earlier that many prefer group dating to forestall sexual opportunities. Those who do get involved in sex at an early age are often the ones who see no future, have no other way to feel "I'm okay; I'm somebody!" Even youngsters into heavy sex with many partners have been known to change the pattern when career or personal development opportunities arise.

You laid the groundwork for an honest discussion of sex and dating when you told your eleven- or twelve-year-olds (when a question or incident provided the opportunity) that as they get older they might feel strongly toward someone with whom they may want to have sex. At the same time, in all that you did with your youngsters, you helped them develop their self-respect. Express confidence in your teens' ability to act in a way that maintains self-respect, and remind them to allow themselves time to grow up and have the freedom to make choices that pregnancy and/or early marriage won't permit.

It is reasonable to express your attitude without imposing it on them. It's important to explain the relationship of mutual respect and commitment that should surround a sexual involvement. We do not think it's helpful to warn teens that sexual activity is bad and that they must not engage in it. Such warnings didn't work for many of us or, when they did, they made it hard for some of us to enjoy sex later on.

You should also explain that it's okay for them to choose to postpone sex until after marriage. Some will experiment—without deep love—out of curiosity or some other need. This does not make them bad. The important thing is that they act to prevent harm to themselves. You must provide them with information on contraceptive techniques and the practice of safe sex. They should fully understand the risks and dangers of sexually transmitted diseases (STDs) and Acquired Immunodeficiency Syndrome (AIDS). The incidence of STDs and AIDS is increasing in teenagers. Teens who have been given all the independence they could handle from early childhood on—and your help in solving problems they could not deal with effectively—are best able to accommodate to the changing personal rules guiding today's behavior.

My teenage boy thinks of dark-skinned girls only as a "piece of pussy." How did he get such an attitude?

That's the wrong attitude for him to have toward any woman. Black boys who disrespect darker girls and consider them as more sexual than girls with lighter skin are harboring racist attitudes. Perhaps your son is insecure and abuses girls to bolster a weak ego. He sounds like a budding male chauvinist who should be taught to see girls as equals, not as objects for sexual exploitation. You also need to talk to him about his prejudiced attitudes toward dark skin.

How can we prevent our teenager from confusing sexual attraction with love?

Because many Americans feel guilty about purely sexual attraction, they call their sexual feelings "being in love." Let your child know that sexual feelings are normal and acceptable, but that love develops over a period of time in a close relationship.

Should my teenager be allowed to be alone in his room with a friend of the opposite sex?

Teenagers occasionally want to be alone, out of the sight of adults or siblings, but these desires are not necessarily sexually motivated. However, if you as a parent feel uncomfortable with this arrangement, do not permit it and explain your feelings to your teenager. He may not agree, but if your relationship has been a good one, he will probably respect your wishes.

I recently learned that my thirteen- and fourteen-year-olds participated in a mixed skinny-dipping party at a beach. How should a parent handle this kind of behavior?

Talk to your children about the nature of the party to ascertain whether it was merely swimming or if group sexual activity was involved. Group sexual activity should be discouraged, because it gives rise to risks and psychological dangers that even very mature adults are unable to handle. If nudity has too many sexual overtones for your family, you should certainly ask your children to avoid such activities with members of the opposite sex. Skinny-dipping (or nude swimming) is becoming acceptable in some communities in light of changing values toward nudity. In communities where it is illegal, your children should be made aware of the law and the possibility of arrest.

I overheard a conversation among my fourteen-year-old son and his friends regarding several boys having sexual relations with one girl during the same gathering. What should I do?

Your son should be counseled against such behavior. Participation in "gang bangs" is antisocial behavior that often leads to serious exploitation and possible rape of girls. Except for paid prostitutes, most girls would not permit such acts unless they were too intoxicated by liquor or drugs to resist. In that event, the young men would be engaging in rape, for which they would have to face serious legal consequences if convicted. Such action shows a lack of respect on the part of the boys—both for themselves and for the girl, even if they pay for her services. Group performance is a most unhealthy form of sexual expression. Some boys can be pressured into these types of activities by peer influence. Participants in group sexual activity also run the risk of contracting rapidly spreading venereal disease. In addition, boys who take part in "gang bangs" may later experience a great deal of guilt, which leads to feelings of low self-worth. But it is worse for a girl who is raped and sexually abused—her psychological scars are usually severe.

A friend of mine overheard her son and his friends, including my sixteen-year-old, arranging a contest to discover who could seduce the largest number of girls during summer vacation. What advice should I give my son?

Your son may be suffering from feelings of inadequacy or rebellion, so it would be helpful to talk to him about the meaning of his planned behavior. Discussing this type of unnecessary sexual activity shows a complete lack of respect for females. Much of the unconventional sexual behavior or fantasies of teenagers, especially boys, stems from curiosity about sex coupled with insufficient sex education from parents and schools. But don't be too alarmed: Boys who fantasize about great female conquests seldom carry them out. They're usually indulging in male bravado to impress the other members of their group.

My shy seventeen-year-old son is uncomfortable with girls. He can't dance or talk to them on the phone, and when asked about girlfriends, he becomes embarrassed. Should we be alarmed?

Shy boys can best overcome their fear of girls through participation in social activities, community work, and other group projects in which girls also participate. As in most instances, you can help by talking to your son about any special concerns he may have about social situations with members of the opposite sex. Listen carefully for indications of fear of sex; if it surfaces, help him understand that relationships with the opposite sex need not be sexual until both are ready to make them so. Don't become alarmed if your son seems disinterested in girls during his high school and early college years unless he shows signs of a general social withdrawal. Boys become comfortable with girls at different stages.

My nineteen-year-old daughter wants to live with her boyfriend. How should I react?

Such living arrangements, which were frowned upon in the past, are more socially acceptable today. Living with someone is probably preferable to premature marriage. Sharing a home is much like a trial marriage and *may* help a person make a wise choice of a permanent marriage partner—although divorces are about as common among trial-marriage couples as among traditional ones. Also, there is no proof that trial arrangements lead to *better* marriages even when the marriages last. Discuss the pros and cons of her plans and make your point of view known. But the ultimate decision is hers. Condemn your daughter and her boyfriend? Are they humane people? Take into account that some of us did secretly, with less commitment to each other, what they are doing openly. Remember?

Our daughter is coming home from college for a long weekend with her boyfriend. The two of them share an apartment in their college community, but my husband and I object to their sharing a room in our house. Are we being unreasonable?

We think your objection is perfectly reasonable. The key issue here is respect for the values of parents in their own home. Young people can't always understand why parents cherish certain values, but the important fact remains that they *do*. Just as your daughter expects you to accept her college living arrangement—expecting you to continue sending her allowance and tuition—she and her boyfriend should respect your wishes regarding sleeping arrangements in your home.

Does premarital sex lead to marriage problems?

Seldom. A person who experiences deep guilt in connection with premarital sex is ripe for marital problems. Although today's sexual attitudes are more liberal, some people still sanction a double standard: premarital sex is a no-no for women but okay for men. Such mind-sets have strong male chauvinistic origins. What is okay for the gander must be okay for the goose.

What is the best age for a young person to marry?

For many decades, most people married in their late teens and early twenties. More recently, young people have been postponing marriage until their later years. We believe that each person should develop fully before taking on the responsibilities of marriage and parenthood, because a large number of early marriages end in social hardship and divorce. Mature adults are likely to be better parents and have the financial security necessary to raise a family. Therefore, postponing marriage to the middle and late twenties would probably benefit the black family and community.

Adolescents often have a problem with intimacy, with deep emotional closeness. This varies with their upbringing. In general, the more secure and self-confident they are, the less fear teenagers will have about being close to another individual. Young adults who have identity and self-image problems may be unable to cope with the level of intimacy and give-and-take required in a marriage. Through their activities and associations with friends during adolescence, they gradually learn about the subtleties of close relationships—particularly between males and females. This gives marriage a better chance of succeeding. In addition, full educational development gives a teen a better opportunity in the job market and a better chance in marriage.

SEX EDUCATION

Have black families been too strict about sex in the past?

Frequently, yes. Because blacks have been accused of being sexually loose, many families have adopted a strict puritanical approach in raising their children. Such an upbringing may cause excessive guilt and emotional conflict about normal sexual activity. Many people cannot fully enjoy sex for five or six years after marriage—if ever—because of such feelings. Today, however, many black families err in not setting enough limits on early sexual behavior and in not providing adequate sexual information. As a result, many black teenagers become pregnant and a high proportion end up as unwed mothers. The way in which black families influence their children's behavior needs much more study and attention.

How can we better help our teenagers learn about sex?

As we have stressed from the start, sex education should begin early in life and keep pace with a child's growing understanding. Adolescent boys and girls have many questions about sex because of their bodily changes—breasts, body hair, shape —and strong sexual urges. Now those long-pent-up sexual urges have the possibility of leading all the way to full expression— intercourse. Boys and girls are often anxious and full of questions: When, how, with whom? What will it be like? Will I be respected? Ashamed? Guilty? And so on. Your child may feel uncomfortable discussing these subjects with you, so books and other sources of information should be made available to them. But you should be knowledgeable about sex; the purpose of all your chats about sex with your younger child was to pave the way for a smoother transition into adolescent and adult sex life. For a more detailed account of what you and your child should discuss together, see Chapter 7 and the following information.

How is sexual interest expressed in adolescence?

Early adolescents may continue the hitting, teasing, sexual jokes, and jingles prevalent among preteens. Much of the telephone gossip of thirteen- to fifteen-year-old girls centers around boys, and boys tease one another about their interest in girls. Boys and girls masturbate, and some may indulge in petting. Some boys may exhibit their pubic hair and penises in a small group. There may also be physical contact—boy-boy and girl-girl. Sometimes boy-girl genital contact without intercourse takes place.

Many youngsters begin to have sexual intercourse in adolescence, but a large number still abstain until after the age of twenty, or even wait until marriage. Early adolescent intercourse may prove to be overwhelming for the youngsters. For some, intercourse is a way to establish adulthood and end the confusion and anxiety of adolescence. Unfortunately, it usually doesn't accomplish that end, because sexual intercourse involves other social relationship demands for which young teens are not prepared; guilt, confusion, and anxiety result.

Teens who can't stand intimate contact may ridicule, expose, or put each other down in one way or another. One or both— usually the girl—end up feeling used and guilty. We have also heard boys express guilt about using a girl, although, among many males, "seducing a girl" is still a badge of manhood. Some men never lose their adolescent need to prove their adequacy. Sex for them is not a warm, shared experience but a matter of domination and conquest.

Some black fathers encourage their sons as young as twelve and thirteen to "get some" to be a man. Is this good advice for young teenagers?

No. Young black boys should not be made to feel that masculinity derives from the number of different women one takes to bed. This can make sex a matter of domination and conquest to the detriment of females—and males. It can lead to dissatisfaction with married sex life or having only one partner. There is much more to masculinity or femininity than sexual performance. Again, it is not wise to push youngsters into a situation for which they may not be ready; they may be made to feel *inadequate* as a man. Fathers who do this are using their sons to relive their own past while claiming to "school" them.

What should I do if I surprise my fourteen-year-old son masturbating?

If he is alone, it is best to excuse yourself and leave. You might explain at the first opportunity that you know that boys and girls masturbate and there is no reason for him to be embarrassed or guilty. If he is with a friend or two, it is a different situation—part of the urge to show off or exhibit himself. There is still no cause for alarm because such incidents occur from time to time as teens experiment with their feelings, sexuality, and ways to express them.

If it is a first occasion you might say, "Okay, boys, let's stop it and get dressed. We know that you do that in private." We hope by now that you have already discussed all the major aspects of sex, including masturbation. A second incidence should cause you to be more firm, yet try to find out the cause—is it defiance, testing, or an inability to control the urge? Should group masturbation occur again, it's advisable to seek professional help.

Threats are useless and produce unnecessary guilt and defiance. Even if you don't say anything, the likelihood of a repeat group masturbation session is slim. But it is better to comment, because then there is no confusion about where you stand and you have made it clear that sexuality doesn't alarm you.

What is a "wet dream"? Is it a bad sign?

A wet dream, orgasm (sexual climax) accompanied by the discharge of semen experienced by a sleeping boy in response to sexual tension, is a perfectly normal occurrence, especially in adolescence. Wet dream semen should not be confused with a puslike discharge from the penis, which may be due to venereal infection. Many girls have orgasms in their sleep, but without a discharge of fluid; again, this is normal.

Can you tell us more about the process of discharging semen?

The male discharge of semen during sexual orgasm is called ejaculation. During climax, rhythmic contractions of the fibers of the penis force the emission of sperm and other fluids from the male sex glands through the opening of the penis. Because the ejaculation can be quite powerful, it has become known as "shooting" or "coming." A male can usually sense the onset of ejaculation and withdraw his penis from the vagina during intercourse. This practice (coitus interruptus) is used as a method of birth control, but it is highly unreliable and should not be practiced.

Is oral-genital sex perverted?

It is part of normal sexuality. Girls and boys should not be made to feel "dirty" if they ask questions about this form of activity. Couples who do not use contraceptive techniques often indulge in oral-genital sex in place of intercourse. As with sexual intercourse, there is a great danger of contracting STDs and AIDS through oral-genital sex.

What are some of the old wives' tales about masturbation?

It has often been said that acne (pimples) is caused by masturbation; that it can cause girls to walk crooked or become bow-legged; that it can cause hair to grow on the palm of one's hand; that masturbation can make one go crazy or cause other mental problems; and so on. Any mental problem that might surface is likely to result from feelings of guilt about this normal human activity. No physical problems result from masturbation—except sore genitals when the stimulation is vigorous or excessive.

There's so much pornography available on newsstands. Should we let our children bring sex or "girlie" magazines into the house?

Teenagers have ways of reading what they want. However, you should not buy such magazines for them. Interest in these magazines is a part of normal human curiosity about sex. Reading them has not been shown to be damaging to the normal sexual development of most teenagers. However, such magazines are usually sexist and portray women in derogatory and exploitive ways, which, if taken at face value, may interfere with healthy boy-girl friendships. Make your teens aware of the sexist orientation of many of these magazines and their tendency to exploit. Teens so prepared may then be encouraged to adopt your negative view and avoid reading these publications, or at least approach them without being duped by their content. If we don't overreact to sex, the attraction of the forbidden and the mystical quality will disappear. Sex will remain an important, but not unduly emphasized, part of human relationships. A teen's constant preoccupation with magazines or viewing X-rated videos may signal a problem. If you note such behavior, seek help for your youngsters.

Should mothers not kiss their teenage boys? My son gets annoyed when I kiss him.

Many a teenage boy feels it's "sissyish" to be kissed by his mother. This unfortunate attitude probably stems from a fear of developing sexual feelings toward the mother. It's okay to kiss your son, but don't act in a seductive or sexual way, and don't kiss him passionately. If he strongly objects to your kisses, don't force them on him.

Are black men sexual studs?

No. For reasons that are not entirely clear, some young black boys and girls consider solitary masturbation unnatural and therefore pet and complete intercourse for sexual gratification. Some black teenage boys, particularly those reared in predominantly female environments, have a special need to prove their manhood through sexual conquests. But overall the sexual patterns of blacks are normal and not unlike those of other ethnic or socioeconomic class groups. The stud image is a stereotype that is part of the myth that black people are "animalistic." Again, young black men should not be made to feel that they have to be super-sexual performers. Such overcompensation is misdirected use of energy.

Is it true that black men's penises are larger than white men's?

No one knows for sure. The normal range of the erect penis in both white and black men is 5 to 7 inches, but in both groups it can be larger or smaller. However, the size of a penis has little to do with a man's ability to satisfy a woman sexually. Boys' preoccupation with the size of their penis is a waste of time. Nevertheless, many still require reassurance.

Do frequent and early sexual intercourse and masturbation lead to enlargement of the penis?

No. Penis size is determined by biological factors and inheritance. Exercise of this organ cannot make it larger.

Is there a high rate of homosexuality among blacks?

Although the rate of homosexuality among black men is unknown, it is probably similar to that of white males. Although there is no totally reliable data, most current reports suggest that about ten percent of American men are primarily homosexual; and about five percent of American women are primarily lesbian. Some people believe that there are more black gay men today, but this may be due to their increased visibility as more are coming out of the closet. The increased strength of the gay movement and a lessening of social discrimination have led to a growing sense of gay pride.

How about the rate of homosexuality among black females?

No one knows much about black female homosexuals. They exist, but their numbers and styles of behavior have not been well researched. However, memberships in national black gay and lesbian organizations are increasing.

Is it true that the absence of fathers from black homes contributes to black boys becoming homosexual?

Some social scientists believe that the absence of male role models may make it difficult for young boys to develop a masculine identity. However, most boys who grow up in fatherless homes do *not* become homosexual. At the same time, many homosexuals grew up in homes where fathers were present. The reasons for homosexuality are complex and depend on a variety of biological and environmental factors.

Will a girl who is a tomboy at age twelve and thirteen become a homosexual?

Usually not. "Tomboy" is an inappropriate label to apply to girls who have an interest in sports and active adventure. Labels like "tomboy" or "sissy" restrict the potential of both girls and boys to have a broad choice of male and female role models. Energetic and active girls can be as feminine as those who surround themselves with dolls and play house.

Are young boys or girls who engage in homosexual acts destined to become homosexuals?

No. Teenagers satisfy many different questions about sex with buddies and girlfriends, and curiosity about homosexuality is no exception. Most do not engage in truly homosexual acts; they may experiment with a disguised form of such activity with total innocence of its implications. Actual homosexual behavior is infrequent and often exploratory. Open interest in homosexual acts usually disappears when a boy or girl commits to an opposite-sex style. All of us maintain some level of same-sex interest and should not be afraid of our feelings. They are more affectual (emotional) than sexual. A measure of the anger and rage that some people direct toward homosexuals is due to fear that their openness will weaken our control of our own feelings.

Teasing, rejecting, or ridiculing a youngster who displays signs of homosexual interests can make matters worse. If a youngster is upset by her homosexual interests or behavior, her parents should arrange to have her consult with a psychiatrist, psychologist, or social worker. Homosexual clinicians are also available if your child would prefer to see one. If no conflict is evident, nothing should be done. Our society is adopting more liberal attitudes toward homosexuality, no longer considering it an "antisocial disorder." Discrimination against homosexuals is cruel and un-American. Signs of homophobia and gay bashing in your teens should be dealt with in the same way as any other form of bigotry.

What is meant by the term "bisexual"?

It is usually applied to a person who engages in sexual relations with persons of both sexes. Bisexuality is apparently more common than professionals had first speculated. According to some data about one-third of American males have engaged in same-sex activity to the point of orgasm.

Even though some professionals consider gay and bisexual behavior normal, should it be discouraged because of the risk of spreading AIDS? I know a lot of black men who have died of AIDS.

AIDS, which has devastated many members of the gay community, appears to be transmitted primarily through anal intercourse or the penetration of bodily fluids into broken skin. These conditions facilitate the transmission of HIV (human immunodeficiency virus), which causes AIDS. The immune system is severely weakened so that opportunistic infections and tumors lead to death. Although drugs like AZT slow the progress of AIDS, they are not curatives.

The spread of AIDS among gay men has slowed thanks to publicity about safer sex practices, including the use of condoms. AIDS is also transmitted among intravenous drug users, however, which has led to increasing rates of infection in poor and minority communities. In addition, AIDS can be transmitted by heterosexual intercourse with infected partners. Therefore, promiscuous sex, whether homosexual or heterosexual, should be more strongly discouraged than ever. More AIDS education programs are sorely needed in the African-American community.

MENSTRUATION AND CONTRACEPTION

At what age does menstruation occur?

Menstruation usually starts between the ages of nine and sixteen, with the average age around twelve and a half to thirteen years. The average menstrual cycle is about four to six days, but variations are common. If your daughter has not begun to menstruate by the time she is sixteen, consult a physician. Have your daughter see a doctor even before that time if, in addition to absence of menstruation, she had not developed breasts or pubic or underarm hair.

It is important to explain to your daughter that each person is different; that girls start to menstruate at different times; that some may not be regular at first; and that a few women never have regular menstrual periods. Tell her that these differences do not make one woman better than another. Differences simply mean that people are different, nothing more.

Can playing around with boys bring about early menstruation?

No. The onset of menstruation varies from person to person depending on each girl's particular physical, hereditary, and environmental circumstances. A girl who menstruates at an early age is neither "fast" nor "more female."

What is the biological importance of menstruation?

Menstruation marks the biological beginning of womanhood.

It merely signifies that a girl has the capability to reproduce—
to become pregnant. The female begins bleeding from her uterus
(womb) as a perfectly normal and healthy condition of growing
up. Women who counsel girls about menses must be careful not
to impart negative attitudes or information that may cause them
to fear and dislike everything associated with menstruation. For
example, menstrual cramps and pain are not uncommon. Some
females have very little pain, whereas others have a great deal.
Each woman is sensitive to the individual rhythm of her body.

What should I do if my daughter develops PMS (premenstrual syndrome)?

Don't be too quick to conclude that your child has PMS unless
symptoms such as bloatedness, irritability, depression, fatigue,
headaches, and other complaints occur with regularity during
the week or two before the flow begins. The complaints vary
from one woman to another. If you suspect that your daughter
is not just having normal mood changes, have her keep careful
monthly records of her symptoms before consulting her physician. Over-the-counter medications relieve some symptoms.

Does the start of menstruation mean that a girl is also capable of having an orgasm?

The ability to have an orgasm has nothing to do with menstruation. Some girls may experience orgasm from masturbation
before the onset of menstruation, whereas others may not have
one until many years after the first menses.

Is it important to get a doctor's advice at the time of the first period?

If your daughter is under regular medical care, report the
onset of menstruation to the doctor at her next regular physical
examination. If she has not been seeing a doctor regularly, she
should start to do so. It is important for the practitioner to develop a history of her physical condition. Females run a high
risk of cancer of the breast and cervix. Teach your daughter, from
the onset of menstruation, to pay careful attention to her physical
condition. The menstrual cycle and minor problems associated
with it often warn of a serious health problem. As a teenager
gets older, it is important that she develop the habit of visiting

a doctor at least once a year for a Pap smear, which is a quick and painless cancer-screening test of the cervix, and a breast examination.

What should parents tell their daughters about douching?

Young girls frequently report that they see their mother's douche bag in the bathroom but don't know what it's used for. Girls should be taught about douching, including the information that it is unnecessary because the body has the ability to cleanse itself, particularly at their age. Older women generally douche to cleanse the vagina after sexual intercourse, because it's faster than nature. Some doctors feel that using chemical preparations can eventually (particularly with frequent use) be harmful to the tissues of the vagina. In addition, douching may also spread infections into the cervix and uterus. Above all, tell your daughter that douching is an entirely *ineffective* method of contraception and should not be used for this purpose.

Is it okay for teenagers to use tampons, or should they use sanitary napkins?

Tampons are perfectly acceptable for use by young teenagers. In response to another commonly raised question, most girls who are virgins can use tampons without difficulty. However, they—and all women—must practice good hygiene and follow the instructions on the package insert.

A small number of women run the risk of developing toxic shock syndrome, which develops from an overgrowth of the staphylococcus bacterium. Because this illness can be fatal, any woman who develops a high fever or other signs of an infection should see a physician immediately.

Does menstruation weaken girls to the extent that they cannot participate in normal physical and athletic activity?

Menstruation is not an illness, and there is no reason for a girl to curtail any of her regular activities because of it. The major issue is that teenagers, who are often careless, don't keep themselves as clean as they should or change their sanitary protection often enough during their periods. If they observe hygienic precautions, they can continue all regular activities, unless, of course, they are subject to menstrual cramps that *may* diminish their physical strength. If a female has an illness that might restrict her activity, however, she should follow the advice of her physician.

Is bathing during menstruation harmful?

No. Bathing or showering is particularly necessary during menstruation. Tampons may be worn in the bath, but sanitary pads should be removed in preparation for bathing.

How about feminine hygiene sprays?

These sprays are largely perfumed powder. A spray is neither a medication nor a substitute for soap and water, and most doctors do not recommend them. Buying sprays is a waste of money. Even worse, sprays may cause irritation and rash in women who are sensitive to the chemicals they contain.

Exactly how does the menstrual cycle relate to pregnancy?

Menstruation involves a cycle or process. The appearance of blood is only one part of the total menstrual cycle. Some time between the eighth and twentieth day after the first day of bleeding is when a girl is most likely to become pregnant. The ovum or egg within the girl's body becomes fertile and could unite with a sperm from the male should intercourse take place. This union of egg and sperm produces conception and the development of a baby begins. Some people have sexual intercourse during presumably "safe" periods—the first to eighth day after the start of a period and three or four days before a period. This so-called rhythm method of avoiding pregnancy is *highly risky*.

Can a girl become pregnant without having sexual intercourse?

Rarely. A girl may feel guilty and fear that she has become pregnant after petting with a boy or experiencing an orgasm, or if the boy fondled her in sensitive spots or she touched male genitals. But pregnancy occurs only when a male sperm unites with a fertile egg, which usually happens when a male ejaculates with his penis directly inside a female's vagina. It is possible, however, for a boy to "come" just outside the vagina and for sperm to enter the vagina and result in pregnancy.

When the opportunity arises or youngsters ask questions about artificial insemination, explain that in some few cases, when a man's sperm is unable to adhere to an ovum, a male donor can ejaculate into a tube so that, with the consent of a husband and wife, a physician can later insert the sperm into the female's uterus or near the cervix or uterus opening to attempt to achieve conception.

Can a girl get pregnant only if she has an orgasm during intercourse?

Orgasm is unrelated to becoming pregnant. If male ejaculation occurs inside her vagina, a girl can become pregnant whether or not she experienced an orgasm.

Doesn't telling adolescent girls about contraception give them license to engage in sexual intercourse?

No. Telling your daughter about contraceptive measures does not mean that you are encouraging her to engage freely in sexual intercourse. For many generations, parents have made the mistake of thinking that they could delay sexual relations among adolescents by not telling them about sex. This is a dangerous myth. There is no scientific basis for the belief that information about matters relating to sexuality increases sexual activity. Remember that teens generally engage in sexual activity because of strong pressures—sexual urges, curiosity, peer pressure, search for companionship, a sense of adequacy—and it is unlikely that strong threats of punishment will prevent it. On the contrary, such threats may cause youngsters to "do it" just to prove their independence or to "fix" you. In spite of the strongest indoctrination against sexual activity, many young people still engage in sex and many girls become pregnant. Again, it is best to give advice that will help your child make wise decisions about sex and health matters but not to forbid the act. (See our discussion in the "Boy-Girl Relations" section of this chapter.) Information about sex, contraception, venereal disease, AIDS, and such, can lessen the influence of myths and fears about pregnancy and disease.

Can a girl become pregnant the first time she has sexual intercourse?

Yes, if she is fertile at the time. Unfortunately, many girls do become pregnant the first time they have intercourse, which is why it is important to inform young women about sex and contraception *before* their initiation into sexual activity. Some women still believe that only regular intercourse can result in pregnancy. A few believe that they can get pregnant only when they enjoy the act. The sad fact is that women can become pregnant after a brutal and painful rape.

What should I do if my daughter is raped?

Take her to a doctor immediately and report it to the police. Unfortunately, it's been said that many police departments do not pursue the rapists of black women because of prejudice and indifference. Black women should demand protection and speak out strongly against rape and violence in their communities. In addition, women must guard against and report date rape, which occurs when a male friend or acquaintance overpowers them against their will.

Rape victims need a great deal of sympathetic emotional support. Take your daughter to a rape crisis center for counseling. She may develop fears of being alone or traveling alone or become generally distrustful of men. The important thing is to help her understand that the act does not make her a bad, tainted, worthless, or doomed person. Encourage your daughter to bring charges against the rapist and not wrongfully blame herself. Your continued respect for her is more important than what you say.

How can a girl avoid being raped?

In general, girls should not pick up strange men, and they should refrain from walking alone in dark, secluded places. However, once a rapist attacks, a girl's first concern should be to protect her life. If the rapist is armed and violent, she is probably best advised to give in to avoid physical injury. Afterward, she should report the incident to the police immediately. Women should not hesitate to report date rape as well, rather than make excuses for the perpetrators. The men and women police officers who handle rape cases have been specially trained, which helps to relieve the embarrassment rape victims feel when filing a complaint.

Is it all right for a girl to be sexually aggressive with a boy if she is feeling excited?

It's not a question of right or wrong. Young women today are much more sexually aggressive than they were a few decades ago. Females have as much right as males to express their sexual desires. Men and women must be sensitive to the attitudes and values of their mates in deciding how aggressive or passive to be. As much as they may deny it, men also have different degrees of passivity and aggression in sexual activity.

Given strong evidence that my daughter is engaging in sexual intercourse or is on the verge of doing so, should I encourage her to use the pill?

Not necessarily. The overall effects of the pill on a female's system during her lifetime are still unknown. Oral contraceptives are readily available and simple to take, but they may not be the best method for a young, developing female. In addition, your daughter is probably not engaging in sexual intercourse so frequently that a measure as dramatic as the pill is necessary. Spermicidal sponges are available. A diaphragm, which can be inserted before intercourse and taken out hours later, is effective. Many adults underestimate the ability of young girls to use a diaphragm properly. It should not be overlooked as a method, since its effects on body functions are not as severe as those of the pill and IUDs (intrauterine devices).

Girls can keep their own supply of condoms (rubbers) on hand and insist that their partners use them. Condoms are inexpensive and easy to put in place when unplanned intercourse takes place. Condoms, which offer one of the best protections against contracting sexually transmitted diseases and AIDS, are the recommended form of contraception for the sexually active who have multiple partners.

Suppose our religion forbids the use of contraceptives?

Many religious concepts pose dilemmas for those who have to adjust in a modern society. In deciding about contraception, each person must weigh a religion's requirements against the possibility of pregnancy. It appears, unofficially at least, that many religious groups have come to accept the practice of birth control, as well as intercourse for pleasure and not just procreation.

Do women need to have children to feel fulfilled?

As more and more women find new opportunities for careers, they feel fulfilled without being mothers. Many women have personal reasons for not wishing to have children. They should not submit to pressure to become parents. No man or woman should bring children into the world out of a sense of obligation to relatives or society.

What is the best number of children for a married couple to have?

That is hard to say. All things considered, the optimum number of children is how many a woman wants and thinks she and/or the father can support. There is no particular virtue in having a great number of children who cannot be adequately provided for. The most important question parents should ask is how many children they can adequately care for with their energy level, and social, psychological, and financial resources.

If we think our daughter is pregnant but she denies it, what steps should we take?

You must take your daughter's word. If she exhibits uncommon symptoms of minor illness, seems to be gaining a lot of weight, and sleeps more than usual, express concern about her health and suggest that she make an appointment with a doctor. If you make it clear that you want to help rather than criticize or ostracize her, she is less likely to resist.

How should we proceed if our daughter gets pregnant out of wedlock?

The important options of families when an unmarried, teenage high school girl gets pregnant are getting married, placing the baby for adoption, having an abortion, or keeping the child. If both the girl and the boy want to get married and are reasonably mature, and resources are available for this potential family to provide an environment for the healthy development of a child, the pregnancy should be accepted and prenatal care undertaken immediately.

Occasionally, one of the families may have the resources and desire to rear the child in an extended family situation. In any arrangement, the welfare of the unborn child should be the most important consideration.

What if the teenager doesn't want an abortion?

If a girl does not want an abortion even though it appears to be the best solution, the parents should first make sure that she is not resisting out of fear for her health or in an effort to hurt her parents. An emotionally uninvolved professional person can help the family explore and answer these questions. Parents and any others involved should talk with the teenager about the demands and responsibilities of rearing a child and indicate whether they are prepared to give her financial as well as psychological support. If possible, the father of the unborn child should be consulted to clarify his intentions about providing for the mother and the child. When the boy's position is clear, it is often easier for the girl to make decisions.

An important solution for your daughter might be to have the baby and place it for adoption, although black babies have more difficulty being adopted than white babies. Many pro-life young people opt for this choice.

Traditionally, many girls have looked upon pregnancy as a means of identifying with the adult world. Some have used pregnancy as a means to get and keep the man they love. These are not good reasons to have a baby.

What if abortion is forbidden by our religious teachings?

Many religious faiths are beginning to accept abortion and do not consider it murder or a sin. Each woman must examine her beliefs and make the best decision for her future well-being. We feel that neglect of an unwanted child is abhorrent and must be weighed against other moral considerations.

*Which pills, laxatives, tonics, or concoctions work best to abort
a baby in the first months of pregnancy?*

For a normal, healthy, pregnant female no generally prescribed oral means for abortion exist in America. Scientists have
developed an abortion pill that can be used during the first
trimester but, as of this writing, it is available only in foreign
countries. It may soon be available in the United States, however.
Many girls who think they are pregnant take laxatives or pills
to bring on a period. If these products induce bleeding, there
was no pregnancy. Parents can help their daughters prevent
unnecessary sickness by explaining that such concoctions cannot
abort a fetus. Should a miscarriage occur, it would be the result
of a weakness in the mother's system or the fetus, not of pills.
A girl who has a miscarriage should be attended to by a doctor
as soon as possible.

*Will douching immediately following intercourse prevent
pregnancy?*

No. Douching is not a contraceptive method.

*If we cannot afford to travel to a state where abortion is legal,
should we seek out local illegal means?*

No. Back-alley abortions may cause permanent sterility and
even death. Social agencies in nearly every major city in this
country will make arrangements for consenting pregnant teenagers and their parents to go to a clinic where legal abortions
are performed under sanitary medical conditions. These agencies
also provide helpful educational information to pregnant women.

*Will undergoing an abortion prevent a woman from having
another child?*

No. In the past, when illegal abortions were carried out under
crude circumstances, complications resulted that sometimes per-
manently injured the woman's reproductive organs. An abortion
performed by a doctor is usually safe, and the woman can become
pregnant again.

*Can an abortion lead to having a deformed child the next time
you become pregnant?*

No. The probability of having a normal child after an uncomplicated abortion is as good as it was before.

What about guilt feelings following an abortion?

Any woman, regardless of age, should have proper counseling before submitting to an abortion. Parents and close friends can be especially supportive at the time, and doctors and nursing personnel can be helpful during the procedure. Legal abortion has lessened the guilt that women once carried about it.

What is a vasectomy?

A vasectomy is a minor operation, done under local anesthesia, in which the vas deferens (the tube that carries sperm to the penis) is tied, causing the male to become sterile.

Does a vasectomy cause impotency (inability to have an erection)?

No. The operation does not have a physiological effect on a man's capability to achieve erection. When impotency occurs after vasectomy, it usually stems from psychological problems.

Is impotency more or less common among black males than white males?

There are no accurate or reliable data to suggest that there is any difference in the number of white and black males who suffer from impotency.

Can a vasectomy be reversed?

Not reliably. It was once believed that a vasectomy resulted in permanent sterility. Recent studies and new techniques indicate that some males who have successfully had the procedure reversed have regained their fertility. However, there remains a serious lack of information on the effects of vasectomy.

Should black male youths be encouraged to consider vasectomy as a means of contraception?

Many black males have associated manhood with fertility because they are subject to racial oppression and have been denied rights, both social and economic, enjoyed by white males in society. As long as such oppression continues, these attitudes are likely to prevail and many black males will object to vasectomy as a means of contraception. Childless young black men should not be encouraged to have this operation. Feelings about having children may change, and the odds against successfully reversing the operation are still significant.

With all the contraceptives on the market for women and the legalization of abortion, why should a male consider such an operation?

Abortion, as well as many of the contraceptives on the market, including the pill, often cause women physical and emotional hardships. Vasectomy is a fairly minor procedure with few disadvantages for males.

SEXUALLY TRANSMITTED DISEASES AND AIDS

What causes VD?

Sexually transmitted disease (STDs), or venereal diseases, are almost always contracted through direct sexual contact. Most doctors believe they cannot be passed along through bathtubs or toilet seats. The most common STDs are chlamydia, trichomoniasis, gonorrhea, and syphilis.

Chlamydia, a bacterium that lives in cells, can be sexually transmitted. It causes infection in the male urethra (genital canal) and epididymis (ducts in which sperm are stored); in the female it can infect the urethra, cervix, uterus, and fallopian tubes. Women can develop pelvic inflammatory disease, which can lead to serious complications and infertility. Since 1980, chlamydia has become the most common STD in America. It responds well to treatment with antibiotics. Male partners should also be treated to prevent reinfection.

Trichomoniasis is caused by a protozoan organism found in 30 to 40 percent of male partners of infected women. Although the infection may be asymptomatic, it can produce vaginal irritation, discharge, and foul odor. The vagina becomes sore and tender, and urination (passing water) can cause burning. Medications are available to treat the infection in women and their male partners. Consult a physician should any of these symptoms appear.

Gonorrhea is generally easier to detect in males than in females. In usually three to five days after sexual contact with an infected person, a puslike discharge from the penis appears and burning irritation occurs with urination. Girls may develop a green or yellow-green discharge or experience lower abdominal pain. However, about 80 percent of infected women show no symptoms. Gonorrheal infection can also occur in the rectum or anus in men and women who have anal intercourse with an infected partner. Gonorrhea should be treated by a doctor immediately because serious complications, including sterility, fever, heart trouble, and even death can result. Treatment, with antibiotics, is painless. Some physicians recommend that sexually active women in nonmonogamous relationships be tested for gonorrhea at least once a year, whether or not they have symptoms. The test procedure is simple and painless.

Syphilis is less common but more dangerous than gonorrhea. The first sign is usually a sore on the genitals, on the lips, or in the oral cavity (mouth, tongue) if oral-genital sex was involved, or in the anus through anal intercourse, about three to four weeks after contact, as early as ten days after contact, or as long as three months after contact. It may later disappear with or without treatment, and a skin rash appears in the later or second stage. See a physician if you suspect syphilis. A simple blood test can often reveal the infection. Treatment is with antibiotics. Untreated syphilis can develop into extremely serious complications of the heart, brain, nervous system, and other parts of the body.

A man's use of a condom (rubber) offers some protection against spreading VD but is not absolutely safe. Anyone who suspects the presence of an STD should seek treatment promptly and inform sexual partners so that they may also seek immediate medical attention.

What effect does an STD have on the child of a woman who becomes pregnant while carrying the disease?

The child of an untreated woman can be born with syphilis and suffer serious medical consequences. Women who receive prenatal care are routinely tested for syphilis infection. If syphilis is discovered and treated early, the baby is not harmed.

Are there other STDs besides the well-known ones?

Yes. An organism called gardnerella vaginalis can cause vaginitis with a foul odor and discharge. Because the disease organisms can also be carried by men, treatment should be sought by the male partners as well.

Another infection that can be sexually transmitted, but may develop in women alone because many normally harbor yeast in the vagina, is *candida albicans*. The infection may be transmitted from a male partner, but it can also develop from changes in a woman's body, pregnancy, improper hygiene, or taking antibiotics. When the vaginal flora changes, a yeast infection may occur as an opportunistic infection. Even tight underwear with poor ventilation may precipitate an outbreak. Yeast infections produce irritation, burning, and a cheeselike white vaginal discharge. Physicians usually treat an infected woman, but her male partners should be treated as well. An over-the-counter antifungal medication for self-treatment is available for women who have recurrent infections.

Genital herpes, a widespread and unpleasant STD, is caused by a virus—herpes simplex. The first infection causes painful genital sores, blisters, pain, and severe itching. In addition, headaches, fever, muscle aches, and other general symptoms may occur. The sore may last from two to three weeks. After the first outbreak, the virus remains in the system and episodes can recur throughout life. There is no cure, but some medications may help to alleviate symptoms. The herpes virus can be transmitted from mother to fetus during pregnancy or delivery. People should refrain from sexual relations while the virus is active, and use condoms at all other times to prevent infecting partners.

Another STD that is receiving increasing attention is genital warts caused by the human papilloma virus (HPV). Warts can occur on both the genitals and the anus. Venereal warts and herpes infection are two of the commonest STDs. HPV infection is associated with increased risks for cancer in men and women, especially cancer of the cervix. Anyone with HPV should refrain from sexual contact and seek treatment. After the warts are removed, regular checkups are important. The faithful use of condoms helps prevent the spread of HPV.

Information on other STDs can be found in most sex manuals. Any person who has unusual itching, swelling, ulcers, or sores or warts around or on the sex organs should consult a physician.

How does a person contract AIDS?

AIDS can be transmitted through homosexual or heterosexual contact with an infected person, by the sharing of infected needles among intravenous drug users—when blood or other infected fluids come in contact with a wound or cut in another person—and by transfusions with infected blood. The virus can spread from pregnant women to their children. The disease may incubate for many years before symptoms appear. The person's immune system is destroyed and the disease is ultimately fatal. Although treatment may prolong life and reduce symptoms, no cure has yet been found. Several laboratories are working to develop an effective vaccine.

The best treatment is prevention: practicing safe sex with few partners, avoiding anal intercourse, and regularly using condoms with virus-killing spermicides.

What are "crabs"?

"Crabs," tiny lice that invade the pubic hair, can come from dirty linen and toilet seats as well as through sexual intercourse. They usually crawl about the genital area, causing itching. A doctor can prescribe medication to apply to the infected area that makes the crabs disappear in a day or so.

Is strong itching or an unusual discharge in women a sign of an STD?

Not necessarily; often it is not. Females sometimes have other infections in and around the vagina, which are caused by changes in body chemistry and minor illnesses of one type or other. Various forms of vaginitis (minor infections in the vagina) sometimes occur and recur. It is important for a female's mental and physical well-being that she consult a doctor whenever she has an unusual discharge with an unpleasant odor, itching, or irritation. The causes can usually be diagnosed, and prescribed medication can quickly clear up minor infections. Advise your daughter not to delay seeking medical attention when she feels any discomfort in the vaginal area.

Girls often avoid bringing such problems to the attention of their parents because they fear that the parents will think they have been engaging in intercourse. Parents' overriding concern for female adolescents during these trying years of sexual development should be the good physical and mental health of their children. (See our discussions in the "Values, Morals, and Attitudes" and "Boy-Girl Relations" sections of this chapter.) You're ahead of the game when you have developed a way of responding that encourages your youngsters to approach you with any problem or issue, as we hope you have.

PROSTITUTION

Is a woman who has sexual relations with several different men a prostitute?

No. The key factor in prostitution is engaging in sexual intercourse for a fee, often with strangers on a one-time basis. Many girls and women who are not prostitutes have frequent sexual intercourse and with different partners.

Why do some teenage girls, especially in large urban areas, turn to prostitution?

There are numerous reasons, but for many the major reason is economic. Young girls learn from older women, pimps, or friends that they can earn money through prostitution. For a girl who comes from a poor home and has no skills for employment and therefore no job prospects, prostitution offers a means to secure money for clothes and other items teenagers desire. Some girls become prostitutes because they are drug addicts in desperate need of money to support their habit. However, some girls become prostitutes because they are dependent, have a poor self-image, or are rebelling against parents whom they wish to punish. Many prostitutes were victims of sexual abuse as children, which may cause them to devalue themselves and their relationships with men. But we also know girls from middle-class homes who work as prostitutes.

Parents can usually prevent prostitution by providing sound sex education as well as an accepting, caring atmosphere in the home, thereby discouraging rebellious, antisocial behavior in their children. Good preparation in dealing with "slicksters," exploiters, and child abusers also helps. Trusting, idealistic girls who deny the realities of the world are sometimes led or forced into prostitution. Occasionally, even with the best parental guidance, a young woman may drift into prostitution because of deep emotional conflicts.

At what age are girls likely to turn to prostitution?

This varies with the emotional and physical development of the girl and the supply and demand for females in a given low-income community. With the increasing economic and social deterioration of many inner-city communities, girls are turning to prostitution at younger and younger ages. Some who are obviously in their early teens can be seen on street corners at night.

Do female gangs encourage girls to practice prostitution?

Yes. Teenage girls may be trapped into prostitution through association with people who already engage in this trade. Prostitutes are often forced by their pimps to recruit new girls. In some cases, however, a young girl who has experienced sexual assault may feel guilty, choose to engage in prostitution, and seek out others with similar aspirations. In numerous cases, it is not the influence of other girls, but attraction to a boy who aspires to be a pimp that gets a girl involved in this activity.

How do prostitutes function psychologically?

There are few good studies about the emotional and psychological development and functioning of girls who engage in prostitution. We do know that many eventually abandon this kind of life, get jobs, marry, and have families. Others stay in prostitution into late adulthood, stopping only when they are no longer marketable. Women who don't want to remain in prostitution but can't handle self-damaging psychological forces can frequently be helped by psychological treatment.

Is prostitution confined to the black ghetto and lower classes?

No. Prostitution, which is as old as civilization, occurs at all social and economic levels in white as well as black communities. Whether prostitution is recognized as a social problem is determined by the values of a given society. Prostitution is legal in some countries and in the state of Nevada. In one respect, it is quasi-legal in our society: the male consumers are rarely prosecuted; it's mostly the females who are arrested. White prostitutes are usually found in the lucrative call-girl establishments of larger cities.

Contrary to popular belief, prostitution is not widespread within ghetto areas. Prostitutes usually operate in or near bars, and in commercial districts of cities where males from outside the black community congregate. Males—often white—come into the black community and "hunt" for young black girls on streets or blocks known to be frequented by prostitutes. Traditionally, a smaller percentage of black men than white men patronize prostitutes.

What is the relationship between pimps and prostitutes?

A pimp is usually a male upon whom girls depend for direction and protection in prostitution activities. Life in the streets is a competitive marketplace similar to business and industry. Prostitution *is* a business enterprise, with the pimp usually the manager. He determines when, where, and how the girls work. Ordinarily all moneys are turned over to the pimp, who allots a given amount to each woman; he often manages all housing, health care, purchasing, and other aspects of the girl's life. He also helps to keep her out of jail and provides for legal counsel if she's arrested.

The pimp-prostitute arrangement is obviously a master-slave relationship—economic exploitation, physical abuse, and psychological damage for the prostitute; material and social gain for the pimp. Pimps are most undesirable models for black youths. Male prostitutes who solicit homosexuals usually do not require pimps.

Why do girls cooperate with pimps?

The two greatest reasons for the pimp-prostitute relationship are romantic attraction and protection and security. Many girls become emotionally attached to their pimps, who are then able to control the girls' behavior. Pimps also lure runaways into prostitution by offering them security, a place to live, and protection. In addition, as a male, the pimp can protect the prostitute from assaults by emotionally unbalanced consumers and other street hustlers.

Are certain types of males more likely to become pimps than others?

Some young black men see pimping as a way of making big money and gaining status. Charm and charisma, ability to manipulate people, and attraction to a risky and promiscuous lifestyle are the characteristics of most pimps. Little is known about what makes one young man rather than others in the same environment turn out to be a pimp, although many pimps have a deep dislike for women. We suspect that a number of these young men could do well in a legitimate business or in government if they had the proper role models and the opportunities to move in these directions.

What can parents or other adults do to help girls who may be engaged in prostitution?

Parents who discover that a daughter is practicing prostitution are usually hurt, angry, and embarrassed. People tend to despise or reject such girls. But many prostitutes get involved even when they don't want to and need a parent's help to get out. Some may even rebuff a parent who tries to come to their aid. Having painted themselves into a corner by ignoring parental advice, they are too embarrassed or guilty to openly admit their desire for help. In such a case, it is best to offer assistance and maintain contact until your daughter is able to accept it.

A number of youth programs in large cities are attempting to get these girls (especially the younger teens) off the streets and into educational and recreational programs to redirect their interest and train them for a variety of jobs. But there are too few such programs for adolescents, and there is a need for more centers where young people can receive counseling and education, develop confidence, and enjoy healthy recreation. Community-based residential centers are also needed.

RELIGION

My teenagers, who have been attending Sunday school and church since they were very young, recently began to resist going to church. Should they be forced to attend regularly?

Youngsters who have been exposed to church and are now rejecting it should be allowed that right. On the other hand, teenagers who continue to find churchgoing important should be encouraged. The important issue is that morality and teaching what is right must also take place outside the church—in the home and in the community. As we mentioned earlier, physical attendance at church doesn't necessarily make for a good Christian.

My teenagers say that church is racist, dull, and irrelevant to modern life. Can the church still offer them opportunities for healthy social activities?

Yes. Ministers in many communities are making the church relevant to today's issues among blacks. The church remains an important institution for social action and interaction, with black awareness programs, clubs, dances, art, music, athletic programs, and so on. It is still a place where many black youngsters develop organizational and leadership skills. It is an important base or place of belonging that reduces the sense of alienation and rejection for many black youths in the larger society. Support, rather than attack, this important black institution, and challenge your teen to help it become the more relevant force it needs to be. You must also keep in mind that the church has played a major role in the civil rights movement under the leadership of Dr. Martin Luther King, Jr., the Reverend Jesse Jackson, and other fighters for justice and equality.

However, we do believe that black churches should not depict Jesus Christ and the Madonna exclusively as white; they should also be shown as black, brown, and yellow. God and His disciples are universal symbols that should be represented by all racial groups. It is important for the self-image of black youths to see all-powerful and all-good African images, too!

Our youngsters claim that belonging to a particular religion tends to create animosity among people, and cite the Irish Catholic-Protestant and Arab-Israeli conflicts. How can a parent reply to that?

It is best to acknowledge the divisive nature of "our faith" carried too far or "used" to justify exploitation and abuse of others who believe or worship differently. We sincerely hope that you reject this misuse of religion. Point out that humane people should recognize the brotherhood of all people and accept different religious forms without using difference for selfish political or economic ends.

Are young people less religious than formerly?

It is difficult to ascertain whether youths today are less religious. Fewer attend church, but this may be related to weakened family and extended family structures, particularly in inner-city neighborhoods. Churches must do more to attract teenagers with programs and activities geared to their lifestyles and interests.

The desire for spiritual enlightenment and devotion can take various forms. Many changes are taking place within organized religion; young people are engaging in new forms of religious activities, ranging from silent meditation to dramatic expressions of spiritual devotion. Some are involved in community service activities in order to find spiritual meaning.

My fourteen-year-old says she is an atheist even though we are religious people. What could be wrong with her?

Nothing is wrong with her. Many young people question religious beliefs they earlier took for granted. Accept her questioning. You should respect her atheistic views just as she should respect your religious viewpoint. Adolescence is the period when teenagers explore new ideas. Their deep attachments to a particular ideology may come and go quickly. Your daughter is more likely to reconsider her views if you respect her opinion than if you try to force her to accept yours.

My sixteen-year-old son is interested in joining the Black Muslims and it frightens me. Is it a real religion?

The Black Muslims (the Nation of Islam) comprise a religious order in the United States founded by the Honorable Elijah Muhammed. It is based, with some modification, on traditional Muslim teachings derived from the Koran. Malcolm X, a great African-American leader, embraced this religion.

The practices of the Muslims differ significantly from the Christian faith. The Nation of Islam requires strict discipline from its members. The group, which has had considerable success in rehabilitating wayward black youths, is strongly dedicated to fighting racism and white oppression.

My teenage daughter, a college freshman, is in some Christian group that demands all her time and thought, and she is neglecting her school work. It almost sounds like a cult. What should I do?

Some religious sects are very demanding of their members, requiring total devotion. A few are on the fringes of bona fide religions, but others do represent cults into which individuals are blindly led and exploited spiritually and financially.

Talk to your daughter about her school responsibilities and the reasonable allocation of her time. Refrain from challenging her religious beliefs, but emphasize that most constructive Christian groups would encourage her to devote adequate attention to her studies.

MENTAL HEALTH

Are adolescents more likely to have an emotional breakdown than older people?

As mentioned earlier, adolescence is generally a period of great emotional turmoil fired by deep personal drives. Teenagers experience the onset of sexual interests and search for independence. Some of them may break down emotionally under such stress. Fortunately, most teens manage to channel their sexual urges and drives into constructive activities and learning behavior. Most youths are able to move through adolescence without serious emotional disturbance.

What is schizophrenia?

Schizophrenia, which frequently manifests itself during adolescence, is a mental disorder to which some youngsters are genetically predisposed and in which thinking is deranged. A schizophrenic person has strange ideas and may hear voices and see things that are not present in reality. He may imagine he is a famous person or that he has special magical abilities. Paranoid schizophrenics may think people are plotting against or trying to hurt them. Schizophrenics are usually withdrawn and have trouble making friends; a teenager, however, may be withdrawn and noncommunicative without being schizophrenic. Schizophrenics may become unruly; teenagers occasionally have extreme temporary upsets in which they act strange but are not schizophrenic. Unresolved questions about race, sex, and adequacy, as well as hidden and open family conflict can cause schizophrenics to become upset; an upset youngster's behavior is often a cry for help for the entire family.

What should be done for a teenager who exhibits symptoms of schizophrenia?

Take the youngster to see a doctor, privately or in a hospital clinic. Some hospitalization may be necessary. Medications are available to help schizophrenics recover; some people never become ill again. With the additional help of psychotherapy and counseling, many people can lead useful and productive lives. It is frequently necessary for the entire family to be involved in the treatment. Never reject or make fun of a child with mental problems.

Do other mental disorders affect teenagers?

Yes, a few, the most common being severe anxiety, overactivity, and depression.

Severe to moderate depression can seriously handicap a

teenager—or anyone else. If your child becomes extremely depressed, withdrawn, fatigued, neglects her personal responsibilities, is agitated, can't sleep, and has a decreased appetite for several weeks, she may be experiencing a serious depression. Some teens may show manic (overstimulated) behavior followed by a depression. Psychiatrists have found a hereditary predisposition to these disorders. In any case, if your child is affected, consult a psychiatrist for help. Many effective medications are available for the treatment of depression and manic-depressive disorder.

If a teenager has prolonged periods of anxiety or panic reactions, try to discuss her problems with her. If this does not help, consult a doctor, social worker, local hospital, or mental health clinic.

Finally, teens may develop a variety of personality disorders, including antisocial personality problems that lead to criminality.

Is it true that black teens don't develop eating disorders?

Apparently, anorexia nervosa disorder—characterized by a pathological fear of weight gain leading to faulty eating habits and excessive weight loss—is much more common in white middle- and upper-middle-class adolescents, mostly girls. However, blacks, too, can develop this life-threatening illness, which requires medical treatment.

The incidence of bulimia   the practice (usually of a young female) of binging on food, then inducing vomiting in order to remain thin, is undocumented among blacks, but it may occur.

A far more serious eating disorder for black teenagers is overeating, which results in a high rate of obesity, especially among females. This puts them at high risk for diabetes, hypertension, heart disease, and stroke. Obesity requires medical treatment that includes a regimen of good nutrition and exercise.

My friend's daughter had a craving for and ate a lot of laundry starch during her pregnancy. What is that all about?

In the past, particularly in the South, young black women ate clay and starch during pregnancy, thinking that it was good for the growing fetus. But that is just an old wives' tale. Actually, women who eat too much household starch develop anemia, which can endanger them and their babies. Today, black women rarely eat such compounds. This practice should be strongly discouraged.

Is it true that blacks don't commit suicide?

No. Young black men in cities have long had a high suicide rate, which in the past decades has been increasing. Their suicide rate is becoming equal to that of young white males in cities. Overall, the black suicide rate remains about half the white rate. More than 1,000 black men and 300 black women commit suicide each year. Percentage figures indicate that the suicide rate among unmarried teenage females (black and white) is about ten times the national average. Therefore, depression in a teenager should be taken seriously.

A person who is not eating or sleeping well and is easily upset and tearful may be depressed, even though he or she is not "dragging." Report such symptoms to your doctor. People in danger of committing suicide may become argumentative and difficult in an effort to drive away family and friends and break all social contacts. Friends feel attacked, hit back, or desert without considering the pattern. It sometimes follows the loss of a boyfriend, close family members, and so on. If you find that youngsters are breaking social ties, persuade them to seek professional help. Pointing out that you think they are trying to drive you away because they are in trouble, upset, feeling bad, or whatever, is one way to raise the issue. Unfortunately, some victims give no warning nor are they always depressed.

Is drug overdosage (O.D.) a form of suicide?

Although O.D.'s are officially, counted as accident statistics, we suspect that some of them are suicides. But it is impossible to tell whether an overdose is related to suicidal intentions. In some large cities, overdoses of heroin and cocaine are becoming a significant cause of death among young black men and women. Certainly, teens who take risks with lethal drugs may be expressing an unconscious wish to commit suicide.

Does daydreaming in teenagers signify emotional trouble?

No. Everyone daydreams. It is normal to do so and it is

normal for adolescents to daydream more than people of other ages. If their daydreaming leads to the neglect of personal responsibilities or withdrawal from social contacts, however, it deserves investigation. Excessive daydreaming may be an attempt to avoid dealing with the realities of daily life. A teenager who confuses daydreams with reality needs professional help.

How can I persuade a teen who needs help to go for treatment?

Be truthful and don't use scare tactics or deception. When the area of difficulty is limited—school trouble, sadness, or depression—indicate that you're aware that the teen is doing okay in other areas but you are concerned about and want her to get help with her school problem or become happier or whatever. Teens struggling with new urges and ideas may feel they are about to go crazy, and blacks in this state of mind may fear being hospitalized under unfavorable conditions.

Suggest that the teen talk with a mental health worker, an idea that may not have occurred to her as an acceptable alternative. Thus, when a youngster's problems are not extreme, you can help by saying that you understand that she is not crazy before you explain the why, when, and what of treatment. It may be helpful for you to consult with the mental health worker beforehand on how to bring up the subject of seeking help with the teenager. Once you have made your initial contact and visit with the youngster and helper, encourage an older teen to make her own appointments.

Should the problem require hospitalization, use basically the same approach, but don't promise to do more than stand by or assist the youngster in obtaining whatever will help her get on the road to recovery.

DRUGS AND DRUG ABUSE

Should teenagers be allowed to smoke?

Cigarette smoking, which has been proved to be very dangerous to health, should be strongly discouraged. It can cause lung cancer and contribute to heart and other lung diseases.

Pregnant women who smoke can damage the fetus and give birth to at-risk, low-weight babies. Explain these risks to the teenager. In addition, make them aware that cigarette smoking is highly addictive and once started the habit can be extremely difficult to break. Unfortunately, despite many warnings, teenagers continue to take up smoking in great numbers. After you have advised against it, your child will still have the final choice. But if smoking irritates other members of the family, the smoker should not be allowed to impose his or her self-pollution on others. Parents and family members who smoke provide bad role models. Secondhand smoke may precipitate potentially fatal asthma attacks in children. If you smoke, stop if you can, for your own health and that of your children.

Why are young people so quick to start smoking when they know it's dangerous?

They want to feel sophisticated and grown up. Smoking may also be a way of rebelling. It seems like a hip thing to do and may increase their feelings of belonging with their group. Death from lung cancer or other diseases at age fifty or sixty seems too remote to represent a real danger to young people. Cigarette advertising, which presents smokers as cool, attractive, and masterful, is one of the reasons we suggest that you teach your child early in life to "see through" advertisers' messages.

Should we let our teenagers smoke marijuana?

Smoking marijuana (grass, pot, reefers) should be discouraged. Explain the legal risks. Remember that it is illegal to smoke marijuana, and although in some states the penalties for using it are as minor as those for traffic tickets, young blacks may be selectively arrested by police officers and receive stiff penalties. The health risks of smoking pot are similar to those of smoking cigarettes—increased risk of cancer and heart and lung disease. In addition, chronic use of pot can produce paranoia, panic reactions, distortions in perception and thought, and memory loss. Users may lose motivation and develop school and work problems. Pot smokers are impaired drivers and should not operate motor vehicles or other machinery. Tests for the presence of traces of marijuana in the urine are administered to those involved in accidents and in random drug checks of various employees. A positive finding can cost you your job. But parents who themselves smoke pot would be hypocritical to insist that their children refrain. They should know that they are putting themselves and their children at risk, and seek help.

Should we allow our teenagers to smoke marijuana at home?

Some parents allow their children to smoke marijuana at home because they feel that if they *do* smoke, home is a safer environment than the street or other unfavorable settings. But such parents are helping their child break a law. Besides, youngsters who smoke at home often do so away from home anyway. We don't think it's a good idea, especially when you consider the effects on other family members, particularly younger children.

How can we try to prevent our youngsters from smoking marijuana or taking drugs?

It is less what you say or do now than what you did in the past. Teenagers who feel adequate, have ambition and direction, and can handle frustration are less likely to turn to drugs. Teens who are not under extreme peer pressure to use drugs are also less inclined to do so. In any case, discussion and education about drugs can be helpful in the prevention of drug usage. Scare tactics are less productive than helping youngsters understand that using drugs can prevent their full enjoyment of life, limit opportunities, and cause them a number of personal and social problems.

With early teens or late preteens, it is useful to discuss the issue of smoking marijuana and drugs calmly and objectively. Look at books written on the subject and make the ones you consider best available to your youngsters. Let it be known, early in your discussion and without undue emotion, that you disapprove of the use of drugs. Youngsters may point out that other youngsters are taking drugs or smoking pot and that they could do the same without your knowledge. One effective response is, "You could, but why would you *have* to smoke or take drugs?" Interestingly enough, many youngsters have never asked themselves this question. It can lead to other questions about what they want for themselves and whether drugs might help them achieve their ambition. Fortunately, the number of teenagers who smoke marijuana has been decreasing in recent years.

If marijuana is so harmful, why do people smoke it?

People generally say that it makes them feel good and that experiences take on a greater intensity. Some claim to feel more relaxed. Marijuana is reported to enhance the pleasure of listening to music, tasting food, and sex, and produce a temporary euphoria. However, some people claim to feel no effects from marijuana, whereas others have experienced severe anxiety and paranoid reactions.

Teens may argue that marijuana is less harmful to the body than alcohol, but this is no justification for its use. Youngsters often take drugs of any type to feel more sophisticated and grown up. Suggest constructive ways for your child to establish maturity to help decrease the need for rebellion and pot smoking.

Can marijuana make you drunk as alcohol does?

No, not exactly. Marijuana can make a person as light-headed, sleepy, and sluggish but usually not as uncoordinated. Alcohol intoxication leads to loss of coordination and staggering. Both alcohol and marijuana may make a person feel uninhibited. Judgment is impaired with both a "high" from alcohol and from marijuana. It is dangerous to drive an automobile or engage in other precision activities when under the influence of either drug because they interfere with alertness and reaction time.

My seventeen-year-old son smokes marijuana a lot and has no motivation to make something of himself. How can I get him to stop?

Excessive marijuana smoking may be a sign of deep emotional disturbance and serve as an escape from life's problems. Many teens having trouble making career choices, lifestyle choices, and so on, just "cop out" on drugs. If you cannot reach your son through discussion, obtain the services of a mental health worker.

If my child smokes marijuana, could he become a pusher?

It's possible, but it doesn't always happen. Unfortunately, although marijuana may be considered a less harmful drug, a marijuana pusher is usually pressured into pushing other drugs, namely, crack cocaine and heroin. Young people are attracted to many illegal activities in the black community, as they are to this one, for the monetary gain. When education and jobs are unavailable, teenagers turn to other ways of making money. Feeling they have nothing to lose if they are caught, they find it easy to engage in unlawful deeds. Encouraging your youngster to think in terms of a future goal *may* help. Point out the risks he will take and the people he will hurt as a pusher of illegal drugs of any kind.

Doesn't smoking marijuana always lead to the use of hard drugs?

Not necessarily, but it may. Contact with the drug culture, in which it is one of many drugs, might lead a person to use harder drugs through social exposure.

The big problem in my neighborhood isn't pot but crack. What is crack?

Crack is a form of cocaine that is processed into a "rock" and can be smoked. It is less expensive and has caused an epidemic of drug users and pushers in the inner city. The personal and social effects of crack have been devastating to the black community.

How does crack affect people?

Crack is an extremely powerful stimulant that can speed up the heartbeat and breathing. It can constrict blood vessels and, consequently, raise blood pressure, which can cause strokes and heart attacks. Users have been known to drop dead on the spot after just one dose.

Crack usually produces a quick high that may disappear in thirty minutes, when users require another "hit." They feel euphoric, talkative, energetic, and powerful. They may feel more alert and less inhibited than usual. Chronic users develop sleeping problems, impaired judgment, irritability, and sometimes severe paranoia and other bouts of "craziness."

What's a crack baby?

Women who take crack while pregnant can damage the fetus with even one "hit." The babies may suffer small strokes and other brain damage. They do not develop properly and are emotionally distant and irritable. Many have a variety of learning disabilities. These children are probably damaged for life, and will require special management. It is urgent that community and health officials take every action possible to prevent pregnant women from taking crack and other forms of cocaine.

Why does the use of crack lead to so much crime and killing?

The crack trade has been so profitable that many young people have become pushers to earn quick money. Turf battles occur, which are settled by gunfights and gang-style executions. Also, people on cocaine are frequently paranoid, hyper, and combative. In other words, they are likely to strike out and be quick on the trigger—and guns are readily available. The homicide rate among young black males has risen significantly as a result, and many more are incarcerated.

Do you think there is a conspiracy on the part of whites in power to spread drugs in the black community?

We do not think there is a conscious conspiracy, but we do think that officials are often indifferent to many social ills in the inner city and treat them with benign and malignant neglect. Certainly, the government and federal law enforcers have not done enough to keep drugs out of the country and to capture the "big players" in the drug trade.

But we should make every effort to work with community groups and the police to eliminate the scourge of the crack plague from our neighborhoods.

What are "downers"? Are they dangerous?

"Downers" usually refer to sedative or sleeping medications, the most common being barbiturates, which are highly addicting. Overdoses, particularly when mixed with alcohol, can lead to death. Withdrawal symptoms of people addicted to barbiturates can include convulsions. Anyone so addicted requires close medical supervision.

What are tranquilizers?

They are a variety of calming drugs, the most common being Serax, Xanax, Valium, and Librium.

There is a high level of consumption of tranquilizers, particularly among girls and young women. Are these drugs dangerous?

Tranquilizers can cause dependency and addiction. Taken in heavy dosages over a consistent period of time, they can be as dangerous as barbiturates. Although these drugs are available only with a doctor's prescription, increasing amounts are being pushed on the illegal market.

Is it harmful to take tranquilizers with alcohol?

Both tranquilizers and alcohol are drugs. When taken together, they enhance each other's effects. This is also true of illegal drugs such as marijuana and cocaine. It is dangerous to mix drugs—mixing any drugs can be fatal.

What is "speed"?

Speed (also known as uppers) is the name given to a group of stimulant drugs such as amphetamines. They can make one feel more alert and awake. Large quantities can produce extreme nervousness and rapid heartbeat. Speed, which is habit forming, can also cause psychoses. Over-the-counter diet pills usually contain speed-type ingredients.

What are LSD and mescaline?

LSD (lysergic acid diethylamide), "acid," and mescaline are hallucinogenic drugs. They can make users see things that are not there, interfere with thinking, and make a person psychotic. These drugs are extremely dangerous and should not be used.

Is heroin as dangerous as it is said to be?

Yes. Heroin produces a feeling of great happiness and being on top of the world, but it is strongly addicting. People can quickly become dependent on heroin and must then devote their lives to acquiring money to buy the drug. Much of the crime in the black community is committed by heroin and cocaine addicts. There are hundreds of thousands of heroin addicts, a disproportionate number of whom are black youths.

Sharing needles among drug addicts is a major way of spreading AIDS in the inner cities.

Should cities give clean needles to drug addicts to try to stop the spread of AIDS?

We think there is some risk of addicts feeling that, by dispensing clean needles, officials accept or condone drug use, but the risks of contracting the deadly AIDS virus outweigh these concerns. Attempts should be made to provide addicts with clean needles and discourage needle sharing. A few cities have tried such programs, but authorities have difficulty in obtaining the cooperation of the drug addicts.

Do methadone programs help heroin addicts?

They may help in some cases. Methadone is a drug chemically related to heroin that can be taken orally and reduces the desire for heroin. Clinics supply addicts with methadone under medical control. Eventually, through therapy programs, an attempt is made to withdraw the addict from all drugs. The important aspect of methadone maintenance is the psychotherapy and related therapy program that addicts are required to attend. Unfortunately, not enough drug treatment programs are available.

Why do some blacks oppose methadone programs?

Because the program has not reduced the amount of drug addiction in the community. Methadone itself is addicting, and addicts have sold it to others. A number have died of methadone overdosage. In addition, many black leaders fear that methadone is just a social control program to cut down crime, and that unscrupulous politicians could use it to manipulate addicts by threatening to withhold treatment.

What is the best way to treat heroin and cocaine addicts?

No one knows for sure, but ex-addicts claim a high rate of

success in rehabilitating other addicts. Increasing numbers of residential detoxification programs are available for individuals involved in substance abuse, which includes alcohol, heroin, cocaine, and other addictions. The most important factor in breaking the habit is an addict's own resolve to stop.

Do many teenagers experiment with mixtures of various drugs?

Sadly, reports indicate that teenagers often mix several drugs such as marijuana and crack or marijuana and various pills. They frequently mix these drugs with alcohol, which leads to serious impairment in judgment, physical coordination, and alertness. As mentioned earlier, all such practices of drug mixing simply heighten the seriousness of the drugs' effects and increase the chances or overdose and death.

What is the cause of the increased use of drugs among black youths?

The causes of drug use and abuse in our society are too numerous for discussion in this book. However, the widespread availability of drugs clearly creates a situation where young people have increasing access to drugs, leading to the likelihood that they will try and continue to use them. Also, black youths are more frustrated and victimized than others by poverty, joblessness, lack of recreation, and other social problems. Such conditions are fertile soil for drug addiction. Unfortunately, the wide use of drugs will not decrease significantly until these conditions are corrected.

Is it true that alcohol can damage the body?

Yes. Every year many black men and women die from liver cirrhosis brought on by consumption of excessive alcohol. Chronic drinkers often develop brain damage and a psychosis (i.e., they "go crazy"). Many lose their memory and judgment. Chronic alcoholics undergo a slow deterioration of the personality as well as the body. Pregnant women who drink excessively can damage the fetus and produce babies with fetal alcohol syndrome. Such children suffer stunted growth and are mentally retarded.

Should teenagers be permitted to drink?

There is no reason why teens shouldn't taste wine and other alcoholic drinks, under adult supervision, on occasion. It is important for young people to learn how to drink in moderation. Youngsters who are denied that lesson within a family often drink too much the first time they are away from home. Explain the dangers of excessive and continual drinking. Not infrequently, a person collapses and dies after consuming great quantities of alcohol. People who function well have their lives under control, including when and how much alcohol to drink. Do not insist or tell your teen that it's cool or grown up to drink alcohol if the youngster doesn't want to.

Is it possible for an adolescent to become an alcoholic?

Yes, it is. Alcoholism often begins in adolescence. Teenagers who drink excessively have personal problems. An anxious or depressed youngster may turn to alcohol, a highly addictive drug, as a release. Parents must try to get to the bottom of the problem or seek professional help for such a child.

Does the common practice in some countries of serving the entire family a moderate amount of wine or beer with meals encourage alcoholism in adolescents?

There is little scientific evidence on which to base a factual answer to this question. However, light wines at meals add pleasure to dining, and there is no reason for the entire family not to partake of them, even if children are given only a taste. But we feel that families should not encourage regular drinking of any type.

Can't drinking alcohol be a good release for a young person under pressure?

Yes, if it's indulged in maturely and not resorted to as the only means to relieve pressure. However, many crimes of violence and fatal accidents in the black community involve intoxicated people. Drunk driving has led to a large number of senseless fatalities, bringing tragedy to many families. No one should drink and drive and, rightfully, serious penalties are imposed on people apprehended as drunk drivers. Drivers who refuse to submit to a Breathalyzer test receive an automatic suspension of their driver's license and additional punishments.

Alcoholic parents cause family breakdowns. They frequently abuse and neglect their children. In addition, a large number of cases of domestic violence, homicides in general, and accidents are associated with the abuse of alcohol.

Does alcoholism run in families?

Sometimes. It is believed that certain persons may have a greater psychological or physiological tendency to become alcoholic, but this susceptibility is not necessarily hereditary. Children of alcoholics are more likely to become alcoholics themselves because of the breakdown and stresses of the home. For complex reasons, many children imitate a parent's life pattern.

What can we do to help young alcoholics?

All alcoholics should be referred for medical help. Many special programs are available for them at hospitals and clinics. Various self-help alcoholic recovery groups are successful in treating alcoholics who want to break their habit and can provide information about other such programs. Youth-directed, self-help, antialcoholism programs are emerging in a number of communities.

VIOLENCE AND CRIME

Does any one factor cause black youths to become juvenile delinquents?

The two most important factors associated with juvenile delinquency are a poverty environment and a difficult family life. Because of racism, past and present, blacks have more than their share of both. However, the rate of juvenile delinquency is high among whites in disadvantaged environments as well.

Some of the kids on the block think it's okay to shoplift. Is it?

No. It's unfortunate when our youths try to justify antisocial behavior. Some have adopted the philosophy that the exploitative white store owner steals from the people by charging high prices for inferior merchandise. But these same youngsters steal from black shop owners as well. They think shoplifting is a means of getting what belongs to the people, but it doesn't work. The shop owner merely raises prices accordingly, and thereby shifts the cost to other customers in the community. Some black-owned supermarkets have gone bankrupt because the locals stole so much merchandise. It is important to impress on children that shoplifting is a criminal offense that can lead to serious punishment.

Do black teenagers really shoplift more than whites?

We don't know. There are reports, however, that many teenage shoplifters are white youngsters from middle-class backgrounds who have the money to pay for what they take. They steal for attention, as a form of rebellion against their parents and authority, and for other more personal and deeper emotional reasons. The problem for black teens, however, is that, when caught, they are prosecuted more often than white. Black youths are more likely to be sent to detention homes where they may begin a pattern of crime and antisocial behavior.

What is selling "hot" goods?

Procuring "hot" goods, a form of organized shoplifting or burglarizing for profit, is most popular among the street cultures and is frequently related to raising money for drugs. Many young men and women involved in prostitution also "boost" the clothes needed for their nighttime "business." In addition, they may take orders for specific articles from persons who are willing to buy stolen merchandise. Thus, the thief is not merely shoplifting or burglarizing for himself, but derives income from selling "hot" merchandise.

While my daughter was shopping with several other girls, one of them was seen shoplifting, but they were all accused of doing it. What can a parent do in a case like this?

Store security agents are generally very hard on groups of teenagers shopping together, whether they are black or white, but black youths encounter more abuse. Guilt by association is a common cause of much teenage difficulty with the law. Although teens usually prefer to shop in groups, they should be aware that they are sometimes considered "suspicious." Black youths in stores have been falsely accused and harassed by security agents. When that happens, parents should assist their children in making complaints against the store.

Is shoplifting widespread among teens generally?

No. As with most illegal activities, only a small percentage of teenagers engage in shoplifting. Most youths are trustworthy and spend their money to purchase goods. As a matter of fact, the teenage consumer market amounts to billions of dollars, especially for such items as clothes, records, tapes, musical instruments, cosmetics, cars, and other items related to recreation and glamour.

Is it true that store personnel discriminate against teenagers?

There are complaints of discrimination and unprovoked abuse from store managers and salespersons toward teenagers generally, and black teenagers feel these problems even more severely. For example, many of the musical and videotapes sold are defective; when teenagers attempt to return them, however, they are treated indifferently and often not reimbursed as readily as adults. We know several instances of a teen being refused a return, but when the parent took back the same merchandise, it was accepted. Parents should serve as advocates for their children when such discrimination occurs.

What can be done about teenagers' shoplifting problems?

First, we must realize that much of the problem rests not within the teenage population but with the nature of our society. America is becoming more and more materialistic, and youths who grow up under the widespread influence of TV commercials and advertisements are encouraged to acquire goods that neither they nor their parents can afford. In addition, the motivation to accumulate a range of materialistic symbols fits right into the adolescent's struggle for identity, social acceptance, and a sense of security. Thus, teenagers are extremely vulnerable to the advertising of goods.

If their parents can't provide them with items they feel they must have, and they can't find employment (unemployment for black inner-city teens has been known to hover around 40 to 60 percent), stealing becomes a real option for many young people, especially when parental guidance is lax. Black teens, in fact, have had epidemics of murders associated with stealing designer sneakers, jackets, and other articles right off the person of other youths. Perhaps the problem of stealing will never be solved without a change in values and a deemphasis of the importance of material possessions. Again, if you prepared your child, from an early age, to understand that he can't have everything and that's okay, the problem is less likely to arise.

We are upset that young blacks are so violent with one another. How can we help prevent violence?

That is an important question. Murder, the leading cause of death among young black men, is still on the rise. Malcolm X once warned, "My experience has been that in many instances where you find Negroes talking about nonviolence, they are not nonviolent with each other, and they're not loving with each other, or forgiving with each other." We cannot make excuses for the violence we inflict on one another. Many homicides that occur in ghettos are related to the drug addiction problem and competition among pushers, particularly of crack. Other murders are associated with robbery and domestic disputes. Women are increasingly victims of rape, battery, and homicide. One disturbing development has been the sharp increase in gang killings related to the increased availability of handguns and automatic weapons. Random "drive-by" shootings by gang members have terrorized communities. Many innocent black children and bystanders have been killed this way. Alleviation of slums and poverty will help decrease the amount of violence, as well as gun-control legislation. Blacks should take an active part in gun- and drug-control campaigns and support the establishment of homicide prevention centers at clinics and in other community agencies.

Building African-American pride will help. But the way we raise our children *from the beginning* and the way we teach them to handle anger, conflict, and frustration will help most. If we punish them in a violent manner, thus encouraging them to be violent when others bother them—without first seeking a peaceful but honorable solution—there is little reason to expect them to act in a nonviolent manner as teens and adults. (See our previous discussions about handling anger, confrontations, frustrations, and aggressions.)

My eighteen-year-old son wants to keep a gun in the house because he says he needs it for "protection." What should we do?

Some neighborhoods are tough, but keeping a gun in the home is dangerous. In a fit of anger, one family member may use it against another. Many impulsive killings in the black community occur in this fashion. Also, with a gun available, your child might be too quick to settle a street argument by "shooting it out." Such an episode may mean death or jail for your child and unnecessary slaying of other blacks. Very young children have discovered guns in their home and accidentally shot and killed young siblings or friends. Unless there is a clear and present danger, *no family member should be permitted to keep a gun in the house.* The legal possession of guns requires registration and a license in most sections of the country.

If you must keep a gun, we hope that you established a safe practice long ago: nobody throws at, hits, or otherwise attacks anyone else while angry. Children who have learned to hit other things, take a walk or run—*not a drive*—to relieve anger are less likely as teens to turn to the gun immediately. If you haven't already started the practice, now is the time to do so.

My teens hate police officers. This can mean trouble. How can I persuade them to be open-minded about the police?

This is a very real problem. We all know that too many police officers are more respectful of whites than blacks, particularly of educated, middle-income whites. Many blacks have been badly abused by police. At the same time, police officers are symbols of authority. Their mistreatment of people says, "You are unimportant, of low value; you don't belong." Such abuse and rejection brings out anger and rage. (See our discussion of black college youths in this chapter.) Our communities have long suffered from inadequate police protection, and better police-community relations are needed.

We must organize and continue to press for improved police practices in our communities. At the same time we must encourage our youths to see police officers as individuals and respect those who deserve it and to work through our organizations and the political system to remove or change the behavior of abusive members.

Black police officers are in a particularly difficult position. Some have risked promotions to fight racism in their departments, yet find themselves the targets of black anger. They are perhaps best able to limit abuse of blacks because they are on the inside. We hurt ourselves when we attack the very people who have the greatest chance of making the police not only protect us, but treat us with respect. Encourage your sons and daughters to think through such issues.

What should our children do if they are arrested?

Advise your children never to run from police who attempt to stop them, because they could be killed. If pursued and detained they must not fight with, curse, or antagonize the police, even if they are abusive, because the situation may be life-threatening. Youngsters should know that when they are questioned, they are not required to give any information except their name and address. However, they should also be instructed to respond immediately and politely to other questions, even if the reply is a refusal. If the police officer seems too threatening they should respond to questions to protect their well-being. They should try as best as they can not to incriminate themselves in their responses. Later they can report police misbehavior. Even though the police may search them for weapons, this is no time to fight police abuse. Should abuse occur, victims should try to remember the details and gather all possible evidence. If possible, enlist the aid of your church or civil and human rights group to censure and punish offenders.

If arrested, your child should ask to call you immediately and you should respond immediately. Your rapid response may benefit your child's case. You have to be supportive at this critical time even though you may be angry with the youngsters. If you

can afford to, obtain the services of a private lawyer at once. If
that is beyond your means, contact your local Legal Aid Society
for help. If you cannot retain an outside lawyer, the court will
usually appoint a public defender for your child.

Nationally, about 50 percent of prison inmates are young
blacks. Too many of our young men are in jail.

What can we do about teenage crime? For example, should I turn in a teen who commits a crime against our family?

If the crime involves more than a minor infraction that can
be settled privately between you and the youngster's family, it
is reasonable to seek police protection. On the other hand, it
may be dangerous for you to act as a regular informer about
matters that do not concern you. Teenage crime is a very complicated problem, one that relates to everything from neglectful
or troubled parents through economic and racial exploitation to
the corruption and immoral behavior of local and national public
officials.

In some heavy crime areas, citizens have formed groups to
look out for one another, work with police and, in some instances, try to attack some of the problems that cause youth to
turn to crime. This is a sensible approach. It is unwise and
dangerous to attempt to capture suspected criminals.

What is bail and how do we handle it?

Bail is money that must be paid so that an arrested person
can be released from jail while awaiting trial. On a minor charge,
the police may authorize bail; on a major charge, a judge decides.
However, the determination of bail can be discretionary. A judge
may set bail at any amount she chooses or deny bail for serious
crimes. The primary purpose of bail payments is to ensure the
appearance of an arrested person in court for trial. Factors that
determine a person's risk include length of time at her present
residence, school or job status, family ties in the area, criminal
record, and so on. The bail system is unfair to the poor who
have no ready cash. Bondsmen (people who take responsibility
for an arrested person's release) are usually required to pay 5 to
10 percent of the court-determined amount of bail. Bondsmen
have wide latitude on what they can demand as security—jew-

elry, your bankbook, the title to your house—and they are free to refuse a case. If the defendant does not appear for trial, the total amount of bail must be paid to the court.

What is probation?

Probation is a term used by the court to indicate that a person who is convicted of a crime can be released with certain restrictions on her behavior for a specified period of time. Probation is commonly prescribed in place of a jail sentence. A person who violates probation is usually imprisoned. Probation is considered a form of rehabilitation, because the probationer is allowed to function in the community while under supervision of the court system.

What is a pardon?

Pardon is official release from or reduction of the legal penalties of an offense or forgiveness for a criminal offense, usually by a governor, a committee appointed by a governor, or the president.

What is parole?

Parole is the term applied when a prisoner is released on good behavior before having served his or her full sentence. Prisoners ordinarily are not eligible for parole until they have served a prescribed length of the actual sentence. Parole, like probation, places restrictions on an ex-inmate's activities. A person who violates parole may be returned to jail, generally for the full balance of the original sentence.

What is extradition?

Extradition is the surrender for trial of an alleged criminal by the state where he or she is apprehended to the state where the crime was allegedly committed.

What can we do to ease the life of our child who is sentenced to a jail term?

Write and visit frequently. Contributing small amounts of money and gifts goes a long way toward making a prisoner's time more tolerable. Books of various types, especially about problems and achievement in the black community can be useful to persons in prison. Malcolm X and other leaders in the black community have used their time in prison to increase their awareness through reading and writing.

Encourage your adolescent to use the time and any available programs for self-development. Help him understand that this is the most important contribution he can make toward solving some of the complex problems in the black community. By self-development, we mean putting effort into improving work, school, and social skills, including honesty, self-discipline, and a realistic commitment to constructive goals. Some young people, with good family support, are able to use their prison confinement to turn their lives around.

What should we do when our youngster is released?

Ex-prisoners need a great deal of help to get back on their feet, including moral and financial support. Financial support, help in finding a place to live, and aid in finding a job are crucial. Have your son or daughter contact local rehabilitated ex-inmate groups; they can offer assistance and suggestions. Social rejection often makes it difficult for an ex-prisoner to be rehabilitated.

There is much talk about closing detention homes and other prison systems used to incarcerate young people. Is it really a good form of rehabilitation to allow criminals back into the community?

The issue of rehabilitation is very complex. Years of experience have shown that the so-called rehabilitation programs inside prison walls are largely ineffective, as proved by the high rates of repeated crime and return to prison. In recent years, however, some prisons have established military-type boot camps with intense, structured, and disciplined programs to rehabilitate inmates. These programs are more successful with certain inmates than routine jail programs. Nonetheless, what happens after an inmate is released from any of these programs is crucial. Clearly, something in the way a person relates to his or her family, community, and outside environment must be changed if criminal behavior is to be reduced. In addition, because so many criminals are victims of their life circumstances, the total community should take greater responsibility in helping youths adopt noncriminal behavior. Careful screening of inmates for readiness is certainly needed for such programs to survive.

What is a halfway house?

A halfway house is a community facility to which prison or mental hospitals may send inmates or the recuperating mentally ill as the first step in returning them out into the community and normal routines. The halfway house, a step along the road to rehabilitation, is a progressive reform.

EDUCATION

You mentioned in Chapter 6 the importance of maintaining close contact with our youngsters' schools. But how can we handle our teenager who becomes embarrassed about parents visiting the school and says that he doesn't want his parents poking into school affairs?

If you began visiting your child's school when he was in kindergarten or elementary school, he learned at an early age that your concern is for him to have the best possible learning experience. If your teen nevertheless now displays resentment about your interest in school, point out that it's still part of your parental responsibility and general concern that school be a good experience for him. If he still objects, you might arrange to visit teachers while he is not in class. You can also participate in parent-teacher associations and committees. Attending school plays, performances, and sporting events is another way of showing interest without trespassing on his privacy.

Should parents encourage teenagers to participate in such school, social, and civic organizations as student councils, clubs, and other competitive leadership activities?

Yes. Leadership interests and skills are learned early. But keep in mind that not everybody is a leader. Even if you yourself are in a leadership position, it does not necessarily mean that your child will want to follow in your footsteps. You must be very sensitive to each child's inclinations. Support and encourage a child who expresses leadership interests, but don't push a child who is not motivated to take charge. The desire may develop later, if a child doesn't bury it because you are leaning on her too hard. Perhaps only one in a family of several children exhibits leadership characteristics; if so, try not to emphasize that child's accomplishments more than the activities of the others. We know of black students who criticize other black youngsters for taking leadership roles in racially mixed schools and programs. These objectors fail to realize that, as a group, we need to encourage all the people we can beg, borrow, or steal who are interested in and capable of holding executive and leadership positions among blacks and in racially mixed settings. Some of the critics are jealous, afraid of competition with whites, or just plain alienated. Help your youngster to understand the feeling but to "keep on keeping on" everywhere.

How can parents best encourage leadership?

Take an active interest in your child's school activities. Ask questions and express your support to the child who wants to get involved by talking about your own involvement in school or that of close friends. Explain to your child that the process of leadership is learned from experience. He should know, too, that leadership styles vary, from the flamboyant up-front person to the individual who works quietly in the background. Also point out that even good leaders need good teams, and that successes are made partly by good managers behind the scenes. In other words, there are many ways and roles to be played in changing an institution or society for the better. Suggest that your child read biographies and autobiographies of great African-American and white leaders who have described their childhood. Many of these personality profiles record early leadership activity in school and church.

Should parents object if no provision exists to provide a mechanism for student participation in leadership activities in a school?

Yes, student participation in school offers an early opportunity for leadership experiences, especially for black children who have few opportunities to take part in activities that prepare them for influential roles in society. Student involvement is necessary at various levels in the operation of schools, including classroom activities, curriculum selection and development, school personnel training and sensitivity, and student government. If the opportunity to participate in school policies and programs is not available in your children's school, find out why, and try to promote it. Lacking democracy in their school life, children may well grow up without an understanding of how democracy should work in the larger society.

What should we do if our son reports that a teacher has directed racist remarks to individual students or to the class?

Report such remarks to the principal and request his or her assistance and intervention. It would also be helpful to bring up racial problems of this nature at parent-teacher association meetings. Race relations workshops for the teachers may be effective. See our discussion in Chapter 6.

What does the talk about student rights in junior and senior high school mean?

From disruptions that have occurred in junior and senior high schools over the years, officials and educators have come to realize that schools must establish basic codes indicating student rights and responsibilities. Rights policies teach students social obligations, and many teachers and law organizations advise educational institutions to develop codes that spell out student rights, responsibilities, and mechanisms for carrying out such codes. Many school systems have already done so.

What can parents do about junior and senior high school students who don't apply themselves to studying or other activities that develop their intellect, but merely goof off for hours and days at a time?

One of the major problems is that the cause is not obvious, and, even when known, it is difficult to correct. Work habits, comfort, and pleasure in getting a job done become ingrained most easily in the seven- to twelve-year age range. The planning, organizing, and discipline to accomplish tasks developed in this early period leads to achievement, which then feeds on itself until one is almost addicted to working or mastering a task—for example, math, English, learning to sew, or perfecting the hook shot. Praise, approval, and respect or admiration from parents or peers lead to the development of positive standards and determination that can remain with us all our lives.

For children who fail, for any reason, to acquire such values, goofing off at work or play can become the rule. Little parental support, poor teaching, schools where few children are interested in learning, a specific learning problem, or an undetected health problem such as poor vision and hearing can underlie failure. Efforts to conceal failure lead to more failure, frustration, and a lack of interest in academic work. If other areas for growth are not available—athletics, the arts—youngsters may miss the opportunity to develop mastery or work skills and take refuge in goofing off. Even though a child may want to do well at some point, she may have difficulty attaining her goal. It is important to have such students examined for a learning disability that may have been overlooked in the past. Testing for specific learning disorders has become quite sophisticated, and treatment programs have proved to be effective.

Wouldn't a more flexible, community-oriented, or Afro-centric school program help such youngsters?

It has been said that including relevant social issues in the curriculum in schools that do not require active teens to follow rigid programs would help. Students who feel frustrated and inept can benefit from such an approach. Schools must offer courses that are culturally applicable to their student population. Predominantly black schools need to increase their focus on Afro-centric history to help build a sense of pride, belonging, and self-esteem. Students who feel that they have some control over their course of studies can achieve at a higher level than those who do not. It has been demonstrated that disciplined students benefit most from loosely structured, independent programs. It is also true that undisciplined students can't concentrate on black studies, social issues, and other matters that should concern them.

What can be done for such teens?

Parents, teachers, or counselors should talk with them and point out what they see as the problem. One approach is to encourage these youngsters to get involved in programs that require hard physical work, routine, determination, planning, organizing, and even token punishment for less than the best effort. You can help them transfer the learned skills and experienced pride to academic areas. We have seen youngsters develop the incentive they need after getting involved in demanding athletic and wilderness programs, and also in well-structured and well-organized choral groups and other activities. Many floundering high school students do well after experiencing the discipline of military life. Sometimes you can motivate youngsters to achieve, complete, or master very simple tasks, then move on to more complex ones, eventually getting them back on the achievement track.

My very bright fourteen-year-old won't work because some of his contemporaries call him odd. How can I bring him to his senses?

Occasionally, teenagers are made to feel guilty by friends because they are "too smart." Blacks in some neighborhoods have an anti-intellectual attitude and persecute and ridicule students who take their studies seriously. They are called "dork" or "white" or worse. Such pressure may cause a black teenager to fear success and try to fit in with his group. If this happens, he will resist doing homework and other academic chores. In this case, you should actively support your child's academic interests and make an effort to introduce him to other youngsters with similar goals, or adults who have attained success in his field of interest. Seek out church, school, YMCA, and other programs for talented youngsters.

You must stress the importance of independent thinking. If you have allowed him to be an independent thinker at home, your teen is less likely to be negatively influenced by peers. Do not encourage your youngster to isolate himself from friends of his choice. This often requires such children to compromise a little and play different roles, but bright students have the capacity to do so. We have seen youngsters who can be "one of the gang" yet "do their thing" with the books and participate in extracurricular activities. When the pressures are severe and nothing can be done, the best solution might be to transfer your youngster to another school or send him away to school if at all feasible. Many schools offer scholarship aid for bright students.

Can there be other causes of poor performance in a youngster who "has it" intellectually?

Yes. Struggles with parents, for one: "You want me to make all A's; therefore, in the name of independence, I will make all C's." "You want me to make good grades, go to college, and become a banker and live like you; therefore, in the name of independence, I will strum a guitar in the park and live a life of genteel poverty, but one with love." That may be okay, but make him understand that what you are asking of him is for his benefit, not yours!

Comfort in high school and fear of failure in the larger world is another cause. Some black teens, particularly those from low-income backgrounds, have mixed feelings and guilt about "leaving my people" or "joining the Establishment." They may purposely fail in high school to escape facing these issues. For some, there are too many confusing issues, too many choices. Their answer is to do nothing. Personal emotional conflicts, as well as many other factors, may be behind the lack of effort.

How can parents help?

The tendency is to call such teens lazy kids who have "more opportunities than I ever had." If the struggle is with you, back off. We discussed the method earlier. Indicate that you know they are having trouble and ask what you can do to help. Assure youngsters that you want to assist them achieve what they want for themselves. They may gradually reveal their confusion or fear, often indirectly in spontaneous comments: "Who wants to go to college anyway?" (Fear of failure?) Reassure them. Try to make them realize that they don't have to resolve every question and issue on the spot. Explain that teens can benefit black people throughout life by developing their talents and using them humanely. Remind them that they don't have to be a Martin Luther King, Jr., or a Thurgood Marshall to make a contribution, that they don't have to make a giant footprint on the sand; they simply have to work up to their ability in whatever they undertake, even algebra, and be a fair, caring person. But in anything they pursue, exerting the maximum effort is the key ingredient to success.

Don't ignore an obvious serious emotional problem because you think it will reflect badly on you. Seek help to avoid its becoming a greater problem later on.

My teen doesn't have any study problems. How can I ensure the continuation of this happy state of affairs?

Keep on—as you have been doing from the child's early years—to expect your youngster to study, to do homework and to learn outside of school for himself, not just because he wants to please you. Setting a strict nightly schedule for such pursuits may be effective for one child but not for others. Many teenagers who spend the required number of hours in their rooms each evening do more daydreaming than studying. Ask your son to work out a plan to complete his work, play, and other activities at times that are convenient and appropriate for him. Even teenagers who are getting along well need help in developing good activity programs and study habits, particularly as their work loads increase. If you are unable to help your child plan his study routines, you can arrange for him to be referred to a school study skills counselor.

Shouldn't a child who is doing poorly in a subject be required to spend more time studying that subject?

Maybe, but in most cases not by himself. Requiring a boy who is doing poorly in math to go to his room to tackle his math problems undoubtedly frustrates him further. Students who are having trouble with certain subjects usually require assistance from someone who can help them overcome their specific learning blocks before they can understand their homework assignments. Simple commonsense tests can be applied to difficulties youngsters have with certain subjects. If your son has trouble with math each year, it is likely that he never learned the basics; therefore, math becomes more difficult each succeeding year. If your son continues to find it hard to deal with a particular subject, especially math and English, it is important that teachers use several types of approaches to attempt to make the content clear to the child. Remedial courses and tutorial instruction are frequently necessary to accomplish the goal.

What should a parent do when a child brings home a report card with poor grades in schoolwork and conduct?

A report card, in many ways, is not an adequate measure of a child's educational progress and does not always indicate the true educational needs of a pupil. Poor report cards should be considered signals that something is wrong in the child's school relationships. You must take the time to have a three-way conference with the teacher(s) and your child concerning her progress in school. Do not simply chastise your youngster and sign her report card.

Our daughter has dropped out of high school. What can I do?

Attempt to discover the underlying problem and get help for her. She may have dropped out for any of the reasons given in the preceding discussions, and many more besides. Urge her to return to school—the one she left or elsewhere. Some private schools provide scholarships for such students. If nothing works, don't condemn her. Help her plan for the future. After working a year or two, she may want to return to school or study for a GED (graduate equivalency development) degree offered by community groups.

Should children be consulted before their parents decide to send them to schools outside their community?

Yes. Furthermore, parents should explain their reasons for such changes and clearly express their expectations. Too often children are arbitrarily sent away without being given an opportunity to discuss the importance of quality education to their development; as a result, their performance in a new school frequently shows no improvement. A child who is sent to a residential school may feel that her parents are just trying to get rid of her. When youngsters are transferred from a predominantly black school to one that is predominantly white, you need to help them understand the social and economic reasons for some of the differences they will observe and prepare them for possible racial confrontations. See our discussion in this chapter about preparing black teens to enter predominantly white colleges.

How should parents treat a black child attending a predominantly white school who shows disrespect for his family and parents whom he considers deprived, unqualified, uneducated, and inferior?

Several reports from parents indicate that this type of behavior is not uncommon, especially as the number of such educational opportunities increase. Parents must be prepared to counter such impressions with convincing historical information about blacks, confidently expressing pride in African-American people. In addition, it is important that your youngster participate in enough positive black experiences so that he can deduce for himself that there are strengths in the black community. A parent with strong negative feelings about being black can serve to further convince the youth that he is right. When the problem is extreme, it may be necessary to arrange for the child to visit black institutions where he can observe blacks functioning in responsible positions of authority and settings that refute his negative impressions. It is probably not wise, however, to remove a child from a predominantly white school environment and place him in a predominantly black one if he objects. Under these conditions, he will see only what he wants to see.

My son wants to become a famous athlete but doesn't put enough time into his high school studies. Is that okay?

No. Your son's academic studies should come first. He should not neglect classroom work in favor of sports. Many black folk heroes have been athletes, singers, musicians, and movie stars, and many black youths try to emulate them. You must remind your son that very few people can earn a living as athletes or in other highly visible and popular professions. Encourage him to develop any skill he has and channel it into a legitimate area. But young black men and women should know that most people "make it" as teachers, doctors, lawyers, electricians, technicians, truck drivers, and so on. Thus it is important for your son to strike a balance—enough basketball, music, or other interest, and enough attention to academic studies. Help him seek excellence everywhere rather than fame somewhere. This approach may lead to the fame he desires, but will provide him with alternative skills, which will lessen his disappointment if he doesn't make it to the top as an athlete or musician.

When my daughter goes to her room to study, she turns on the radio full blast. Can she really learn anything that way?

Surprisingly, some people can study effectively under such conditions. If she is getting her work done, fine. If the loud radio or cassette playing is disturbing others, however, ask her to reduce the sound level or wear headphones. The volume of music is often a bone of contention between black and white teens at college or wherever they may live together. The same rules that apply at home should be observed everywhere. Any racial animosities that exist should be discussed directly and separately without interference from a boom box that is too loud to allow concentration, work, or sleep.

The school dropout rate was very high in the early 1960s. Are many black teenagers still out of school?

Yes. About one-third of all black teenagers are not in school. The dropout rate of black teens from college is also high. Of those not in school, more than one-third are unemployed, as well.

Should we encourage all our children to go to college?

Yes, but don't force them to attend. Youngsters who are made to go to college are often unhappy, drop out, and waste money. Some students are better suited to careers in service occupations—for example, auto mechanic, plumber, electrician, truck driver, or construction worker—which do not require a college degree. Many positions in technological fields require only a year or two of college or other training. These jobs pay very good salaries. Help your teens seek out the necessary training for these occupations, but be sure to encourage them to at least complete high school.

Why do a number of black youngsters have trouble at predominantly white colleges?

The adjustment to college can be difficult for all youngsters, black or white, rich or poor. It frequently involves a move from a situation in which they were comfortable socially, good academically, and known by many students and adults to one of a community of strangers as good as or better than they academically. The transition comes at a time when teens are rejecting parental and societal values and customs and attempting to find themselves and their own values and customs.

In addition, black youths are discarding a negative societal attitude and still seeking a positive black identity. They need to be active and to make blackness and the world okay, right now, yesterday. Because of past racism they find too few black authority figures, too many of whom have little power; thus it is sometimes hard to regard them as models and "evidence" that they can make it.

Again because of past hardships, many black students have encountered modest to little competition, whereas many white students have been in highly competitive settings since nursery school. The parents of many whites are decision makers and community leaders who enjoy financial security and "contacts."

Outright and subtle racist acts are a major cause of difficulty. For example: security guard yells at a black student to get off the grass in a tone that he ordinarily uses to address "town blacks" but not students. He changes his attitude on discovering that the black is a student. Situation: rude white authority figure; emerging black determined to be a man; guilt over different status accorded town blacks; probably a penalty for a violent response. Outcome: rage and anger and perhaps acting-out.

All these factors affect a person's self-confidence, sense of "belonging," right to be a future leader, and, in turn, the ability to perform socially and academically. These are some of the reasons many bright African-American youngsters do not perform as well as some of their white equals. Many catch up late in their college career, in professional school, or on the job after they experience enough success to assert "I am and I can."

How have black students responded?

Attack and withdrawal—some healthy, some not so healthy.

Attack has ranged from protest tactics to disciplined academic and social action. Withdrawal, designed to create social comfort, has ranged from black living quarters to individual apathy, paralysis, and failure. Although African-American studies programs and cultural and social programs have been useful as middle-ground and necessary awareness approaches, even here, in some cases, there is protective withdrawal. The most troublesome outcome has been the destructive black-on-black attacks—on black peers of different color, income, and style, on black faculty (and vice versa), and on occasion even on black townspeople. Some black students are still struggling with feelings of self-negation and inferiority. We have seen too many bright black youngsters—whose negative responses are self-defeating—drop out or barely make it, therefore lacking the necessary grades or skills to go on to professional schools. Black-on-black conflict is tragic but understandable. On the other hand, cooperation and mutual trust are growing among African-American students and faculty as they unite to cope with increasing numbers of racist incidents on campuses.

How can we help?

Parents, teachers, and community leaders must be more understanding. We must help black youngsters, before and during college, think through the maze of complex issues they face. We have heard many black leaders condemn the youngsters and talk about "the hard times we endured"—less money, *no* black faculty, blatant discrimination, and so on. What our generation did not have was the five to ten years of sensitization to the severity of racism during our social awareness period, when we were eight to eighteen years old. In addition we had less incentive to do something about it, other than to learn and graduate.

As individuals and as a black community we must fight racism in colleges and universities, and everywhere else. But to achieve the numbers to do this, we must see that more black students get through, achieving well, in spite of racism. If we are honest with our teenagers rather than minimizing their concerns and feelings, we can make a positive contribution.

Encourage youngsters to participate in black campus affairs and legitimate causes, but stress that good academic performance comes *first*. Well-trained professionals have more power to effect change than students, although students can help keep us honest. Every social problem that concerns youngsters now will be around, in some form, four or eight years in the future. Remind students that they must determine who—peers, black or white faculty—are sincere, remind them that it's what they *do* rather than how much noise they make.

In a tactful way, you might remind them that they have to experience a system before they can understand how to effect change in it; that they have to follow before they can lead. You might also suggest that they can help the black cause through service. Some college towns with a large black student population lack enough tutors, scout leaders, Big Brothers or Big Sisters, and mentors for younger students; they would welcome the assistance of volunteers for these positions.

Some black students, because of limited previous experience, attempt to make appointments with busy people on short notice, show up late or fail to appear without apology, fail to acknowledge unusual assistance, and so on. Parents and teachers in charge of precollege programs should make sure that students are taught social skills.

Is it true that black women outnumber black men on most college campuses?

Yes. Even at many black colleges, females outnumber male students at ratios of two or three to one and higher. Black males, for a variety of social and psychological reasons, are not succeeding academically at the same level as their female counterparts.

This problem has been a source of stress and conflict among black students. Black females complain that they have no one to date, that the black males are threatened by and avoid them. The availability of black males is also diminished because some date white women; black females are more reluctant to date interracially. These issues have led to severe and angry conflicts between black male and female students on campus.

Many organizations are working to help black boys achieve academic skills so that they can find their way to college and professional education.

Should we encourage our children to attend a predominantly white college?

Ask your children to think about what they want from a college—academic superiority, social life, prestige, and such—but urge them to make their own choice. There is no reason why they *must* attend a predominantly white school. Some black students feel more comfortable in a predominantly black atmosphere. Black colleges usually provide a broader range of role models for blacks and have played an important role in developing African-American leaders. The quality of academic offerings in black colleges is being strengthened by increasing numbers of well-trained black faculty. On the other hand, many "white" colleges enroll enough black and other minority students to keep your youngsters from feeling isolated. However, students on black campuses do not have to cope with the stress that accompanies subtle and overt forms of racism.

Black students should not write off predominantly white colleges for fear of competing with whites. They should select a college that can provide them with a good education oriented toward their career goals.

My district wants to establish an all-black-male high school because teachers think they can give the students a better education in such a setting. Does that make any sense?

It makes some sense and, given the critical state of black male failure, it is certainly worthy of experiment.

Schools in the inner city are already de facto segregated, so all-male schools do not represent a radical departure. As recently as the 1960s, a number of schools in urban areas were for one sex only. These institutions could provide discipline and education without having to deal with the day-to-day distractions of teenagers who devote much of their energy to attracting the opposite sex. Also, much exaggerated macho behavior and male violence in schools is associated with slights and incidents related to boy-girl relations. Same-sex schools may be beneficial to both males and females if they are not deemed discriminatory.

Some people feel that establishing manhood and self-esteem in young black males requires special male-modeled, Afro-centric programs. Our experience suggests that Afro-centric programs alone are not sufficient without an otherwise strong curriculum. However, something is needed to counter the negative statements that society makes about black people. Students must feel adequate so they can learn to deal with other peoples' negative attitudes.

Legally such schools are required to enroll students regardless of race or gender. Black males should not be forced to attend such schools. Enrollment should be voluntary and require parental consent, and parents and teachers should be sure that these males do not feel stigmatized or isolated. Therefore, it is important that teachers and administrators are representative of both genders and different races. It is often wrongly assumed that such schools would have only black male teachers. We say these alternative approaches must not support de jure segregation. Such schools may have some merit, but this remains to be demonstrated.

My son is gay. Can you recommend the best type of college for him to attend?

The discrimination gays and lesbians still suffer in society is reflected on college campuses. In general, large urban colleges provide more diversity and support groups for gay and lesbian students. Some small progressive colleges are also hospitable to the gay community.

In recent years, gay and lesbian rights groups have established legitimate campus organizations and fought successfully to gain equal rights for these students.

Above all, your son's confidence that he has your support and that of the family will go a long way toward helping him cope with the pressures that many gays and lesbians have to face in society.

My daughter wants to major in African-American studies in college. Isn't that a waste of time?

African-American studies should be considered the same as any other major field of study, no less or no more. We need competent and knowledgeable blacks in the field of African-American studies as we do in all other fields. But your daughter should not select that area solely to resolve identity problems or to prove her blackness or because she has heard that it is "easy." That attitude in itself may indicate she is a victim of tactics used by some to discredit black studies. Such programs are important in enhancing a student's understanding of white racism and black consciousness. As with any liberal arts major, she would be wise to select a backup major in another field to maximize her future job opportunities.

CAREERS AND EMPLOYMENT

How can we guide our teenager in selecting a career?

First, encourage your child to explore the many career possibilities available. Although some parents attempt to fulfill their own dreams through the careers of their children, it is unwise to try to force a teenager into a career primarily to satisfy your desires. Encourage your youngster to make his own career decision with parental assistance. Discuss such issues as the satisfaction, income, employment conditions, and opportunities a particular career offers to help the youngster determine whether that field is for him. Have your teenager arrange to talk to people in particular and related fields in which he may have an interest.

Although school guidance counselors should be the best source of career information, they are not always prepared to offer that kind of assistance. Many community organizations sponsor educational counseling services. Check with the Urban League, NAACP, the United Negro College Fund, and other national or local education action groups for advice or referral to appropriate programs. Counseling programs are available in most urban areas at the YMCA, YWCA, and neighborhood youth agencies. Local community colleges are expanding their counseling services, and many colleges and universities provide transitional counseling and tutorial services for high school students.

Earlier you mentioned the high unemployment rate among black teenagers. What are some of the causes?

First, it must be clearly understood that black teenagers are highly desirous of employment, despite the involvement of some in illicit money-making enterprises. But the number of jobs and training programs available is not sufficient to meet the demands. Many black teenage high school dropouts lack the skills required for white-collar jobs. Discrimination by unions bars young blacks from apprenticeship programs and high-paying blue-collar jobs. Because many of the available jobs are so far from the areas where black youths live, no public transportation exists to make the jobs accessible.

Should black teenagers be encouraged to take jobs while they're still in school?

Yes, as long as the hours are not so demanding that they interfere with school performance. Jobs can serve important purposes for teenagers. In addition to earning money, jobs help them learn new skills, requirements, and responsibilities. Job experience also provides young people with training in scheduling their time and accepting authority. On the job, they may gain practical experience in race-related problems with which they will have to cope in the future.

What is the best way for a black teenager to get a job?

Check with your local youth employment center for jobs. A city's Chamber of Commerce or mayor's office may sponsor special programs for young people. A number of community groups in large urban areas specialize in job placement. Newspapers and radio broadcasts can be a source of information. It is probably best to supervise a timid youngster's job-seeking efforts. In any case, you should express an interest in the type of work and the kind of pay and treatment your child is receiving on the job. A teenager who seeks a summer job must start hunting for one well in advance.

Some youngsters are not aware that appearance, personality, and style are important elements in securing and holding a job. A youngster who has been taught to make a "good show" all along has an advantage. A person who exhibits good work habits—arrives on time, does good work, and is cordial to others—has the best chance of holding a job. Of course this does not mean that anyone must submit to ill treatment. If a youngster must stop abuse, there is a way to do it that will increase the respect she gets when dealing with reasonable people, rather than cost her the job. Parents, teachers, counselors, and others should have taught youngsters these skills, but if they have not, it is better to teach them now, rather than after a few work failures.

We know of work programs run by well-meaning liberal whites who were unable to tell poorly groomed black youngsters that they were handicapped because of their appearance. A person who can't say, "Look, man"—or however you put it—"you're not going to make it if you don't shape up," and give sound advice, should not be a counselor in that type of program.

Is it true that black children are less motivated to succeed in jobs than youths from other groups?

No. The level of motivation among black youths ranges from high to low, as it does among other racial groups. A child's aspirations are determined largely by her environment. She assesses her life chances in reference to the people with whom she identifies. The motivation to achieve is directly related to the past encouragement and support she has received for work efforts, and to her belief that she has opportunities or access to satisfying work experiences.

Should we allow our son to drop out of school to join the armed services or later volunteer?

You should encourage your son to remain in school. The military services prefer to enlist high school graduates. Should your son decide to join the armed services later, he will improve his chances for advancement if he has a high school or college education. Once he decides to join and is accepted, urge him to take advantage of the education and training programs offered in these services. Remind him of these opportunities even if he has no initial interest. The discipline developed in the service sometimes makes it possible for a youngster who could not previously concentrate on schoolwork to pursue educational or training programs later on.

Black men should join the army if they really want to do so. It is important for blacks to attain positions of authority within all the branches of the armed services. In addition, the army can help young men and women develop discipline, a sense of responsibility, and maturity.

Does racial discrimination still exist in the armed services?

Yes. Black military personnel indicate that discrimination still exists, but it is more subtle than the open bigotry of the past. Nonetheless, blacks have more opportunity for training and advancement than ever before. Some black men and women feel that there is more racial equality in the navy, army, marines and air force than in civilian life.

Should girls enlist in the military? Doesn't it offer educational opportunities and a chance to travel?

As girls and young women consider careers, they will find the military a reasonable option, because it offers valuable educational and travel opportunities. Other programs, such as the Peace Corps, also offer training and travel programs that aid in providing services to nations developing economically and educationally. Keep in mind, however, that the primary purpose of the military is preparing for war, and make certain that your youngster considers this fact before making her decision.

Should black youths be advised to join the police forces of this nation, including the FBI?

Yes, if they have an interest in doing so. There is a need for black input and control of the social organizations and institutions that affect the African-American community. Often, indifferent law-enforcement officers have neither shown proper respect for nor enforced the laws consistently in the black community. It is hoped that black officers can bring a more positive attitude and a greater commitment to, and understanding of, black community problems. But hiring more black officers hasn't, in and of itself, reduced black crime and violence, the causes of which are varied and complex.

What careers do you think will be important for black youths to consider in the future?

Blacks have traditionally been involved in the service sector, including teaching, medical care, and social work. These are important areas, but we need blacks in all fields in order to obtain our fair share of leadership positions. More African-Americans are needed in business and economic development, technological and computer fields, politics and government—at the local, state, and federal levels—foreign affairs (especially focused around Africa and the Caribbean) and social planning.

Are enough blacks entering the professions?

No. The number of black college graduates increased in the 1970s and 1980s but has since decreased. Active affirmative action programs have disappeared at many colleges and increases in financial costs have been prohibitive to many black students who are more likely to come from impoverished backgrounds. We still have a long way to go to achieve proportional representation. Black men and women represent about 12 percent of the U.S. population, but only about 2 to 3 percent of all doctors and dentists and 1.5 percent of all engineers. In recent years, the number of blacks earning doctorate degrees has decreased significantly.

COMMUNITY INVOLVEMENT AND POLITICAL ACTION

How can we involve our teens in building a stronger African-American community?

You have made a start if over the years you have exposed your youngsters to community activities through your own involvement. At adolescence, youngsters begin to look beyond their own needs. They identify with community ideas, ideals, and causes as a way of establishing their own identity. Service to others and the community helps them establish their humanity. Teenagers should become involved in community self-help activities, particularly in programs catering to younger children. Too few black college students are involved in community activities because the advantages of service and the opportunities to serve or to help others are not introduced at elementary school level. Teenagers should also participate in programs that educate them about the nature of racism and provide them with realistic humanistic strategies to reduce this problem in our society. The attitudes and awareness gained during adolescence are carried into adulthood.

What clubs or organizations should we encourage our teenage children to join?

Teenagers can become involved in the activities of major civil rights groups as well as in local community groups. The NAACP, the National Urban League, the Southern Christian Leadership Conference, the Congress of Racial Equality, and Operation PUSH (People United to Serve Humanity) welcome the active participation of black youths. Sororities and fraternities whose members work on community projects also offer social opportunities.

Are there other groups?

Yes. There are church organizations, Muslim youth groups, and many emerging community-based youth organizations. Most large cities staff agencies that sponsor programs for youth or referral services. YMCA and YWCAs have community-based branches that offer special programming for young people, supplementing local community action agencies. Teenagers and young adults should be encouraged and aided in establishing their own organizations that sponsor special programs in the community, such as antidrug and anticrime projects, clean-up campaigns, educational tutoring and mentoring programs, Big Sister or Big Brother programs with preschoolers, and various other educational, recreational, and community development projects. Active programs for teenage mothers and some for teen fathers have also been instituted.

Should we permit our children to join groups that advocate self-defense?

Many of these groups are involved in constructive programs, including economic and community development, free food programs, free medical clinics, and political activity. Most have advocated violence only in self-defense. Because of police confrontation, however, there is a danger to your youngster's well-being as a member of any of these groups. Be sure to discuss *all* the pros and cons of joining such a group with your teenager. If you feel that it is dangerous, unnecessary, and you don't want your child to join, say so in a calm, rational manner. But it is unwise to tell a teen that she cannot and must not join, because that can be the stimulus to join secretly, even when she really doesn't want to, and you may never know about it.

Should we encourage our eighteen-year-old to vote?

By all means. But again, teenagers learn by example. If you want your eighteen-year-old to vote, you should vote. If he went to the polls with you when he was nine or ten, he is more likely to want to vote when he can. The black community needs to exercise its political strength through the ballot box. Too many eligible black adults are not registered to vote, and many of those who are registered fail to vote. The Reverend Jesse Jackson's campaigns for the presidential nomination in the 1980s did a great deal to draw more blacks into the political process. The number of elected black officials has increased significantly in recent years. African-American participation in politics, which has a significant and ready payoff, is one of the important avenues for social change.

My son recently turned eighteen; however, he refuses to register to vote. He says voting won't make a difference for black people. What can I say to change his mind?

This very unfortunate point of view is held by some young people. Explain to your son that changes come about through many kinds of strategies, the ballot being a prominent one. Malcolm X said that we must work to liberate black people through any means necessary, and voting is clearly a significant means. The give-and-take of the political process isn't apparent on a daily basis, but if you don't stay involved at every opportunity, you'll rarely see results. Having something that people need makes you more powerful, and they must pay attention to you and your needs. If we African-Americans don't vote and remain interested and involved in the overall political process, our needs will be ignored because we will not be the margin of victory in an election or a force to be reckoned with at a city council hearing.

The complicated political and economic shifts taking place in the 1990s will leave cities unable to educate black children, provide recreational services, and improve conditions in the community. Tax revenues are limited, city infrastructures are in urgent need of repair, and affordable housing is in short supply. Yet black public officials point out that even blacks who vote believe that they have fulfilled their civic duty and leave the polls with no thought to providing the visible support that those they elected need in the ongoing battles against resistant police departments, city councils, and other powerful public and private officials.

We can dream of dramatic actions that will bring about rapid change. But, in reality, the only thing we can count on is a day-to-day effort in the political and economic arenas. Help your youngster think about the role he is or isn't playing, can or can't play. Is he in groups that have ties with decision makers—unions, political clubs, and such? We love the art or aesthetic aspect of African-American culture, but if we don't encourage our youngsters to pay more attention to the political and economic sides, our communities are going to be even more troubled in a few years.

School and other programs at every level should develop ways to make participation in the larger political process familiar to everyone.

How should teenagers go about registering to vote?

Most cities maintain a voter registration section in City Hall where people can register during regular office hours. Some large cities have community-based agencies where residents can register in their own neighborhoods. During major local and national election periods, officials establish special voter registration times and places, and publicize them in the news media. Because voter registration is often closed for several weeks before major elections, it is not wise to wait until a year in which elections are held to register to vote. Young people should register on their eighteenth birthday, or soon thereafter.

What should a black youth do if denied registration at City Hall?

People are denied the opportunity to register because they fail to take proof of their birthdate and residency with them. Be certain that your youngster has written proof of these two statistics when applying for registration. There is no other reason to deny an American citizen the privilege of voting. Race, literacy tests, voting fees, and other devices are *illegal*.

Is it a fact that a youth who has been in trouble with the law cannot register to vote?

Juvenile delinquency and other misdemeanors such as traffic offenses do not disqualify a youth from voting privileges. Generally, the only crimes that would prevent an eighteen-year-old from voting are felonies or election fraud. Check the rules in your particular state, because voting regulations vary from state to state.

What address should an eighteen-year-old who plans to be away at college use as residency, home or college?

Students in general should maintain residency in their hometown to vote in elections of local importance. It is relatively simple to obtain an absentee ballot. Ask for details at your local registration office.

What does voter education entail?

Voter education can take many forms, from basic instruction on how to use voting machines to information on complex tax issues. Only a few city governments in America provide adequate nonpartisan voter education, so citizens have to rely on private sources or political campaigns for necessary information. Unfortunately, when people register to vote in most cities of this nation they are not even instructed on how to use the voting machines. Schools or community groups in your area should conduct voter education courses in which children, beginning in their preteens, can practice using voting booths.

Candidates for political office frequently hold meetings, all-day conferences, "meet the candidates nights," and related activities to inform voters of key issues. Local chapters of the NAACP, churches, and the League of Women Voters are usually good sources for voter information.

What should a registered young voter—or anyone—do if he is told he's not registered when he goes to the polls on Election Day?

Don't just walk away. If you know you are registered, ask the clerk at the polls to check further. If nothing happens, go to the main office at City Hall or the place where you originally registered. You can call the Board of Elections if City Hall happens to be closed on Election Day. Many communities issue voter registration identification cards. In communities that use this procedure, each voter is responsible for presenting such identification at the polls. Encourage a youngster to clear up what are usually bureaucratic misunderstandings so that he can at least be assured of being able to vote in the next election. Urge and assist him to contact a civil rights group if he is denied either registration or the vote.

What if a young voter gets confused in the voting booth and doesn't know what to do or can't find her candidate's name on the ballot?

A person who feels pressured will often panic. Instruct the young voter to take her time and read the ballot carefully. Even though a long line of people may be waiting, there is no limit to the length of time she may take in the voting booth. If the young voter has a problem with the levers, she should not be embarrassed to call the booth attendant for assistance. Anyone can become confused at times.

What is bloc voting?

Bloc voting usually refers to a special-interest group supporting one candidate or issue. For instance, the entire black community might vote only for black candidates on the ballot. Many political critics discourage bloc voting, but ethnic groups have used it effectively for decades to get their candidates into office. We believe that it is important to vote for the candidate, black or white, who will best meet your needs and the needs of your community.

CHAPTER 9

A Final Word

You have now read many questions and answers with some general and specific discussion on rearing the black child. We hope that our responses have been helpful to you, whether you are a parent, teacher, social worker, or friend. We realize that we have not answered all of your questions—a book of this length can only begin to discuss the issues that relate to black child development. But we have tried to provide general approaches to child rearing that you can apply to your specific problems in helping black children in your home and community. Someday soon, we hope that all middle and high schools will have required courses in child rearing for girls and boys to help prepare them for one of the most important and rewarding tasks of their adulthood: being a parent. Most of us become parents in our lifetime and it is not acceptable for young people to be steeped in ignorance or questionable folklore when they begin their critical journey as mothers and fathers.

This book then should be a basic guide to you and a source of important information. But you, the parent or caretaker, still remain the best judge—the final "expert"—on how to rear your child. We urge you to continue to rely on your basic, good common sense in coping with the everyday issues involving your youngsters. Respect your children as individuals and they will respect you. Remember that your task is to improve your skill in becoming an effective child-developer and that your goal is to produce a healthy, strong, and mature black adult who is able to cope, achieve, and constructively bring about change in America.

We want to stress that some of the information you want to provide your children with and some of the ideas you want to help them think through are complicated and sometimes threatening. Thus, you must always play it by ear. You want to use words and give explanations suitable to your child's age. You don't want to jam information or ideas down your child's throat when he or she is not ready (can't understand) to hear it. You don't have to explain anything all at once. If you are able to talk about anger, race, sex, drugs, and other highly charged subjects, your youngster will open the topic, or make it known that it is okay for you to open the topic, for discussion.

But sometimes we all get tired and emotionally taxed in caring for our young. We adults too are only human and cannot expect perfection in ourselves. We will make mistakes; that is part of life. No single mistake, usually not even many mistakes, will "break" or hurt your child as long as you genuinely care and you are doing your best. Even your best is not enough in some situations, but that is all you can do.

There are times when we all need support and guidance. This is a fact for which we need not feel ashamed. Stand ready to consult the books suggested on the following pages that deal with specific issues in child rearing. We urge you to seek help in assisting your youngster whenever situations arise that overwhelm you. Talk to your friends, speak to your clergyperson, teacher, pediatrician and social worker, and don't be afraid to consult with a psychologist or psychiatrist when the need arises. Don't be embarrassed to ask questions and seek advice—none of us has the wisdom to know all the answers. Many persons both professional and nonprofessional can be an important resource to you as you struggle to raise a healthy black child in this often harsh world.

Social problems of poverty and racism continue to affect a great many people in the black community. But, today African-Americans are attempting to look beyond the basic struggle for survival and want to participate fully in the dreams and opportunities shared by all citizens. Raising strong black children will help these dreams to come true. Although your job is important, it does not help to get uptight. Relax and enjoy your children.

If this book contributes just a small bit to these goals, our efforts in writing this volume will be time well spent. We are satisfied that there will be a brighter future for all our sons and daughters.

Suggested Reading

There are many books about child-rearing practices that can easily be found in the child-rearing section of most libraries and bookstores. These books deal with a wide range of issues from pregnancy, nutrition, education, discipline, divorce, and many others. Similarly, libraries and bookstores have sections on the African-American experience; books dealing with black history, the civil rights movements, and interesting autobiographies are available. It is important for parents to take the initiative in finding materials that can be useful to them in helping to raise a black child successfully.

These are a few suggested books that we believe would be of special interest to parents and teachers of black children:

Children's Television Workshop. *Family Living Series*. New York: Prentice-Hall, 1989.

Clark, Kenneth B. *Prejudice and Your Child*. Middleton, CT: Wesleyan University Press (1963) 1988.

Coles, Robert. *The Moral Life of Children*. Boston: Houghton Mifflin, 1986.

Comer, James P. *Maggie's American Dream: The Life and Times of a Black Family*. New York: New American Library, 1988.

Cosby, Bill. *Childhood*. New York: Putnam, 1991.

Cosby, Bill. *Fatherhood*. New York: Doubleday, 1986.

Feldman, S. Shirley & Glen R. Elliott, eds. *At the Threshold: The*

Developing Adolescent. Cambridge, MA: Harvard University Press, 1990.

Gibbs, Jewelle Taylor & Larke Nahme Huang, et al. *Children of Color: Psychological Interventions with Minority Youth*. San Francisco: Jossey-Bass, 1990.

Hopson, Darlene Powell & Derek S. Hopson. *Different and Wonderful: Raising Black Children in a Race-Conscious Society*. New York: Prentice Hall Press, 1990.

Jaynes, Gerald David & Robin M. Williams, eds. *A Common Destiny: Blacks and American Society*. Washington, D.C.: National Academy Press, 1989.

Kozol, Jonathan. *Savage Inequalities: Children in America's Schools*. New York: Crown Publishers, 1991.

Lightfoot, Sara Lawrence. *Balm in Gilead*. Reading, MA: Addison-Wesley, 1988.

Lovejoy, Frederick H., Jr. & David Estridge, eds. *Boston Children's Hospital: The New Child Health Encyclopedia*. New York: Delacorte Press, 1987.

McAdoo, Harriette Pipes & John Lewis McAdoo, eds. *Black Children: Social, Educational, and Parental Environments*. Newburg Park, CA: Sage Publications, 1985.

Méeks, Carolyn. *Prescriptions for Parenting*. New York: Warner Books, 1990.

Pinderhughes, Elaine. *Understanding Race, Ethnicity and Power*. New York: Free Press, 1989.

Powell, Douglas. *Teenagers: When to Worry and What to Do*. New York: Doubleday, 1986.

Pruett, Kyle D. *The Nurturing Father*. New York: Warner Books, 1987.

Steinberg, Laurence & Ann Levine. *You and Your Adolescent*. New York: Harper & Row, 1990.

Taffei, Ron, with Melinda Blau. *Parenting by Heart*. Reading, MA: Addison-Wesley, 1991.

Index

open classroom, 182, 203–205
opportunities for educated blacks, 12, 223–24
parent-school interaction, 175–81, 190–95, 392–93
peer pressure and, 396–97
political, 228–29
poor performance by intelligent student, 397–99
public education, problems of, 187–90
punctuality, 184–85
racism and racial pride, 178–81, 210–14, 394
report cards, 399
residential schools, 399–400
role of black community in, 223–25, 227–28
separate schools for black males, 2, 405–406
sex education, 267–70, 336, 340–48
student rights policies, 394
study routine, 398, 401
subjects, difficulties with certain, 398–99
support services, 222–23
teacher-pupil interaction, 185–87, 195–202
undisciplined adolescent, 394–96
of very young, 206–10
violence and hostility, 215–19
withdrawn or timid student, 219–22
work habits, failure to develop good, 394–95
Eight-year-old, see Five- to eight-year-old
Ejaculation, 292, 343
Eleven-year-old, see Nine- to twelve-year-old
Emancipation, 8
Emotional breakdown, 369–70
Emotional development of nine- to twelve-year-old, 245–50
Employment, 319, 407–11
during adolescence, 319, 407–11
contributing to family finances, 319
finding, 408–409
motivation and, 409
saving part of earnings, 319
see also Careers; Unemployment
English:
black, 211–12, 225–26

standard, 211–12, 225–26
Exhibitionism, 308–309
Expectations:
of parent, 225, 255, 256, 257, 259
of teacher, 186–87, 203, 257
Exploitative parents, 260
Extradition, 390

Failure, fear of, 397
Fairness, 270
of teachers, 198–99
see also Morality; Rules
Fairy tales, 121
Families:
activities together, 167–73, 253–54, 333
disrespect for, 400
exploitation by, 260
father-controlled, 98–99
healthy, 99
neglect by, 260
Fantasy, see "Make-believe"
Father(s):
child's favoring of, 94–95
-controlled family, 98–99
fatherless child, 95–97, 185–86
flirtation with, 310
of preschoolers, 94–95
"putting down" child's, 95
quality time with, 94
support payments, 114
see also Stepfathers
Favorites:
of parent, 100
of teacher, 219–20
FBI, 410
Fears:
creating unnecessary, 133
of nine- to twelve-year-old, 245–46
of two-year-old, 55–56
Feeding:
baby feeding himself, 28
of frustrated child, 72
of infant, 44–45
Feminine hygiene sprays, 351
Fetal alcohol syndrome, 19, 381
Fighting:
during adolescence, 298
by five- to eight-year-old, 123–24, 149–50, 248–49
by nine- to twelve-year-old, 248–49
racial slurs leading to, 123–24
in school, 200–201